THE LITTLE WONDER

ROBERT WINDER was Literary Editor of the *Independent* and Deputy Editor of *Granta*. He is the author of three novels as well as several works of non-fiction, including *Hell for Leather: A Modern Cricket Journey* and *Bloody Foreigners: The Story of Immigration to Britain*. For some years he was a genuine all-rounder – not quite a bowler, and not quite a batsman – for Harold Pinter's Gaieties Cricket Club.

THE LITTLE WONDER

The Remarkable History of Wisden

Robert Winder

BLOOMSBURY

LONDON · NEW DELHI · NEW YORK · SYDNEY

First published in Great Britain 2013

This paperback edition published in 2014

Copyright © 2013 by Robert Winder

Foreword copyright © 2013 by David Kynaston

Published in the UK in 2013 by
John Wisden & Co.
An imprint of Bloomsbury Publishing Plc
50 Bedford Square, London WC1B 3DP

www.wisden.com
www.bloomsbury.com
Bloomsbury is a trademark of Bloomsbury Publishing Plc

Bloomsbury Publishing, London, New Delhi, New York and Sydney

A CIP catalogue record for this book
is available from the British Library

ISBN 978 1 4088 4679 7

10 9 8 7 6 5 4 3 2 1

Typeset by Saxon Graphics Ltd, Derby
Printed and bound in Great Britain by CPI Group (UK) Ltd, Croydon CR0 4YY

To the unseen hands that crafted – and continue to craft – Wisden

Contents

Foreword

I suspect we all have our own "special" *Wisden*, usually going back to childhood. My cricket-watching began on 4 June 1959 – a seven year old in my grandparents' house in Shropshire, the retrospectively somewhat improbable pair of Arthur Milton and Ken Taylor opening the batting against India, a far from full day's coverage on BBC television – and I was hooked. Rummaging among my father's *Wisden*s soon ensued, and I found myself intensely drawn to the 1957 edition, less because of its record of the feats of Jim Laker, not quite comprehending their enormity, more because of that almost fairy-tale sequence of selectorial coups during the 1956 Ashes series: in the Third Test at Headingley, "severely criticised" for choosing the long-discarded Cyril Washbrook, who then with Peter May turned it round on the first day; in the Fourth at Old Trafford, "sprang a surprise" by naming the Rev David Sheppard, "who had given up cricket to take up Holy Orders", but now scored a century; and in the Fifth at The Oval, "enjoyed yet another triumph" when they summoned Denis Compton, minus right knee-cap. I also loved the photographs of the series: the crouching, black-hatted umpire raising his left hand for Laker's final wicket, the weirdly balletic poses of Laker's leg trap, above all "Lucky Escape for England", with Colin Cowdrey and Peter Richardson both hopelessly stranded halfway down the pitch but somehow surviving.

Serious addiction followed. I suspect I craved reassurance in my life (my parents divorced when I was nine) and each spring my father buying the new *Wisden* helped to provide it. I treasured the immutable certainties, as every year the English cricket season followed the same preordained pattern – and every year, *Wisden* faithfully recorded it in an equally unvarying format. I loved too the advertisements at the start

(Foster & Co, "Hosiers and Club Colour Specialists"), the quirkier records (could A. E. J. Collins *really* have scored 628 not out in a house match?), the slightly rag-bag feel of "Other Matches at Lord's", the often stern assessments in the county overviews, the pleasing variety of birthplaces in the lists of county players, E. M. Wellings sounding off about the inadequacies of public school cricket, the strange allure in the overseas section of teams like Griqualand West and East Punjab, and – maybe best of all – the books round-up by John Arlott, often with that sentence appended about how "the normal dictates of reviewing" precluded him from noticing his own books. I also devised a game by which I would take an old Almanack and follow an individual cricketer (usually a batsman) through a whole season, tracing his ups and downs. A. C. Revill of Derbyshire was for some reason a particular favourite; but years later, when I happened to be introduced to him on the boundary at Basingstoke, I felt too embarrassed to mention it.

Wisden was of course a national institution long before the 1950s, and remains so in the twenty-first century. Why? The answer is surely that the Almanack, like cricket itself, represents something deep in the English psyche. I am not thinking here of those famed Victorian qualities like fair play and character-building (which in my view we are contemptuously cynical about at our peril); rather, I have in mind the somewhat narrower – and undoubtedly often unimaginative – attributes of cautious empiricism and patient, incremental accumulation, mistrustful of theory or rhetoric or even the grand gesture. It is the conservative tradition of W. G. Grace, stating bluntly that there is no such thing as a crisis in cricket, only the next ball; of Hampshire's Phil Mead, tucking the ball behind square leg to move from 49 to 50 and murmuring as he started running that that was another bag of coal for the winter; and, in our times, of the unashamedly pragmatic Graham Gooch, in such explicit contrast to the more elegant but less fiercely self-disciplined David Gower. Put another way, it is a view of cricket as ultimately defined by getting the runs and the wickets in the book; and year on year, for a century and a half, the book that has mattered most is *Wisden*.

Robert Winder is a real writer, with a strong sense of the inherent tragi-comedy of both life and cricket, and in this hugely enjoyable, illuminating anniversary account he does full justice to the Almanack's long and mainly distinguished history. His attitude is that of a critical friend: unfailingly humane in his treatment, but never shirking an unfavourable judgement. This is entirely as it should be, for *Wisden* itself has been transformed in the last quarter of a century or so – from a semi-mouthpiece of the establishment into a much more independent (and much more readable) recorder and appraiser of the game. Of course, cricket itself has changed even more fundamentally during these years, but it still at heart remains, in any format and in any context, an intense physical and psychological battle between bowler and batsman. As long as that contest continues to grip an audience, the play will continue; and all being well, the not-so-little wonder will still be here to memorialise it for posterity.

David Kynaston
January 2013

Advertisement from Wisden *1937*

Introduction

In the Book

Cricket, like most sports, inspires happy delusions. Braced by a post-match drink or two, most players can rewrite the story of their day by forgiving themselves the odd blemish and improving on what they actually achieved; as night falls they can shrug aside their real-life efforts and conjure up, for a dreamy moment, the innings they almost, if only, to all intents and purposes, more or less and very nearly played.

There is a straightforward response to such fabrications. The batsman fuming at a dismal lbw decision, the fielder itching to explain how he must have lost the ball in the sun, the bowler swearing blind that he heard a nick ... all these can be silenced by the simplest cricketing observation of all: "well, it's in the book".

The book in question is the scorebook, and it does not lie. We can huff and puff, exonerate, revise and excuse as much as we like, but down in the scorebook the cold arithmetic of what actually happened is there for all to see. If only this, if only that ... The batsman out first ball is out for a duck, no matter how fervently and frequently he replays the awful moment in his mind's eye; a missed catch is a drop, however intricate and extenuating the context; and wickets claimed in the post-match bar do not count, even if the bowler believes them "deserved". This is one of cricket's better-known laws: much as it inspires fantasies of grand deeds on summer afternoons, it metes out its rewards in frosty, undebatable facts and figures. "Look in the book," we say to batsmen, as they scowl their way to the pavilion, protesting that the umpire can't see straight. "Check the scorebook," we tell the bowler, as he grinds his teeth, adamant that our pad was bang in front of the stumps. "No use arguing," we smile, week after week and year after year – "it's what's in the book that counts."

The scorebook is not quite the game's final arbiter, however. There remains a higher authority, a book of books sometimes known, to the chagrin of the thing itself, as cricket's "bible". In truth it has often been eccentric, even fallible, and has rarely been so all encompassing as this sobriquet suggests.* Its full name is *Wisden Cricketers' Almanack*, though it has not always been so called. Early editions (the first was in 1864) were simply *The Cricketer's Almanack*, but in 1869 the apostrophe was nudged one space to the right to form the plural and in 1870 the founder's name was included to create *John Wisden's Cricketers' Almanack*. Minor variations such as these would one day become antiquarian clues, like the hallmarks on silver, but at this stage the book was simply a buff-covered catalogue of scores and records: a casual glance revealed little more than pages filled with names and figures. But longevity has lent it poetry. It can claim to be the oldest continuously published book in the world (*Who's Who* was born in 1849, but is not renewed so thoroughly each year), so it has become a collector's item; but it is also, thanks to the algebraic purity of the cricket scorecard, which preserves old games in statistical aspic, a reservoir of sporting nostalgia. As the cricket-loving playwright Harold Pinter (one of two Nobel Prize winners for Literature in its pages) told a *Sunday Times* interviewer in 2005: "Sometimes, when I feel a little exhausted with it all, and the world is sitting heavily on my head, I pick up a *Wisden* and read about Len Hutton's 37 in 24 minutes in Sydney in 1946."

Wisden certainly assumes a keen interest in cricket, but it also (perhaps even more intensely) appeals to the bibliophile, the reader whose first love is books. It lures the numerate, who can see the purest drama in a game that can be narrated entirely in figures, and which occasionally throws up orderly flukes: a score of 123 for 4, with batsman 5 on 6, batsman 7 on 8 and the last man having scored 9 ... or 90. As the mathematician G. H. Hardy once wrote: "If I knew I was going to die today, I think I should still want to hear the cricket scores." And as luck would have it, cricket is unusual in that it has appealed, down the years,

---

* "All faiths need a sacred text," said the former Archbishop of Canterbury, Robert Runcie, in a speech to the guests at the *Wisden* dinner in 1997. "It's a big help if the faithful come to believe it is well nigh infallible."

to plenty of people who are not themselves cricketers. "There is no other game," wrote the essayist E. V. Lucas in 1933, "at which the confirmed duffer is so persistent and undepressed." As a result, perhaps, it has often found favour with literary types: a hundred years ago England's authors could (and did – and still do) put out a handy team that in those days included, among others: Arthur Conan Doyle, J. M. Barrie, E. W. Hornung, A. A. Milne and P. G. Wodehouse. "The very names of a cricket bat and ball make English fingers tingle," wrote William Hazlitt; while the novelist and poet George Meredith talked of "the ancient rapture of a first of May cricketing day on a sunny green meadow, with an ocean of a day before us, and well-braced spirits for the match". There are countless examples of this sort of thing; entire anthologies have been dipped in purple ink; and cricket has often been rustled up as a conservative model of Merrie England. Yet somehow, through two *fins de siècle*, a pair of world wars, various moral scandals, assorted financial upheavals and social commotions, plus a barrage of other shaves and scrapes, *Wisden* has chronicled, with stately devotion, the entire small world of English cricket. In the process it has given a ceremonial twist to the famous phrase: to be "in" *Wisden* – to have one's meagre efforts recorded, ranked and in some cases applauded – truly is to be "in the book". Inclusion confers a rare sort of immortality – at least I hope it does, since I, like countless others, feel a tremor of pride to know that thanks to a few lucky wickets taken 30 summers ago my own name appears, once, in minuscule print, at the feet of the giants and legends who stalk its stately pages. I am far from alone. Being in *Wisden* is like being in *Who's Who* – a frail, sepia-tinged feather in anyone's cap.

What follows is the story of a unique publication. Naturally, an exhaustive volume of cricket information, some 1,800 pages of compressed print, may not conform to our usual idea of a central character, but in its own idiosyncratic way the story of *Wisden* does possess the kind of trajectory we expect from Victorian novels. It opens with a conception and a birth before advancing through growing pains to maturity, breasting the storms and vicissitudes of ceaseless change. Above all, it is the story of a survivor: the modest seed planted in 1864 grew into a sturdy plant which has somehow, through a mixture of tenacity, optimism and luck, clung on to its place in the life of the game. It has proved, quite literally, a hardy annual, though by now it seems more monument than plant – a fixed point, like a stone circle or church spire, in the rush of modern life. For 150 years it has watched and annotated the cricket pageant that unfurls each summer, embedding it in a social history of the country that sustained it for so long.

Of course, it is obvious that not everyone likes cricket. We live at a time when passers-by stroll across park cricket grounds, or set up picnics in the outfield, quite oblivious to the fact that they are intruding upon a significant boundary. For many modern Britons the game is fusty, quaint, old-hat and impossibly tedious (though it might be ventured that anyone who finds it slow has never faced, or contemplated facing, a real fast bowler). This is partly because it has stood for so long as an emblem of upper-class, public-school Englishness that is no longer fashionable or a source of pride. And since modern players curse, quarrel and trick the authorities as freely as anyone, cricket's own much-vaunted code of fair play can often seem shopworn and hypocritical. Illegal bowling, sexual escapades, temper tantrums, umpiring disputes, ball-tampering, gambling, match-fixing – there's been more than enough bad form over the years to undermine cricket's claim to be character-forming. But there is no denying the fact that the game *was* used as a moral PR exercise and a weapon in class one-upmanship. Edwardian England, through the cult of "muscular Christianity", saw it as an elevated pursuit and sent it across the British Empire as a dramatic example of manly endeavour, stuffed with all the virtues London wished to broadcast as its own: patience, steadfastness, honesty, leadership, courage, sportsmanship, camaraderie and of course the much-vaunted "amateur spirit". Many of its idioms – the need to "play up" with a "straight bat" while risking being "stumped", "trapped in front" or "caught out" on a "sticky wicket" – lie deep in the reflexes of England's proverbial life.

What thirst or need in the national mood did it answer, this careful compilation of cricket facts? According to one early reviewer (in the *Nottinghamshire Guardian*) it was especially useful as "a proof of deciding wagers", but its durability, the way it became a pillar of England's sporting culture, suggests that it touched a deeper nerve. Are there ways in which it did not just reflect but actually shape that elusive beast – the national identity? These are questions to which there is no simple answer, because cricket is a rich sport, susceptible to many interpretations, urges and needs. Not the least of its rare qualities is the fact that the outcome, the actual result, can be its least compelling feature. Cricket grounds on the final day, with a win or loss imminent, are often deserted, while day one, when all was uncertain, was a sell-out. Few games inspire so casual an attitude to the see-saw business of victory and defeat, are so content to shake hands and agree on a draw. This does not mean that winning and losing are trivial: the will to win shapes every twitch of every muscle, as well as each minor adjustment to the field. And since defeat can be a slow, gradual submission it can be excruciating. But success and failure come in many forms. It is possible to play brilliantly in a defeat, or to fail in a victory. When the game is done, the outcome dissolves into the mist, leaving individual achievements – that memorable catch, that wonderful stroke, that unplayable ball – standing proud in the memory like sculptures. Cricket is only rarely a knockout affair; more commonly it forms into a series or a season. And cricketers know better than most that fate operates in mysterious ways – no one plays well all the time, so the game's humbling moments – the golden duck, the fumbled catch or misfield – are never far away. Being dismissed may feel like dying – not for nothing is a reprieve known as a "life" – but cricket offers plenty of opportunities for resurrection.* The match may be short, but the game is long.

So while it may well be the slowest game in the world (the Test between South Africa and England in 1938 went on for ten days, and still didn't reach a conclusion) it is also, as the speed gun attests, one of the fastest. It is sedate yet dangerous, tranquil yet nerve-shredding. It is a team game in which personal triumph and disaster can be exposed as twin imposters; yet it encourages and celebrates individual feats. The cosiest dressing room can harbour bitter rivalries: few team-mates in other sports are so rude as cricketers awaiting their turn, gleefully

---

* Cricket's vocabulary is saturated with such imagery. A batsman who is dropped is "given a life", while an lbw victim is trapped "dead in front". It is possible, and at times necessary, to play with a "dead" bat, while nervous tailenders often have to see off the "death bowlers". When it is all over there is still time for a "post-mortem".

shredding the faults of the so-called comrades insultingly placed higher
in the batting order. As a result, many of the game's magic moments
concern personal milestones – Lara's 501 not out, Laker's 19-wicket
haul, Sobers's six sixes – rather than collective efforts. It is hardly *au
courant* to be even slightly poetic about cricket, but the game does
share the flickering charm of a waterfall or a flame: a stream of constant
change is held within the boundary of a stable, familiar form. True
disciples can stare at it for hours, as into a winter fireplace.

If cricket is variegated enough to be, as has so often been said, "more
than a game" (as well as "only a game") then this may also be because
its history has been stitched into the fabric of everyday life – in England,
at least. It is a midsummer sport whose alluring qualities, in the
sentimental accolades that echo down the years, blend with familiar
images: long shadows on bright grass, swallows and linnets above the
oaks, warm beer foaming in the pump room behind the pavilion. The
most famous author of this thesis was Neville Cardus, the cricket and
music critic of the *Manchester Guardian*, who saw it simply as part of
England: "Cricket, as I know and love it, is part of that holiday time
which is the Englishman's heritage – a playtime in homely countryside
… Wherever cricket is taken, England and the flavours of an English
summer go with it." This is sugary, to be sure (it has often seemed that
the National Trust could profitably issue Cardus fudge and tea towels),
but at that time, in England, it had real force. In the days before air
travel and television, cricket was as seasonal as strawberries: "The game
comes to us modestly on spring's rainy days … and after the last drawing
of stumps a leaf falls from a tree and a faint mist touches the field."

Raymond Robertson-Glasgow, many of whose writings on cricket
were humorous, also allowed himself a serious moment along these
lines. "Cricket," he wrote, "lives next door to the elements of life: it
brings with it the rare smell of mown grass, pleasant breezes in the face,
panoramas of rolling meadows and green hedges." And while it is
tempting (especially at a time when the game is increasingly Indian in
accent and flavour) to ascribe such fragrant ruminations to sentimental
whimsy, we cannot level the same charge at the war poet Edmund
Blunden, who gave patriotic idealism a sombre edge when he
contemplated, in his book *Cricket Country*, a pursuit that seemed, seen
through the prism of trench war, distinctly more than idle fun. Cricket,

he wrote, "does not terminate at the boundary, but is reflected beyond, is echoed and varied out there among the gardens and barns, the dells and the thickets, and belongs to some wider field". It has long been thought part of the rural pageant of the English summer, in other words, a polish on the furniture of our shires and counties; but it has also been readily anointed by high society, glad to parade itself not at cultural events (like Salzburg or Bayreuth) but at sporting galas – Henley, Ascot, Lord's – turning these into ceremonial, even royal events. This element, weak now, does endure in the marquees and pennants, blazers, ties and tea intervals that stud the game still.

In the 21st century, sighing cadences such as these can seem stale and complacent, and in modern cricket literature they have usually been supplanted by an equally limiting cliché to the effect that cricket is just a fussy pastime for well-born dolts with too much time on their hands. Certainly it is true that few sports are so shimmering with nostalgia: cricket has been on the slide for centuries, and the Golden Age, as has been said, is by definition in the past. Today's fans watch Pietersen and pine for Gower, just as Gower's pined for Cowdrey, and Cowdrey's for Hutton, and Hutton's for Hobbs. And elderly Victorians sneered at anyone who had the gall to compare Hobbs with the master himself: Grace. This may be biologically determined: we may experience our most fervent love for the game as children, after which everything seems diminished. Blunden, attempting to capture cricket's "grace without a name", felt it was something to do with "eternal youthfulness", and perhaps it was this that appealed also to J. M. Barrie when he filled his own sketches of Neverland, the fantasy kingdom of the boy who never grew up, with endless cricket pitches.

If it feeds a boyish appetite the Almanack is also, thanks to the resolute consistency with which it thumps down each year, part of the ageing process. It has always been full of memorials and obituaries, fond recollections and rose-tinted glances back in time. In 1969 John Arlott, reviewing it, wrote: "No other annual devotes so much, or such faithful, attention to the dead," and he meant it as a compliment. *Wisden*, he understood, was a book not just about cricket bits and bobs, but about the passing of time. Each new volume cast an ever-longer shadow, like a gravestone, reminding collectors that they were one year older. In "The Love Song of J. Alfred Prufrock" T. S. Eliot had conjured a lonely life measured out in coffee spoons. *Wisden* allowed cricket-lovers to mark their own mounting years by building a yellow brick wall.

This does not prevent cricket, like the world, from moving with the times. The game began life in the 18th century as a rural frolic, was adopted by the Victorian elite as a stylish pastime with en-suite morality play, and then developed into a commercialised product of the leisure industry. The way it has been played, thought about, talked of and written about has shifted many times over the years, and is shifting still. Yet *Wisden*'s calm style (we might call it *chunky-yellow*) has somehow managed to thread a path through the sequence of fads. The more it changes, the more it stays the same. And while it is clear that sport – deriving as it does from "disporting", the pursuit of pleasure through play – is on one level mere innocent fun, it is not a coincidence that it shares that word "play" with the theatre. Both are forms of narrative drama, though in cricket's case it is unscripted: neither performers nor spectators know whether their play will have a happy or a sad ending, be a thriller, a tragedy, a comedy or an epic. Whatever form it takes, it has often (usually unconsciously) presented the game not only as a form of innocent fun but as a telling allegory of social qualities – obedience, honour and in particular class distinction. More than most sports, cricket was able first to absorb the class-conscious tendencies of the society in which it was born, and then become an evangelist for those same characteristics. By 1832 there were two strands of cricket, and in her book *Our Village* Mary Mitford, describing a country cricket match, expressed the contrast by sneering at "people who make a trade of that noble sport", saluting instead the village game in which two neighbouring parishes played "for honour and a supper, glory and half a crown a man". The very first *Wisden* could not help but be embroiled in this conversation. It was a tacit comment on relations between amateur and professional; and so, even more directly, was the hundredth, when the distinction was finally abolished.* It may be going too far to

---

* Even when it had been annulled, the gulf between amateurs and professionals still yawned. "They looked down on us," recalled Fred Trueman in his autobiography. "Pros were pros and amateurs amateurs, even after 1962," wrote Barry Knight, the Essex, Leicestershire and England all-rounder. "You always felt they wanted amateur captains."

say that class tension has been the book's main subject, but it has been an ever-present fault-line in most of the many stories *Wisden* has to tell.

If cricket is more than a game in this way, it follows that *Wisden* is more than a book, and that what follows is more than a literary tale; it is the story of a sport, a business, an idea, an institution and a people. For 150 years *Wisden* has been the mouthpiece or voice of cricket; its annual editorial celebrates high achievement, frowns on sharp practice and lays down the law on matters great and small. Against heavy odds it has captured an audience of people stirred not only by cricket but also by words about cricket. This is where cricketers loiter in the dreary winter months, reliving the highs and lows of their seasons in the sun. In 1893 the editor, Sydney Pardon, wrote: "A friend of mine – not wont to be demonstrative – assured me the other day that he had no pleasanter evenings in the whole year than when the appearance of *Wisden* enabled him to fight the battles of the cricket season over again." The sentiment was echoed in 1964 by Thomas Moult, who put the Almanack at the centre – who needs skylarks or Grecian urns? – of his poem "Close of Play":

> *Well, what's a crimson hearth for, and the lamp*
> *Of winter nights, and these plump yellow books*
> *That cherish Wisden's soul and bear his stamp…?*

Satirists like presenting this sort of thing as the moaning of overgrown schoolboys, but there is more to it than that. If it is an English trait to live in the past, then *Wisden* is one of the means by which we can make brief visits to it. The private yearning for "eternal youthfulness" merges with a national urge for a pre-industrial sanctuary, a green place where larks are on the wing and there is honey still for tea. Early cricket writers depicted this as a rustic theme park, as English as the flash of a kingfisher's wing or a stand of beech trees; more recent works, led by C. L. R. James, prefer to see it as an expression of social-political forces. Somehow, *Wisden* has navigated a course between these poles. On the surface a conservative publication, with eyes trained on the past, it has often aspired to be, at least in its own terms, idealistic as well.

The golf writer Bernard Darwin, grandson of the great evolutionist, once wrote that the playing-field dreamers who gathered at the cricket were, while easy to caricature, not necessarily quite as dumb as they seemed. "Because men meet at Lord's or St Andrews," he reasoned, "it does not follow that they talk about nothing but cricket or golf." Then, as now, sport was both a dramatic spectacle and a cocktail party. And while it is common these days to sneer at the latter (in its modern form: corporate hospitality) the sport recorded so respectfully in *Wisden* also involved a balancing act between these qualities: the game, the only-a-game, and the more-than-a-game.

When C. L. R. James, enlisting Kipling to his belief that cricket was both an expression of political energy and a sharp manifestation of high culture, famously asked "What do they know of cricket who only cricket know?" he was praising a sport rich enough to deserve solemn narration. He went on to express a connoisseur's dismay at the historians who, in narrating Victorian Britain, barely mentioned one of its greatest heroes – W. G. Grace – an omission that suggests only that most historians are not themselves athletes, and enjoy disparaging physical skill (despite the fact that cricket, unusually, attracts a range of physiques – gangly, dumpy, huge or lightweight). Thus it is common today to hear, when Grace's name is mentioned, cynical remarks about his shamateur status – so much so that *this* is now more or less the received view; it poses as subversive while being the orthodox line. These days, the more radical and edgy proposition is that Grace – the patriarch whose "doings" dominated *Wisden*'s own youth – really was one of the men who, by blending cricket's many streams into "one great winding river" (as his contemporary Ranjitsinhji wrote) helped make us what we are. Certainly, as Bernard Darwin wrote (not in *Wisden*, alas), Grace was "far better known by sight than any man in England ... he had only to pass through a village street in a motor car for windows to be thrown up and fingers to be pointed".

Wisden was born at a particular moment, in the hungry intellectual, industrial and sporting furnace of mid-Victorian England. It remains a clear echo of the time when the *Oxford English Dictionary* (1857), Crockford's *Clerical Dictionary* (1858), *Palgrave's Golden Treasury* (1861), *Whitaker's Almanack* (1868), the *Dictionary of National Biography* (1885) and other edifices of scholarship appeared. Through its theme, cricket, it echoes a distant past, and while we no longer build cathedrals there is something medieval about the enterprise; one imagines a scaffold teeming with labourers: it feels finely chiselled by a thousand hands. If any book could have turrets, pinnacles, buttresses, niches and shadowy corners with hidden treasures, it is *Wisden*.*

We can hardly doubt that the early editors would be amazed to see a modern edition; they might even struggle to grasp the scale of the project. But though the decor has changed, the essential lines of the vessel they launched are intact. I like to think that if they could leaf through a present volume, scanning the kaleidoscope of exploits and implosions strewn across each page, they would smile. After all, anyone can get a century: the trick is to go on and on. As *Wisden* celebrates its 150th edition, I propose to retrace its steps to see how it came to be what it has been and, somehow, still is.

To put it another way: we should begin, as they say, at the beginning.

---

* Gideon Haigh put his finger on this ancient-monument aspect of *Wisden* in the introduction to his 2007 anthology of unusual occurrences in *Wisden*, *Parachutist at Fine Leg*, where he called it "mysterious … a statistical Stonehenge".

Advertisement from Wisden *1886*

I

The Birth Pang

Two-thirds of the way through the 19th century a small advertisement appeared in the classified columns of the *Bradford Observer*. "On the 8th of February," it said, "will be published THE CRICKETER'S ALMANACK for 1864, containing the Laws of Cricket, Quoits and Bowls, together with full and accurate Scores of the Matches between the Two Elevens." It was not strident; it was hardly claiming to be a must-read. But there was a quiet authority in this simple announcement, which at least hinted, along with its declared intention to be "full and accurate", at greater things to come. Its chief selling point – the book's full name – was not even mentioned.

The publication appeared a few weeks later, in March. Its unpretentious title did not suggest anything out of the ordinary: it claimed only to be *The Cricketer's Almanack for the year 1864, being bissextile or Leap Year, and the 28th of the Reign of HER MAJESTY QUEEN VICTORIA containing the Laws of Cricket as revised by the Marylebone Club ...* Behind these fine-sounding formalities lay a plain paper-bound booklet whose bland buff wrapper contained 112 pages of semi-arcane facts and figures, with not a word of explanation – it could have been a railway timetable or a stock price gazette. The cover, which was also the title page, promised an exhaustive collection of lists, tables, "extraordinary matches" and "other interesting information", but the most cursory flick-through revealed only a sequence of cricket scorecards and a summary of the game's already fiddly laws. To pad things out there were sections on horse racing – complete histories of the Derby, the Oaks and the St Leger – and guides to other pastimes, including some now-forgotten Victorian ones such as "knurr and spell" (a Yorkshire-born outdoor pursuit in which players would see how far they could whack a conker-sized ball, the "knurr", with their stick (or "spell"). The deaths of certain poets (Crabbe and Berenger) were soberly noted, and there was a collection of whimsical "extras", such as the date (1121) when "the Arabian horse was introduced to Britain". Finally, there was a brief but vehement note on the execution of Charles I, which seemed, given its Catholic-Royalist slant, to have been written by a surviving member of the Stuart line. Readers were told that the condemned monarch, in his final moments, summoned up all the "kingly dignity of which he possessed no small share" to rise above "this mockery of a trial". If it strikes us as significant that the historical episode given most weight in the book concerns a regicide, a toppling of the established order, we must note too that the book's sympathies lay with the victim-king, not with his supplanters.

That was not the end of it. There was a list of lunar movements and a "calendar" of noteworthy dates. Alert readers could enjoy the fact that the Gunpowder Plot and the Battle of Inkerman fell on the same day – 5 November – but could also learn that the Cambridge term would begin on 13 January and fly-fishing on 15 March. If by some chance they did not already know that the interest on Indian bonds would be paid on 31 March, that the mutiny on the *Bounty* fell on 31 April 1789, or that Bosworth was fought on 22 August 1485 ... well, *Wisden* was happy to come to their rescue.

It was an inexpensive volume, modestly priced – one shilling, plus a penny postage for those who subscribed by mail. It was printed by W. H. Crockford of Blackheath, a junior relative of the John Crockford whose *Clerical Dictionary*, now half a dozen years old, would go on to become the *Wisden* of the church. A *Times* journalist, W. H. Knight, assisted with the gathering and laying out of the information, but this was not an elaborate publication: it contained more numbers than words. There were signs of a delicate class ambiguity, too. Only a page into the very first *Wisden* it was not clear at whom it was aimed. On the one hand it served the growing popular audience for cricket data uncovered by the boom in newspapers and other bulletins (such as *Bell's Life*) eager to record the "doings" of top players. Thus it relished the fact that 22 June was the "first recorded match at Lord's present ground, 1814", or that 17 September was the day when "11 Single beat

11 Married women by 7 runs" at Parson's Green. Did anyone not know that the first Eton v Winchester match was on 4 August 1826, or that 15 February had been immortalised by Barrett, who "scored 13 runs at one hit" on the ice at Harewood in 1838? They did now.

On the other hand the new book seemed also to crave the approval of the hunting-shooting-fishing set, chaps who owned racehorses, read poetry, held railway bonds, sighed over the misfortunes of kings and had sons at Oxford. Much prominence was given to the dates of the Queen's birth, the Battle of Waterloo and the conversion of St Paul (mysteriously supposed to have taken place on 25 January). And the small print was crammed with parlour-game quiz-fodder. A gentleman scanning the list of Derby and Oaks winners might easily have believed that this new *Wisden* thingy was some sort of guide to aristocratic quirks: from Lord Egremont's Assassin and the Duke of Grafton's Whisker to Lord Lowther's Spaniel, Lord Clermont's Trifle and Lord Chesterfield's Industry. He (the launch editor seemed to have in mind a male reader) might also have reached for the snuff-box while trying to comprehend the finer points of bowls: "all bowls that rub or set after passing the parallel are taken off the green, except they rub or set upon a bowl belonging to the playing party". But he would soon have been able to discourse knowledgeably on the recent history of the university rowing matches, could have won any guessing game involving the lengths of Britain's canals (the shortest being Brecknock and Abergavenny, built in 1758) and would have been able to regale the other fellows at the club with a hundred enticing details concerning Britain's far-flung Empire – from the Battle of Copenhagen in 1804 and the Opium dispute of 1834, to the blocking of Canton harbour in 1840, or the terrible day the British were "repulsed" at Peiho in 1859. As a final flourish, there were some unsettling footnotes scattered like wildflowers among the cricket lists. "The graces of the modern tea table", readers were informed in one haughty aside, "were quite unknown to the country folk" until "the reigns of the Georges". And a moment's silence, please, for the January day in 1861, when the great brass bell of Woolwich, for so long rung to "call and disperse the labourers", was cracked by frost.

It would be easy to smile at this high-minded thread in the first *Wisden* as merely a symptom of the Victorian faith in and fondness for education – the evangelising reflex that had so recently inspired the founding of grand museums for science, geology and natural history in South Kensington. The autodidactic thirst for self-improvement – the impulse behind Samuel Smiles and all the other self-help manuals of the time – was also an informing presence, along with the blunt instinct for statistical summaries that was suddenly central to a people that depended on tide charts and railway schedules. But something else glimmers through this eccentric intellectual decor. In surrounding his new publication with echoes of the school history syllabus, and adding a ribbon of patriotic poetry and science, Wisden was, like a proud parent with upmarket ambitions, firmly aligning cricket with upper-class taste.

But any readers who imagined, from this eccentric surface noise, that *Wisden* was a frivolous comic (its nose ever so slightly in the air) would have been soothed by the fact that the first major item was a guide to the laws laid down by MCC. There was nothing grandiose – only a modest catalogue of bare facts – but there was something ostentatious about these faintly stuffy *thou-shalt-nots*. Along with the earnest tributes to the Queen and MCC on the cover, it suggested that *Wisden* was already positioning itself as a guardian of the game, a ceremonial keeper of its code.

It is evident that this code was already, in 1864, precarious, in ways we recognise today. The role of gambling in sport was deep-rooted enough to make it necessary to emphasise, in print, that "No umpires shall be allowed to bet." Some sartorial habits still required legislation, too. Fielders were asked not to stop the ball with their hats, and in a specific ruling that was broadened when helmets were introduced more than a hundred years later, the penalty for breaching this law was abrupt: "the ball shall be considered dead, and the opposition party should add five runs to their score". Not everyone knows that when modern players store helmets behind the wicketkeeper in case they need to be worn by a close fielder, they risk triggering a very old law.

One 1864 law that *has* faded from view is the one designed to discourage players from sharing bats. "When one of the strikers shall have been put out, the use of the bat shall not be allowed to any person until the next striker shall come in." Was this a defence against bat-tampering, or a rule against using the bat as a weapon?

Either way, this was the first hint that *Wisden* was coming into the world at a time of energetic change. Historians make a distinction between long-term and short-term causes – an abrupt division that sits quite happily with the way the world was turning in 1863. It was not evident at the time, but in retrospect we can see that this was, in a way, the great Victorian moment, the time when all the forces unleashed in the 19th century flowed together and raised up a storm-surge of change. Across the Atlantic, the disunited states of America were locked in a traumatic and bloody war (echoing, for the British, recent horrors in India – in Amritsar, Lucknow and Calcutta). At home there were less lethal but equally resounding cultural forces at work, shaking the religious, scientific and political facts of mid-Victorian life. The heretical findings of Charles Darwin (not to mention Marx and Engels, whose revolutionary notions were gaining currency every year) created an unsettled climate of opinion that was only darkened, in 1861, by the sudden death of Prince Albert and the mourning-tragedy of Queen Victoria (too inconsolable even to attend the funeral, she wore black for the next four decades). English life felt raw and stirred, like freshly turned soil, and even the surface tremors of the subterranean Darwinian-Industrial-Imperial convulsion were sufficient to make this a time of tremendous and unnerving renewal.

The most obvious of these commotions was the expansion of the railway. Since the opening of the first line (Stockton to Darlington) in 1825, some 10,000 miles of track had been laid. Britain was suddenly mobile; a rural population was sucked into the mills and factories rising in the cities. The population of Leeds, Liverpool and Manchester boomed from 348,000 in 1821 to 885,000 40 years later. This is where Dickensian England was born, a squalid milieu described in 1844 by Engels and Marx in *The Condition of the Working Class in Britain*, and by Dickens himself, in more jaunty but equally trenchant terms, in novel after novel.

This rapid creation of a metropolitan working class, combined with the heightened mobility offered by the panting new steam trains (the amazing new service on the London Underground emerged in January 1863) generated an audience for sporting spectacle that had never existed before, because it turned out that what this new population wanted to do on its well-earned holy days (and strike days) was play and attend sport; the country's favourite games – football, racing, cricket – grew towards this bright new sun, and, under the influence of the robust Victorian urge to classify and tabulate, began to organise and codify themselves into clubs and leagues.

This brave new edifice of sport as public entertainment (supplanting the baiting of bears and bulls, which had been banned in the mid-1830s) was fertilised, of course, by one of the railway's most creative by-products: the postal service. The advent of the penny stamp in 1840 cracked open an enormous new world of private interaction (its effects not unlike, perhaps, the revolution in social networks on the internet in our own recent years). But it also made it possible to create far-flung fixture lists for sports teams. Cricket, until this period a rustic pursuit, was not slow to join the party.

The second great force was ostensibly a mere shiver, yet its effects on cricket were equally dramatic. One of the by-products of the Industrial Revolution was mechanical mowing, which gave England not just a taste for well-groomed lawns but a new way of preparing playing fields. Until the mid-century a horse-drawn scythe was the best available method, but this was too rough and ready to create anything we would today recognise as a cricket wicket – Lord's, it was said, was "all ridge and furrow". By the same token, golf, even in Scotland, was a winter game. Only when frost kept the grass down could a well-struck ball be found – in summer it was impossible to locate until those clever Victorian engineers devised ways to shave the land into fairways. Many years later (in 1892) the Hon. R. H. Lyttelton would write, in *Wisden* itself: "Of all the inventions that ever worked a revolution in cricket, nothing had more effect than the heavy roller and the mowing machine." Ancient methods simply could not compete. "The old scythe, however deftly wielded, left a tuft of grass here and there ..."

Of course, this is only a blunt-crayon sketch of a swarming, contradictory era. The teeming commotions of 19th-century Britain are a vast subject, certainly – too various to be summarised in a handful of paragraphs. But *Wisden* did not spring from nowhere. It did not drift in on a sea breeze, like a stray weed, to germinate in a crack in the English pavement. It was a fruit of the clanking native ecology. The prevailing turns of English life had created the kind of society – rapidly industrialising, imperially haughty and philosophically tense – that might want or need a book like *Wisden*. It was a society that was also generating new museums and libraries, new journals and clubs, new churches, new schools, new allegiances ... even new towns.

Other sports were responding to the same bracing change. Golf's first Open championship came at Prestwick in 1860, and the Football Association was formed in 1863. Based on the rules favoured by Eton, Westminster and Charterhouse (even football has a public-school ancestry, which it rarely celebrates) this was an attempt to legislate for the difference between soccer and its bastard child, rugby. It led in 1872 to the emergence of a separate Rugby Union – and to England's first "lawn" tennis club at Leamington Spa: another game that owed its existence to the impact of steel blades on grass.

There were other, deeper tensions in the air. Cricket, like society as a whole, was being tugged in two directions. On the one hand it was an upper-class pursuit, a decorous gambling medium for sporting gentlemen of leisure. But now it was turning demotic. The urban masses were quick to develop a fresh conception of the game – not as a recreation for the well dressed but as paid work, and entertainment. This was a radical alteration: in the mid-19th century cricket ceased to be a pastoral pageant attended by ladies in ballgowns, and became an urban theatre of playful combat.

There had been paid professionals in the game for years – mainly bowlers, paid £5 a match to work up a sweat while their so-called betters demonstrated the "art" of batsmanship to admiring, double-barrelled relatives. In 1844 Lord's retained a staff of ten professionals to bowl in the nets at well-heeled members, and thought of them in much the same way as it thought of the unlettered lads who cleaned the knives and boots. But the annual Gents v Players match at Lord's was rapidly establishing itself as one of the guaranteed high points of the English summer, and had no small amount of "edge" to it, since the Gents were struggling to compete with their skilled inferiors. Meanwhile, in the steam-driven whirl of mid-century England, something quite new was emerging. In 1846 William Clarke founded a team of cricket professionals, named it the "All-England XI", and travelled the country like a circus troupe.

In one sense Clarke was the Kerry Packer of mid-19th century England: he scooped top players into a boisterous caravan – George

Parr from Nottingham, the Lillywhites from Sussex, Fuller Pilch and Alfred Mynn from Kent, and many others. He himself was still an employee at Lord's, paid a few pounds to bowl to MCC members when they felt like refining the rare batsmanship they had learned at Harrow or Eton, but he soon found himself the leading cricket impresario in the land, collecting up to £70 per game, only half of which he felt minded to distribute to his team. In 1847 he staged ten fixtures and hired new players. By 1851 he found himself in charge of a full-fledged, breakaway rebel tour playing 34 games a season. It was a major medium for gambling – the 1847 game in Manchester was said to have inspired some £30–£40,000 in side wagers – but this was in keeping with its rollicking, feasting-and-drinking approach to life. By 1852 the All-England XI even had a song, complete with a sentimental chorus: "Both peasant and peer / Find ecstasy here / Then Cricket for ever, my boys!"

William Clarke's originality lay in the way he tested the value of cricket's artisans in the laissez-faire free market beloved of Victorian ideologues, and made them stars. Of these the brightest was Parr: in the Eleven's second season he scored 100 at Leicester, 78 at York and 64 at Manchester, on pitches we would now deem unplayable. He was such a favourite at Trent Bridge – the ground he developed in Nottingham – that the tree at square leg (a favourite scoring area) was named after him.

Two of Clarke's hirelings, Alfred Mynn and Nicholas Felix, were in theory amateurs – neither had paid jobs in cricket. But nor did they have the kind of private incomes needed to shrug aside petty financial considerations and play as Gentlemen. The "travelling expenses" they received from Clarke amounted to wages, and everyone knew it. Meanwhile, the All-England Eleven acquired a uniform – white shirts, with red polka dots or stripes, and tall top hats – and criss-crossed the country like carnival gangs of actors or jockeys. And they were box office. When word spread that they were coming to take on the town's best XI, 16 or 22, marquees would go up around the field, cricket gear would be stacked up for sale, food and drink would be piled high and gala meals planned. It was common for the local teams to field oversized teams – in a nice inversion of the usual class habits, the quality of the touring professionals was countered by sheer quantity. Crowds gathered at the station for a raucous first glimpse of the visiting stars, most of whom had enjoyed a bottle or two on the train and did not look formidable. It was festival cricket: if Eton and Harrow could have days like this, then why couldn't Doncaster, Huddersfield, Glasgow or Bristol? Fireworks crackled in the sky; balloons popped on the breeze.

There were mixed feelings about this development. On the one hand it lured an audience of new fans – it "tended to a healthy circulation of the life blood of cricket, inoculating and vaccinating every wandering rustic with the principles of the national game". But it was also a clear challenge (especially since the Players were beginning to beat the Gentlemen with unseemly ease) to the established order. The anthem may have raised a foaming cup to the idea of cricket as a playground where toffs and labourers could mingle on equal terms, but the rise of professional cricket inspired the opposite reaction too. The Reverend James Pycroft, an Oxford-educated barrister in holy orders, sneered at the "travelling circus" and called it "a very serious nuisance". His words were echoed by the novelist Anthony Trollope, who described it as "the monster nuisance of the day". The game was splitting into factions.

Benjamin Disraeli's 1845 novel *Sybil* had aired the notion of there being "two nations", and when Dickens took up the theme in *Hard Times* (with its biting portrait of industrial grime in "Coketown") in 1854, no one could deny the presence of such a split. It was often seen as a divide between north and south (the north being where grim factories cranked out industrial wealth, the south being the pampered pavilion where the money was counted), but it was chiefly a rupture along crude class lines. MCC was the opposite of avant-garde, and bridled at the notion that cricket might belong to the common man. One of its leading lights, the Hon. Robert Grimston, famously took a look at the new-fangled mowing device at work on the hallowed turf and paid some navvies a sovereign to smash it up with pickaxes. Even in these early days, progress was not something to be accepted without a scowl.

There was powerful cultural support for the lofty view of things taken by MCC and Lord's. They had absorbed the high-minded Victorian preachers who saw cricket as a way of life, a moral exercise, a noble calling for refined gentlemen of leisure. Thus the "home of cricket" celebrated the amateur ideal (it was said that cricket was the Church of England at play) and took as its text the already-famous line in Thomas Hughes's novel *Tom Brown's Schooldays* (1857), which booked cricket a seat at the high table of English culture by having its hero declare, in a line that has become corny over the years, that it was "more than a game … an institution". The Reverend Pycroft asserted, from his imaginary pulpit, that "all who would succeed in the head-work of life must also learn to unbend in play", and he found an attentive ear in the network of public schools establishing themselves in England's county towns. In 1853 G. E. L. Cotton (the model for the schoolmaster in Hughes's novel) wrote that cricket "merges the individual into the eleven; he doesn't play so that he may win but that his side may win". This was an idea gripping enough to become one of the key empire-building concepts, and it flourished. In 1845 Harrow possessed eight acres of sports fields, but by the turn of the century the school owned nearly 150.

With hindsight it is clear that this belief derived not only from Christian tradition but also from a half-baked Darwinism: the survival of the fittest reduced to a mere fitness craze. But the idea that a healthy mind required a healthy body (*mens sana in corpore sano*) soon felt like a classical truth. Strangely (to us) it was a notion of manliness that had little to do with virility – on the contrary, it was the way that "primitive" urges could be mastered. It defined itself as the opposite of secret homosexual feelings, the enemy of idle dreams. As the Reverend Charles Kingsley (more famous for his children's story *The Water Babies*) put it: "Through sport, boys acquire virtues which no books can give them; not merely daring and endurance but, better still, temper, self-restraint, fairness, honour, and unenvious approbation of another's success."

Sometimes this ennobling pastime required self-sacrifice. When the Rev. Robert Hooper was asked to play for Cambridge against Oxford in 1848 (the great year of European revolutionary fervour) he was obliged to decline on the grounds that he had (as his obituary in the 1919 *Wisden* was proud to point out) made a commitment to play elsewhere "which I could not honourably throw over". The elevation of this sort of cricket-sacrifice as a beau idéal of English manhood may have seemed theatrical; in due course, in Flanders, "playing the game" would take on a graver significance.

It was no coincidence, given all this, that when France conducted an inquiry into its feeble capitulation in the Franco-Prussian war in 1870, it should conclude that its elite was too introverted, too cerebral, altogether too lily-livered. One aristocrat actually visited England, in an attempt to discover the secret of their more soldierly products. He saw the embryonic sports event at Much Wenlock, in Shropshire, where Dr William Penny Brookes had in 1850 founded a festival to promote "the moral, physical and intellectual improvement" of the local citizenry; and he also visited the famous public schools, with their emphasis on team sports. He was the Baron de Coubertin, and he was so impressed that he began work, when he returned to France, on the concept that eventually emerged as the modern Olympic movement.

This elite form of the game found its expression in smart clubs, amateur versions of the professional elevens, with Latin-inflected names – I Zingari, Quidnuncs, Incogniti – and rainbow-coloured caps. There was a semi-automatic reflex in such circles to feel that blue blood was a prerequisite for civilised cricket: in 1841 the MCC presidency ceased to be appointed by a committee, and new presidents were simply nominated by their retiring predecessors. They did not look far beyond their immediate circle. In the years immediately following 1841 the office was held by 17 earls, three marquises, three viscounts, eight barons, two baronets and only one non-aristocrat. The upper-class reflex extended to a sense that even cricket skill was a function of social standing, and that, as the Reverend Pycroft put it, "a peculiar kind of caution" characterised the professional approach. He insisted not only on there being such a thing as a "correct" method ("underhand bowling requires an upright bat") but also that cricket was a distinctly virile pursuit. He scorned the "listless and effeminate" style that was "creeping", he felt, even into Etonian cricket.

All this might seem to have little to do with *Wisden*, but the creation and cultivation of this amateur ideal was to become one of the endless gusts blowing through the Almanack's long life; it is not a coincidence that it was part of the compost in which *Wisden* grew. And amateurism at this time was much more than a question of merely not being paid – that was only the surface definition. It was a full-blown philosophical system, which assumed a particular approach to life and promoted specific virtues. A century later, it is easy to find instances of amateurs paid more than their professional team-mates, and to see this as typical Victorian "hypocrisy". But that is a little beside the point, because amateurism was larger than that: it was an evangelical worldview that

filtered Christian ideas through athletic endeavour, a form of zeal. It
did not hold that cricket was a way of life – a tawdry notion – but that
cricket could be an exemplary part of a life filled with other pleasures,
and other obligations.

It is significant that this idea was rising to prominence, like an
ascending star, in the year of *Wisden*'s birth, since the tussle between the
amateur and the professional spirit would go on to dominate the
Almanack for a hundred years or more. In 1864 cricket was already
seen by its most high-minded spokesmen as a game of two halves:
cavaliers and aesthetes on the one hand, and money-grubbing labourers
on the other. We can see these rival factions forming like armies on
opposite sides of an invisible valley: the game that was supposed to
bring them together also served as a way of affirming their differences.
In polite society the professional "players" were often disparaged as
joyless hirelings, turning a beautiful game into a mere trade. So perhaps
it was no accident that the first *Wisden* included so many Civil War
echoes. The battle between royalists and roundheads was being fought
all over again – this time on the playing fields of Eton, Harrow, Lord's
and Leamington. No one knew that at this time the professional
"Elevens" were in fact at the very height of their popularity. It was clear
only that the nearly national game was splitting into camps, and that the
future was up for grabs. There were schisms aplenty, the most telling of
which was the fault-line developing between north and south. After
another quarrel over umpiring, the men of Nottingham were refusing
to play against Surrey altogether, and would stick to their decision for
half a dozen years. Something, it seemed, would have to give.

An even bigger controversy, as it happens, was an already familiar
one: dubious bowling. Convention still insisted that the arm must not
be raised above the shoulder, but this was under challenge from bowlers
who, looking for bounce on the improving wickets of the day, wanted
to deliver the ball from a greater height. In 1822 a Kent bowler called
Willes had been no-balled, in a game against MCC at Lord's, for raising
his hand to shoulder-height (round-arm). He had been inspired (so runs
the rural myth) by his sister Christina, who lifted her arm to escape the
stays of her dress. Now, in a fit of pique, he tossed the ball away, climbed
on to his horse and clopped off, never to play a senior game again. Five
years later Sussex, led by William Lillywhite, bowled out England using

the round-arm style, and nine England players marched off in a huff, refusing to resume "unless the Sussex bowlers bowled fair".

In what now seems a typically British compromise – the legislation by precedent that underpins the Common Law itself – there was an initial attempt to resist change, followed by a giving-in to the inevitable. The following May, MCC insisted that both arm and hand must be "below the elbow", but in 1835, after further incidents, round-arm bowling was legitimised: "If the hand be above the shoulder in delivery," ran the new law, storing up trouble for the future, "the umpire must call no-ball."

Now, a generation later, it was happening again. Bowlers were delivering the ball with their arms *above* the shoulder, putting both umpires and lawmakers on the spot. In the summer of 1863 a Cambridge Blue called Tom Collins was no-balled five times in succession for raising his arm too high in the Varsity match. It came hard on the heels of an even more prominent ruckus in 1862, when one of the country's top professionals, Edgar Willsher of Kent, was no-balled *six* times in a row at The Oval – by none other than John Lillywhite, William Lillywhite's son. It was a dramatic episode, not least because it came at a time when professional cricket seemed to have the wind in its sails. The Players had beaten the Gents in their last 12 games; contests between the two leading elevens (All-England, and United All-England) were fast becoming the top fixtures of the summer, and the 1857 game drew a crowd of 20,000 over three days. So the no-balling of Willsher felt like a crisis even at the time.

It has sometimes been supposed that the entire episode was pre-arranged. Willsher, despite a lanky and "cadaverous" appearance caused by the fact that he had only one lung, was one of England's premier cricketers. On the first day he bowled six overs and took two wickets without being no-balled at all. Day two was different. His first over was delivered in "breathless silence"; then the trouble started. Lillywhite called "No-ball" again and again, and the game crashed. George Parr and eight professionals on the England side stormed off the pitch, and the talking began. The Players sensed a southern conspiracy, and vowed never to play against Surrey again; in a desperate attempt to soothe wounded feelings, John Lillywhite was replaced as an umpire. But as before these initial fumbling attempts to uphold the existing law failed; the rules were stretched to accommodate overarm bowling, and the whole game changed.

There was nothing new about such disputes, of course, but they tended to follow the same pattern. Each time the law changed, players began to press up against the next redoubt. The 1864 Laws allowed for a raised arm, but stood firm on the subject of throwing, insisting that bowlers deliver the ball with a straight arm: "the ball must be bowled. If thrown or jerked, the umpire shall call *No-Ball*." But this too was tricky to enforce now that cricket was becoming professional. Livelihoods were at stake; a man's career could be ruined on the capricious whim of an ill-tempered umpire. The Players, lacking the resources of the better-off Gentlemen, and in no position to put the purity of cricket aesthetics on an aesthetic pedestal above commercial facts, formed a huddle in which breaches of even this rule were overlooked.

William Clarke understood that the carousel would spin only as long as the team played like champions, and he did his own considerable best to keep the standard high: between 1848 and 1854 he took 2,327 wickets, more than 300 a year, all over the country. This allowed him to rise above the occasional complaint inspired by the fact that he did not always share the proceeds. One player in particular refused to ply his trade to line the pockets of another man. His name was John Wisden – creator of the Almanack that bears his name; though few have heard of him, he is a household name. In the true Dickensian temper of the times, he wanted and asked for more.

2

The Little Wonder

Of his life we know only the bare facts. John Wisden was born at Crown Street, Brighton on 5 September 1826 – to a builder called William (some accounts call him Thomas) and his wife Lucy. He had a brother (also William, which makes sense) and a sister (Johanna) and attended a school, Middle Street, which remains proud of his having stared out of a classroom window all those decades ago. In truth he might have made only the smallest dent in the life of the world had he not, in a Copperfield-like twist of fate, been sent to work as a pot-boy (washer-up) for a local hero called Tom Box, the leading wicketkeeper of the day. Young "Johnny" Wisden was soon put to work as an apprentice fielder or "longstop boy", scrambling after the ball as it raced between the tents that fringed the pitch (there was no firm "boundary" in those days – indeed it was common to complete half a dozen runs while the ball was being retrieved from the cat's cradle of canvas flaps and rope), and before long he was earning extra pennies for this work on Brighton's Montpelier ground. The simple business of tossing the ball back gave him a strong arm, and while he did not know it, he had entered a world in which sport was spreading beyond the gentry, in which ball-skills might even be a route to advancement. The boy Wisden absorbed the nuances of cricket with unusual, knee-high intensity, and in 1838, as a minuscule 12-year-old, he was selected as one of "Eleven Youths of Brighton" to play against Lewes.

A dozen years later he was a whippy underarm bowler for Sussex against Kent. He was always tiny (topping out at five foot four and seven stone), but height and bounce were not an issue in these days before overarm bowling. Cricket was a game of guile, not brawn, and

Wisden's deeds as a professional were soon a matter of public record. In
the decade to come he would play 82 matches for Sussex, bagging 578
wickets and becoming known as the "Sussex Pet", the "Little Marvel"
or, most resonantly, as the "Little Wonder" (a sobriquet inspired by the
1840 Derby winner). Opponents saw him, more pragmatically, as a
"deadly trundler". On 15 July 1850 – a date noted in the calendar in the
first Almanack – the Little Wonder memorably "bowled all the wickets"
("without assistance" from the fielders) in a North v South match at
Lord's, a feat which today's *Wisden* confirms as still unique in first-
class cricket – it was said that his deliveries "without exaggeration
turned a yard from the off". Nor was this his only high point that year:
he took nine wickets for Young v Old at Lord's and another nine
playing as a professional guest (in place of Lord Guernsey, a later president of MCC) for the Lords and Commoners against the blue-bloods
of I Zingari, at Vincent Square, in London. On a tour of America he
took six wickets in consecutive balls, and the following year took ten
again, this time against a "Fourteen" of Sheffield.

He was a feared opponent, in other words, causing mayhem across
the country with his "fast and ripping" off-cutters. It is hard to state his
career statistics with complete accuracy, but according to *A Wisden
Century* (the brief history published to mark the company's centenary
year in 1950) he took, in the 12 seasons from 1848–59, 2,707 wickets at
an average of 225 per season. Some modern archives give him a
career-haul of only 1,109 wickets, at an average of 10.32, which makes
it clear only that the age in which he played needed a *Wisden* to keep
track of his achievements. In 1851 alone he took 455 wickets, an
amazing feat even in an age that favoured bowlers* – it was possibly
only because he was often playing the 18 of Huddersfield or the 22 of
Bath. He was a batsman of repute as well, hitting centuries against Kent
and Yorkshire (148, in the debut first-class match at Sheffield's Bramall
Lane). So when England's top fast bowler, John Jackson, was rebuked

---

* The 455-wicket haul comes from *Wisden* itself (1963) where it is claimed it
came from 43 games. But Cricinfo gives John Wisden only 340 wickets (in 38
games). This remains a dazzling haul, but it reminds us that even records can
be flexible.

for failing ever to achieve the fabled ten-wicket haul, he retorted: "No, but for North against South I got nine and lamed Johnny Wisden so he could not bat. That was as good as ten, eh?"

In 1847 Wisden joined Clarke's All-England XI and rapidly became one of its – and the country's – most noted performers. He and Clarke made a potent pair: three years later, they would open the bowling for the Players at Lord's and continue unchanged for the entire match, with Wisden taking eight wickets and Clarke a dozen. In 1848 Wisden spent a year playing country house cricket in Cambridgeshire for Captain Alexander's Auberries XI, but he returned to the professional circuit when he befriended George Parr, the Nottingham star or "crack" who in due course would take over from Clarke. In 1849 he and Parr became business partners as well as team-mates when, with the backing of MCC luminaries such Lord Guernsey (who took the field with them in the 1850 Young v Old game) they leased an eight-acre site in fashionable Leamington, near Warwick, levelled it, and announced (in the *Royal Leamington Courier and Warwickshire Standard*) the formation of "Messrs Parr and Wisden's Cricket Club". The launch was marked with bells, whistles and an archery gala. According to the *Illustrated London News*, a lone bugler introduced a German band; spectators quaffed and wagered in the beer tents; and "many feats of skill and dexterity were performed".

The first major match (in September) pitted the home side, Leamington, against the United All-England XI (Wisden himself bowled William Clarke for nine, had the great Alfred Mynn caught for nought, and struck 52 not out) and this was followed by a North v South game in which Wisden scored 48 for the North. The following season there were fixtures against MCC, I Zingari and the Gentlemen of Warwickshire. It even seems that Wisden was preparing to settle in the Midlands: in 1849 he became engaged to Parr's sister, Annie, and the following year he and Parr opened a cricket equipment shop near the ground. The March 1851 census, meanwhile, lists a Brighton-born man called "John Wisdoe … Creekiter" in Leamington Priors. But Annie Parr died before the couple could tie the knot, leaving Wisden grieving and alone. In 1852 he became the coach at Harrow School in north-west London, and the ground, the sports shop, and the Little Wonder's thoughts of a life in Leamington were wound up.

Nor did the association with William Clarke survive this change in Wisden's fortunes. According to the memoir of a contemporary (William Caffyn's *Seventy-One Not Out*) there was widespread resentment of the extent to which Clarke was "coining money" – an anonymous correspondent to the journal *Bell's Life*, a so-called "Lover of Cricket" publicly decried Clarke's grand airs and tight grip on the purse strings – he charged £70 for a fixture, but paid his team-players only £4 per match. This was in line with what MCC paid its professionals, but in the summer of 1852 Wisden, like his contemporary Oliver Twist (the novel was published in 1837) demanded second helpings. Clarke "answered him somewhat roughly, and caused a breach between them". Things moved rather fast after that. In September of that year Wisden, along with Jemmy Dean (a bowler so sharp he was nicknamed "Dean Swift"), John Lillywhite and a dozen others, met in Sheffield and signed a declaration that they would no longer play "for or against" Clarke "in consequence of the treatment they have received from him". Two years later, when Clarke got up a North v South match, Wisden and Dean opted out. By then they had founded their own rival enterprise: the United All-England Eleven (UAE), launched at Portsmouth in 1852. At the age of 26 – not young, but by no means old – Wisden was showing both an entrepreneurial streak and a brass neck: this was a clear assault on Clarke's lucrative monopoly.

Wisden was a minor iconoclast who liked to plough his own furrow – he favoured a wide straw hat when all around him were sporting toppers, and was later one of the first senior players to wear a cap. But he also had social aspirations. As cricket coach at Harrow School (a prestigious engagement thought worthy of notice in *The Times*) he taught cricket's finer points to the sons of dukes while running, below-stairs as it were, his own professional tour and planning other ventures. He stayed at Harrow for four years, and was fondly recalled by former pupils as a kindly and diligent mentor – not least, perhaps, because none of the teams under his guidance lost to Eton.

It turned out that Clarke was close to the end of his cricketing life. He played his last game in 1856 and died a few months later. It meant that the two senior Elevens could bury their mutual hatchets and band together to rebuff the newcomers. Parr took over the leadership of the All-England Eleven and quickly repaired relations with Wisden's breakaway outfit. The 1857 game between their respective Elevens generated a tidy sum for a newly constituted Cricketers' Fund Friendly Society into which members could pay one guinea a year and, should they ever be destitute, draw down a pound or two a week to help them through to better times. Wisden himself became the secretary, and the annual match at Lord's was a high point of the cricket calendar. Big crowds flocked to see two well-matched teams, studded with the brightest "cracks" in the game – including the Little Wonder. It was a tentative sign – alarming, in some circles – that professional cricket might one day be financially independent.

The breach with Clarke was a sign that the pugnacious little all-rounder, mid-career, was eager to branch into new arenas and seize whatever business opportunities he could. His brother William ran a sports shop in Brighton, and he now had his own experience of shopkeeping in Leamington. In 1855 he and Fred Lillywhite joined forces to open a "cricket and cigar" shop at number 2 New Coventry Street, near Leicester Square in London. Lillywhite, also a Sussex man (born in Hove) was already a publisher: his scorecard printing operation was a money-spinner (sometimes earning above £20 in a single match) and his annual *Guide to Cricketers,* launched in 1849, was a useful advertising forum for his other ventures.* In 1857 he announced a "large work of cricket scores" that looks to have been the model for *Wisden* itself: it was printed by W. H. Crockford, on the Blackheath Road in Greenwich.

---

* Fred Lillywhite's *Guide to Cricketers* was only the first in a labyrinthine library of similar publications produced by the Lillywhite family in the coming years. It began life as *The Young Cricketer's Guide*, became *Lillywhite's Guide to Cricketers* in its third year, and then changed to *The Original Lillywhite's Guide to Cricketers*. In 1865 it was folded into an annual *Companion* (the so-called "Green Lilly") published by Fred's brother (and Wisden's Sussex team-mate) John Lillywhite. In 1885 another brother, James Lillywhite, folded this into his own *Annual* (the "Red Lilly"). Clear? Bear in mind that there was also a *cousin* called James Lillywhite, who captained England in the first ever Test match against Australia, and you have the makings of a creaking Victorian mystery. This was the swirling, energetic and confusing market in cricket records to which *Wisden*, in time, would seek to bring order and clarity.

Wisden was initially a junior partner in the joint venture: in 1862 the Reverend Pycroft failed even to mention him when he wrote, in *London Society Magazine*, that "the name of Frederick Lillywhite is fast becoming known in foreign parts for bats and balls". But Wisden was not willing to accept second place for long. In 1856 Fred Lillywhite's *Guide to Cricketers* (1856) generously said that Wisden "may be termed the best 'every day' bowler we have". But this kind remark from his partner did not stop Wisden from seeing the Lillywhite model as one he could imitate and supplant.

Shopkeeping was hard work, but Wisden had placed himself at the bustling centre of Britain's colossal Empire. If his spirits ever flagged, he could refresh them by walking round the corner to Leicester Square, where James Wyld's "Great Globe" had been making crowds gasp with wonder since 1851. Visitors could climb ladders inside the giant sphere (some 60 feet high) and inspect a scale model of the planet – complete with mountain ranges and rivers – up close. It was an inspiring vision of a thrilling yet conquerable world, designed to lift the imperial heart. There, in the depths of Africa, was where Dr Livingstone was pressing into the interior! Crane your neck and you could see the icy north-west passage. And there, on the far stairs, was where Florence Nightingale had tended our stricken troops. Wyld's globe stood there for a decade, though interest steadily waned until in 1862 it was taken down and sold for scrap.

Wisden was a professional sportsman, dependent on the game for his living while proud to sell a bat or a fishing rod to make ends meet. But there was already a thriving cottage industry in sporting supplies – the Penshurst-based Duke & Sons had won a royal medal at Prince Albert's Great Exhibition of Art and Manufacture in 1851 – and Wisden was quick to push into this booming new market. He had a keen sense of duty, though, and after his own brush with Clarke was mindful of the financial plights afflicting ex-players who, with fees tied to appearances, could be penniless if they were hurt. In 1868 he bought a pub, The Swan, near Petworth, Sussex, changed its name to The Cricketers, and handed it over to his old friend and co-founder of the United All-England Eleven, James "Jemmy" Dean, to "remain a tenant for as long as he should think fit". Between times he wrote an instruction manual: *Cricket, and How to Play It*, which was published in 1866, the year of the third Almanack. He was assisted in the literary part of this project by a *Times* journalist called George Pardon, a keen writer on cricket, bowls, billiards and whist whose pseudonym ("Rawdon Crawley" or "Captain Crawley") was inspired by a character in Thackeray's 1847 novel *Vanity Fair* and who would, in due course, play a major role in *Wisden*'s affairs. The co-authors emphasised psychological readiness as much as technical skill: a successful player needed to be "wary, yet bold; self-possessed, yet cautious; strong, yet gentle; firm, yet manly". Bowlers, however, were encouraged to be wily; they should be "full of surprises, twists, screws, turns, rises and other dodges".

These varied labours won Wisden a new nickname: "The Cardinal". He was an almost-eminent Victorian, the subject of four portraits, the best of which (by William Bromley in 1850 – he also painted George Parr, giving him a top hat and a bow tie in place of Wisden's cap and cravat) is in the Lord's Museum to this day. After a bright career on the pitch, Wisden was preparing for an equally full life after cricket.

In theory he could have forged a powerful partnership with Fred Lillywhite. In 1854 the two appeared together on a new "cricketing belt" made of smart elastic and clasped in a buckle featuring their likeness. And in the spring of 1858 they launched an eye-catching new product when they bought the patent to a bowling machine called the "Catapulta", a bow-and-arrow design that could project balls at any pace at gentlemen wishing to practise. It was based on a machine designed by Nicholas Wanostracht, who played under the name "Felix" and who, as a classical scholar, was inspired by Roman siege engines. According to some reports, Wisden and Parr had already promoted this cumbersome gadget in their Leamington shop. But in April and May of 1854, as the Light Brigade prepared to embark for the Crimean campaign, they showed the machine off (with the assistance of Fred's brother John) at Lord's and The Oval, securing "upwards of twenty" orders. But they did not remain a joint venture for long. Fred Lillywhite was by all accounts not the easiest man to have dealings with, and later that summer he left Wisden in sole custody of the New Coventry Street store and set up on his own at The Oval. The break was announced in the "Partnerships dissolved" column of *The Times* at the end of the year.

We do not know the precise cause of the split. In the summer of 1858 the usual advertisements appeared in which they still listed themselves as a collaboration. But in August it was announced, in *The Era* and elsewhere, that the New Coventry Street shop was now called Wisden & Co ("late F. Lillywhite and Wisden"). As it happened, Fred Lillywhite's brother John actually ducked out of the Gents v Players match at Lord's on 20 July (he was listed as "absent through illness", but the fact that his wife gave birth to twins that weekend may also have detained him) only to place a notice in *The Era* on 25 July which suggested he had been rather busy with other things too. The notice "begs respectfully to announce" the opening of a new warehouse in Euston Square, with an "immense stock" of sports gear. He and Wisden had been friends and fellow players for years, but it must have pleased the Little Wonder when, in the Married v Single match of 10 August, he bowled John Lillywhite out twice.

Either way, the collapse of the partnership certainly made for a sticky atmosphere the following year, when Wisden agreed to join a cricket tour of America along with – who else – Fred Lillywhite himself. The tour was a groundbreaking union between six members of Parr's All-England Eleven, and half a dozen from Wisden's United All-England Eleven. They were offered £50 a man for the trip – a tidy sum – but actually made nearly twice that (£90). Wisden and Lillywhite were by now on frosty terms. We cannot say for sure that this is when Wisden hatched the idea of publishing his own cricket journal, but it was almost certainly on his mind. As they travelled through America Lillywhite was recording and publishing scores as they went – lugging a heavy printing press at all times. He was also writing a memoir – the first tour diary – in which Wisden was credited with quipping, on the juddering voyage across the Atlantic, with soup plates and teacups crashing to the floor, that the pitch needed "the immediate use of the heavy roller".

Many of the cricketers, wrote Lillywhite, were "exceedingly desirous of putting foot on land again" and one, Caffyn, said he "would not venture to leave England again under any circumstances … no more water". Wisden himself was a "thorough sailor, enjoying both his meals and his pipe" – but although the team won all its matches, the arduous nature of the travelling (it was a 7,500-mile round trip, in late October) led to "frosty" conditions in Montreal and Rochester and strained relations in the touring party; both Parr and Wisden fell out with Lillywhite. Wisden began the tour batting at No. 3, rarely made double figures, and slid down to No. 9 – a descent no cricketer could enjoy, and there are other signs of ill-feeling between the two. He and Parr were pointedly omitted from the list of players thanked at the end of Lillywhite's diary – indeed he noted with feeling that "no assistance was received" from the leaders of the "two celebrated Elevens". Parr, Lillywhite would later write in his *Guide*, was "an able manager (when out of his bedroom) in America". Wisden, meanwhile, was conspicuously absent from the adverts (Duke's and Lillywhites both featured large) and the commemorative belt produced as a souvenir of the tour bore only 11 players from the 12-strong party, under the legend, "England's Champions". Wisden, always easy to spot in photographs (usually the smallest figure), was left off.

He was confident enough on his own, however, planting a series of plain notices in the classified columns of various publications announcing that "John Wisden and Co (formerly F. Lillywhite and Wisden)" was open for business. The item ran weekly for a year in the *Era*, the *Morning Chronicle*, the *Bradford Observer* and elsewhere, often appearing with a similar item about Robert Dark's store in the tennis court at Lord's, with its proud claim to be the "sole inventor and manufacturer of the tubular India rubber glove". Wisden also, in January 1861, advertised in *The Times* for a "shopman ... who thoroughly understands business and bookkeeping". Even in this matter he wanted only the best: "No need to apply without a first-class character."

The clearest sign of his growing status as a retailer came in 1859 and 1862, however, when he produced booklets modelled on Lillywhite's 1857 "List of Matches". Addressed to "Regiments and Cricket Clubs", the "list of prices" laid out the products on sale at New Coventry Street, and showed J. Wisden & Co to be already stocking a broad range of sporting necessities: the "treble whalebone handle bat", the "ebony-top" or "brass-ferruled" stumps, "double-seamed" balls (in various sizes), "superior" flannel for "trowsers and jackets", the "best Electro registered belts" and much more. There were boxing gloves and fives balls, leather boots and leg guards, spiked shoes and portraits (including a photograph of the England 12 who faced an American 22 back in 1859), rackets, "foot balls" (still two words), travelling cases and pipes (with a bat-and-ball emblem on the bowl). There were tobaccos ("Virginia Shag and Bristol Birdseye") and "foreign cigars". There was a mention of J. Wisden & Co's new "Private" guard, which "gives so much confidence to batsmen" – today we would call it a box. And there was a sketch of the famous Catapulta, which had been "worked in the presence of thousands" at Lord's and The Oval, was the "acme of perfection", and was so easy to use that it could even "be managed by a Lady, if set at a moderate or medium pace".

The emphasis on smoking may seem odd today, but in the mid-19th century it was a fashionable necessity. The Canadians Richard Benson and William Hedges had not yet opened their store next to Philip Morris in Bond Street (near Marlborough Street, which gave its name to a famous brand). But tobacco was an aromatic part of a gentleman's life. An 1856 advertisement, in the *Era*, for the Coventry Street store of "Lillywhite and Wisden" offered "foreign cigars not to be equalled", along with various other exotic pipes and cigars. The shop, it claimed, was "well patronised by the noblemen and gentlemen of the Marylebone and other cricket clubs".

By 1859, when John Wisden was running the show on his own, such notices did not even mention tobacco, which suggests that Lillywhite may have been keener on this line of business. But price lists for John Wisden & Co show that the firm did continue to sell cigars well into the 20th century. And why not, when no less an authority than Alfred Dunhill, in *The Pipe Book* (1924), was happy to pronounce that tobacco was "the sole narcotic that can be employed repeatedly and even continuously without bringing in its train either physical discomfort or other ill effects".

The most important thing about the 1857 price list is not the glimpse of the retail trade it offers nor even the illustration of the tidy New Coventry Street store, festooned with bats and racquets, that graces the cover of the 1862 version. This brief 16-page work has the same proportions, the same typeface, the same point size and many of the same design features (bold and capital letters) as the Almanack. No printer is thanked, but even a non-betting man would wager that it came from the steam press of W. H. Crockford, which would print the first *Wisden* just two years later.

It was evidently a success, which was just as well, since John Lillywhite was now moving his own sports arcade from Euston Square to Piccadilly, where it towered for over a century. He was parking his tank on Wisden's lawn, and Wisden, hampered by a rackets injury, his playing days behind him but with business growing fast and the Almanack taking shape in his mind, retired from cricket for good. There was no late flourish. He played his last three games in September 1863, in Godalming, Stockton-on-Tees and Newcastle-upon-Tyne, but his top score was ten and he took just one wicket. In the years to come he would occasionally stand as an umpire (sometimes with his friend Jemmy Dean at the other end) in games involving his own United All-England Eleven. But his days as a significant player were over.

This is how things stood in the years preceding *Wisden*'s birth. London in 1863 was a swirl of busy novelties, flecked by the tension between amateur cricket and the new professional circuit. George Parr, captain of the All-England XI playing Surrey on the fateful day of Willsher's no-balls, had long refused to face players from that county. But now, invited to assemble a team to tour Australia, he swallowed his pride and invited Surrey's stars. Overseas tours were a natural extension of the cricket-circus concept pioneered by the Elevens: a travelling troupe of globetrotters could descend on a faraway place for a game and a gala dinner (with toasts) and collect fees for entertaining the locals. In their wake they threw up a brisk commerce in bats and balls. Wisden was retiring at a vexed but lively moment in the story of the game.

There were other new faces on the scene. In 1863 Lord's acknowledged the formation of Hampshire and Yorkshire, confirming that a third major strand in the game – county cricket – was rising to prominence. Perhaps the future would not be one in which amateurs and professionals were inevitably rivals – in county cricket they could be team-mates too. In 1864 and 1865 three more (Lancashire, Middlesex, Worcestershire) entered the list, and a whole new cricketing arrangement seemed likely. But if growth was in the air, so was change. What we might call the soul of the game – few doubted that it had one – seemed up for grabs.

Lord's itself, though long known as the "home" of cricket – players measured their careers from the time they played their first game there, and thoughts were already turning to the 50th anniversary of the ground, which had been founded in 1814, the year before Waterloo – was also the subject of an ownership dispute. Through the 1850s it was notoriously shabby: "heavy clay, badly drained with a rough outfield, and treacherous". And MCC was such an upper-crust outfit that the cricket ground was abandoned as soon as the shooting season opened in mid-August. So when the lease needed renewing in 1860 MCC declined even to bid for it. The title to Thomas Lord's famous old ground, held by James Henry Dark, was bought for £7,000 by a property speculator called Isaac Moses, who promptly proposed to raise the ground rent for cricket from £150 per year to £550. The future was fraught, to say the least. If an august institution like Lord's could be a mere toy for commercial adventurers, nothing was sacred. Two years later, Lord's was saved when a keen MCC member, gin distiller, politician and cricketer (for Harrow and Middlesex), William Nicholson, financed a buyback. He did not make the loan public, but when he died in 1909 the Almanack thanked him effusively: "There is no doubt that he saved Lord's from the builders," it ran. "But for him the ground might have been built over." The sum in question – "a long way into five figures" allowed MCC to buy the freehold to the ground and secure cricket's occupation of it. And though *Wisden* was never an in-house journal, it was happy to pass on the message that whatever one might say about the role of the amateur in high-level cricket there was a crisp financial truth at the heart of it: amateurs were financial patrons, and cricket depended on them.

The property deal meant a nice profit for Moses (over £10,000), but it was further evidence that cricket in the 1860s stood at an uncertain crossroads. The *Sporting Life* went so far as to argue for a "Cricket Parliament" to replace those useless blue-bloods at Lord's, perhaps not aware that one of them had just secured its fabled future.

In one sense Wisden was embarked on just such a mission himself. He was now a senior figure in the game, and in June 1863, one week after his United All-England XI had played its annual benefit match against the All-England XI at Lord's, with proceeds going to the Cricketers' Fund Benefit Society, he was re-elected as its honorary secretary. This was a significant post. The fund was a co-operative created for luckless cricketers and their families, but also a sign that full-time cricket was emerging from the commercial tangle – something like a gold rush or a scramble for advantage – and donning respectable robes of office. Wisden was proposed by his friend Parr, but also by John Lillywhite and Willsher, a hint that the combatants in the great no-ball drama of the previous summer might have acted in concert, since they seemed to harbour no ill-feeling about the episode. It clearly meant a good deal to Wisden himself – he retained the position until the end of his days.

The success of the fund was a further indication that cricket was able, by forming teams and staging matches, to create a market independent of amateur patronage. Back in 1862 the proprietors of the Café de Paris in Melbourne (Messrs Spiers and Pond) had invited Parr to bring a team to Australia. Each player was offered £150, enough to tempt even a noted amateur like E. M. Grace (older brother of W. G.) to play under the captaincy of a professional. But aside from launching a grand old rivalry when the team sailed out in the winter of 1863-4, the tour was an eye-opening success. It generated profits of roughly £11,000 for the sponsors, easily enough to finance the sponsors' return to London. And John Wisden was able to devote a good chunk of his second Almanack, in 1865, to his old friend's "doings" in Australia.

It was an era when much was up for grabs, in other words, and even Wisden's role as secretary of the Cricketers' Fund sharpened the edge of his rivalry with Fred Lillywhite. He was not just a rival sports retailer; he was also (under cover of this sober philanthropic role) a serious cricket impresario. In his *Guide* Lillywhite was severe, telling readers bitterly that Wisden "devotes himself to doing good as a *paid* secretary" to the fund.

It is evident from all this that *Wisden* was by no means conceived as a mouthpiece for the establishment at MCC and Lord's. Far from it. There may have been a diplomatic nod in that direction, but in the stew of contradictory motives it was the opposite idea that had the upper hand. As we have seen, this was an unusual moment in English intellectual history, a time (satirised in Dickens through the factual tyranny of Mr Gradgrind) when the urge to build tables and lists, and impose hierarchies, categories and codes on to new fields of endeavour had never been stronger or more technically feasible. We can also glimpse here the Victorian mania for collecting, the impulse that gave birth to so many museums. But there was a contrary force at work too – the ravenous 19th-century appetite for progress and profit. Its most immediate effect was to extend Wisden's rivalry with the Lillywhites into a new realm; any publicity the book attracted would, if nothing else, boost his equipment business.

There would be one more twist in the story of this rivalry. In 1866 Fred Lillywhite was declared bankrupt and, soon afterwards, died. Wisden himself bought up a supply – some £30 worth – of Lillywhite's own-brand "Registered Scoring-Paper" before, in due course, producing his own version. He was promptly sued by a Kennington businessman called Page, who had bought the copyright in Lillywhite's design, for stealing a proprietary product. But in 1868 the Vice-Chancellor's Court (nudged by evidence contributed by the "eminent cricketers" Parr and Dean) rejected Page's suit, finding (in Wisden's favour) that there could be no copyright in a simple scoring system – sheets of ruled paper – that had been "in common use for many years" and was really no more "proprietary" than a solicitor's bill.

Something else, though, something at once more ambitious and less likely to please the hyphenated surnames at Lord's, glimmered in Wisden's initial concept. His first Almanack was above all a guide to *professional* cricket – the game staged by paid entertainers for the amusement of the public, rather than the game played on country-house lawns for the moral improvement of the nation's gilded youth. This mercenary world was the untilled field, the untold story and the new market. Despite the polite overtures to MCC on the cover, the first edition was a radical volume in that it aspired to be a handbook for a more abrasive form of cricket. That is why the substance of the volume ignored the well-dressed MCC fixture list, the schools and universities, and consisted instead of scorecards from the two leading professional Elevens (Wisden's and Parr's), along with a full history of the matches between the Gents and Players. *The Cricketer's Almanack*, in this first incarnation, aimed to describe and promote this new brand of cricket. Wisden, himself a professional, planned to record the "doings" of these modern entertainers, whom he was not alone in seeing as a spirited new force – and perhaps the future of the game. When Richard Daft wrote his memoir, *Kings of Cricket*, in 1893, he credited these circuses with establishing a new style of cricket artistry: "All-England Eleven v United Eleven was always one of the best of the season ... for really enjoyable games, both for player and spectator alike, there never have been, in my opinion, and never again will be, any to equal those."

A significant cricket tradition was put at risk by this development. The matches between amateurs, or "Gents", and professionals, or "Players", had been regular high points of the English cricketing summer since 1806, but now they faced competition both from county cricket and from all-professional games. Willam Clarke had created a chill in the corridors of MCC when, in 1854, he refused to release his United England professionals to play in a Gents v Players match, and the fixture was also losing prestige thanks to the increasing relative weakness of the amateurs. Since 1806 there had been 53 such encounters, enough to form a statistical sample, and the results made telling reading. At first the Gents enjoyed (as they expected to) the upper hand, winning seven of the first ten fixtures. Since then, however, the Players had seized the upper hand, winning 28 of the next 43 games, sometimes by a big margin (in 1821 they replied to the Gents total of 60 by amassing 278, leading the Gents to give up the match; in 1823 they won by 345 runs; and the following year they put 14 amateurs to the sword by 101 runs). In response, the Gents briefly set aside their well-known addiction to fair play and the amateur spirit by slipping star professionals into their own ranks as guests. In 1829, for instance, they took the field "with Lillywhite" – the opposition's best bowler. This was William Lillywhite, patriarch of the great dynasty that followed him. He took 13 wickets, merrily bowling out his erstwhile team-mates for 24 and 37 to set up a simple win for the Gents. Intriguingly, *Wisden* records that he "hit wicket, 0" when he batted, and it is tempting (on no evidence) to imagine him doing so deliberately, with a wide grin at his defeated professional colleagues.

The Gents pulled the same trick the following year (Lillywhite took six wickets in dismissing the Players for 46), but in 1831 he was permitted to represent the Players again, and skittled eight Gents cheaply. The writing was not just on the wall; it was in the book. The Gents could no longer count on giving the Players a competitive game. In 1833 16 of them were bowled out for 42; in 1836, with seven more players than their opponents, they squeaked a win, but in 1837 they were out for 54 and 35.

By the time John Wisden himself started turning out for the Players, it was hard for the Gents to hold their own. In 1850 he took a five-wicket haul and scored 24; in 1856 he took four in each innings, while the superbly named Julius Caesar (of Godalming) helped himself to a half century; and in 1858 he scored 58 in another easy victory. All these details he would faithfully immortalise in his own book. When it came to the "doings" of the two Elevens, too, he approached the task with due reverence. The introduction to this section actually referred to Wisden's experience as a player by promising to refrain from commenting on the scores under review. "We have abstained from making any remarks concerning the individual play of any man, since, when all are so good it would, perhaps, be invidious to single out any one as being superior to those with whom he has so often played with varied success."

This canniness extended to a shrewd targeting of the northern cricketer. Where Lillywhite alienated them, Wisden – an honorary northerner – took the trouble to post adverts for his new project in regional papers: the *Blackburn Standard*, the *York Herald*, the *Nottinghamshire Guardian*, the *Sheffield Independent* and several others. Thus alerted, these publications soon began to post warm reviews of the Almanack.

He was also nimble enough to catch Lillywhite on the back foot by getting his own book to the bookstalls first, and on 6 February the first review appeared, in the *Sporting Gazette*. "Like its respected publisher, the work is a neat, well got up and unpretending little affair," it ran. While noting that the horse-racing elements were "a strange affair in a cricket work", it was confident that the new publication could give anyone "a pleasant and interesting hour". The next day, the *Era* also gave a terse thumbs-up: "This little work was published by John Wisden, of New Coventry Street, on Wednesday last. Its contents are varied and useful." The writer summarised the book's main items before concluding that it was "an interesting one shillings worth".

In a much smaller four-line note directly beneath this notice, the *Era* stated that this year's *Lillywhite's Guide to Cricketers* would be published in a few weeks' time, that it was lowering the price to one shilling to match Wisden's effort, and that it promised to be "a crusher". In the event, Lillywhite overplayed his hand, including snide remarks about the professionals who were *Wisden*'s chief supporters, such as Nottingham's George Parr ("has been a splendid bat ... his time is now devoted to other purposes"), George Tarrant ("a very fast bowler – fast in every way") and even Wisden himself, who "does nothing for his country, England, or any other eleven".

There were bitter recriminations. "A Lover of the Game" wrote in the *Sheffield and Rotherham Independent* that Lillywhite's guide was "scurrilous" and "vile", while both MCC and Surrey (Lillywhite's landlord at The Oval) demanded that he withdraw his words. The *Sporting Gazette* ran an article called "The True Enemies of Cricket" which attacked Lillywhite's work line by line, calling it "spiteful twaddle" full of "petty malice". He had no option, said the *Nottinghamshire Guardian*, but to "submit" to his own "humiliation" by printing an apology in a subsequent issue. The *Sporting Gazette* was pleased to report further that in claiming to be "under the patronage of the MCC" Lillywhite had badly wounded his own cause: "immediate steps were taken to prevent any such impudent assumptions for the future".

It was a fortunate outcome for Wisden and he took full advantage of the situation, insisting that *his* journal would commit no such faux pas, pass no judgement. He even repeated what he had said about the professional elevens by declaring again: "We of course make no comments upon the matches, leaving the cricketer to form his own opinion with regard to the merits of the men, since a great many of our readers are at least equal, if not superior to ourselves, in arriving at a right judgement of the play."

This may have been a neat piece of flattery, stroking the vanity of his readers. But it was also a shrewd memo to the powers-that-be. It is easy to imagine Fred Lillywhite spluttering through the thick cigar smoke in his Oval printing room when he saw the maddening, superior tone of this quiet boast. Whether it was Wisden himself or one of his publishing associates who contrived this crafty disclaimer, we cannot say. But no one could fail to see that, while conceding that there was indeed such a thing as a "right judgement of the play", *Wisden* was deliberately placing itself above such matters, and happy to make friendly overtures to those in high and useful places.

Thus while the heart of the book might have been a record of the professional game, the surrounding matter doffed its cap to cricket's traditions. There was a list of dates on which cricketers played their first game at Lord's, an achievement already seen as hallowed. It included the day (in May 1787) when Thomas Lord himself scored one and 36 in a two-innings match, and the day when Wisden himself made a modest four and five on debut. Richard Francis had the honour of being included for the day, in June 1793, when he registered a pair (two zeros) on the rotten yet sacred turf.

There followed a collection of the game's "long scores". At this stage, cricket was not a big-hitting game, and big tallies – Julius Caesar's century for England against Kent at Canterbury in 1853, or Wisden's "long score" for Sussex at Tunbridge Wells in 1850 (as chance would have it, the first century to appear on *Wisden*'s pages, on page 24 of the launch edition), or the amazing Mr E. Austen Leigh, who registered a top score of 190 in 1860 – were precious, and deserved all the acclaim they received.

On a lighter note, there was a brief selection of "Extraordinary Matches". Some of these described outlandish, music-hall contests: Left-handers v Right-handers, One Arm v One Leg (a tightly fought draw), or Smokers v Non-smokers (at Lord's – the Non-smokers won). Others were merely memorable. In 1855 the Royal Surrey Militia posted the sublime score of ... 0, after the whiskered gallants of the Queen's regiment failed to trouble the scorer. There were signs, too, that cricket was already an old man's pastime – in an over-60s match in Sheffield, the combined age of the 16-man team was 1,010 years (average: 68). Remarkably, there were only two run-outs.

———

There are several things we can say about the first *Wisden*. As we have seen, it was first and foremost an entrepreneurial inspiration, an attempt to grab a piece of a shifting market. Like some modern internet pioneer, John Wisden aimed to exploit advances in printing, and the boom in sport, and bag a new market. In retrospect, it seems in character that his book should have slipped into the world with so little fanfare. There was nothing resembling the promotional boasting that would attend such a launch today. The single gesture of explanation for the clump of scorecards that comprised the first book were the curt messages To the Reader, which stated simply, in a solemn Gothic typeface, that "we have taken great pains to collect a certain amount of information" about "this noble game ... this glorious pastime". This was an act of sober deference: the players, it proposed, were by definition superior to the game's mere chroniclers. This was a "cricketer's" almanack, a serious publication for serious persons – not a casual reader's toy. A mere scribe could never be more than a mediocre acolyte, faithfully communicating the deeds of his betters.

No stance was better calculated to please the know-your-place nabobs at Lord's. In cricket's great chain of being, in which professionals perforce occupied the rung below the amateur spirit, they at least breathed purer air than mere journalists.

Perhaps Wisden sensed that the professional cricket world he was recording and addressing was already too fractious and unruly to base a business on. He knew this for certain, while the second Almanack was being compiled, in November 1864, when he attended a boisterous meeting at the Bridge House Hotel on London Bridge, at which seven of his United All-England regulars resigned to form a team of their own. What he had done to Clarke was now being done to him. *Bell's Life* reported that "the appearance of so many 'cracks' caused no little commotion" and the outcome of the meeting dismayed the correspondent, who doubted "whether there would be sufficient country demand to fully employ three crack elevens". John Wisden himself, somewhat crestfallen, agreed to continue as treasurer of the UAE for one more year, and the following summer, when he put a team out to play the Sixteen of Trinity College Cambridge, the *Sporting Gazette* was upbeat: "Instead of their being defunct, or rather annihilated, they have risen, à la phoenix, from the long-smouldering ashes of a low-bred jealousy." But Wisden knew the future was neither simple nor certain, and was careful to maintain goodwill at Lord's. The time he had spent coaching Harrow schoolboys was no hindrance either: he knew how to move in smart circles.

The strategy paid off. In 1865, just a year into *Wisden*'s life, MCC withdrew its support for Lillywhite's *Guide* on the grounds that he had "exceeded the fair limits of criticism upon cricketers". There was a gap at the top of the market, and *Wisden* was padded up and ready to go. Moreover, here, in a single quiet flash, was born a voice whose essential aspect – rarefied, slightly fusspot restraint – would echo through English life for a century and a half. *Wisden* was not born fully formed: this first tentative publication was by no means a sign of what was to come – ahead lay decades of patient trial and error. But if anything *was* etched in the original DNA, it was this sober, judicious, ceremonious tone. In time it would be this voice that would make *Wisden* what it became: a calm, unflustered authority on its game, its world.

In March of that year *Wisden* also published a "little, unpretending work" (according to the *Era*) about the previous winter's tour to Australia. Two months later, the *Era* was rewarded when *Wisden* began to place a series of adverts for his shop in its columns, showing, in addressing it to "Noblemen, Gentlemen, Regiments, Colleges and Schools" that he knew where his market lay. In the years to come, *Wisden* would feature in the classified columns of magazines like *Bell's Life*, alongside plugs for silver harnesses, fur seal waistcoats, smoker's bonbons, overland trunks, shooting capes and editions of Byron's poetry. In its very first year, *Wisden* was proposing itself as a routine accessory for the mid-Victorian gentleman's lifestyle.

As it happened, change would soon be imposed on the infant book. Away in the West Country, as yet only a faint blip on the *Wisden* radar, a 15-year-old boy called William Grace was beginning to show signs of more than ordinary promise. His older brother, E. M. Grace, was an established amateur and famous leg-side hitter bound for Australia with Parr's XI in 1863–4. But this younger brother was, it was rumoured, something else. In 42 innings in 1863 he had made 673 runs against some smart opponents, including 86 for West Gloucestershire against Clifton. Picked to represent Bristol and District against George Parr's marauding All-England XI, he came in late and knocked George "Tear 'em" Tarrant, one of the fiercest bowlers in the land, out of the attack. His keenly struck 32 swung the match Bristol's way and set up a grand win (secured by his brother E. M., who took ten wickets in the match). Sadly, the game was not notable enough to be recorded in the first *Wisden*, but Grace himself later called 1863 "the beginning of my serious cricket". The following summer he scored 170 and 56 not out for South Wales against the Gentleman of Sussex – an astonishing effort. And he was still only 16 years old, not yet the bearded Victorian giant – an athletic reincarnation of Darwin or Tennyson – he was destined to become.

John Wisden would soon gain first-hand knowledge of the boy wonder. In June 1865 he stood as an umpire in a game between his own United All-England XI and The Eighteen of Bath. E. M. Grace, the most celebrated player on either side, scored 121 for the Eighteen, but his scrawny little brother also made a mark, taking three wickets and scoring 11. No one could have predicted exactly, or even roughly, what lay in store. But John Wisden's new Almanack was arriving at a moment when the game, already in flux, was about to be altered thoroughly, and for good.

Advertisement from Wisden *1883*

3

Time to Say Grace

It would be nice to say that young William Grace took the pages of *Wisden* by storm, or that his emergence was one of those happy coincidences with which the life of the Almanack (and the game) has been decorated. But he did not. If anything, *Wisden* was slow to applaud the revolutionary scale of Grace's talent, finding him an indecently greedy run-getter ... too crowd-pleasing by half. Something about Grace unnerved the Almanack that should have been his chief celebrant. His tremendous scoring feats were duly noted – the 1867 book could not ignore 2,168 runs at an average of 54.2 (including a double-century – 224 not out at The Oval), but even this spectacular effort (he was still a teenager) was not enough to earn him a place in the Births and Deaths column, *Wisden*'s own proud list of notable cricketers. Was it the fact that he was simply too good, or a touch too grasping? Either way, he wouldn't quite do.

In the years to come, as Grace registered hard-hitting century after hard-hitting century, *Wisden* politely published details of his gargantuan achievements while pursing its lips over the manner in which he accomplished them. Batsmanship was supposed to be an art, or a science – a cultivated pursuit; but in Grace's hands it was mere vulgar "hitting". He was actually willing, to an extent that alarmed the game's traditionalists (numerous, even then) to aim for the vacant acreage at deep midwicket where cattle could in theory safely graze – "cow corner". A true gentleman would not dream of playing in that plebeian direction, but Grace saw it as an open goal. When one vexed bowler told him, in a famous, perhaps fanciful, story, that the shot he had just struck was "not cricket", the great man replied: "It might not be cricket, but it *is* four runs."

No one now believes Grace to have been a one-dimensional player: on the contrary, he is widely held to have conceived and perfected new methods of playing the awkward overarm bowling by attacking off both the front foot and the back. And he was no mere thuggish smiter – one of his claims to fame was as a defensive rampart – the Lord's crowd once rose to him when he kept out four consecutive "shooters" in a row, then considered virtually unplayable. Perhaps it was simply the enormous scale of his achievements that put *Wisden*'s nose out of joint – there seemed something disrespectful in such wild, unprecedented scoring prowess. So when MCC played Notts in 1869, *Wisden* had nothing to say about Grace's 121, preferring to dwell instead on the more modest heroics of Richard Daft. "Tuesday was Daft's day," it declared. "For cool, scientific, cautious and successful defence, this innings was a marvel; *slow* it certainly was, but then it was *sure*."[*]

Grace was rewriting the record book, and the record book didn't like it. Even his most spectacular totals were recorded with a lip-curl of distaste. "Mr Grace's 96 and 127," *Wisden* reported from Canterbury a few weeks later, "were capital antidotes to his nought on the Monday." And when Grace scored 172 (out of 276) for Gloucestershire against MCC, *Wisden* could not resist cavilling that he was "nearly had at cover point when he made only 21". On this occasion *Wisden* handed the garlands to Gordon, whose 53 was "an innings of careful, good defence, clean, hard cutting and excellent cricket". The fact that Grace also took seven wickets for 65 passed without comment.

When he scored 215 for the Gentlemen against the Players at The Oval in 1870 *Wisden* noted that he was "nearly had at short slip" and that the Players fielded "very indifferently". At a benefit match Grace himself, *Wisden* noted, "fielded very inefficiently". This faint applause persisted for many years. Even the report on his 126th century, at Lord's in 1905, felt obliged to point out that though "an exceedingly fine display" the great man had played "one or two faulty strokes".

---

[*] The pledge in *Wisden*'s first edition not to comment on the performance of the star players had not lasted long. The 1865 edition included a "comment" on George Parr's "doings" in Australia – "his leg side hitting is always a treat to witness". Thereafter the Almanack was known as much for its judgement as for its record-keeping.

We do not know what the *Wisden* staff muttered as they studied the annual scores. There are no records, no minutes of their procedures. But the book itself contains whispers that carry down the decades. In 1870 Grace scored nine centuries; in six innings at The Oval he scored 540, and plundered a further 666 runs for MCC. When he scored 170 not out at Lord's, for England against Notts and Yorkshire (57 more than his team-mates put together), the "Compiler" came up with the famous verdict: "Mr Grace first, the rest nowhere." Yet still *Wisden* was often restrained. A few weeks later, when Surrey's tough opener, Harry ("the Stonewaller") Jupp battled his way to 85, it was hailed as "a masterpiece of defence", while Grace's imposing 181 was deemed disfigured by the fact that "when he had made 123 he gave a hot chance to short square leg". History repeated itself in the 1871 Gents v Players game: Grace's half-century attracted no comment, while Jupp's 29 was "an innings so faultlessly played as to elicit the applause of the eleven Gentlemen and all on the ground".

Of course, it might be that by Grace's own unique standards a mere half-century was barely worth mentioning; but that same summer the "crack" was amassing 3,696 runs, an inspired deluge that included two double-centuries, four scores over 150, and four plain tons. It was common knowledge that no one could match him, but *Wisden* still frowned. He was merely, the book said, the "best *and luckiest* batsman in England".

In 1874 he helped himself to 87 for South v North, but the batting honours were awarded to Yardley for his patient 73 – "splendid, perfect cricket ... unsurpassed, brilliant, manly form". His 152 for MCC against Canada was a feat ascribed mainly to the weakness of the opposition: "inasmuch as the hitting was very fine, the fielding was otherwise". Once again, a far lesser effort, Bird's 116, was "beyond question the finest innings played in the match". And in Canterbury, Grace's 98 was judged to be inferior ("one of the easiest chances possible of running out Mr Grace was literally thrown away") to Jupp's 80 – "an innings that for careful, true, scientific cricket was pronounced to have been the very best played during the week".

It is very curious, this disparaging of the master. It is common knowledge now that Grace was not just a sporting colossus but the author of modern batting's style book, so it is a surprise to find that this was not quite a unanimous view at the time. But hindsight, as has been said, is the best historian – and the 1860s were a time of rivalrous flux. In *Wisden*'s case, there was a clear enough ideological split between two warring enthusiasms: one side wanted to record and promote professional cricket, the other was in thrall to the Corinthian ideal and sought to applaud amateur zest. Grace was complicated, because despite his well-documented "shamateurism" – he made more money as a Gentleman cricketer than he did from doctoring – and his quasi-professional level of competitive excellence, he was still, in theory, an amateur. *Wisden*'s editors were lucky to have him, but they didn't seem to know it.

We know next to nothing about the way the early volumes of the Almanack were assembled, but it appears that the two men chiefly responsible for its production were split along roughly these lines. John Wisden was the founder and architect (what the marketing men would now call "the brand") and his original notion envisaged a handbook of the professional game. But the editorial burden fell chiefly on a flowery Victorian sportswriter called W. H. Knight (part of a notable family of journalists – his brother Robert helped found the *Times of India*) who had markedly different leanings. He lived in Hampstead and was on the staff of the *Sporting Life*, and his tastes were not at all aligned with those of his proprietor: he much preferred Eton v Harrow or the Varsity match to the modish tussles between hired professionals. It is no coincidence that the first ever match report (not signed, but almost certainly his work), printed in the second edition of 1865, described not England or Nottinghamshire, or a game involving Grace, Parr or Lillywhite, but the Eton v Harrow match. This was a very different strand of cricket to the one represented by John Wisden himself. It had been a famous encounter ever since Lord Byron turned out for Eton in the first, ramshackle game in 1805, and by now it was a firm part of the social whirl. The 1864 Almanack showed no interest in such affairs, but in its second year it took great pleasure in praising it. "Very capital accommodation was afforded," *Wisden* purred, adding that the marquees were "well stored with strawberries, ices and cooling beverages".

This second *Wisden*, published in 1865, began with a burst of ostentatious humility. On the title page the editor deferentially recorded that it was "the 29th year of the reign of Her Majesty" and thanked subscribers in ever-so-grateful tones. "Induced by the flattering patronage of many of the most distinguished cricketers of the day, they [John Wisden & Co] have ventured upon the publication of a second number." It is interesting in itself that the first person used in the debut Almanack ("We of course make no comments …") has retreated into a more detached third person ("They [John Wisden & Co] …"). It suggests rather markedly that W. H. Knight has had a firmer hand in the publication, and there was a visible change of policy – school and university matches were suddenly prominent. Two years later the Preface (in 1867) made the shift explicit: "In consequence of the great increase in the number of matches, John Wisden & Co have most reluctantly been compelled to limit the Eleven v Twenty Two matches to the 'Results' only, though they are aware that many of their friends are very much interested." The professional game would from now on be treated in condensed form. *Wisden* hoped that any disappointment this might cause would be assuaged by the inclusion of news about clubs such as "Anomalies, Butterflies, Cambridge University, Free Foresters, Incogniti etc." There were others: the Knickerbockers, the Peripatetics and the Household Brigade.

It is possible that *Wisden* was influenced to change in this way by the launch of yet another rival publication in 1864. *The Cricket Chronicle*, edited by Captain Bayley, actually looked more like a later *Wisden* than *Wisden* itself. But it wasn't only a question of design: Bayley's book, which hoped "to be continued annually", devoted a fifth of its pages to school matches. Knight took heed and included Rugby School's match against MCC (along with Eton v Harrow) in 1865. It was the beginning of a major *Wisden* initiative: in 1870 the matches of eight schools would be thus featured; by 1880 the editor was complaining that he could not fit them all in; and by 1894 the first formal review of schools cricket (involving the 24 best-known public schools) would be conducted by one of the period's grandest names: C. B. Fry. None of this was evident in 1865, of course, but it was evident that *Wisden* was, like the Little Wonder himself, nimble and quick on its feet. Bayley's book never appeared again.

We can only guess at the discussions that led, in 1866, to the reinstatement of the professional cricket scores. It was done with little fanfare, in a Note to the Reader: "John Wisden and Co have this year published the matches of the three All-England Elevens, feeling certain, from the great favour with which these celebrated Elevens are received in all parts of the country, that their doings will be read with interest." Whether John Wisden himself put his foot down – he was himself a founder of one of those teams, after all – or whether he and Knight were both pained by their absence, we cannot say. But it is clear that this was a live debate, because in 1865 the scores of the Varsity match were accompanied by a tight-lipped apology. "In our first number," it said, "these [the university] matches were ready for the press; but owing to the observations of one of our friends we did not publish them, though we are well aware that they would have been as interesting to the reader as those recorded." Connoisseurs of newspaper corrections will recognise the reproof behind the tone.

This first Varsity match accorded a match report in *Wisden* happened to produce an Oxford win, an arbitrary fact which had significant consequences: the winner of these contests was henceforth, as a matter of principle, placed first in the season-summaries of future Almanacks, until 1973.

That 1865 explanation is by no means lucid, and we should not jump to conclusions. But it is hard not to speculate that it was Knight who pressed to put the Varsity back where it belonged, ahead of the efforts of cricket's professional tradesmen. It is even possible that the "observations" of a friend, who felt that the university scores did not belong in the Almanack, came from John Wisden himself. Or perhaps we should see it as a sign that the founder, though he had originally intended to create an almanack for professional cricketers, was not blind to the financial logic of including high-society cricket as well. These, after all, were big-money games, with large, well-heeled attendances. He wouldn't have been a very good shopkeeper if he hadn't made sure there was something for them in his new venture. As it happened, the batting summary of those 14 games between All-England and United All-England included his own 142 runs in 17 innings.

In 1867, however, the balance tilted against the professionals once more. And the routine apology was accompanied, later in the volume, by the following explanation: "John Wisden and Co would have gladly given the scores of these Twenty-two matches," it said. "Had they included the scores in full, this little work would have been so increased in size as to render necessary an addition in price."

It is not a mere inference, since the apology and explanation on this subject were the only topics deemed worth sharing with the reader, that this issue was a tense matter for the Almanack. And the reasoning was patently disingenuous: far from bulging at the seams, the 1867 edition was, at 164 pages, some 35 pages *slimmer* than its tubby predecessor. And the following year it shrank still further, back down to 116 pages. What the sidelining of the professionals *did* achieve, of course, was more space for MCC games, public schools, universities, social and regimental games. This would now be *Wisden's* bread and butter, and in W. H. Knight it found a man disposed to relish it to the utmost. As the 1860s advanced, the book turned away from the professional game. Knight, meanwhile, having helped shape the book's strategy, was becoming an increasingly forceful "Compiler". He wrote the first piece of serious prose in the Almanack, a diplomatic tribute to Wisden's old friend and team-mate George Parr ("his style of play has long ranked him the best batsman in England; his leg-side hitting is always a treat to witness, no man approaching him in this particular department of the game"); and also contributed a larger essay on "long scores" – individual innings of 200-plus – inspired by Tylecote's unprecedented 404 not out in a house match at Clifton. As an editor, though, he went rather further, introducing the brief match reports and summaries that would in time become a *Wisden* hallmark.

None of this went unnoticed. In 1865 the *Nottinghamshire Guardian* called the second book "a great improvement" on the first, and the *Era* agreed. It was "not only the first of the cricket annuals for 1865 in the field" but "one of the cheapest and most useful cricket reference books yet published"; the list of professional batting averages was "novel and cleverly compiled". The following year, the *Bradford Observer* expressed the view that *Wisden* was a book which "everyone who takes the least interest in cricket has, or ought to have in his possession".

It is telling that these hurrahs came from the northern counties, the professional motherland of the game, since this was the world the Almanack was honouring. But year by year, and bit by bit, the book became more thorough and coherent. The game was expanding both on the field and off. When Parr's English tourists took on the Twenty Twos of Ballarat and Bendigo in 1864 they earned high praise from the fledgling *Melbourne Age*: "There cannot be a doubt in all unprejudiced minds

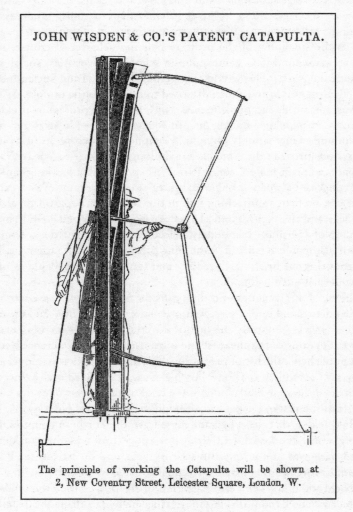

JOHN WISDEN & CO.'S PATENT CATAPULTA.

The principle of working the Catapulta will be shown at
2, New Coventry Street, Leicester Square, London, W.

Advertisement from Wisden *1867*

that the Eleven leaving these shores is greatly superior to anything the colonists have seen before." Cricket was an eager part of the Industrial Revolution, too: in 1867 the Almanack proudly featured an advertisement (taken from the old company price list) for the "Catapulta", the oversized bowling machine whose "principle of working" could still be freely seen at the little old shop off Leicester Square.

The Births and Deaths were squeezed into smaller type, and crammed on to just five pages. And the general knowledge section took on a decidedly sporting tone. Even the Calendar was unmistakeably a list of cricket lore. In the first edition, 16 June marked the date of the Battle of Dettingen (in 1743). The following year it was the day in 1846 when George Parr threw a cricket ball 100 yards 2 feet. Readers of the first book were told that on 20 May (in 1756) Admiral John Byng was shot after a court martial; in 1865 that day marked the first appearance at Lord's of Julius Caesar (who came and saw but, with scores of 13 and 22, cannot be said to have conquered).

Even minor cricket trivia could supplant historic facts. In 1864, 20 March was "the beginning of spring"; in 1865 it was the day in 1751 when the Prince of Wales died following "an internal abscess formed from a blow received in his side when playing cricket". And 2 August, once memorable as the death-day of "Carnot, the French mathematician", was now the 60th anniversary of that first Eton-Harrow game, when Byron, just days before Trafalgar, scored a less than poetic seven and two. At other times, however, *Wisden* was happy to imply that cricket followers might not be indifferent to other walks of life. The 17th of September was – as everyone surely knew – the day when wides were first scored in 1827; but the day before that, the 16th, was the day Moscow burned in 1812, and the day before *that* was the day Brunel died in 1859.

All of which was merely a prelude to the much larger changes that would emerge in the seventh (1870) edition, and we can be certain that Knight played a major role in these, because for the first time his own name appears. The most obvious change was the addition of the founder's name to the title – it was now *John Wisden's Cricketers' Almanack* – and, as if it had been traded, the dropping of the Queen's name from the accompanying rubric. In a move that suggests a growing confidence, plenty of other small-print information about the contents was also removed from the front cover, giving it the appearance of a recognisable brand rather than an information sheet. With more than a hint of false modesty, meanwhile, Knight also broke cover, admitting that "most of the above errors are those of The Compiler of the book, W. H. Knight". This would have been a modest disclaimer had he not awarded capital letters to his humdrum-sounding role. In his Note to Readers "the Compiler" added that "an endeavour has been made to render the little Annual more complete", and went on to explain that it included bowling as well batting, and was thus bringing bat and ball by attempting more "equitably" to tell "the Story of Cricket in 1869". Or, as he put it, a trifle boastfully: "The Compiler has tried to do justice to the Bowler."

Inside he listed "the contents of previous numbers", a hint that *Wisden* was already taking its role as a memorable journal of record seriously. A list of Errata ("Grundy's first match for MCC was in 1851, not 1856 ... Jas. Lillywhite should be credited with two wickets, not three") was an inspired innovation, since it shouted out (it faced the address to the reader at the beginning of the book) the fact that *Wisden* regarded accuracy as sacred, and would strive to rectify even minor slips in its growing archive of sporting facts. Three years later it apologised for stating that Grace scored 995 runs at Lord's (instead of 880) by saying: "The error came through the compiler inadvertently calculating the two innings played at Chorleywood". Could anything be more honourable than bowing one's head in shame over so minor a discrepancy?

The 1870 book continued with a respectful extract of MCC proceedings; summaries on the eight counties whose seasons were featured (Hampshire, Kent, Lancashire, Middlesex, Nottinghamshire, Surrey, Sussex and Yorkshire); and a profile of the Kent bowler Edgar Willsher, the rebel left-armer who by being repeatedly no-balled had helped precipitate the most recent change in the laws. Along with the scores there were detailed match reports of the summer's key events: Cambridge v Oxford at Lord's, Canterbury Week, and MCC v the South of England. Most revolutionary of all, the apostrophe in the title had by now shifted one space to the right (it had become Cricketers' plural in 1869). Plenty has been said about the significance of this small alteration; it is sometimes used as a satirical stick with which to poke fun at cricket – what other game could clutch its cheeks over such a modest change? But it was the surface tremor of a more profound disturbance, and an ironic one: John Wisden, the professional, began by addressing the *idea* of a cricketer – as a model, an abstraction – in the singular; but ended up, guided by Knight, talking to cricketers plural, as a group, as if the Almanack were the in-house magazine of a club. If the move was intended to widen the circle of collegiate subscribers, it risked the opposite by donning a cloak of exclusivity. Anyone could be a *cricketer*, it implied, in spirit if not in fact, and if only for a day. But *cricketers* were a race apart.

It also, more touchingly, introduced an idea that would become one of the book's governing notions in the years to come: that cricket was a family. Of course, it was an unusually manly family (women were only distantly related), but the Almanack could be relied on to celebrate the feats of its favoured sons, help (through the Benefit Fund) those of its members who had fallen on hard times, and mourn its own dead. In one sense it was borrowing the trappings of sentimental soap opera. Entire lineages, broad dynasties, would rise and fall through its quiet, commemorative pages. Since 1865 *Wisden* had carried a list of Births and Deaths for "nearly all" cricketers of note (in 1867 it noted the birth of John Wisden himself) and it is sobering to see, in this book of averages, that the average age of death at this time was not much more than 42 or so. And Knight's 1865 tribute to George Parr put down a marker that *Wisden* would be quick to lay a sword on the shoulder of fine individual achievements. So it was appropriate that, as early as 1872, *Wisden* should publish its very first obituary. Ever since, browsing through the old book has been a little like wandering through a well-groomed graveyard – a bewitching field full of glimmering shades.

The subject of that first obituary was James Henry Dark, the long-time proprietor of Lord's Cricket Ground, who died in 1871. It was another hint that *Wisden* was deliberately seeking to make friendly overtures to MCC and Lord's, and it was a handsome tribute, emphasising the extent to which Dark had been motivated above all by his pure love of cricket. "It should be known that, when more lucrative offers were made him for the ground for building purposes, he rejected them all." Hurrah! Like a true gentleman, he was above mere moneymaking. In much the same spirit, a kindly thought was also spared for the late Stephen Slatter, who had been on the Lord's groundstaff for 44 years. "It is curious," wrote *Wisden*, "that after being in Dark's employ for so long, the same year should see the death of both MASTER and MAN." In this, the very first funeral oration, *Wisden* was turning itself into the cricket family's burial ground. Perhaps it really was wise to slide that apostrophe – cricketers were an extended circle, linked by comparable enthusiasms and shared memories.

The same tone informed the report on that year's North v South game, the proceeds of which were for the benefit of the late H. H. Stephenson, a distinguished MCC luminary who, *Wisden* sighed, "gained troops of friends, but never made an enemy".

Perhaps this was why people began to think of *Wisden* as a bible: it was at once a lawgiver, a celebrant and a mausoleum, and bowed its head to the game's disciples both great and small, high and low. Thus we read, in 1875, that John Lillywhite was "laid in the grave where rest his Father, his Mother and his Wife" at Highgate Cemetery. And the following year we learn that Mr William Davey, "one of the most active, obliging, efficient and courteous officials connected with Canterbury Cricket Week" had passed away, along with George Street, "Ground Keeper" at The Oval. Generations of Englishmen passed through these pages, first as schoolboys, then as Gentlemen (or Players), and finally as umpires, committee men and managers before sinking towards their sad, and inevitable, close of play. Even those whose connection with cricket was brief were included. The Calendar found space to remember Captain Arkwright of the 84th Regiment, killed by an avalanche while ascending Mont Blanc in 1866. The reason for his inclusion? Simple. "He was Captain of Harrow, 1857."

Nowhere was this sense of kinship more evident than in the tender eulogy for the Nottinghamshire batsman George Summers, who died when he was thumped on the head playing against MCC at Lord's (the next man in, Richard Daft, wrapped a towel round his head – the first recorded use of a helmet). The 1871 *Wisden* found a fitting tone for this cruel accident. "A lamentable celebrity will ever attach to this match," it said. "The unassuming manners, excellent conduct and great cricketing abilities of Summers were held in high esteem; and it must be some consolation to his relatives and friends to know that no professional cricketer ever left us who in life was more highly respected, and whose death was so deeply deplored, than George Summers."

To the extent that this turned out to be true, it is primarily because *Wisden* was there, with the appropriate melancholy rhetoric, to render it unforgettable.

———

In 1872 John Wisden moved out of New Coventry Street, the original premises in which he had begun trading in partnership with Fred Lillywhite, and moved a few hundred yards into a new shop at 21 Cranbourn Street, on the western side of Charing Cross Road. In the coming years this would be – as the press advertisements promised – a bulging emporium of new gear, a "mecca for cricket-lovers". John Wisden himself would be there, "radiant with watch and chain of gold", for all the world a well-to-do Dickensian proprietor. Sharp-eyed tourists coming out of Leicester Square station can still see a souvenir of those long-lost days. On the rust-coloured antique tile that forms the facia of the station, a legend stands proudly in bas-relief.* It depicts a pair of cricket bats leaning against a set of stumps, with the words *J. Wisden & Compy* neatly carved around a cricket ball in the centre. Hardly anyone notices it, even the hungry customers waiting at the fast-food kiosk beneath. But what was once a doughty supplier of squash racquets and umpire's coats now offers rice noodles with bamboo shoots, cashew nuts with Hot Asia sauce, and other oriental treats. It takes some mental effort to imagine the shop as it was in the early 1860s, with the great cricketer himself living in rooms above the mound of bats and racquets, boots and sweaters.

None of these outward changes were so telling, though, as the stylistic shift inside the Almanack's increasingly familiar buff covers. Even though John Wisden's name was now in the title, Knight seems increasingly to have been left to his own devices, and his prose gambolled about like a frisky puppy. It was already clear that he was especially gladdened by social highlights, when men from the public schools and Oxbridge enjoyed their days in the sun. Back in 1869 he

---

* The plaque on the tiles above Cranbourn Street was put there in 1908, when the station superstructure was demolished and rebuilt. It remains the only crest of a private company that London Underground has ever permitted on its buildings.

had been happy to report that the match was well attended (despite a five-hour rain delay). And when Oxford won, his reserve melted: "the earnest, exultant Oxford cheers that rang out as wicket after wicket went down were such as none but the young throats of the old country *could* ring out". The 1871 game was a classic, too – a "match of matches". A spiffy crowd – "one of those rare assemblages of fashion, rank and eminent men of the country that meet on no other cricket ground" – saw a nerve-tingling ending (three to win, with three wickets standing) capped by an amazing final hat-trick by the Cambridge bowler, Mr Cobden. Knight's *Wisden* was not lost for words: "The wild rush of thousands across the ground to the pavilion, the waving of hats, sunshades, handkerchiefs, fans and sticks, the loud shouts for Cobden ... all formed a fitting climax to a match so excitingly contested and a result so astoundingly unexpected."

That year's Eton v Harrow match was hardly less exhilarating: "Such an assemblage of rank, fashion and numbers had never before been seen, even at Lord's," wrote Knight. Lord's was "as gay as a bank of summer flowers ... for years and years and years to come, may it continue to be so". Another close finish allowed him to dip his pen in purple again: "Amid shouting, cheering and all that kind of thing, the Captain and prominent players of the two Elevens are carried, jolted, tossed about from pavilion to wicket and back again, and so ended the Eton v Harrow match of 1870."

This was fast becoming the characteristic tone of *Wisden*'s cricket reports. It is somewhat less restrained than the cool, neutral, matter-of-fact voice of later Almanacks, but it was in keeping with the spirit of the times. At times it sounded thoroughly snobbish, and a far cry from the artisan publication suggested back in 1864. When Rugby played Marlborough in front of "an influential and tolerably numerous assemblage", only one or two players were deemed to have "true Cambridge polish". And when Eton and Harrow played in 1871 *Wisden* was quick to tell readers that they did so in front of royalty: the Crown Prince of Prussia, the Marchioness of Lorne and our own Prince Arthur. Knight was jubilant: "The gatherings were as brilliant in rank as they were unprecedentedly large." It was "something wonderful"; it "crawled with all the manhood and beauty of the land ... ladies promenading at luncheon time".

When the Gents took on the Players, moreover, a fixture which, thanks to Grace, was no longer an entirely foregone conclusion, Knight took perceptible pleasure in informing his readers that "the Gentlemen's fielding was infinitely superior".

The match reports in *Wisden* 1874 continued in the same vein. Eton v Harrow "still holds its own as *the* great cricket attraction", drawing a crowd of some 40,000: "as fair and happy a party as ever laughed and lunched", with "nearly a moiety of the Nobility of England". Sadly, there was not enough restraint in this titled mob to prevent an ugly scuffle at the end of the match; and the Secretary of MCC, R. A. Fitzgerald, actually wrote to *Wisden* to put his fury on the record. Owing to the "unseemly conduct of some persons", he said, and "the immoderate expression of feeling" with which the day ended, he had no option but to threaten "a discontinuance of the match".

This was a first in *Wisden*, if not the world: cricket hooliganism, and from fellows in boaters too, hang it all. Whoever would have thought it?

It is easy enough to smile, though we are also free to regret the extent to which this class-conscious cheerleading helped make cricket seem synonymous with English snob-appeal. But we need to remember that this was not just reactionary play-acting on *Wisden*'s part: it was also the commercially wise move. The great amateur matches of which the Almanack was so fond were financial as well as cultural high spots of the summer. The Eton v Harrow matches were box office: the 1870 edition drew a crowd of some 30,000 over the two days, and *Wisden*, taking upon itself the role of cricket's informal accountant, was happy to rake over the numbers – "£790 was taken for admission on the Friday, and £660 on the Saturday ... this being nearly £200 in excess of any previous receipts." These were record takings, and a cause for both celebration and thought. The boisterous and well-turned-out crowds at such games were the market – like it or not; no sensible cricket publication could ignore them.

And as it happened the professional elevens were dying: the play-offs between All-England and United All-England were abandoned in 1867, and in 1870 there was only one occasion on which all 22 players were also Players with a capital P. There had been attempts to repair the rifts, but they came to nothing. On New Year's Eve 1868 there was a meeting at Gregory's Hotel in Rupert Street, hailed by the *Sporting Gazette* as "perhaps the most important ever held by cricketers of this country", at which the South's men pleaded with Parr's northerners to agree to a game, but there was no progress. It was partly – of course – an argument about cash. The Cricketer's Fund had assets of £2,350, but there had been no matches between professional teams on its behalf for two years, at a time when amateur games were attracting more and more attention. The financial as well as the cricketing future was clouded.

And it wasn't only amateur cricket that was seizing the limelight. County cricket – soon to become the foundation of the national game – was being driven centre stage, chiefly by the prodigious feats of W. G. Grace (in 1871 he scored an exhausting 2,739 runs at an average of 78 – at a time, remember, when pitches did not yet encourage batting). And *Wisden* was above all a reporting machine, recording England's cricket life as faithfully, within limits, as it could. John Wisden may have been a professional sportsman once, but now he was a businessman and publisher, and had he stuck to his original plan the Almanack might have sunk without trace. We can detect, from the fact that in 1868 the book was published in partnership with Frederick Maynard, that its existence was precarious, hand-to-mouth, a matter of trial and error. The 1868 edition announced that it was published by "Wisden and Maynard at their cricketing and sports depot", and the same pair of names feature on the 1869 volume (though Maynard has fallen off the title page). It was clearly a short-lived partnership, though since the book was still printed by Crockford in Greenwich it looked the same as it always had. But these were jittery times, and Maynard's bankruptcy (he was a hay salesman in Smithfield) led to the dissolution of the partnership. So while we can sigh at W. H. Knight's more orotund flourishes, his instincts were sound. In making *Wisden* a pillar of the establishment he gave it staying power. The same could not be said of Lillywhite's original *Guide* – deprived of MCC backing, it had expired by 1866.

The tension between professional and amateur cricket would continue to inform England's cricket culture for the next hundred years. But the great Victorian compromise, county cricket (in which both sorts of cricketer could play) was what prevented it from becoming a turf war. The county game, once MCC was able to set out stricter rules preventing professionals from turning out for more than one county, turned out to be an arena in which Gents and Players could be team-mates – to this extent it was fulfilling the dream of cricket as a playground where "peer and peasant" could rub shoulders, or at least share a net. MCC was quick to promote it, and so was *Wisden*. In 1874 it published the MCC proceedings in which a Challenge Cup was mooted (two years after the first FA Cup final, which was played at The Oval) "with a view to promote county cricket". In the event, only five counties jumped at the offer, and when two of those pulled out, the scheme faltered. *Wisden* was on hand, however, to applaud other developments in the shires. When Gloucestershire was finally constituted as a club it declared: "After all is said, written and done, County Cricket Clubs are the real mainstays of the popularity of the game; are productive of the best all-round cricket; are the first to produce to public notice most of the skilled cricketers of the country." Apart from anything else, it was the stage for the grandeur that was Grace.

By now *Wisden* was easing up on its rather po-faced harrying of W. G. Perhaps it was simply because by now the great man was playing as an MCC member (he had been astutely sworn in back in 1869, not least to ward away offers from professional outfits). But the tone of *Wisden*'s commentary softened, and as the years passed for the most part the Almanack was as happy to cheer Grace as the rest of England. When Grace scored 242 for Gents v Players in 1875, the following year's *Wisden* said it was "one of the, if not *the*, best innings he had ever played".

One might have expected Knight to have cheered Grace on with especial vigour if only because he was effectively, through his own towering efforts, reviving the idea of amateur cricket and pushing the all-professional circuses to the margins. Indeed, as the once-mighty "Elevens" faded from view, new amateur venues began to emerge, such as the Prince's Club in Hans Place, just off Sloane Street (where a fellow might leave his Rolls, these days, to pop into Harrods for a haircut). The first committee comprised five earls, one marquess, six lords, two colonels and a quartet of MPs, an "assemblage" very much to *Wisden*'s taste: it predicted that the new pitch would "doubtless be the scene of many a gay, brilliant and aristocratic gathering". In fact it would turn out to be a smart but short-lived arena, chiefly for matches with a military flavour, but *Wisden* was happy to accept it as a major arena from the word go. Intriguingly, given the pressures on cost which the doings of the professional Elevens seem to have inspired, the "Cricket at Prince's" was included in an edition (1873) that was 36 pages larger than before, but at the same modest price – a shilling.

The shifting of *Wisden*'s gaze away from the professional Elevens towards amateur and county cricket had a deep institutional effect: this supportive editorial stance would, over time, both bolster the powers-that-be at Lord's and give the tacit impression that *Wisden* was of their party. Almost a third of the 1870 edition was given over to MCC matches, and its annual proceedings were included in detail, much as if *Wisden* were a cricketing Hansard. Certainly, MCC itself knew where it stood, or wished to stand. The 1872 *Wisden* quoted the president, J. H. Scourfield, as saying that he hoped MCC would "always be looked up to as the highest court of appeal in everything related to cricket". But Knight's *Wisden* was happy to play a similar role, strongly urging an automatic respect for umpires, however erratic: "Their decisions should in every case be strictly obeyed, or there will be no pleasure in the game." He even glossed a list of umpires with the remark: "all the above cricketers are reliable men". One umpire in particular, Robert Thoms, was accorded as much honour as a player. "In the burning hot season of 1868," Wisden reported, "he professionally answered the 'How's that?' query in no fewer than 83 matches."

The idiosyncratic tone of this 1870 volume did not impress everyone; indeed, it inspired the first damning review *Wisden* had ever suffered. The *Sporting Gazette*, long a friend to the Almanack, now felt bound to point out that Knight's floral style was excessive. "A clear half of the contents are simply impertinent," it wrote. "Pretty much everybody is bespattered with praise." While there was no disputing the quality of the factual matter, there was altogether too much tap-dancing: "The statistical portion is most admirably done; that portion which is not statistical is in about as bad taste as it can well be." The reviewer called time on the "barbarously expressed sillinesses" in the book, and begged for a return to "brief, unvarnished descriptions".

It was a telling intervention, but it did not deter Knight from continuing to flatter the Marylebone club. In 1873 he published a speech by the MCC President that was a textbook demonstration of how to appear complacent and stuck-in-the-mud. Alluding to the recent illness of the Prince of Wales as if he were an old friend, the president jested that he could recommend "as a thorough restoration, a gentle dose of cricket, to be taken weekly at Lord's". He went on to plead, in the conservative spirit that was becoming distinctive, that the membership set its face against change as a matter of principle. "Cricket should stand upon its own merit," he said. "An occasional phenomenon would from time to time appear above the cricket horizon, but that was no valid reason why the whole terrestrial sphere of cricket should be disturbed."

This sense that cricket, like a children's playground, should be protected against the noisy encroachments of ordinary life would be a constant refrain in the years that lay ahead. In Victorian England it chimed with a paternalist urge. In the 1876 *Wisden* the MCC President declared that "cricket looks to Lord's as a parent, watchful over her children". This kind of sentiment drifted easily towards jingoism. Cricket was, the president added, "a thoroughly English game … Foreigners might compete with success in the hunting field, but none had yet been found able or willing to wield the willow." It was beyond his ken even to imagine a Bradman, a Sobers or a Tendulkar.

We cannot say that this is the first recorded use of this stodgy epithet about willow-wielding, but it may well be; it is of a piece with the mawkish tone. And, of course, this is precisely the kind of bland rhetoric that has, repeated over the decades since, given cricket a bad name in some quarters – made it a euphemism for dozy old codgers having a placid snooze, content to ignore the complications of the "real world".

Fortunately, even these early Almanacks were not single-minded: they were a broad church. W. H. Knight may have had keen tendencies in favour of a soft-focus, heart-of-England idea of cricket, but his proprietor (however remote he may have been from the detailed composition of the book as he developed his sports equipment business) was more interested in the grittier expressions of the high-level game. So while *Wisden* dwelt lovingly on the top amateur matches, it also described the development of international cricket tours (which resembled the travelling circuses of the 1850s) in eager terms. In 1868 England went to North America, where a Grace-less XI bowled out the Twenty Two of Canada for 28 (16 of them for nought). And in the same year a team of Aboriginal Australians sailed to England – with grand southern-hemisphere names: Bullocky, Tiger, King Cole, Dick-a-Dick – to be put in their place by the titled bigwigs of MCC: Lieutenant-Colonel Bathurst, Viscount Downe et al.

But something else was being filtered through the prism of W. H. Knight's rosy worldview. In paying obeisance to the world of MCC and amateur cricket, to the world of Eton v Harrow and the Varsity match, he was laying down the subtle foundations of a value system which would, as the years advanced, become the cultural template of the English game. It might not have been deliberate, but in referring to himself as "the Compiler" Knight was putting his weight behind a singular and specific concept of the game. Even when it came to batting, he implied, "compiling" or "accumulating" was superior to "hitting", however dramatic. Patience, chancelessness and the kind of obduracy that encouraged well-schooled batsmen to leave the bad ball as if it were a hissing viper ... these were the qualities he praised. In so doing he was laying down one of the abiding criteria by which cricket would be judged for generations.

In this light it was possible to upbraid one promising Old Etonian Cambridge batsman (who scored 124 against Sussex, 110 against Surrey, 156 against the Gentlemen of Sussex, and 50 in the Varsity match) for "his too eager desire to hit". No great future was predicted for him unless he could effect "a visible improvement in his defence".

As it turned out, the insistence on aesthetic rigour was also an effective business ploy – the Almanack was announcing clearly that it stood for the highest standards of both play and conduct, and in any case, the multitudes who milled through Lord's to watch Cambridge or Harrow were all putative readers – but it had telling long-term implications. For the next century and a half, the hierarchical ideas embedded into *Wisden* by Knight would help shape the mental framework of English cricket. Other nations – colonies, for the most part – might brim with native talent, but none thought of batting as a science or art, as "batsmanship". These assumptions also led *Wisden* to develop a voice – pedantic, grudging, picky, a little superior – which, while it inspired bottomless devotion in some readers, seemed to many others just a touch too sniffy.

One reason why Knight and others were so keen to depict cricket as a gentleman's game was that in many ways it was by no means gentle.

Outsiders could see it as a sedate pastime for flannelled toffs on privileged fields, but cricketers knew that the game could be violent: the roll call of those who have had noses split, eyes crushed, skulls cracked or teeth dislodged by balls spitting off a length was always long. *Wisden* itself recorded not just the shocking death of George Summers but many other such incidents, such as the moment when a Mr Prestwick, in a game at Gorton, "was struck by a cricket ball on the temple, from which he died". In this sense cricket fitted neatly with the Victorian virility cult, in which any upstanding chap worth his salt ought to be able to take a crack in the ribs without wincing. It might even be that the game's emphasis on etiquette – respect for umpires, applause for opponents, playing a straight bat – grew up as a response to such sharp hazards, much as table manners evolved in response to the lethal possibilities of enemies dining together, clutching knives. Cricket courtesy became the means by which its intrinsic violence – I am going to hurl this missile at you as fast as I can – was contained and tempered.

We may be reading too much into W. H. Knight's slightly fawning style. If *Wisden* had not survived for so long it would seem no more than typical of the period. By inventing the tone of a publication that would stand near the summit of the game for the following century and more, however, Knight's assumptions were able to work their way into cricket's bloodstream. He was, one might say, laying down the lore.

But we are getting ahead of ourselves. Grace wasn't finished yet.

"THE CRICKETERS' ALMANACK."

CONTENTS OF THE FIFTEEN NUMBERS.

Advertisement from Wisden *1878*

4

Golden Times

In 1876 the Gents and the Players met three times in London, on nine consecutive days at the end of June, at Lord's, The Oval, and the brand-new Prince's club near Hyde Park Corner. It was a major event, and W. H. Knight had little option but to concede that these were the "front rank matches of the season". Never fond of the professional spirit, he did not miss the opportunity to criticise the "very liberal policy" which handed the professional hirelings £10 a day – double the Lord's rate – as a dangerous precedent. Nor was he impressed that the entrance charge at The Oval – a shilling – was twice the price of Lord's. Even the fact that The Oval crowd was twice the size of the one at Lord's did not please him: at least the Lord's fans, he was relieved to say, were of the "old cricket-enjoying, undemonstrative sort". He seemed to have forgotten the near-riot at the 1873 Eton v Harrow match.

Still, he was glad to report that after drawing the first game (in which Grace made 90) the Gents came out on top in the other two. "To record that Mr Grace was lustily cheered is to faintly state the reception awarded him," he wrote. When the great man pummelled 169 in the final match, including an outrageous seven when he drove the ball "as far as it would go past the little chestnut tree", Knight sighed. "Ah, that seven was a hit. The ring of it tingles in this compiler's ear whenever he recalls it."

No one knew it yet, but Grace was at this point embarked on the most astonishing orgy of run-getting the game, England and the world had seen or thought possible. In the summer of 1876 he scored 400 not out for the United South of England (against a weak team, it must be said: the 22 of Grimsby), but also made 344 for MCC against Kent, 318 for Gloucester against Yorkshire, and 213 for Knole Park against the

Incogniti. Some 2,622 runs later he ended the season with an average of 50 plus – for the ninth time. He was a major force with the ball too, taking more than a thousand wickets in the decade as if to emphasise that he could have achieved as much renown as a bowler.

In going on to amass a career total of more than 54,000 runs, achieved in a manner that redefined what was possible, Grace presented *Wisden* with a contradiction. On the one hand he was rescuing the amateur code by making Gents v Players matches competitive, pumping fresh life into the belief that amateurism was superior to the grim professional way. On the other hand he was also promoting the contrary ideal. The forceful, abrasive approach for which he was becoming famed was at best quasi-professional and at worst – perish the thought – not even quite cricket.

Somehow, in a single career, he was staging a one-man enactment of the great social drama of English cricket, taking both parts at once. He hadn't attended the "right" schools (Rudgway House, in the mining *quartier* of Bristol, was not exactly Rugby), but he was a Gent. And he was a doctor, a public-spirited figure who could stay up all night at the bed of a sick patient and still be alert enough to flay the bowling the next day. But in other ways he acted like the most brazen Player. He was even willing, damn his eyes, to stand up to the gilded blue-bloods of Lord's by insisting on a valuation of his own skill and labour. He knew that his name on a team sheet could double ticket prices (from threepence to sixpence), but his unwillingness to settle for less than he was worth seemed, to the fellows with walrus moustaches, nothing more than a base form of money-grubbing. His match fees (or "expenses") were indeed legendary: it took £1,500 (£150,000 in today's money) to persuade him to tour Australia in 1874, when most senior professionals were lucky to get £200.

It wasn't only the money, though. He was by some distance more combative than the amateur ideal allowed – happy to push rules as far as he could, running out batsmen who backed up too far, bowling deliberate donkey drops or taunting opponents. Stories of unsporting behaviour swarmed about him like flies: the time he pretended to return a ball to the bowler before running out the deceived opponent, who had wandered out of his ground; or the time he asked an innocent student to toss him the ball, only to insist that the youth be given out for handling it.

The Old Etonian Lord Harris went so far as to write that Grace's persistent appealing almost amounted to intimidation ("It was within the laws of cricket, but that was all"). That was the famous year when, at the age of 47, Grace hit a thousand runs by the end of May – a greedy novelty. Nothing like it had been seen before, and *Wisden*, the game's recording angel, was by now happy to ride the bow-wave of his popularity. Yet years later, in an otherwise fulsome obituary in the 1916 edition, Harris could not resist mentioning that when it came to sportsmanship Grace could at times be "very rigid in demanding his full rights".

While more than willing to frown at his haughty cheek, *Wisden* liked to present him as a chivalrous force for good too. In 1887 the match between Lancashire and Gloucestershire was marred by a horrendous injury to Lancashire's A. C. M. Croome (an Oxford Blue in cricket and athletics) who dived into the railings on the boundary at Old Trafford and put a dreadful gash in his throat. He might have died had not Grace himself saved the day. "It was of vital importance that the injured part be kept absolutely still," wrote Croome later.* "His hand never shook all that time … It would have been a remarkable feat of endurance under any circumstances, but the Old Man had been fielding out for over four hundred runs and done his share of bowling."

Thus are myths born, and *Wisden* was on hand to record this one for posterity. More to the point, this exemplary doctoring suggested something more than a mere ability to multi-task. It encapsulated all of cricket's best hopes for itself – that far from being an eccentric pastime for the *jeunesse dorée*, it was a spiritual testing ground. Our dim modern world tends instead to offer heavy drinking – a Botham all-nighter, a Flintoff morning-after – as the more entertaining and demotic mark of a noble soul.

Either way, the sheer scope of Grace's achievement tended to put his so-called flaws in the shade. Indeed it is partly this very ambiguity in

---

* Croome recovered well, and went on to become a cricket writer for *The Times* and golf correspondent of the *Sporting Life*. It is possible, since he was a *Times* colleague of Sydney Pardon, that he contributed the odd word of *Wisden* too.

Grace's reputation that makes him so suggestive a figure. He was an amateur, yet as grasping as the greediest hireling. He took the game seriously, elevated it to new heights of effectiveness, and pushed the rules to the limit; yet he could also be a true Corinthian. At once an artist and a pragmatist, he proved that the two could co-exist, that excellence need not be dour. Ranjitsinhji memorably wrote that Grace united the many streams of English cricket into one broad river, and it was true: in seizing the competing strands in the game's social culture, and braiding them into one record-shattering career, he allowed the country to sustain the impossible wish that such things might be routinely true.

As if mirroring this mini-drama, the early editions of *Wisden* were shaped by this tug-of-war between the two world views. The plain fact was that fine rhetoric about cricket as a haven where social classes could meet and mingle could not disguise the gulfs that kept them apart. And truth be told, cricket did not try too hard to conceal them. Professionals had distinct dressing rooms, their own entrance on to the pitch, third-class rather than first-class travel, separate lodgings and even separate tables at mealtimes. It was apartheid, and *Wisden*, eager to address cricketers as a community of like-minded souls, did not wish to alienate either party. Even when, years later, the England players threatened to strike before The Oval Test against Australia in 1896 – demanding £20 a day, double the usual fee – the Almanack bent over backwards to find the action "right in principle" yet "ill-judged and inopportune" in practice.

———

Grace was the chief show in town, but not the only one. He was part of a much larger burgeoning, as imperial Britain marched into uncharted worlds from Manitoba to Mashonaland, from the Sudan to the Great Barrier Reef. John Speke's famous cable to London – "The Nile is found" arrived in 1863; the Suez Canal opened in 1869, and two years later Stanley was setting off to find Livingstone. Stirring exploits were the order of the day, and they were not yet controversial – on the contrary, they seemed evangelically justified. Cricket was implicated too (the army had orders to build a cricket ground at every barracks in the land), but *Wisden*'s chief duty in the last years of the 19th century was more mundane: to celebrate the formation and growth of the County Championship, which was rapidly becoming the bedrock of English cricket. W. H. Knight's enthusiasm for the great old amateur play-offs did not blind him to the importance of this development, and *Wisden* took due note of it.

In 1873 there were only nine official counties – Derbyshire, Gloucestershire, Kent, Lancashire, Middlesex, Nottinghamshire, Surrey, Sussex and Yorkshire – and though they did not play the same number of games there was an understanding that the county with the fewest number of defeats was the champion – cricket was still seen very much as a game of defence in which artful batsmen tried to defy charging (paid) bowlers. Survival counted for more than winning, the frank pursuit of which was unworthy.

Wisden helped change this by proposing a scoring system that gave more currency to victories. In 1875, for instance, Lancashire and Notts lost once, making them joint-winners, but *Wisden* took the unusual step of declaring Notts champions on the grounds that they had *won* more games. Similarly, in 1886 Notts (with 7 wins) were again anointed ahead of Surrey (12 wins) on the grounds that they had *lost* fewer. *Wisden* pointed out that the Notts season was "perhaps less brilliant", and this time MCC agreed. A new system – one point for a win, half for a draw – was approved in 1887.

Even so, counties were still competing with amateur clubs for prestige and crowds. In 1881 a decisive game between Lancashire and Middlesex at Lord's was cancelled in favour of a Harrow Wanderers fixture. This was not seen as remarkable; it wasn't until 1890 that the Championship was recognised as the centrepiece of the season. One reason was that it could be drab. When *Wisden* saw Surrey spend nearly 40 overs scoring just 16 runs against Notts in 1880, it was obliged to confess that this was "slow cricket".

Knight, meanwhile, was nodding politely to Lord's by devoting more space to the "doings" of MCC, committing *Wisden* to the social scenery of school and university gatherings rather than the "first-class" game. Of the Varsity match he wrote, "the playing portion of the ground was crowded by a brilliant company promenading o'er the old turf ... vehicles were filled with pleasant picnic parties." Eton v Harrow, meanwhile, attracted an even more "wondrous assemblage of rank and privilege" to the "best of all outdoor pleasures – an England cricket match". Getting carried away, he proposed "Luncheon at Lord's" as a subject for a national painting, since it was "such a scene as can only be seen in this glorious old cricketing England of ours".

There were some who winced at this. In 1875 the *Sporting Gazette* criticised the sugary praise handed out to schoolboy cricketers and begged for a more austere approach. "We are quite unable to see how a schoolboy can be a 'magnificent' bat or 'capital judge of the game' at the somewhat early age of, say, nineteen." And in 1878 *Bell's Life* added that Knight's "style is as quaint as his matter is valuable". But Knight was not so giddy as he sometimes sounded. He was not a well man, and if anything his eulogistic style flowed not from complacency but from a desire to put a sweet face on things. Either way, he did bend *Wisden* to his own tastes, introducing long sections on matches between MCC and schools, and other pukka contests. If nothing else, the list of MCC's opponents gives us a glimpse of what we might term the schools premiership, circa 1875: Eton, Charterhouse, Clifton, Harrow, Malvern, Rugby, Tonbridge, Uppingham, Westminster and Winchester.

And if upholding standards meant growling at the plebeian nature of the crowd, then so be it: "The applause was indiscriminating," he wrote of a Gents v Players game at The Oval. "The 'Bravos', 'Go Alongs' and 'Run it Outs' being as freely given to all sorts of hits, whilst a finely bowled over, scientifically played, was as frequently slighted by silence." In Knight's mind there were hierarchies not just of cricket skill, but of cricket *observation*. Even the crowd should be courteous. It is possible too that the precious note disguised a firm appreciation of new trends. He could rarely quell a lyrical urge, so the 1878 *Wisden* looked forward to the visits of teams from Australia, America and India, who would play friendly contests "all round our dear old country – the birthplace and home of this fine old game". Even here, though, there is a distinct hint that he was glimpsing cricket's international future.

In any case, he was by now singing from the same hymn sheet as his publisher, John Wisden himself, who was savvy enough to boast, by 1875, that he and his firm were "Cricketing Outfitters to the Army, Navy and Public Schools". In 1880 he provided special cricket apparel – scarlet shirts and black caps – for the Huntsmen v Jockeys match at

Lord's. He knew where his market was, and on which side it was buttered. Meanwhile, apart from the odd rebuke, Knight was mostly hitting the mark, too, in the public eye. In 1874, when *Wisden* marked its first decade, the *Sporting Gazette* said "the mere fact that it has appeared for such a length of time is sufficient guarantee of its worth". It sits oddly with our misplaced sense of Victorian England as a staid, rigid society that anyone might describe ten years as "such a length of time". In truth it was a period of roaring, hectic change, with few fixed points. It is significant that *Wisden*, at this early point in its life, already seemed like one of them.

It cannot be said that Knight was ahead of his time, however, because if anything he was making up lost ground. To its eternal embarrassment, *Wisden* ignored the very first Test match between England and Australia in Melbourne (a famous 45-run win for Australia) in March 1877. In an echo of the now-ancient rivalry, this was in part political: the England team was captained by James Lillywhite, and his brother John's *Cricketers' Companion* featured extensive coverage of the tour. *Wisden*, famously, looked the other way, and did not even recognise the match until 1976, when a preview of Test cricket's centenary gave it a chance to publish that historical first scorecard for the first time, 99 years late. In another sense it reflected a deeper and more entrenched class reflex: the MCC nabobs could hardly help seeing England v Australia as an echo of Gents v Players – with England the Gents, naturally.

There were other signs that the annual remained a chancy, hand-to-mouth affair. In 1877 and 1878 some combination of haste and folly led, with Knight's attention slipping, to the publication of a hasty "Calendar" based heavily on the previous year's weather reports. In the space that once held the deaths of Charles I and David Hume, or spared a thought for giants of the past such as Hillyer of Kent or Beldham of Surrey, readers now were merely told that various dates in January and February saw "destructive gales … floods … rain … heavy snow fall … furious gale … snowstorm … hard frost".

We have no minutes to tell us how this list was received, but – actions speaking louder than words – it clearly went down badly. The Calendar was promptly dropped for good in the 1879 edition, Knight's last. Fittingly enough, this volume opened with the following important announcement – printed on the contents page, so no one could miss it:

"The Committee of MCC passed the following resolution: *that no Gentleman ought to make a profit by his services in the cricket field.*"

It was official. The amateur ideal had the support of both Lord's and *Wisden*. But the phrasing was interesting, because it did not, in stating its contempt for "profit", insist that Gents actually suffer a loss. In keeping open the system by which this open-hearted breed could enjoy expenses, it prolonged one of cricket's central tensions.

The other significant MCC news concerned the ground. It had improved since the days when Grace picked gravel out of the wicket while he batted, and *Wisden* was impressed. "Five and twenty years attendance at Lord's," wrote Knight, for once looking back without a pang, "fails to bring to mind the old battlefield looking so smooth, so firm, so well covered with herbage, so free from spots and blotches."

At the end of the 1878 season, on 3 September, a London steamer called the *Princess Alice* had sunk in what became known as "the Thames Calamity" – the boat went down in four minutes, drowning 640 passengers. John Wisden was quick to respond: his old friends staged a North v South match for the relief fund, and the touring Australians also played an England XI at The Oval. Perhaps as a result of this, Knight's farewell edition paid tribute to the Australians, who played a hundred matches in their four-month stay, "railing it by night and match-playing by day". As so often, nothing is so resonant as the dry bones of the itinerary, which involved a two-day game in Scarborough on the Monday and Tuesday, another at Prince's Club in London on the Wednesday and Thursday, another in Glasgow on the Friday and Saturday, and then a one-day rest on the Sabbath before the next two-day game at Sunderland, with a banquet, starting on the following Monday. Those fragile modern souls who grumble about the punishing county grind? They must be joking.

With the Calendar gone there was room for a solemn new section: "Deaths". It was not quite an obituaries section – it was simply a list of 18 names, but it carried a strong, quasi-religious implication: that cricketers could be united in the grave, arms linked in the national memory – and that they deserved to be remembered, like soldiers. It would be fanciful to suggest that Knight was motivated by an inkling of his own mortality, but in the August of 1879, with the cricket season not yet done, he died, thus submitting himself as an entry in the new section. The 1880 *Wisden* duly tells us that he was "long a martyr to a painful disease" but was a "pains-taking and conscientious compiler" to the end. Sadly, he did not live to see the admiring notice of his final edition in *Bell's Life*. Reviewing it alongside the two Lillywhites publications (one in its 34th year, the other in only its third) the laurels were handed to *Wisden*. It was "far the most complete and valuable" of the annuals and "a marvel of cheapness".

With Knight no more, and the proprietor himself busy with his retail business and charitable works, *Wisden* stood at a crossroads. It might easily have folded its tents and vanished. But it remained a more than useful adjunct to the sports equipment side, so it staggered on. The new editor, George West, was a 29-year-old journalist on *The Field* who was related to a famous old cricketer called Squire Osbaldeston, and who, in the year he took charge of Wisden, also became cricket correspondent of *The Times*. From the first he struck a mournful note, recalling the winter of 1879–80 with a "shiver and a shudder" and telling his readers that the "cold, nipping, bronchitis-creating winds seemed loth to leave the land they had so sorely stricken with distress, disease and death". The only silver lining was the grand sight of cricket on ice: in Cambridge, between the Town and the University; on a pond near Gateshead; under a frosty moon in Windsor Park; at the Sheffield Skating Club; on Christ Church College meadow in Oxford; and on a frozen dam in Chesterfield.

It is hard to imagine Knight smiling at such frivolities – it was hardly "scientific" cricket. But in one sense West had little option, since the endless winter was followed by an equally bad summer – "the wettest ever known at Lord's". Abandoned games littered the pages of *Wisden* like the hulks of ships: MCC v Sussex and Oxford, Middlesex v Gloucester, Gents v Players ... all washouts. The Whitsun match, a benefit for Alfred Shaw, was a high-profile occasion: some 12,000 spectators were expected. But the weather intervened with a vengeance. *Wisden*'s new editor called it "the most dismal, dreary, depressing, drenchingly wet Whit-Monday the oldest holidaymaker could remember; not one gleam of hope ... all was rain, rain, rain."

W. G. Grace – contrary to his reputation as a tough nut – asked that the proceeds of his own benefit be advanced to the luckless Shaw, but that game was ruined too, by elements "ever more perverse". For the men who inserted weather news into the 1877 Calendar this was sharp revenge. MCC played Kent in "frequent and drenching rain showers", and Notts in a "heavy and protracted storm". It went on and on.

If the wittering about bad weather would have offended Knight's ghost, worse was to come, because one of the first sections to feel the pinch was schools cricket. "The compiler of the book regrets his inability to find space for his usual brief notices of MCC's annual matches with the Public School Elevens," wrote West, adding that this has "yearly been one of his most pleasant tasks", but a chronic misprint – "PVBLIC SCHOOL MATCHES FOR 1178" – suggested that his heart was not in it.

Actually, the most likely explanation here is that John Wisden himself was, with a young new editor still feeling his way, seizing the opportunity to exploit the book's commercial potential. Certainly, readers of the 1880 edition could have been forgiven for thinking that they were reading a sales catalogue: the book was stuffed with adverts not only for Wisden's own-brand cricket and tennis equipment, but also for various other publications (the *Sporting Life*, the *Cricket and Football Times*, the *Manchester Guardian*, the *Sportsman* and the *Illustrated Sporting News*). Nottinghamshire County Cricket Club took space, as did Crockford's Steam Printing Works. And like all publications in this period there were plugs for various medical cure-alls: Clarke's Blood Mixture (for "old sores, ulcerated legs, cancerous ulcers, glandular swellings") and "Woodcock's wind pills, for all forms of biliousness".

It was not the most impressive edition, and some years later a memoir of *Wisden*'s first 50 years would admit that at this time the Almanack "fell upon evil days". It was bad timing, because in 1882 Australia beat England at The Oval by seven runs (their first victory on English soil) to ignite the rivalry that would become the Ashes. James Lillywhite's *Cricketer's Annual* gave 23 pages to the event, but *Wisden* barely noticed it, missing one of the great stories of the period. But things were about to get worse, because on 8 April 1884 John Wisden himself collapsed and died (from cancer) in the old sport and curiosity shop at 21 Cranbourn Street, Leicester Square, which was also, as *The Times* reported in a brief notice, "his house".

It was the end of an era, and it felt like it, because two days later Robert Grimston, MCC President, also died. *Wisden*'s old friend Jemmy Dean, meanwhile, had died three years earlier, on Christmas Day, in his upstairs bedroom at the Cricketers pub on the South Downs (where Wisden was a regular visitor – the two of them would go shooting together) and now the Little Wonder had gone too. Several newspapers noted his passing, but few dwelt on his life in depth. *The Times* called him a "once-celebrated cricketer", but otherwise it was left to the Almanack to say he was a "splendid all-round cricketer" and a "quiet, unassuming and thoroughly upright man". *Bailey's Magazine of Sports and Pastimes* (a close contemporary of *Wisden*, founded in 1860) concurred, adding that he had accomplished a remarkable journey up through the apparently fixed barriers of the class system. He was "a really good all-round man … well-mannered and quiet in his demeanour, and during his career on the tented field he acquired the confidence of the first noblemen and gentlemen of England. There is no one in the humbler walks of life to whom cricket owes more." In his singular, quiet way he had actually fulfilled one of cricket's earliest fantasies: that it could erase the distinctions between a pot-boy and a duke. Though he was buried in Brompton Cemetery, at 2 o'clock in the afternoon, in an unmarked grave, he was no pauper: his estate was worth £4,233 9s 9d – a handsome legacy.

The only glimpse of his funeral comes in Volume XIV of *Scores and Biographies*, an ambitious ongoing publication that aimed to list all the matches that had ever been played. Two carriages followed the hearse, led by the chief mourner, John's brother William. There was, ran the report, "a comparatively small number of spectators considering the worth and well-known ability of the deceased". This was a sad hint that Wisden might not have been *quite* so widely loved as we like to think – but one of the named mourners was his long-time printer and collaborator, W. H. Crockford, "compiler of several numbers of *Wisden's Cricketers' Almanack*".

Since he had never married, he had no descendants, so it was his sister Johanna who inherited his estate. But the company was bought from the estate by John Wisden & Co's 28-year-old, Hampshire-born general manager, Henry Luff. He had already been involved in the

Almanack: in 1882 he compiled, "at considerable sacrifice of time", the bowling averages, and was thanked for his "zeal and untiring exertions" by George West. Now he also took charge of the Cranbourn Street business under whose auspices the book was produced. It was soon clear that something radical was needed when, thanks to West's ill health, the 1886 *Wisden* nearly failed to appear. It emerged, many months late, with a sheepish apology: "Messrs John Wisden & Co desire to express their regret at the delay which has occurred in its publication – a circumstance due to the long-continued indisposition of the Compiler." No one knew it at the time, but the fact that it did eventually stagger into print turned out to be of great significance once *Wisden* became a collectable antique, since it preserved the precious continuity without which its value would have been much weakened.

Luff said farewell to George West (who recovered to remain cricket correspondent of *The Times* until his death in 1896) and also (almost certainly) turned to a new printer. Between 1887 and 1893 no printer was named, and it is unlikely that W. H. Crockford, after more than two decades, would suddenly have dropped its own name. But Luff's main task was to rejuvenate the book by turning to a new generation, not just to keep the flame alight, but also to transform it into an inextinguishable blaze. A few years earlier, in 1880, 16 years after the birth of *Wisden*, Charles Pardon and his two brothers took over the cricket side of George Kelly King's Sporting Press Agency, and placed journalists at important matches in order to submit match reviews to newspapers and journals. It was called the Fleet Street Cricket Reporting Agency, and it was a sign of the times: a child of both the cricket and the publishing boom. It was to them that Luff turned. At the end of the 1886 season Charles Pardon became editor of the following year's Almanack, setting in motion a family involvement that would last for nearly 40 years.

The three Pardon brothers – Charles, Sydney, and Edgar – were a new breed: not ageing cricket fans with time on their hands, but young men (Charles was 36, and Sydney 31) on the clacking ground floor of a new trade: sports journalism. Their father George had been a jobbing writer, producing guides for Cassell and Routledge and 20-odd books on billiards, whist, chess and other "parlour pastimes" under the *nom de plume* Captain Crawley. In that guise he had, as we have seen, helped John Wisden himself with his book *Cricket and How to Play It* back in 1866.* The publisher (Darton and Hodge) had advised readers that the cricketer had been responsible for "all the practical instruction" but that Crawley (or Pardon) had supplied "the literary part of the work". The book made nothing like so great an impact as the Almanack, which was then in its third year. But in forging that original connection with the Pardon family Wisden had bequeathed a substantial dowry to the book that carried his name. George Pardon's sons found themselves prompted by many of the same technical advances that had played midwife to *Wisden* itself. New ideas – such as wireless telegraphy and industrial-age printing – were opening up fresh forms of media, and Pardon reporters soon fanned out in search of top-class games so they could send back trim summaries of what they saw. In time the Cricket Reporting Agency (CRA) would become the Reuters of the sports world. For now, *Wisden* offered them something more modest: a winter job.

Charles Pardon had been born in 1850, John Wisden's greatest year as a player. He lived in a mansion block off Oxford Street and, like his father, wrote books on card games (sometimes using his father's old pseudonym, Rawdon Crawley). His first edition, in 1887, was the first to feature the editor's name on the cover, and in his note to readers he admitted that *Wisden* had "suffered during the last few years from irregularities in time of publication", while promising the "numerous subscribers" that they would "receive it regularly in future". He featured a description of two visiting teams – the touring Australians and also a team of Parsees from India – though the latter of these was so weak, he felt, that "we have not thought it worth while to print any of the scores". This was a telling step forward, and he followed the 1882 Australian tour of England for both *Bell's Life* and his own book; he had also collaborated with his brothers (and with Stewart Caine) on a book about the 1884 tour.

---

* The title had quite a long life. When Bobby Abel published his own book in 1895 he borrowed not just Wisden's title but much of the contents too – his book included reminiscences concerning players (such as Jackson and Willsher) from before his own time. Gilbert Jessop used the same title, again, for his instructional book in 1925.

From now on, *Wisden* would regard international cricket not as a coarse interruption of the distinguished English season, but as the summit of the game.

Pardon's debut edition also included a four-page essay on the counties, the first major piece of opinion-forming writing in *Wisden*; and he promised that the following year he would provide yet more space to "the less important counties". Even before his feet were wet, he was recognising the value of completeness as a publishing idea.

Pardon's work drew a warm response. *Reynolds* said: "the fact it has run through 24 editions testifies to the confidence reposed in the intelligence contained in its pages". The *Aberdeen Journal* called it "the largest and best of the cricket yearbooks" and, though regretting there was not more Scottish cricket, declared it a "wonder". The *Penny Illustrated Paper* singled out the editor, saying that Pardon had put out the book with "his usual acumen" before giving voice to a thought that would become common: "This is just the sort of book to enable a cricketer to fight his battles over again with, as he sits by the fireside and glances through its pages."

The tributes poured in. The *Hampshire Telegraph* said it "teems with matter of the deepest interest", the *Dundee Courier* felt "there was no room left for improvement", and the *Glasgow Herald* thought it "indispensable". The *Bristol Mercury* hoped that a copy would "find its way into the pocket of every cricketer in the British Isles".

It helped that the new editor was already well known. As *Bell's Life* wrote: "All the cricket world knows Mr Charles F. Pardon, and therefore need no recommendation from this pen – he is the Editor of this admirable volume, than which nothing more emphatic could be said in its favour." In washing away Knight's windy mannerisms, Pardon gave *Wisden* the clout and dignity of an archive, a work of record.

His greatest legacy, however, was the introduction, in 1889, of "medallion portraits" of the "Six Great Bowlers" of the previous season. Inspired partly by the developing technology that allowed for the printing of photographs (the portraits were supplied by Messrs Hawkins of Brighton), this was the embryo that in time would become one of *Wisden*'s most popular features, the Cricketers of the Year. Sadly, however, his death a year later meant that he would not be able to watch this seedling flower.

If Charles Pardon had not died young he would in all likelihood have maintained this impressive form. But he was able to produce only four editions of the Almanack before falling ill in April, 1890. He stayed at home for a week with congested lungs but, according to the papers, "a fatal result was not anticipated" until, on the afternoon of 18 April, his heart failed. He had already achieved renown, though. He was buried in Brompton Cemetery, near the remains of John Wisden himself, before a mourning-crowd of 100 journalists, who laid what the *Pall Mall Gazette* called "forty or fifty beautiful wreaths". The news was reported in Leeds, Bristol, Aberdeen and Dundee, and his contribution to the Almanack was much praised: in 1891 the *Leeds Mercury* called the book "a classic", while the *Morning Post* referred to it simply as "an institution".

There was no difficulty finding a successor: the mantle passed seamlessly ("the task fell upon me") to his brother Sydney. Five years younger, he would prove much the more durable, editing 35 volumes, polishing *Wisden*'s essential lines and nudging it towards the heart of the country's cricket life. Variously described as a "small, frail" man, with "small feet, small hands and long, tapering fingers", he had a high, domed forehead, a gentle voice and "twinkling, restless eyes". He loved theatre, music and racing, wrote about them all for *The Times*, and was a walking encyclopedia on these and other fields. According to his colleague Stewart Caine, who wrote a warm memoir years later, he was "possessed of mental powers of no common order", and these, combined with untiring dedication and sense of duty, allowed him to turn cricket-writing into a high calling. A creature of his time, he was a solemn evangelist for high standards both on and off the field of play, and never lost his sense that Englishmen were a cut above ordinary mortals. "No power on earth," wrote Caine, "could have made him write anything of which he was not absolutely convinced."

As a result, though he had never played the game himself, he was a recognised authority on all matters to do with bats and balls. When Yorkshire announced that it was raising the wages of its ten first-team professionals to £2 a week, he declared that it "excited a feeling of anxiety, not to say alarm". While affecting to speak on behalf of less affluent counties who could not afford such rates, he could not hide his horror of handing over such sums to cricketers. "To represent the average professional as an ill-treated or downtrodden individual is, I think, a gross exaggeration." This may have been true, but the clamour for more generous terms was growing all the time. How could it not when W. G. Grace – who as an amateur was not permitted to earn money from his "services on the cricket field" – was able to pocket a lavish sum from his own testimonials in the summer of 1895, which Grace himself referred to as "a period of lionising"?* It has been estimated that Grace's earnings from cricket averaged out at the present-day equivalent of £100,000 per year – not bad, since in theory he was not paid at all. Indeed, the 1897 *Wisden* carried a notice from Surrey CCC insisting that, contrary to "various rumours" (following a tense flare-up in which England's players threatened to strike if their fee was not doubled – to £20 a man), W. G. Grace was paid £10 to play at The Oval and "not one farthing" more. In his Notes, Sydney Pardon was aware of these foibles but forgiving. "Mr W. G. Grace's position has for years, as everyone knows, been an anomalous one," he wrote. "But 'nice customs curtsey to kings', as the saying goes, and the work he has done in popularising cricket outweighs a hundredfold every other consideration." Not everyone knew that he was quoting Shakespeare's *Henry V*, but the meaning was clear: Grace was a one-off. It must have made the theatre-lover in Pardon smile to think that with this small echo of English kingship he was delivering a little touch of Sydney in the night.

Would John Wisden have turned in his grave to see his own Almanack taking the amateur's part? Would he have laughed at the fact that the word "amateur" was gaining a second meaning – "contemptibly inept", as the *Oxford Dictionary* put it? Either way, the authority Pardon brought to such debates was making *Wisden* a force to be reckoned with. The *Sporting Library* reckoned the 1894 Almanack to be "one of the best shillingsworth to be had ... Mr Pardon is to be unreservedly complimented"; the following year the same publication asserted that "the simple fact of being edited by Mr Sydney H. Pardon is of itself

---

* According to Simon Rae's *W. G. Grace: A Life* (1998) three separate benefit funds were launched to raise money for the great man that year – an MCC appeal, a Gloucestershire campaign and a *Daily Telegraph* testimonial. The public response was lavish. In all they raised £9,073 8s 3d – more than a million pounds in today's money.

sufficient recommendation"; and in 1898, not afraid to repeat itself: "The fact that it is edited by Mr Sydney H. Pardon is a guarantee of its accuracy." In 1899 it polished the same words again – perhaps there was nothing else to say. By then the tussle with the Lillywhite publications was virtually over: the *Companion* had closed in 1885 and though the *Annual* would continue until 1900, *Wisden* would soon have the field to itself. It could not resist a last dig, however, in 1904, when its obituary of Arthur Haygarth, the indefatigable compiler of *Scores and Biographies*, made a point of emphasising that though it was published by Lillywhites, Haygarth himself had produced "every line": "The statement inserted at the commencement of the first volume that the Lillywhites assisted in its compilation being altogether inaccurate, and inserted merely to suit their own ends."

Pardon's great quarrel at this time, however, concerned a subject that had plagued cricket for decades: illegal bowling. In the days of the professional elevens it was overarm deliveries that were rocking the boat; now it was bowling with a bent arm, or "throwing". As the century turned, Pardon became half-obsessed with it. His finest hopes for the game – his faith in cricket as a civilised pursuit – seemed put at risk by "unfair bowling", and he was happy to use his high status to stamp it out. Neither a pedant nor a quibbler, he rejected the idea that it was a vexed subject by appealing to the core wisdom of the game itself. "To the argument that it is impossible to distinguish between throwing and legitimate bowling," he wrote, "I attach no importance whatever. A throw may be difficult to define in words, but to the eye of a practical and unbiased cricketer it is, I think, very obvious."

In the 1895 *Wisden* he gave the topic a thorough airing by inviting a number of cricket luminaries – famous amateurs for the most part – to address the subject. He was not coy: he named-and-shamed the subjects of the "most serious complaints" as being "Mold, Captain Hedley, Mr C. B. Fry, and Hardstaff". Since Fry, in particular, was one of the most vivid heroes of the contemporary game, this was a buccaneering assault. His argument was that professional umpires, mindful of the career-breaking nature of their power over players, "persistently shirked their duty".

Some 21 correspondents took up the challenge, and Pardon published their replies at length. Almost all conceded it was a significant problem; some confessed to feeling sick about it. The great man himself, W. G., too canny to alienate the umpires, hedged his bets, admitting there was a "growing throwing nuisance" while confessing he had "no idea" how to prevent it. But his brother E. M. Grace freely urged umpires to be braver, or more honest, or both; R. A. H. Mitchell suggested that MCC appoint a roving "special umpire" to assess the legitimacy of county bowlers. I. D. Walker added that such umpires must be "amateur" (code for unbiased), and Mr L. C. H. Palairet agreed, pointing out that it was unfair to ask umpires to "watch a man's hand and foot exactly at the same time". Lord Hawke refined the idea by emphasising that bowlers must never be warned they were under suspicion, since all of them could bowl legally if they wished. These were the great cricket men of the time, and their presence in this forum confirmed that *Wisden* was something like the game's senior common room.

Pardon returned to this subject in 1898 ("Throwing: A Note") and 1899, worrying at it like a terrier. His particular bugbear was Arthur Mold, who had been controversial for years (and successful too – he once took 16 Kent wickets for 111 runs) until 1899, when he was repeatedly no-balled. Pardon had little sympathy: "I regard Mold as the luckiest of men to have gone through nearly a dozen seasons before being no-balled." He felt the same about C. B. Fry, who was forced to give up bowling altogether when he too was no-balled; it was, Pardon felt, merely "a case of long delayed justice".

Perhaps fanned by these remarks in the Almanack, the issue finally burst into flames in the summer of 1900, when Mold was no-balled at Trent Bridge by a firm Australian umpire, James Phillips, who was vilified in some quarters for exceeding his brief (the following season he no-balled him 16 further times, in a match at Old Trafford). Pardon disagreed, and praised him for having "the courage to act when other umpires were content to express their opinions in private". His bravery in squaring up to the problem had, *Wisden* declared, wrought "a great improvement". All of this was covered in detail in the 1901 Almanack, the Preface to which stated that Pardon had "something to say on the subject". What followed was the first "Notes by the Editor", a feature that would become one of the most important elements of *Wisden*'s appeal. The 1902 "Notes" again fussed away at the same topic, expressing delight that cricketers had acted to outlaw foul bowling and repeating his support for Phillips.

We cannot quite say, however, that the entire concept of these Notes grew out of the campaign against throwing; there were other precedents. The *Nottinghamshire Guardian*, in a review of *Wisden*, had actually suggested something similar as long ago as 1878. "A short article on the leading features of cricket during the past season might with advantage have found a place," it wrote. "There is generally something which gives a distinctive mark to the season ... the writer on cricket should watch for such changes." Charles Pardon took the hint in 1889, his penultimate volume, by offering a lengthy article called "Some Questions of the Day" in which he shared his thoughts on such matters as the best way to start a match ("in the great majority of cases it is best to toss") and the diplomatic niceties surrounding umpires.

But it was the subject of throwing, pressing at his nerves, that led his brother Sydney to create a permanent space for such reflections. They were soon an annual fixture, a summer-scented Christmas sermon. Pardon had plenty on his chest: whether railing against gimmicky changes to the lbw law or disparaging a bowler for serving up "tosh", he was never slow to thump a tub. But he usually did so in exalted language. When he died the Oxford, Surrey and England alumnus Sir Henry Leveson-Gower (pronounced "Loosen-Gore") wrote that "no better judge, no fairer critic, no better writer ever existed" – kind words which carried the clear implication that these were the sort of qualities for which cricket was to some extent synonymous.

Though a less pretentious writer than W. H. Knight, Pardon did not find it hard to square himself with the principles laid down in *Wisden*'s early years regarding the importance of tradition and the amateur ideal. He was always glad to accept as his editorial mission the need to protect cricket from the teeming vulgarities of modern life. His most consistent theme was that tradition mattered, in itself, more than any of the expedient vagaries prompted by fashion, commerce or politics. He would have admired the later cliché that form was temporary, class permanent, because for him the ideals of the past were not just a guide, but an aspiration. Thus he was scornful when the idea of a two-division championship was mooted, with promotion and relegation to attract spectator interest. As usual, he had a precise disregard for any suggestion that cricket, with all its finesse, imitate its proletarian rival, soccer. "The idea of a county with the traditions of Surrey or Nottinghamshire being relegated to the second-class as the result of one bad season couldn't be entertained for a moment. A system which answers very well for football could not do at all for cricket."

———

While all this was going on, county cricket was entering its second great phase: the Championship was officially recognised as such in 1890, a belated concession to the fact that *Wisden*, among others, had been lauding champion counties since 1873, and the concept had gripped the public mind for years. But things took a step forward in 1895, when five teams – Derbyshire, Essex, Hampshire, Leicestershire and Warwickshire – joined the elite. The process was complete when Worcestershire (in 1899), Northamptonshire (in 1905) and Glamorgan (in 1921) brought the number of combatants up to 17 – a group that would remain settled for more than seventy years (until Durham became a first-class county in 1992).

The map of these first-class counties made for a curious but intriguing sight, neatly describing the commercial and political geography of the country: cricket had an agglomeration of members in the south-east, supplemented by a band angled up the Midlands from Somerset to Nottingham, with another heartland straddling the Pennines. The class distinction was also a geographical one – between the leafy Home Counties on the one hand and the industrial conurbations on the other. Whole swathes of England remained barely touched, and would henceforth be classified as "minor", though this meant only that they were mostly rural regions where urban professional cricket had not quite taken root.

There were also regions, of course, where professional cricket *had* taken root, in a way *Wisden* could no longer quite countenance. Its own roots might have been in the professional circuses of which John Wisden himself had been such an active part, but the Almanack that bore his name no longer wanted much to do with scurvy schemes like that. So in 1892, when the Lancashire League was officially constituted as a club cricket competition backed by salaried professional cricketers, *Wisden* saw it as a rival, and a low-class one at that. So far as the gentlemen of Lord's were concerned (the milieu in which *Wisden* was increasingly at home) a cricket professional was a species of labourer, however skilled or dedicated. The Lancashire League upended this arrangement by treating its professional recruits as heroes, and since they were both willing and able to pay more than the counties, they soon attracted an array of great stars. In time the Lancashire League would hire, welcome and be thrilled by some of cricket's most glamorous figures – from the first generation of great West Indians such as Learie Constantine, George Headley and the three Ws (Walcott, Weekes and Worrell) to Australians like Lindwall, Chappell, Lillee and Waugh. Some England internationals started life in these combative arenas. In their early days, Hedley Verity and Frank Tyson – an English Literature graduate from Durham University – both played for Middleton in the Lancashire League.

Wisden, however, shunned it, preferring to dwell on the traditional amateur pageants down south. School and university games remained major events, and the Almanack lavished them with attention, treating them as seriously as international games. In 1894, for instance, it devoted much space to a discussion of the Oxbridge match, which was disfigured by a notable ruction when Oxford, nine wickets down, needed eight runs to avoid the follow-on, and actually discussed the idea of getting out on purpose, to bat again while the wicket was still good. Cambridge promptly bowled a series of deliberate wides in order to ensure that *they* would bat first in the second innings.

Somewhat surprisingly, *Wisden* defended this seemingly brazen manipulation of the Laws, revealing the Pooterish tendency to stand up for strict, fussy letter-of-the-law ideas of fair play that cricket's detractors have always enjoyed. Conceding runs on purpose might have seemed a bold enough contravention of the "spirit" of the game, but *Wisden* preferred to urge that the law be changed. Sure enough, MCC amended the follow-on regulations such that the bowling side could now *choose* whether to enforce it or not, removing at a stroke the incentive to make mischief with it.

Amateur duels such as these remained at the heart of *Wisden*'s universe – a giddy whirl at Lord's, haloed with Britain's imperial glory, made St John's Wood feel like the bright sun at the centre of things. No encounter was more dramatic than the Eton v Harrow match of 1910, a game Eton looked certain to lose (at one point they were nine down in their second innings and only four runs ahead) until Robert St Leger

Fowler had one of the grandest days ever seen on a cricket pitch. First he smacked 64 to set a target (55) for Harrow to chase; then he took eight for 23 to win the game by nine runs. W. H. Knight would have fainted; even Pardon's more level-headed *Wisden* was moved: "The scene of enthusiasm at the finish was quite indescribable," it wrote, adding that it would "be known for all time as Fowler's match" before concluding that "in the whole history of cricket there has been nothing more sensational".

The "doings" of MCC still commanded detailed coverage, even when they were, to say the least, routine. Thus the 1911 *Wisden* learned that the drainage of the ground had been "thoroughly overhauled", that the sale of newspapers was being suspended and that the "refreshment department" had made a loss of £140. This attentiveness to MCC encouraged *Wisden* to publish some rather minor amendments to the game's regulations. In 1919 it announced, like a town crier delivering a proclamation, that the expenses payable to amateurs would be fixed at "30s per diem" while the match fee for professionals would be £20, that the tea interval in Test matches would be fixed at 4.30 p.m., and that "Umpires shall be appointed by Ballot and shall be paid £10 per match". This would become part of *Wisden*'s routine service: as late as 1930 it would alert subscribers to the fact that "a maximum of seven minutes actual rolling" when the pitch was being tidied up between innings had become the law. If the publication of such details seemed de trop, it was also pragmatic: it made *Wisden* seem official, part of the ruling class.

Clubs and schools would need a copy close to hand to settle disputes, and for many years it would often be assumed that the Almanack was produced at Lord's. It never was, but it was by no means unhelpful if people believed it.

The social games still drew amazing crowds – they were the commercial salvation of Lord's, at least. Some 10,000 people had stayed to watch that famous Harrow run-chase, more than twenty times the number who might today be expected to watch the equivalent game. Anyone could scoff at amateur cricket, but no one could deny that it was box office.

Nor, whatever the brilliance of these student festivals, was there any hiding the fact that cricket was fast becoming a professional sport. In 1875, the year before Grace's *annus mirabilis*, 14 of the top 20 in the batting averages were amateur; a decade later the reverse was the case

– 13 of the best 20 were professional, along with 17 of the top 20 bowlers. Fortunately, as Grace entered the dusk of his career, other stars were twinkling to the fore. *Wisden* featured them in annual portraits, and what a roll call it was: Fry, Ranjitsinhji (in 1897, the Golden Jubilee), Trumper, Rhodes, Bosanquet ("how he manages to bowl his off-break with apparently a leg-break action one cannot pretend to say") and many others. No wonder this era is referred to as cricket's Golden Age. And it was not just *Wisden*'s luck to have such glowing subjects – some of the magic flowed the other way, from the sheer fact of their being celebrated in *Wisden*. As it approached its own apogee, *Wisden* had the power not just to reflect greatness, but to confer it. And it could catch glimmers, as if from a great distance, of future stars. In 1902 a young fellow named J. Hobbs had played four games for Cambridgeshire, it noted, scoring 35 at an average of 8.75.

So while the amateur matches were still giddy events, the Gents' match against the Players remained the big one – especially at the turn of the century, when (the ghost of Reverend Pycroft must have been pinching himself) amateurs almost held the whip hand – in 1899 the first five England batsmen were all amateurs. In 1900 *Wisden* recorded the grand occasion at Lord's when R. E. Foster scored a hundred in each innings for the Gents, but was on the losing side thanks to 163 from J. T. Brown, the highest score ever recorded in the fixture by a Player. *Wisden* still handed the laurels to Foster for his patience, however – "sternly restraining all desire to hit, he was at the wickets nearly half an hour before he made his first run". This was not a reversion to the Almanack's early impatience with mere "hitting", because once settled, Foster cut loose: "not often have first-rate professional bowlers been treated more lightly".

In the 1888 *Wisden* a new note was struck. The former England captain A. G. Steel began an essay on county cricket with the leisurely air of a man settling down with a brandy after dinner at the Ritz. "I was sitting in the smoking room of a country house one night last autumn," he wrote, and in a flash *Wisden*'s world changed. From now on it would be something more than a dry-as-dust record of names and numbers; it would carry a literary cloak and cane. It would also extend its gaze to

PRINCE RANJITSINHJI

In his "Jubilee Book of Cricket," says:

"BATTING."

"The first thing that strikes one is that in order to Bat well a player must provide himself with a suitable instrument in the shape of a bat. It makes all the difference in the world whether he has, or has not, an instrument made in the proper way and of proper materials; and one which is entirely suitable for him. A Cricketer cannot be too careful in this respect. **Experience teaches how much advantage there is in the possession of a good bat.**

There are many different kinds of Handles of a Resilient nature made now-a-days.

Personally I use one of WISDEN'S.

Most players now-a-days use India-rubber Covers for their Handles, or sometimes Wash Leather, both are good.

Keen Cricketers take great care of their bats, treating them almost as works of art.

Care should be taken also to secure comfortable well-fitting Pads and Gloves—an ill-fitting pair of Pads prevents a Batsman moving about easily, and consequently helps to tire him out— Toy-shop Batting Gloves are perfectly useless. **I recommend Gloves fitted with Thick Black India-rubber,**

Such as are supplied by WISDEN.

Remember, good tools do not necessarily make good workmen, but good workmen usually have good tools, and what is more take care of them."

embrace the merely quirky, and there certainly did seem to be curiosities aplenty in this period. In 1897 Highbury Park School took on Islington High and managed, despite being bowled out for 21, to win by an innings and 16 runs. Islington's first innings re-created the achievement of Royal Surrey Militia in 1855 by notching 11 noughts.

Pardon, meanwhile, was introducing new features almost every year. Without ever seeming to give the Almanack a radical overhaul, he trimmed the edges, restored the lawn, planted new shrubs and cleared the beds as part of a thorough overhaul. In 1892 he published a full bibliography of cricket writing, which, twice updated in the coming years, embraced works from *The Cricket Match* of 1706 to *Hints to Young Players* of 1893, and indicated that *Wisden* took literature as seriously as it took wicketkeeping. In the same year (1892) he turned the meek list of significant "Deaths" into a fully-fledged Obituaries section (just in time to pay tribute to George Parr, one of the book's first friends). Thirteen one-time cricketers were included, some of them with just one line, but some of them with a substantial paragraph. They were listed not in alphabetical sequence, but in the chronological order of their death. George Wells of Sussex and Middlesex was "one of the shortest men who ever acquired a reputation in the cricket field"; Surrey's Edward Barratt bowled "left arm with a tremendous break"; Richard Pilling, the subject of a *Wisden* portrait in 1891 for his wicketkeeping for England, fell to influenza and consumption at the age of 36; while G. E. Jeffrey owed his inclusion to his feats for Cambridge in the Varsity match of 1873. George Parr himself was described simply as "the best bat in England".

This commemorative language was increasingly in keeping with the solemn, formal mood of the publication. But Pardon was also a man of strong opinions, which he was unafraid to voice. In 1895 he expanded the comment section to include the round-table on throwing, and he balanced it with less controversial articles on "Cricketers Past and Present" and "The South African team in England". He improved his brother's list of batting averages by putting amateurs and professionals together, and the following year assembled a special number on Grace, who had reached his hundredth century, and with the Almanack now at 524 pages he made it available in a hardback, clothbound edition (for two shillings). The Grace *festschrift* was illustrated by a full-page portrait of the "crack" himself, gently raising his bat from a stance open enough to suggest a man looking to score on the leg side.

"The Five Cricketers of the Year" was a calm refinement of a feature that had been launched in 1889 by Pardon's brother, Charles, and had since become one of *Wisden*'s most popular initiatives. In 1892 Sydney Pardon stated that the "portraits" had proved so "acceptable" that "there is no likelihood of the Almanack ever again being published without one". Beginning with "Six Great Bowlers" (1889), "Five Wicket Keepers" (1891) and "Five All-round Cricketers" (1894) it showed that *Wisden* was not only a severe taskmaster when it came to laws and etiquette, but a celebrant, an anointer, a bestower of fame. To some extent it was simply a means to exploit new technology – the delightful advance in photographic printing. Messrs Hawkins of Brighton continued to provided the "medallion portraits", and *Wisden* liked to comment on their "excellence" while promising that "the faces will be easily recognised" – no small thing in the pre-television age, when it was rare actually to glimpse a player. But the selection of outstanding performers was also an effective talking point which reflected *Wisden*'s abiding respect for solo performances. Cricket might be a team game, but it was also a forum for individual heroics. In the accolade's first year, 1889, all the named players were bowlers. In the second year, as if losing confidence in the point of the enterprise, *nine* professional batsmen were picked out. Charles Pardon actually distanced himself from this decision, pointing out that it was the proprietors' choice, not his own, but whoever was responsible, it led to a dazzling omission. Louis Hall, Frank Sugg ... these were fine players, but they could hardly hold a candle to W. G. Grace. The decision to honour only professional cricketers meant that Surrey's Robert Henderson, who had a high score that year of 63, was included, while Grace, with his usual blizzard of centuries, was not.[*]

In keeping with *Wisden*'s new respect for international cricket, the Almanack was happy to include Australians (such as George Giffen, or Albert and Harry Trott) in its hall of fame. It was a powerful accolade.

---

[*] In *Wisden* 1893 Pardon wrote: "If the portrait of our greatest cricketer should ever be presented to the readers ... it will, we fancy, appear by itself."

"For an Australian to have his portrait in *Wisden*," wrote Gideon Haigh, looking back over a hundred years of Anglo-Australian rivalry, "was to make it in front of an audience that mattered."

It was nothing so overt as a blackballing, but it remains a curiosity that the supreme player of the age was not selected until the award's eighth year, in 1896. Pardon was almost apologetic, confessing that "it had been intended for some years" to publish Grace's portrait, and he signed off with a fanfare: "Having known Mr Grace for many years, and seen him make a goodly proportion of his 107 hundreds, I can truthfully say that my feeling of delight when he succeeds, or disappointment when he fails, has not become less keen with the lapse of time." In 1907, again as if making up for lost time, he referred to Grace unreservedly as "the great deity".*

None of this could quite disguise the peculiarity of the omission. Grace had been *the* cricketer, a genuine "nonpareil", for over a decade, yet *Wisden*, perhaps flinching at so populist a gesture, hesitated before honouring him. Perhaps Wisden felt no need to illustrate so famous a face. Or perhaps it was a sign of the Almanack's confidence that it could ignore him for so long: a lesser publication would surely have grabbed at the chance to claim some of his undoubted lustre for the new award. As it was, the accolade did not quite become authoritative until Grace had been named. And as luck would have it, 1895 had been a special year even by Grace's exorbitant standards. One of the awkward features of the award is that it cannot be won twice, so some players win it before they reach their peak, but in overlooking Grace for so many years, *Wisden* ended up capturing him at his towering best.

Over a hundred years later, in 1993, a new editor of the Almanack, Matthew Engel, would write (in his newspaper, the *Guardian*) that "the right to choose *Wisden*'s Five probably constitutes the most enjoyable exercise of arbitrary power open to a mere mortal since the Emperor Alegabulus disported himself on the Palatine Mount with the richest wines, the rarest aromatics and a chorus of Syrian damsels." Alas, the

---

* Since this was the first hardback edition, and also contained the first full-length photographic portrait – Grace himself, gently lifting his bat – it has become a highly valued volume. In 2007 a rare copy of this one edition fetched £21,000.

emperor himself is not available to confirm the truth of this arresting comparison, but we get the drift. The selection of the *Wisden* Five is an unfashionable procedure – no polls or public phone-ins; only the editor counts. As a result, the list emerges as if from swirling tea leaves, or like a puff of smoke from the Vatican. *Wisden* becomes an oracle, lofty, shrouded in mist. This has remained, for over a century, one of the Almanack's most forceful contributions to the ongoing life of the game.

The celebration of individuals was part of a tendency that ran counter to the game's professed faith in the team ethic. Victory or defeat counted for less, in the end, than virtuoso leaps. And the Cricketer of the Year portraits clearly had a cheering effect on sales. The 1889 edition was the first to have a second printing, and by 1892 Pardon could fill 448 pages (four times as many as in 1864, and for the same price: a shilling) while expressing pleasure at the "constantly growing circulation". He was also pleased to thank the team at the Cricket Reporting Agency, by whom he had been greatly "assisted". This included two later editors (Hubert Preston and Stewart Caine) and his brother Edgar, the subject of a warm obituary when he died in 1897. "Of late he practically divided with me the duties of Editor," wrote Pardon of the second brother he had lost. "His interest in *Wisden* was extremely keen."

Thanks to them all, *Wisden* continued to draw admiring reviews. The *Times* said that the 1893 edition "maintains its good name as an accurate and exhaustive survey", and referred to the 1895 volume as "the standard record of the cricket year". As a result, it approached its own half-century in confident mood. "Having survived other annuals which at one time dealt with cricket," wrote Pardon in 1909, thinking back to the days of the Lillywhite guides, "it now has the field very much to itself." He hoped, however, that far from making it complacent, this allowed it to be "more exhaustive than ever".

His instincts remained conservative. He dismissed plans to increase the width of the stumps by one inch as needless "tinkering", and was dubious about C. B. Fry's proposal to introduce a knockout cup. "I am not alone in thinking that now-a-days we have too many matches." There were even times when cricket did not seem all-encompassing. In 1900 A. G. Steel wrote, thinking of South Africa, "At the moment of writing one hears nothing but War! War! War! What numbers of gallant young soldier cricketers have gone to the front?" The connection

between cricket and war would soon be even more intense, but that
didn't mean that the game could be ignored. Within a sentence or two
Steel was discussing the gloomy rise of the draw, or the pitch
"improvements" that were fostering a "tedious and weary style of play
… batsmen working slowly on for hours". Cricket was unique in that
it permitted leisurely conversation – between balls, between overs, over
lunch or tea, and between days. It was only natural that the Almanack,
in representing it, should grow ever more discursive as well.

It was not yet the book of records it would one day become. In 1892
there were only three pages of such material, and they were haphazard:
the Non-Smokers who scored 803 at East Melbourne held the lead in
"big scores", and W. G. Grace's 344 in 1876 was still "the best individual
first-class score ever made". But these were sketchy glimpses of unusual
events, not authoritative benchmarks. If anything, *Wisden* was making
its name as a guiding hand rather than a statistician. Following his
influential debate about throwing, Pardon gave the Almanack's pages
over to similar round-robin discussions on the etiquette of the
follow-on in 1894 and the lbw law in 1899.

Wisden was meanwhile becoming conscious of its own value as a
monument. The 1892 Bibliography mentioned that "only a few copies
remain" of the early editions, and reported that a complete run might
"realise" as much as ten guineas. And Pardon's Notes became an
energetic campaigning force within the game, urging changes to the
laws or playing conditions, admitting that "at times" he had been
accused of "making too much of this throwing question" while cheering
the fact that English bowling had since become "uniformly fair and
above suspicion", setting his face against "stonewalling cricket",
discoursing on umpires, rejecting calls for shorter boundaries and
harrying the England selectors. The Notes were still slotted in just after
the Public Schools, and were only two or three pages long, but slowly
they assumed a wider-ranging brief and delivered not just arguments
on specific points but a review of the previous season. Thus 1906 was
"by general consent one of the most brilliant of recent years"; there
never were such "lamentations from county committees on the score of
poverty" as in the washed-out summer of 1910; and, wouldn't you
know it, the following year was much brighter ("Never in an English
summer has been so much sunshine") and the game duly "flourished".

Year after year, meanwhile, the one-paragraph match reports vibrated with miniature cameos which, taken as an ensemble, still paint a vivid picture of the game in progress: "Heavy rain prevented a ball being bowled on the opening day ... Hobbs took the chief honours ... the home side's display was painfully slow ... Jessop and Ranjitsinhji were seen at their very best ... the pitch became more difficult as the day advanced ... Before a run had been scored two men were out, and half the wickets fell for three ... the players, overcome by the cold, left the field for a little while ... it will be noted that extras played an important part in the match, no fewer than 92 byes being given away ... Essex batted in a sedate manner ... Yorkshire had a humiliating experience ... there never seemed much chance of arriving at definite result."

Page after page rolled by, like the view from a train window. And it wasn't only the incidents that created the sense of a great pageant unfolding across the country; it was the language – such a haughty and self-confident way to write about a mere game! Pardon's *Wisden* was investing cricket with a degree of seriousness which few sports could even dream about. And best of all it was, as the adverts promised, "published every Christmas". The very first *Wisden* (an account of the 1863 season) had been published in February 1864, and since then, as often as not, they were small enough to appear before the festive season. In the years to come it would become too large to be produced in such short order, and would struggle even to come out before the start of the following season; but at this stage it was still sufficiently trim to be produced before Santa Claus loaded up his sleigh. And of course it was an ideal gift: wintering cricketers could haul it out of their stocking and drink their fill of summer memories.

The business of which the Almanack was a small yet prestigious part was thriving, too. Henry Luff turned out to be more energetic than the original proprietor himself, who was in truth no more than a cricketer-turned-shopkeeper. Luff soon began to turn a retail business into a manufacturer, though some of his first steps were clumsy. In 1894 his own cricket ball – Luff and Week's "Marvel" ball – was advertised in the Almanack, but two years later he was sued in the High Court by Duke's, the venerable Penshurst-based ball-maker, for misleading customers and deliberately mispricing the Duke's ball, which he also stocked. The manager of the Cranbourn Street shop, William Smith, admitted that he had indeed been selling the number four Duke's ball for the price of the superior number one ball, thus overcharging by two shillings and leaving customers with the impression that the Duke's was a "bad ball".

It was a faux pas, but not a terminal one. Luff responded by placing an order for 13,000 boxes of balls from Smith & Ives, who had opened a factory in Tonbridge. He soon realised that this was a large enough order to keep the firm going on its own, so he acquired the factory and turned it into a John Wisden & Co production facility. Ives used the proceeds to build a new factory for himself elsewhere in Tonbridge, and the seeds of a long-running local rivalry were sown: with Twort's in Southborough, there were now four major cricket-ball makers within a few miles of one another.

The new red-brick "manufactory" in Quarry Hill, Tonbridge meant that Luff could start producing other own-brand equipment, like the "Exceller" bat originally made by Crawford's, with its novel strip of rubber in the handle to give it added spring. This was promoted both in *Wisden* and in the sales catalogues as part of a broad list of goods the company was offering to the Edwardian sporting world. Luff opened a shop in Great Newport Street, and developed links with overseas retailers, so that classified advertisements would appear in newspapers in Australia and New Zealand announcing the arrival of the new range of Wisden bats, racquets, balls and polo sticks – "direct from the manufacturer".

We do not know whether it was an affection for John Wisden the man, or mere corporate pride, that led him to give his old proprietor's name to his three sons – Harry Claude Wisden Luff, Ernest Constantine Wisden Luff, and Cyril Montagu Wisden Luff. He did become, like the founder, Secretary of the Cricketers' Fund Friendly Society, a position he held for the rest of his days. And it is clear he was a careful bookkeeper. In 1897 the fund attracted £480 5s in revenue, and disbursed almost exactly the same amount, £480 7s, in payments to cricket's most needy families. The Fund also played a significant role in the game's social life. The annual meeting usually took place at Lord's, often in the evening after the Gents v Players match. It was keenly supported by grand figures within the game such as Lord Harris (who became president in

Advertisement from Wisden *1911*

1912, and marked the occasion with a speech about the disgraceful new habit of going off for bad light, something the old generation would *never* have done) and Lord Hawke.

Luff understood the impact a famous player could have on sales. In 1903 W. G. Grace himself came to John Wisden & Co showroom to show off a new table cricket game. Luff collected bats, too, and in 1907 held an auction in the showroom (the bidding on Grace's blade, the following year's *Wisden* reported, reached £50). And he was well aware of the Almanack's power to mark occasions in a ceremonial way. Back in 1882, when John Wisden himself was still alive, Luff had dropped into Billy Murdoch's Australian tourists' team hotel in Covent Garden to give them a framed copy of the scorecard from their historic victory at The Oval. And in November 1897 he presented a specially bound, signed copy of the brand-new *Wisden* (hot off the presses and "with Henry Luff's kindest regards") to the Australian captain, G. H. S. Trott, congratulating him on the way he had "handled" (that is, led) his team on the tour to England in 1896. A true cricket fan, in 1896 and 1898 he went to Waterloo to wave off England touring parties (to the West Indies and South Africa). And when his health began to fail in 1908 he boarded a ship to Australia to watch England, chiefly for restorative reasons, though he found time to give interviews in which he blamed "bad captaincy" for the defeat in Sydney.[*]

In 1910, following his death after a long illness, his sons took over. The oldest, Harry Claude, was his chief executor, and he also took over his father's position as Secretary of the Cricketers' Fund (in November 1911 he gratefully accepted a donation of £155 from Surrey CCC, half the proceeds of a match at The Oval between England and Warwickshire, the champion county). It was a sign of how much the company had grown that Luff left an estate worth £35,604, a considerable sum. Helped by a strong following wind (the billowing market in sport and leisure) he had turned John Wisden & Co from a shop-and-book outfit

---

[*] In 1904 Luff also presented Pelham Warner with a generous wedding present: a complete set of *Wisden* from 1864 to 1904. They were, noted Warner years later in his autobiography, *Long Innings*, "magnificently bound". He continued to add to the set an annual copy, "bound in similar fashion", right up to the end of his life.

into a significant sports brand. But he did not live to see the day, in February 1911, when the company won a prized Royal Warrant and became "Athletic Outfitter to the King" – a terrific seal of approval from the new monarch, George V, who ascended to the throne following the death of Edward VII in 1910. The obituary of Henry Luff actually appeared in the same section (now covering 20 cricket-related deaths) as the lines dedicated to the late King, in which *Wisden* could not resist pointing out – standards were standards – that despite having a wicket laid out for his own use at Fenner's, in Cambridge, "it cannot be said that he ever showed much aptitude for cricket".

In that 1911 volume Pardon too made a point of thanking Luff. "I must not omit a tribute to his unvarying kindness. He gave me a perfectly free hand in conducting the Almanack, and our relations were always of the pleasantest nature." It is not clear how we should read this use of "conducted". Did Pardon see himself as the leader of an orchestra, or the fusspot at the back of the bus? Either way, it was a fine gesture.

As executor of his father's estate, it fell to Harry to sign the Royal Warrant, but he would later play no role in the company's future. A keen golfer (he came second in the English Challenge Cup back in 1907), he became a 2nd Lieutenant in the Royal Garrison Artillery in 1917. It was his brother Ernest Constantine who moved into Cranbourn Street and took charge of the business.

At least the Almanack was in experienced and confident hands: Sydney Pardon was approaching *Wisden*'s own 50th edition, in 1913, with a keen awareness of its high place in the cricketing scheme of things. The Almanack was the game's record-keeper, but also its memory and to some extent its conscience: by now it was beginning to feel irreplaceable. And though it is impossible to inspect the 1913 edition in modern times without shivering at what was about to befall the world it describes, no one at the time sensed that the Golden Age (of which they were an enthusiastic part) was about to dissolve in blood. In commemorating its own half-century, the 1913 edition bursts with a pride and optimism that only hindsight renders foolish. In the light of what lay ahead, some of its observations seem beside the point. But how was Pardon to know, when he complained about "one of the most appalling summers ever known, even in England", that things were about to get much worse? The Almanack was still only a shilling (for the softback version), but not much else was unchanged. The original cover had been buff; and some of the covers since had been a buff-pink shade. But since 1887 it had been a vivid yellow – more or less the colour of spring's first daffodil or primrose. At 849 pages it was a monster, barely recognisable as the child of the slim 1864 pamphlet, and its well-organised pages embraced a much bigger game than the tipsy caravan celebrated in the early days.

Appropriately enough, it featured an illustrated memoir of its founder. Conceding that John Wisden was "only a name to the present generation", it set things right with five brief "reminiscences". Fred Ponsonby Fane, who played with Wisden for ten years, recalled him as a "fast-medium" who, in the Fast v Slow matches, played for Fast, and who preferred a straw hat to a topper. Sir Kenelm Digby, a Harrovian, recalled his old coach as a "great favourite" with a "genial disposition", whose bowling was always "on the spot". Canon McCormick emphasised that he was "small in stature, but well made" and "consistent rather than brilliant or original".

There followed an account, by Pardon himself, of the book's first 50 years – further confirmation of the extent to which *Wisden* had become part of the world on which it reported. The centrepiece of the season under review, however, an ambitious "triangular" tournament between England, Australia and South Africa, did not come up with a story fitting the occasion. This was partly because the weather did its best to put a dampener on things. "Practically every important match was ruined by rain," wrote one morose reporter – and the financial fallout was duly noted. Receipts from Kent's Canterbury Festival were £100 worse than usual, while Yorkshire, the County Champions, actually lost £1,000. Inevitably, there was plenty of brainstorming about possible remedies for this, but none found favour with Pardon. When the Australian demon bowler, Spofforth, suggested in *The Sportsman* that two runs be docked from any batsman facing a maiden over, Pardon was firm. It was "an absurd proposition ... contrary to the true spirit of cricket". This spirit may be easier to evoke than it is to define, but Pardon was rarely so haughty as when donning the shield and lance and riding to the defence of cricket's noble ideals. "Cricket does not stand in need of alteration," he declared. "It must not be tampered with to please people who vainly think that it can have the concentrated excitement of an hour and a half's football."

This tone – with its grandiose sense that cricket is by definition superior to all other games – may have put more people off cricket than any other aspect of the sport, but there was some logic in Pardon's sense of himself as the defender of a dignified institution. In 1864 there had been only 21 games at Lord's, though it was already a sacred place, MCC having supported the game since 1788. So when in 1851 Wisden and Parr levelled their new field in Leamington Spa they had every reason to think, given the power of cricket in Nottinghamshire and the north, that it could rival or even supplant the imperious London club. But now, in 1913, MCC was taking part in 163 matches all over the country, including the most important fixtures of the year. County cricket had settled into a groove that would last a hundred years; international cricket, though in its infancy, was growing fast, and the stars of the Golden Age were genuine national celebrities. To be editor of *Wisden* in 1913 was no small thing.

It was certainly attractive to advertisers. The Jubilee edition was stuffed with pleas on behalf of all the usual sporting supplies, but also for tents and marquees (by Alfred Dunhill), grass seeds, a "special renovating mixture for pastures" and a full set of English-country-garden flowers: asters, phlox, nasturtiums and pansies. And it went down well with readers too. The *Manchester Guardian* called it "as near perfection as any human work may be expected to be" – a decent review by any standards.

In one sense cricket's wheel had come full circle: *Wisden* had been conceived in 1863, in the midst of a crisis about overarm bowling – and now, on its 50th birthday, it was still struggling to define what constituted a legitimate delivery. In other respects things had changed a great deal. Having been born in the year W. G. Grace announced himself as the game's biggest hitter, in all senses of the word, *Wisden* had been able to narrate both the formation of county cricket and the beginnings of the international game. But it could not rest on these laurels for long. At home Emily Davison was throwing herself under the king's horse at Epsom, signalling to the British public that major change was in the air. Cricket grounds could now be reached by motor car: *Wisden* itself recorded the historic moment when the Northamptonshire team opened up a whole new world of cricket bags in the boot, and maps on the dashboard, when they travelled to Gloucestershire by road in 1911. Across Europe, meanwhile, ignorant armies were beginning to form like waves. An Austrian Archduke was about to visit one of his upstart provinces, Serbia. It was horrifying enough when the *Titanic* steamed into an iceberg in 1912, but this was only a tame metaphor for the deadly collision that was now, in this cricketing high noon, only just around the corner.

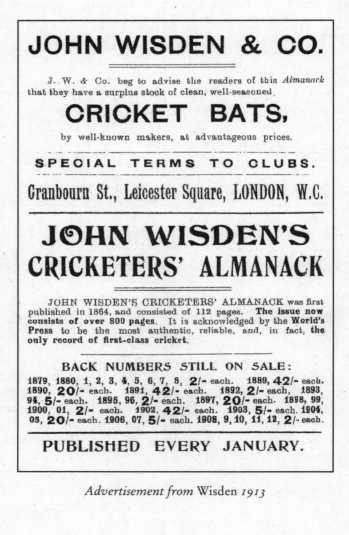
Advertisement from Wisden *1913*

5

Somewhere in Flanders

The summer of 1914 still gleams in the English imagination as a season of gilded innocence, a sepia-kissed last gasp of pleasure before the thud of war said goodbye to all that for ever. Hindsight has led us to drape it in pathos: in our nostalgic mind's eye we can't help but see hawthorn coming into blossom, corn waving in the breeze, hollyhocks in flower, meadows bright with lambs and rabbits, and cricketers lolling on calm green acres serenely unaware of the horrors that lie just over the horizon.

Wisden readers who turned (or still turn) to the 1915 edition in search of a grand response to the coming catastrophe may have been disappointed, however, because the Almanack fell some way short of rising to this sombre occasion. "Writing in the early days of the New Year," ran Pardon's Notes, "it is impossible to take other than a gloomy view with regard to the immediate future of cricket. Never before has the game been in such a plight." This was a weak way of putting it, and in the years to come it would even be cited as evidence that cricket was the toy of a small-minded clique. In Pardon's defence we can note that he was writing in January 1915, when the hellish scale of the conflict was not yet conceivable. But there is no hiding the fact that he *was* voicing a fond wish – that the game was not just a playful escape from the trials of everyday life, but actually superior to it, a dreamy playground that was (like Wodehouse's Blandings, which coincidentally made its first appearance in 1915, or J. M. Barrie's Neverland) a coherent world in itself. While admitting with a sigh that county cricket in 1915 was "out of the question", Pardon paid tribute to his Cricketer of the Year, George Gunn (later to become, in partnership with Moore, a noted bat maker) for all the world as if nothing were amiss: "His easy style and quickness in judging the length of a ball," he wrote, "suggest that, as a boy at Trent Bridge, he studied Arthur Shrewsbury's methods." He went on to carp at the wartime spoilsports who were looking to restrict all – not just first-class – cricket: "I hope no attempt will be made to close the game down entirely." In these grim times, losing Surrey v Yorkshire might be a necessary sacrifice – but the Varsity match? Unthinkable!

There might not ever be a good time for war, but in *Wisden*'s case the outbreak of hostilities was genuinely awkward, since apart from the fact that it rendered the book's prime subject – cricket – somewhat lame, it came at a time when the firm had just taken a nervous step forward. Henry Luff's ambitions for the firm outlived him: in May 1914 John Wisden & Co was incorporated as a limited company. Only one of Luff's sons, Ernest Constantine, was on the original board, and even he was not in the chair. That position was taken by James Fabian, of the chartered accountancy firm Singleton, Fabian & Co. One of his colleagues, Albert Tilley, was also appointed to the board, and these two controlled the lion's share of the stock, functioning almost like brokers as other shareholders came and went. The first group of shareholders (11,000 shares were issued) formed a close circle involving founders, relatives, or connections in the world of cricket. Ernest Luff took 1,500, and his brother Cyril (from Hove, Sussex) 1,250; the older brother, Harry, surprisingly, took none. A baronet called George Elliot Armstrong (founder of a dining club for retired naval officers) and his mother, Alice Fitzroy, bought blocks of shares, as did the banker Henry Hoare. These were solid, pillar-of-society backers. The first board meeting took place at the Singleton, Fabian offices in Staple Inn, London in May 1914.

The minutes were written out in a handsome red leather book, in beautiful antique copperplate handwriting. They give off a nice sense of occasion, but also a vague whiff of men not sure, now they have attained this grand position, quite what to do. The first resolution was that the certificate of incorporation be framed (it remains on the firm's wall in Hampshire today); the second was that Alex Smith be appointed Secretary, and the third was that the company bank would be the London County and Westminster in London's St James's Square. The final resolution was that Ernest Luff be appointed manager, but they evidently did not have enormous confidence in him: he was empowered by the board to authorise purchases only up to the value of £30 – even at this stage the directors were putting him on a short rein. Perhaps since the firm was part of his own name, he could not help seeing *Wisden* not as a job but as a fiefdom. He was certainly keen to advance a new ball-making twist he had patented: for a ball bound with steel or bronze thread and "lapped with wax". So far as the Almanack was concerned his first act, as manager, was to argue that a price rise would not "seriously affect" sales – and so, after more than half a century, and "owing to the heavy cost of production", the price was raised from one shilling to one and six.

It was not an absurd move, but it was tactless timing, as was the purchase, that same summer, of James Henry Dark's cricket shop at Lord's. John Wisden & Co was looking to expand at an unfortunate moment. And the approaching war with Germany wasn't the only problem. In June 1914 some 300 cricket ball-makers at the John Wisden & Co factory in Tonbridge went on strike, and Luff was invited by the *Observer* to explain the company line. "Strange as it may appear," he said, "I am quite in sympathy with the men's demands." The sum they could earn in a week, around 30 shillings, was "quite inadequate", he felt. He could only apologise for the fact that "the price the trade pays will not permit our acceding to these demands".

There were other signs of the firm's ambition. Albert Tilley reported to the board that A. C. MacLaren (who had the highest first-class score at the time, with 424 for Lancashire against Somerset in 1895) might be willing to "represent the Company generally" for a salary of £50 a year, plus a percentage of sales; a page was paid for in the magazine MacLaren now edited (*The World of Cricket*) for a full year, to advertise the firm's wares; and a 14-year lease was taken out on a new shop at 23 Cranbourn Street. It was not a complicated move: it was right next-door to the old store at number 21. There was a mock-up stumps and bat mounted on the balcony, and a row of bats hung on a rail inside the front window, but curiously, among the wares advertised in large lettering on the glass – boxing gloves, racquets, footballs, croquet, lawn tennis – there was no mention of cricket at all.

These attempts to press forward soon found themselves in a changed atmosphere, however. MacLaren never was signed, and his magazine (which had formerly been known merely as *Cricket*) survived only 14 issues into the war. And by the time the 1915 edition came out, the weight of advertising on behalf of the company's own products struck a commercial note not quite in keeping with the temper of the times. There were blaring notices for the Wisden "Special Crown" ball, with a tribute from Sydney Barnes, who used it to take hatfuls of South African wickets in 1913–14 and was happy to declare it "far less hard to the hands" than any rival. And the "Exceller" bat with which Woolley had broken records for Kent was boosted by Woolley himself ("There are not any Bats made to equal the Wisden Exceller"), Ranjitsinhji ("the very best Bat I have ever used") and Grace "I have made over 1,000 runs with the Bat. I shall be very much obliged if you will make me two more like it."

In these years John Wisden & Co was also proud to proclaim itself a "Complete Golf Outfitters", supplying "every requisite" from brassies, baffies and cleeks to a new range of balls – the "Royal", the "Truflyte" and – in memory of the founder – the "Wonder". It may even have been the first shop in London to sell golf clubs. From 1874 John Wisden was the "sole London agent" for famed Scottish marques like Tom Morris, Robert Forgan and Willie Park. Auction houses still unearth the odd "rut iron" or "lofter" with "John Wisden" stamped on the sole or shaft. The firm was also able to persuade its sporting connections to praise its riding boots, which W. G. Grace thought "the best I have ever seen", and the champion golfer Harry Vardon, a little more emphatic, found "the *very* best I have ever seen".

War meant belt-tightening, and the board was not slow to cut back. Two men at the West Ham factory were dispensed with in 1914, and the following year the entire factory was closed. The firm's travelling salesman (a Mr Thompson) was urged to stop travelling and directed instead to create exclusive partnerships with "one good Sports Outfitter" in each town, who would enjoy a local monopoly on Wisden products. In the autumn of 1914, Ernest Luff informed the board that he had joined the armed forces and requested an "allowance", but he was crisply turned down – "considering all the circumstances". In the event, he did not rush off to war; he continued coming to board meetings until 1916.

It was a mark of *Wisden's* prestige at this time that other products were keen to pay for promotional space in the Almanack. To modern eyes they bring a period tang to the book, giving it antiquarian charm and value. "Get fit on Ivelcon," said one plug for a strengthening brew – "contains many times more nutriment than beef tea, and its flavour is much nicer." There were cartoons boosting an exciting new material, Viyella; news of an exhilarating shave tonic, "Oatine", which "has the effect of softening the beard in a most astonishing manner"; there were silk hunting hats and clip-on rubber boots ("To use them is to know their true value") and hotels conveniently located for Lord's and The Oval ("Electric light and bells throughout").

The house advertisement for the very book the reader must by definition have been inspecting at that moment might have been a last-minute filler. But the notice in the 1915 edition about back numbers (evidence that the company was looking to milk its assets more energetically) put the price of the previous year's edition at £1, a hint that *Wisden* was already a collectable antique whose value would grow rather than decline.

The luckless timing of all this might in retrospect have made *Wisden* look clumsy or – worse – unpatriotic. But while it was hard to present cricket as a casualty of war (who cared about games when men were dying?) there was some logic in cricket's self-pity, because the Great War really did bring down the curtain on what had been a halcyon era. More important, to a larger extent than anyone could yet guess, the game was preparing to contribute something truly central to the war effort: eager young men who had been trained, on the playing fields, in obedient and unquestioning courage. Schools cricket had long been seen as a glory of the English game. In 1898 John Wisden & Co had actually published a small book on "Public School Matches" – a showcase of the game played by Eton, Harrow and Winchester – edited by Sydney Pardon himself. But the schoolboys were about to become heroes in a larger sense.

The years before the war have been known as a golden age ever since: they have been given the sobriquet as a title. And while, of course, this is a generalised cartoon – as even the flowery writings of Cardus indicate, pre-war England had many gritty facets – life was certainly not one big country house party. And industrial England had long since been creating a new class of cricket lover: a dour, urban, no-nonsense fellow with his roots in the professional not the amateur game. It remains the case, however, that when Edwardian England recovered from the death of Queen Victoria and that unpleasant fight against the Boers, it enjoyed the balmiest of peacetimes. The Empire was thriving, Britain ruled oceans of waves, and all seemed prosperous and modern: free schooling (introduced in 1891) and steam-age printing were inspiring a mass market in the pleasurable arts. P. G. Wodehouse, Conan Doyle, Bram Stoker, H. G. Wells and co were pumping out extremely popular literature, much of it of a make-the-world-go-away sort; the quips of Shaw and Wilde were glittering in the London theatres; Elgar and Holst were swelling the concert halls, and sport was taking vivid drama even to the factory-bound masses. There were motor cars on the road, and still more astonishing engines at sea and in the air. The new century was taking wing, and the game did seem, after a period of tremendous flux, to have a settled shape.

Onto this stage stepped an enviable array of talent. The sun was setting on the age of Grace (he played his last game for England in 1899, while *Wisden* records his last innings of all as a 69 not out for Eltham against Grove Park on 25 July 1914), but the new dawn was ushering in a galaxy of fresh cricket luminaries. The amazing C. B. Fry, who scored 94 first-class centuries, played in an FA Cup final for Southampton, set a world record in the long jump and was offered the throne of Albania, was the most dashing. But he was only one of many. His Sussex team-mate, the immigrant "Prince" Ranjitsinhji, matched even Grace by nailing ten centuries in a single summer (1896) and in the three seasons of the *fin de siècle* (1899–1901) scored 8,692 first-class runs; then there was Gilbert Jessop, of whom Fry said that "no man has ever driven the ball so hard" and who once thumped 286 against Sussex in under three hours. The 1914 *Wisden* was also obliged to celebrate Tom Hayward's hundredth century – the second man to achieve this (after Grace) and the first professional, but mostly this was the peak of amateur cricket: B. J. T. Bosanquet (author of the googly), Lord Hawke, Archie MacLaren, Pelham ("Plum") Warner … the list of redoubtable Gents is a long one.

These bright amateur stars made this the high noon of the Edwardian spirit. In 1900 there were 18 amateurs in the top 20 places in the batting averages, not least because the public schools and great universities (cricket remained a preserve of schools with ample playing fields) were as dedicated to cricket as they were to classics; it was a central plank in the education of the young men who would inherit the "great game" that was Britain's mighty Empire. How else could they acquire the necessary qualities: leadership, loyalty, fortitude and *esprit de corps*. As Sir Henry Newbolt's much-mocked poem put it, if a chap's nerves could handle a tight finish at cricket – "A bumping pitch and a blinding light / An hour to play, and the last man in" – they could handle anything. Not for nothing was the imperial assault on Central Asia known as "The Great Game". And while modern sensibilities assume that only class-conscious commentators could imagine public-school cricket to be anything better than well mannered, this was not in those days the case. They were genuine centres of excellence, offering students plenty of leisure time and expert coaching from famous professionals. The standard was high. Gervase Birkbeck was only twelfth man for Eton, but he was good enough to go on and score three centuries for Norfolk.

For the most part the professional game was still a step up, of course. As Grace's influence dwindled, so the Players resumed their easy supremacy over the Gents, thanks to remarkable figures like Barnes, who took 189 wickets in only 27 Tests (17 in one great triumph against South Africa) and still holds the all-time record for the number of wickets in a series; or Frank Woolley, the left-handed professional who batted as elegantly as any Cambridge man (Cardus wrote that there was "all summer in a stroke by Woolley"); or the prodigious George Hirst, who in 1906 scored a stupendous 2,385 runs *and* took 208 wickets. And then there was the young Jack Hobbs, who scored 83 on his England debut in 1907 and went on to stand head and shoulders over all other batsmen of his time.

Though the class division remained strict, one of cricket's proudest boasts was that it provided a forum in which all men might be equal. No one had a better view of this than Ranji, and he was unequivocal. "Go to Lord's," he wrote in *The Jubilee Book of Cricket* (1897). "Analyse the crowd. There are all sorts and conditions of men round the ropes – bricklayers, bank clerks, soldiers, postmen and stockbrokers. Bad men, good men, workers and idlers are all there, and all at one in their keenness over the game. Cricket brings the most opposite characters, the most diverse lives together."

It is not cavilling to note that Ranji was in one sense being generous. The ground might have been a demotic fellowship, but the pavilion was another story. There were very few postmen or bricklayers in Thomas and Frank Verity's new building, which had opened in 1890 after fire ruined its predecessor, and women were excluded from its elegant rooms until 1999. Cricket's "diversity" was in important ways constrained. And while the elite players trod a now-familiar stage – the County Championship – the lower levels were barely connected. The society fixtures – universities, schools and Gents v Players – thrived, all carriages and parasols, while the Lancashire and Yorkshire leagues continued to be regarded as a slightly vulgar cousin of the senior game. Still, Ranji's broad point remains: cricket did throw at least some frail threads across the class divide and, however illusory, they were better than nothing.

Either way, it all came to an abrupt end when war was declared late on 4 August 1914. It was the day after a Bank Holiday in England, and a large crowd (some 15,000) watched Jack Hobbs proceed to a double-century at The Oval. At Lord's, in a schools match, a young batsman called John Howell, from Repton, was scoring 78 not out. It was one of the best days of his young life, but he would not be granted the leisure to enjoy it: he was off to war. For a few weeks cricket stumbled on, but droves of young players – many more than expected – were answering the nation's call and signing up for a chance to bash the Hun. At this stage the whole bally shindig was conceived, at least in the corridors and quadrangles of the public schools, as something of a jaunt.

Within days, the British Expeditionary Force was making its way towards Flanders, while in India Sikh regiments were being prepared for life under fire in Belgium. Hampshire, meantime, were tackling Essex at Bournemouth, and on 2 September, with German troops barely 30 miles from Paris, Yorkshire were engaged in a tricky rearguard action against Sussex. It was unreal, so when, at the end of the month, W. G. Grace sent his notorious letter to *The Sportsman*, it cleared cricket's mind. "Sir," he wrote. "There are many cricketers who are already doing their duty, but many more who do not seem to realise that in all probability they will have to serve either at home or abroad before the war is brought to a conclusion. The fighting on the continent is very severe, and will probably be prolonged. I think the time has come when the county cricket season should be closed, for it is not fitting at a time like the present that able-bodied men should play day after day and pleasure-seekers look on." Embarrassed, the cricket circus folded its tents. For form's sake Surrey were declared champions, by virtue of being in the lead when the lamps went out, but few cared much either way. The game was up. As E. W. Hornung (whose own doomed son left Eton and headed for the guns, declaring that he couldn't wait to "have a plug at those blighters", before dying in Belgium) would write:

> No Lord's this year, no silken lawns on which
> A dignified and dainty throng meanders
> The schools take guard upon a fierier pitch
> Somewhere in Flanders.

The author of this pained lyric was himself a keen cricketer – a regular for the Authors XI led by James Barrie and his own brother-in-law Arthur Conan Doyle. When Doyle suggested that a gentleman-cricketer-thief would make a fine character for a crime caper, Hornung took him at his word and created Raffles, the debonair thief who was only too happy to help himself to a sapphire necklace while knocking up runs on the lawns of country houses. Hornung borrowed freely from cricket's social divide by making cricket an effective disguise for skulduggery. When Raffles himself plays for the Gentlemen against the Players he delivers not just "an exhibition of athletic prowess" but "an intellectual treat". It is the perfect cover. In the best circles, no one could suspect a man who wore an I Zingari blazer.

When *Wisden* appeared in January 1915 the view remained fogged, and Pardon's first instinct was to carry on, as far as possible, as usual. The 1916 *Wisden* did not attempt to write poetry about the war; it simply tried to soldier on as best it could. If it was modesty on Pardon's part that he did not seek to approach the war through rhetoric, then it was also wise. In true *Wisden* style, Pardon trusted the cool recital of facts to express the pity and the poetry of it all. The war was young, but cricketers were joining up in droves, and it fell to *Wisden* to honour them. Of the patriotic-sounding G. B. Eden, captain of Winchester, *Wisden* noted that he "might easily become first-class, and in ordinary circumstances would have been captain again next year, but I am told he has received a commission". Eden was not alone. By the time the Schools XI played MCC on the August Bank Holiday (Eden did not make the team) most of his chums had "answered the country's call". As *Wisden* said, calm as ever: "the great majority of those who were going to the Universities are serving".

Established players answered the same bugle call. Of the five *Wisden* Cricketers of the Year, three were in uniform by the time the book went to press. Percy Fender, embryonic captain of Surrey and England, and the subject of that year's portrait, ended the season as a Lieutenant in the Royal Fusiliers; Donald Knight, "easily the best bat in the Oxford Eleven", was in the 28th London Artists; Johnny Douglas, who scored 72 for the Gents against the Players (and was also a middleweight boxing champion of whom it was said that "nothing shakes his nerve"), joined the Bedfords.

Joining up, of course, very often meant dying, and matters were brought close to home almost immediately. Pardon wrote in his 1915 Preface, dated January: "Mr Ernest D. Allen, who for several years had assisted in the work, joined the Army during the first week in the War." By the time he wrote that, Allen – holder of the London Golfing Society's Challenge Cup and for several years on the staff of the Cricket Reporting Agency, was already dead, shot through the head on New Year's Day 1915.

Wisden had said little about the Boer War, perhaps because "no cricketer of high repute was killed", but this time things were different. The finest public-school players of the pre-war years were just the right age, and just the right class, to lead the futile charge against the enemy guns.

One of the saddest losses, in *Wisden*'s mind, was 2nd Lieutenant John Howell, who had scored a double-century against Uppingham and lit up Lord's with his batting on the day war was declared. He "dominated the match" in such style that "no honours in the game seemed unobtainable". In reviewing his year in the Repton XI *Wisden* was unsentimental. "He is a little dull at times." But it was confident that great things lay ahead. "He must surely take a high place in first-class cricket." It was not to be. Less than a year later he was killed in the Ypres Salient. "Among all the young cricketers who have fallen in this war not one of brighter promise can be named," said his obituary. "He was potentially an England batsman." Similarly, the outstanding batsman in another game at Lord's between the Schools and MCC, a few weeks earlier, was one G. W. E. Whitehead, who had been in the Clifton side for four years, captaining it for two. This was his third outing for the students. In *Wisden*'s eyes he was a "perfect flower of the public schools", but he went on to spend the next four years in the Royal Flying Corps until he was killed on 17 October 1918, just three weeks before the final whistle. He was one of 500 "sons of Clifton" who died in the conflict; another – one of the first to fall, indeed – was Arthur Edward Jeune Collins, who was killed on 11 November 1914 after joining the Royal Engineers. His claim to fame? In 1899, as a 13-year-old at Clifton, he had scored 628 in a house match (still the highest ever individual innings) and been immortalised in *Wisden* the following year in an arithmetic-literary form unique to the Almanack: "a six, four fives, thirty-one fours, thirty-three threes and forty-six twos". The 1915 edition had a more sober duty to perform: his name appeared in a roll call of Deaths that ran, even in this mild first stage of the conflict, to 48 pages.

It may not be easy for a modern reader, a century after these events, to accept *Wisden*'s unabashed affection for the public-school ideal without an ironic shrug. But if the class-bound system of English education can now be held up for inspection (not least for indoctrinating a generation of well-born boys with the deference required to fight such a war) then the young men it produced must be seen not only as privileged beneficiaries but also as victims. Whatever we think about dynastic privilege, the boys themselves really did march off like bright-eyed lambs to slaughter, with an unquestioning sense that this was their fight. When war was declared, these cricket-loving sons of inherited wealth leapt into the fray with well-tutored enthusiasm. Like the wide-eyed greenhorn Raleigh in R. C. Sherriff's play about trench life, *Journey's End*, they had a fervent appetite for the concept of Hun-bashing without the smallest notion of what it might involve. And when they fell, as they did in their thousands, cricket helped provide the language in which they could be mourned. From Abingdon to Wycliffe, chapels bore their names. At King's School in Worcester they were inscribed in a cricket pavilion with the words: "In Memory of those who, having learnt in this place to play the game for the school, played it also for their country."

Wisden was not wrong, then, to detect in the declaration of war a tolling bell for the culture at whose centre the Almanack now stood. In Sydney Pardon's reverent mind "cricketers" and "the public schools" merged into a single sterling model of all that was fine and brave about the English character. Like the young men themselves, what else could *Wisden* do but stiffen the sinews and the upper lip? "Cricketers have made a splendid response to the call to the colours," Pardon wrote, for all the world as if he were a proud headmaster, a dear old Mr Chips, to these young gallants. He wasn't making it up, either. At the 1915 meeting of MCC, the president, Lord Hawke, raised a glass to the fact that some three-quarters of first-class cricketers were in the Army or the Navy. The game, as people kept saying, was afoot.

———

Behind the scenes, business was jittery. A "heavy decrease" in the sale of sports gear obliged John Wisden & Co to lay off staff at 23 Cranbourn Street, and prepare to close down the neighbouring store (number 21) entirely. Worst of all, it emerged late in 1915 that Ernest Luff himself had helped himself to a "considerable sum" – £200 – from company funds, in order to escape, as the minutes put it, "proceedings taken by a creditor". Luff had been given a number of company cheques, signed by James Fabian, and he had made out one of these for £50, payable to himself. The board was aghast. He was warned that if there was "any further tampering with the cash of the company" he would, "in the opinion of his co-directors", be regarded as "unfit" to run the firm. The chairman said that he had spoken to Luff "very strongly", but no one needed to spell out how inappropriate it was for the senior executive to be dipping into the till at such a time. As a precaution, a new man – A. J. Webster Keech (known, for mysterious reasons, as Harry Brevett) – was appointed joint manager. Luff didn't like it – indeed he suggested that since he now looked unlikely to be called up for military duty it was "unnecessary" – but his protestations were ignored. The board did, however, agree that, should Luff indeed be called to arms, the company would be willing to vote him an allowance of half his salary.

A few months later, as the armies on the Somme steeled themselves for another hellish assault on the machine-gun wall, it happened again. This time it seemed that Luff had, contrary to the express decision of the board, incurred debts of £671 to a sheepskin company in an ill-judged attempt to manufacture "leggings" (what we would call pads). And some of the invoices didn't add up – on one occasion he had signed a receipt for £40 but credited the firm with only £20. The directors were stern. This was, said the minutes of a meeting at which Luff himself was present, "very unsatisfactory and unbusinesslike conduct". That winter, they decided it was "no longer possible to retain" his services, made good on their promise to declare him "unfit" and dismissed him – "summarily". As a sign that they were still determined to look forward as a group, however, they renewed the three-year lease (£110 per annum) on the space at 15 and 16 Great Newport Street. Cranbourn Street would remain open until 1928, but where John Wisden had been a shopkeeper, the company that bore his name was now a manufacturer and a chain. Three new directors were appointed, and the business made it through the war: in 1919 the lease on the premises in Great Newport Street was again extended, and the employees at Cranbourn Street were all awarded a bonus worth one month's salary "to mark the appreciation of the board of the work of the staff during the past difficult years". Yet when Ernest Luff's brother Cyril (a shareholder, and at this time a transport engineer in Brighton) wrote to the board in the winter of 1918 hoping to find employment at his father's company, there was "no suitable opening" (he went on to join Gradidge's, a rival sports equipment firm in Tonbridge). Instead, the board signed H. J. W. ("Wally") Hardinge, the former Kent professional who had scored 1,000 runs in a season 18 times, been a Cricketer of the Year in 1915, and played football for England, as the firm's "sole outside representative".

Throughout the war years, the Almanack did not feature in boardroom discussions – it was too small and self-sufficient to need much thought. Pardon was left to his own devices, and if the 1915 volume did not entirely disturb the naive spirit of the times, then the 1916 book made up for it. Thanks to the wartime paper shortage and the abandonment of first-class cricket, it was slim (298 pages instead of the 534 in 1914), but it was decorous at such a moment to be undernourished. Pardon was frank: "The question of coming out at all was seriously considered, but the proprietors decided not to break with the continuity of over half a century," he wrote. The Almanack would summarise the cricket played by schools, universities, amateur clubs or

Advertisement from Wisden *1919*

improvised military teams strengthened by top players in uniform. But he knew that the games "were of no importance", because in truth the book had only one subject: death.

Chief among the victims, in this sad roster, were already-prominent cricketers for whom *Wisden* was the proper chief mourner. Alan Marshal played for Queensland and then, when he came to England, for both Surrey and W. G. Grace's London club. He scored a triple century against Croydon and 245 against Egypt at the Crystal Palace. "He had it in him to be great," *Wisden* thought, "but somehow he missed the position."

Other names jump out like bright nuggets in the mud. There seemed nothing too remarkable about Sub-Lieutenant Rupert Brooke, of the Royal Naval Division, at this time – he was just one of thousands who had fallen, and his end ("died at Lemnos of sunstroke") was not the stuff of medals. But *Wisden*, while noting drily that "he had gained a considerable reputation as a poet", was equally anxious to remind us that he had taken 19 wickets for the Rugby Eleven of 1906. A flick back to the 1907 *Wisden* shows that he played against Marlborough at Lord's, scoring nought (clean bowled) – not quite the stuff of which sonnets were made.

The most moving entries, however, are not those of the already famous, but those relating to the ranks upon ranks of promising lives cut short. Lieutenant James Balfour-Melville of the 3rd Black Watch enjoyed a cracking youth as a batsman for Malvern and Scotland, as well as winning four Oxford Blues for football. Captain Ronald Lagden, meanwhile, was a cricket prodigy at Marlborough College, won four Blues for Oxford at Lord's and also represented the university for football, rackets and hockey (playing rugby for England on the side). Captain C. H. Eyre played at Lord's half a dozen times for Harrow and Cambridge (captaining both) and won on every single occasion. None of this spectacular sporting promise did these young men a blind bit of good in the trenches, but even their untimely death could not inspire *Wisden* to suspend its dry judgement. It glossed Captain Eyre's grand winning run at Lord's by pointing out that he himself played only a minor part. "For this happy experience he was not largely responsible, as in the games with Eton he made only 68 runs in five innings and in the inter-Universities' matches but 75 in six."

By the same token, readers were informed that the late Major William Cautley, though he had won a DSO for gallantry, had spent three years in the Bradfield Eleven but still had "no idea of batting". Even in death, *Wisden* would not let standards slip.

Somehow, these dry, abbreviated reports still carry a muted emotional charge. Major Eustace Crawley was the only man to have scored a century in the Eton v Harrow match *and* the Varsity match. A "skilful and plucky horseman", he was assigned to the 12th Lancers, where he discovered that German howitzers were no respecter of equestrian skill; he fell, as the humdrum saying goes, in the line of duty.

What memories must have writhed in the flailing imaginations of all this doomed youth. Did Percy Banks, when he floundered at Ypres, flash back to the day he scored 103 for Haileybury, an innings *Wisden* called "Trumperesque"? Did 2nd Lieutenant Arthur Bourchier, fatally wounded while supervising a "bomb-throwing" experiment, regret the fact that he was handed that lethal assignment thanks to his background as a "very useful" club cricketer in Devon? And when Captain Geoffrey Dowling of the 7th King's Royal Rifle Corps lay dying from bullet wounds, did he think back proudly to the day he went in No. 10 for Charterhouse, and scored an unlikely 78?

Few other accounts of the Great War capture the nature of this tragedy with quite such ceremonious clarity, intensified as it is by the contrast between boyish pleasure and the deadly trial by fire. There are even, as the list unfolds, ripples of *Wisden*'s enduring subject – class distinction. Sometimes the classless playground glimpsed by Ranjitsinhji is visible in the pile of dead figures. Alphabetical order means that Major Bernard Brodhurst, of the 4th Gurkha Rifles, lies alongside Captain F. S. Brown, of the 5th Manchester Regiment – even though the former took 30 wickets for Clifton, while the latter was merely a "sound bat" for Wigan CC. But mostly the gulf between officers and ranks is as deep and abiding as the one between Gents and Players. Even in the grave, some men have elaborate initials while others are plain surnames.

It comes as a shock to find, appended to the war list, famous men who did not die in action. A. E. Stoddart, having played rugby and cricket for England, shot himself in the head, while Victor Trumper, the cavalier Australian batsman, also died young. In most years *Wisden* would have donned a black armband on their behalf, but in 1916 they seem an afterthought. They were not casualties of war, and *Wisden*'s chief role in this extraordinary edition was to provide passing bells for those who died as cattle.

But, so far as *Wisden* was concerned, the most resonant death of all, if such a thing can be said, was that of cricket's own great father figure, W. G. Grace. In October 1915 he suffered a heart attack triggered, said the mythmakers, as he shook his fist at a German Zeppelin drifting menacingly in the skies above his garden in Eltham, Kent. Who knows: when the appearance of the 1916 edition was being discussed, it might well even have been the fact of Grace's death, and the obligation to remember him in style, that triggered the resolution to go ahead and publish. The Almanack buried him with full cricketing honours: an obituary by Sydney Pardon, a tribute by Lord Harris and some 40 pages of facts and figures about his exorbitant achievements – or, as the front cover put it, "full statistics of Mr Grace's career in the cricket field".

For the most part these are straightforward measurements of greatness – endless runs, endless wickets – but they are also full of small emotional tremors. One can all too easily imagine a quiz question: what connects the following five men – Callaway, Christopherson, Clayton, Cochrane and Coe – apart from the fact that their names all begin with C? Answer: they all bowled W. G. Grace, once, in first-class cricket.

And what do we have here? In a list of "spectacles" – the rare occasions on which the great man scored nought in both innings – we find the day in 1863 in Bath when young William Gilbert, then only 14 years old, was dismissed twice in the match by his own rotter of a brother, E. M. Grace. It must have been a merry journey home that day. *Wisden* noticed such things. *Wisden* remembered. And cricket lovers more than a century later can still stumble across the old names, and wonder who they were.

"Though one's thoughts are concentrated on a far different field," wrote Pardon of Grace, growing fulsome, "I ought to try, before it is too late, to leave on record my recollections of him. The greatest cricketer of all time has passed away. We who gloried in his overwhelming excellence may well think ourselves fortunate."

This was Pardon at his best: forthright, deeply felt and serious. And his analysis of Grace's batsmanship was warm, too. Where his predecessor

W. H. Knight sneered at the young man's "unscientific" leg-side hitting, Pardon preferred to observe that "he excelled all his predecessors in his power of placing the ball on the on-side". Since he also cited Grace's assertion that he "did not indulge in the pull till he was forty", we must infer that the revolutionary aspect of Grace's batting was his forcefulness off the front foot. Until Grace, front-foot play was a bland defensive measure, a game for the "dead bat". Grace (inspired or at least liberated by the steady improvement in playing surfaces during his long career) turned it into an aggressive move, showed Fry, Ranji, Jessop and the others the way to go, and changed the way cricket was played for ever.

Pardon ended with a tender tribute. "Personally, W. G. struck me as the most natural and unspoiled of men. Whenever and wherever one met him he was always the same. There was not the smallest trace of affectation … if anything annoyed him he was quick to show anger, but his little outbursts were soon over. No man who ever won such worldwide fame could have been more modest in speaking of his own doings."

Lord Harris (despite permitting himself a minor quibble over Grace's occasional mulishness) was even more effusive. "He was a land mark, a figure head, a giant, a master man … as well-known by sight to the public as any man in public life." Grace was more than a cricketer, in other words; he was a late-Victorian institution.

It is one measure of Pardon's editorship that his personal acquaintance with cricket and cricketers entitled him to address his subscribers in these amicable terms. Under his stewardship the Almanack had become more than an annual album of sporting facts and figures, and more than a mere bookkeeper. If there was such a thing as the cricketing family, then Grace was its grand bearded patriarch, and *Wisden* the obliging family friend, keeping the children honest and the paperwork straight.

By this stage Pardon had been editor for two decades and was supremely confident. Back in 1910 he had sworn, in a famous phrase, that the England selectors who went into an Oval Test match without a fast bowler had "touched the confines of lunacy" and that "the despised man in the street could not have been guilty of such folly". He never minded admitting that he missed the old days: by nature conservative, he saw himself as a guardian of a distinctly old flame, and accepted that it fell to him to see off any vulgar modern threat. His obituary of Frederick Fryer, a Cambridge captain who had once scored 72 for the

Gents against the Players, suggested that he had "flourished at a time when University cricket was amazingly rich in talent, and attracted more public attention than in later days of numberless county matches".

We can hardly take this complaint about the dominance of county cricket literally, since at the time of writing (January 1918) there had been *no* county matches for over three years. But we need to take due note of the sentimental pressure behind it, since it expresses a powerful aspect of the Great War zeitgeist. The outrageous slaughter in the trenches gave cricket an especially intense glow, fixing it ever more firmly as a pastoral archetype of English summer repose. Of course, some of this was pure fantasy – a hazy dream of sweet afternoons in which the sun always threw cool shadows across fragrant meadow-grass, every opponent was a great sport, every slice of ham delicious, and even the most crushing failure a matter of no importance whatsoever. Edmund Blunden, who survived four years in the army, wrote that during the years of mud and fire, cricket seemed to him "an earthly paradise", and this was a common reflex. Siegfried Sassoon echoed the same stark thought in his poem "Dreamers":

> *I see them in foul dug-outs gnawed by rats*
> *And in the ruined trenches lashed by rain*
> *Dreaming of things they did with balls and bats,*
> *And mocked by hopeless longing to regain*
> *Bank holidays ...*

The English countryside, with all its rituals, never seemed so fine as when it flashed before the mind in a howling mudhole, in mid-February, in some shell-battered corner of northern France. As the *Daily Mirror* put it, in December 1916: "I've just heard of a 'Tommy' who spends his time in the trenches, when he isn't fighting, reading *Wisden's Annual*." I should say. That's the spirit.

The 1916 *Wisden* would go on to become one of the most precious British books of the 20th century – a perfect hardback edition (the holy grail) might fetch up to £8,000 at auction. The small print run had something to do with it, but chiefly it was the book's contents that made it unique. The Grace obituary would have been enough on its own to make it a special case, but more important, this particular

Almanack was seized upon by grieving relatives of the fallen sons commemorated in its famous pages. At any rate, the entire edition sold out – said a grateful prefatory note the following year – "in a few days". And since the book immediately became a cherished family souvenir, few copies were thrown back into the market.

But its appeal is more than antiquarian; it is a rich historical document in its own right. The personal force of the memoirs and the cumulative effect of the death list generate as much heartache as the saddest novel. Nearly a million British troops were shuffling to their end in the killing fields of Passchendaele and the Somme; *Wisden*, inevitably, could only commemorate those who had made a mark with willow or leather, but this was a multitude. In doing so, it established a powerful sense of English cricket as a clan, with its own inimitable rites of passage. The book could not bring the boys back, but it had something special to offer, and it knew it: it could remember them. Cricket knew how to mark such moments: the close of play and the drawing of stumps had an automatic kinship with the going down of the sun.

In 2006 this famous book formed the basis of a crude eBay prank when a vendor offered up an entire attic full of *Wisden*s, including "loads" of wartime copies ("six for 1916") with bids starting at just a pound. The antiquarian world juddered at the news, and one impatient dealer was said to have offered £250,000 for the whole stash without even looking at it. *Wisden* itself was taken in, devoting a page in the 2007 edition to the story. But the whole thing turned out to be a hoax. Very funny.

The next two Almanacks had little option but to repeat themselves. County cricket was suspended for the duration, so school, university and military cricket was the order of the day. But these were soon rendered irrelevant by the swelling obituary section. "The fifty-fourth edition of *Wisden* is of necessity rather a mournful volume," began the 1917 Notes, as they introduced another horrifying list of sawn-off lives. It had already been noticed, in the *Manchester Guardian*, that "*Wisden* allows no man who has had a hand in English county cricket to pass without his tribute" and this habit was about to become the Almanack's defining characteristic. *Wisden* was a graveyard.

Once again there were distinguished players among the fallen. Pardon's 1918 obituary of Colin Blythe quoted Ranjitsinhji himself putting the Kent spinner ahead of the great Rhodes; *Wisden* agreed, calling him "the greatest Kent bowler of modern days". He took an amazing 215 wickets in the 1909 season, and two years earlier, at Headingley, had bowled out South Africa twice, taking 15 wickets in all. He also had two first-class hat-tricks to his name. Now, in 1917, Sergeant Blythe was playing a final couple of games at Lord's before heading off to war. It is hard, looking at his last scorecard, not to imagine the scene. It was the middle of August, and Blythe, a softly spoken left-armer from London's docklands, took just one wicket and was bowled for nought before rushing away early to catch the boat-train to France. One can visualise him taking off his white cricket boots, hoisting his pack high on his shoulder and leaning his way down the platform at Victoria, the smell of Lord's turf still in his nostrils. Two months later, he was dead, just one more name on *Wisden*'s list. Not just any name, though: the Almanack devoted page after page to his bowling achievements.

As chance would have it, one of only two South Africans Blythe did not dismiss in the 1907 Headingley Test was Reggie Schwarz, an English-born googly-merchant and 1908 Cricketer of the Year who had studied under Bosanquet. Not out in both innings, he too would soon be "in *Wisden*" as a casualty; a week after the eleventh hour of the eleventh day, having been wounded twice and somehow survived, he was mown down by influenza.

These are just two men, among so many. The longest "roll of honour", in 1917, ran to 107 dreadful pages. Name after name, man after man, agony after agony. But all of their stories were brushed by moments on a cricket field somewhere, and *Wisden* was ready to receive them into its hallowed fold. Who knows what might have become of them had they survived? Lieutenant K. L. Hutchings topped the batting averages at Tonbridge three years in a row, helped Kent win their first County Championship in 1906, and played twice for England in Australia the following year, scoring 126 in the Melbourne Test. Now he was dead, "struck by a shell, death being instantaneous".

Not everyone was so unlucky. Rohan Mackenzie Chadwick of the Royal Garrison Artillery, a headmaster, curate and sometime opening batsman for Rugby, Cheshire and Dorset, was listed by *Wisden* as having "died of his wounds" on 12 May 1915. However, the information was incorrect, the dead man was actually 2nd Lieutenant Richard Markbarn Chadwick, also of the RGA, who died the following day, aged 20. It seems there had been some "confusion of initials". The Reverend A. H. C. Fargus, who in the 1916 edition was declared lost at sea, presumed dead, was still alive too. He had been "prevented from re-joining the ship", and never embarked on the fatal voyage.

One name glimmers for an unusual reason. In 1913 Percy Jeeves took 106 wickets for Warwickshire; in the truncated 1914 season he took 90 more. This was enough to catch the eye of P. G. Wodehouse, who admired his bowling but, more to the point, needed a good name for a butler-character in a new short story. It was right there in the 1916 *Wisden*, which marked Jeeves's passing – endeavouring, no doubt, to give satisfaction. There are other signs of *Wisden*'s appeal to the bookish as well as the cricket-minded. The obituary of Sir Arthur Conan Doyle hinted that Sherlock himself might have his roots in the pairing of Shacklock (Nottinghamshire) and Holmes (Yorkshire) while the great detective's brother echoes Mycroft, of Derbyshire.

It is evident that by 1917 Pardon had achieved a settled view of his duty in this time of war. Through *Wisden*, he would do his bit to keep cricket alive, defending it when necessary, but chiefly by celebrating the game in whatever incarnation it appeared. He was happy to announce that there had been a "great change of feeling" since the early days of the war, when no one dared use the nets at The Oval for fear of being "jeered at by the men on the tram cars". Two years later, such fears had "quite passed away". War had become a familiar, if acrid, experience and he made no apology for giving it time and space when theatre, music hall, billiards and boxing rings were all cheerfully sanctioned as morale-boosting exercise. "We had all come to regard the nightmare of war as a normal condition," he wrote, adding that cricket was "as legitimate as any other recreation". He even began to brood on the necessity of change when the war ended, on the grounds that there would be a falling off in support. Not surprisingly, this struck him as an opportunity to roll back the volume of county cricket: "It would not be a misfortune if the counties had to be content with shorter programmes."

As if to prepare for this second golden age of amateur cricket (and moved by the scale of the schools' sacrifice in the war) Pardon gave more of the Almanack over to schools cricket. In an odd irony, its status had been lifted even higher by events on the Western Front, which could scarcely do otherwise than recast the class structure of Gents and Players into its military equivalent: officers and men. Winchester, meanwhile, which until then had only ever played Eton College, went so far as to arrange new fixtures against upstart schools like Bradfield, Charterhouse and Wellington – a development that proved, *Wisden* said, an "unqualified success".

Since MCC also played an extended fixture list against schools, travelling the country to spread the word, it felt logical when in 1918 *Wisden* introduced a novelty: in the continuing absence of first-class cricket, the Five Cricketers of the Year would all be schoolboys. This gave rise to one of the sweetest stories in *Wisden*'s long life, because one of the five young cricketers selected in that inaugural list was one Harry Calder, from Cranleigh, who was mostly "fast-medium with an easy action", but had a "dangerous Yorker" and had once taken eight for 21 at The Oval. Calder himself was soon serving abroad, however, and cricket was not at the forefront of his mind. It seems that he did not even know about the award until 1994, when he was 93 years old and living in a South African nursing home. One of *Wisden*'s enduring roles is to keep track of its extended family; in this case it took a long time, but 76 years after the event, *Wisden* was able to remind Calder of his long-lost triumph. Back in 1917 he became (and still is) the youngest-ever Cricketer of the Year; by the time he heard news of it he was the oldest one then alive. He pronounced himself "delighted". Such is cricket; such is *Wisden*.

Not everyone was so fortunate as Calder. The 1917 Almanack carried an errata note stating that Rifleman Hilleard, listed as dead the previous year, had in fact survived. Alas, it later turned out that this correction was itself incorrect – Hilleard really *had* died, as originally stated (his name is on the Menin Gate at Ypres).

With the war over at last, the 1919 edition came blinking out from behind the clouds. Somehow, in the midst of so much carnage, *Wisden* had made it through. The slender wartime editions would forever look the part

– emaciated, deprived – but they had seen it through to the end, and could now start growing again. To mark the occasion Sydney Pardon's salary was increased to a princely 125 guineas per annum. "The long nightmare of the War has come to an end," he wrote.

The primary business of the book was still the roll of honour ("again a terribly long list") and on and on it went, page after page, line after line of young cricket-playing men, in another remarkable *festschrift*. Elsewhere, Pardon was impatient to get down to business. "The present issue of the Almanack is, I hope, the last that will ever come out in such reduced bulk," he wrote, before moving on to the game itself. *Wisden* had loyally continued to publish the minutes of MCC's annual meeting, from which we learn that cricket grounds like Lord's and The Oval were requisitioned by the Army and used to train cadets and manufacture military equipment. We learn too that by 1917 some 3,000 MCC members were "serving with the colours", leading to talks on whether they should be spared their fee, and the consequences for the MCC budget if they were. In the end a neat muddle-through was found: members in the service were offered a refund of half their subscription, on application; and here is the clever thing – one has one's pride, what? – not a single one of them applied.

Pardon noted these goings-on with ceremonious attention to detail, almost as if they were high-level cricket. Compared to previous editions, they almost were. The Long Room at Lord's, *Wisden* had noted in a report on MCC matters in 1918, "is still being used for making hay-nets for horses for the Army. Owing, however, to a reduction in the staff, the number made (about 12,000) has not been so great as last year (about 18,000)." In the absence of batting averages, hay-net production would have to do.

The MCC proceedings alert us, too, to the speed with which, even before the war ended, cricket began to ponder its future. There was plenty of water – none of it clear or blue – between progressives, who wanted to remake the game, and Golden Age conservatives, who wanted the pre-war mood to pick up where it left off. Pardon's *Wisden* was unusual in that it wanted neither of these things: it wanted to turn the clock back even further, to a time when the counties played a less dominant role.

At the first post-war meeting of the counties, in February 1919, it was mooted that games be reduced to two days, to speed things up and attract bigger audiences. There were calls to abolish the tea interval and to award more points for wins than for first-innings leads (an attempt to incentivise positive cricket and cure the pre-war epidemic of drawn games). From Australia came a plan to move from six to eight balls per over. It was even mooted that batsmen could be out for slow scoring or penalised for facing maiden overs, and that boundaries be shortened to encourage big hitting.

In the first post-war *Wisden* Pardon, at his most harrumphing, gave all such notions short shrift; they were "too preposterous to be worth serious consideration". Was it for this that a war had been fought? "The restriction of all county matches to two days strikes me as a sad blunder," he stated. And he took a dim view of the Australian plan to move from a six- to an eight-ball over: "I can see no good, but on the contrary a great deal of harm, in the proposal," he wrote. Longer overs would mean "less and less fast bowling" and a "huge increase in run-getting". The balance between bat and ball was delicate (whisper it, but the so-called Golden Age was in part a time of easy batting on increasingly benign wickets), so tilting the game in favour of run-feasts could hardly be applauded. Pardon did, however, reveal a fondness for the age before boundaries, which knew "the importance of making batsmen work for their runs".

There was more than mere cricket in such conversations. In its reflections on the habits of the summer game, *Wisden* was dramatising a deeper identity crisis, the terms of which were being debated in the topmost corridors of power. Now that the German menace had been repelled at such unbelievable cost, what kind of country did Britain wish to be? The conservative strand wanted Edwardian Britain – which furnished its elite with a most agreeable lifestyle – to stiffen its lip, take a deep breath and shrug off the traumas of gas and shellfire. But this was an elitist dream; thousands of deserving veterans wanted something more: not just a land where the wickets were always true, but a world fit for war-heroes and their long-suffering families.

Wisden, by nature conservative, had quieter hopes. It wanted Canterbury week, legitimate bowling actions, tigerish fielding, correct batting in the Varsity match, and a full house at Lord's for Eton v Harrow. That wasn't too much to ask, surely.

Advertisement from Wisden *1915*

6

Beg your Pardon

The period following the First World War was, not surprisingly, one in which the position of amateur cricket looked parlous. It would be years before the blows to the national consciousness would find bruised expression in discordant music and off-kilter literature, egalitarian politics and a sceptical attitude to landowning and inheritance. But the reflexes of the whole country had been shaken by the carnage in France, and it was impossible to pretend that the conflict had been a bad dream – over now, thank God. Militarised Britain had been (in a later phrase) a nation of lions led by donkeys; it was common knowledge that a generation of fine young men had been led to slaughter for very little gain or purpose. And that was not all: for the first time ever the common man had been abroad and seen up close the leadership qualities of his elders and betters. Never again would he be so deferential. While the United States marked the end of hostilities by prohibiting alcohol, in Britain a slew of reforming politicians were demanding a bolder say in their own, and their country's, future.

On the home front, women had moved into the workplace and could not be wished back to domestic life without friction. Poets, journalists and dramatists all described a civilian world that teemed with grief and anger, shivering with veterans, widows and orphans. So far as cricket went, the pre-war fantasy of Corinthian high jinks – the linen-and-boater culture forged on the playing fields of public schools ... this now seemed a feeble notion. The Edwardian moment – all those cucumber sandwiches in the dappled parkland – was over. The idle rich were living in numbered days.

Had the war been lost the ruling class might have been powerless to resist this great alteration. Victory, however, encouraged the hope that the good old days might be revived. Indeed, the drift towards professional cricket would otherwise have seemed irresistible, given that in 1919 the Gentlemen's batting, in their annual encounter with the Players, was "immeasurably below the standard of pre-war days". This was not a temporary dip – in 1912 there were five Gents in the England team; by 1926 there were just two.

There were still a few outcrops committed to the restoration of past glories, though, and Pardon's *Wisden* was one of them. In one sense – the plain fact of its continuing existence – the Almanack was itself a plucky survivor. The 1919 edition was published in May rather than January, which gave Pardon a chance to include the new fixture list (not settled till February) as well as time to put his foot down over all those new fangled ideas – what the papers were "pleased to call reform or reconstruction". He was especially unenthusiastic about two-day cricket. Modern wickets were too good to permit a finish to such games in decent weather; nor did he relish the idea of playing until a 7.30 close, arguing that the "craving for food" might prove stronger than the appetite for play. All he wanted was for cricket to regain "its old charm".

Meanwhile, there were ceremonial duties to perform. The 376 deaths recorded in the 1919 *Wisden* brought the wartime total to nearly 2,000 – a long and lethal pilgrimage made more heart-wrenching by the fact that many of the men in the list had so nearly made it through. The schoolboy Cricketers of the Year were named, and there were significant one-offs to commemorate, such as the match between the Armed Forces and an England XI got up by Captain Warner. Games such as this had enlivened the war years. When a Warner XI took on an F. S. Jackson XI at Lord's a crowd of 8,000 spectators were warmed by the sight of Air Mechanic Jack Hobbs scoring 86 in what *Wisden* called, as if there were nothing unusual about it, "the finest display of the season".

There was room for some teasing asides as well: the death of the King of Tonga was marked by a notice explaining that cricket had become so popular on his island it had to be banned for six days a week to prevent it from leading people astray. This strain – a fondness for eccentric cricket curios – was becoming a signature *Wisden* habit. In 1922 Pardon included a potted list of Ashes incidents torn from their context and presented as tributes to the rich and variegated nature of "the old game". There was the first occasion on which the result was transmitted by cable; the coincidence by which both captains in the 1905 rubber were born on the same day; the fact that one spectator had "dropped dead from excitement" in a tight run-chase (while another merely "gnawed away the handle of his umbrella"); and the fact that the temperature in the sweltering sun of Adelaide, in 1921, had touched 150 degrees Fahrenheit.

It was good almanackish fun. But with a new cover price of two shillings, the post-war book cost twice as much as the pre-war version; every penny counted. In the spring of 1919, for the first time since 1914, John Wisden & Co was doing well enough to pay a dividend to shareholders as a reward for their patience in the war. But caution remained the watchword: presented with a request for a typewriter, the directors insisted that "it be obtained at the expense not exceeding a sum of £20". And when Harry Brevett, the new manager of the Tonbridge works, spent twice that (£45) on a smarter model, he was soon given three months' notice. If £45 sounds a minor amount to modern ears, we should note that it was over a third of Sydney Pardon's own salary.

Pardon had been in the chair for almost three decades by now, and felt no need to kowtow to anybody as he sought to preserve the golden cricket culture of the pre-war years. This was not a sign that he was some blinkered, dyed-in-the-wool cricket monomaniac. On the contrary, in 1920 he put together a series for *The Times* about the theatre, and even had the nerve to disparage the great-seeming actor Sir Henry Irving: "He followed no model," he wrote. "He founded no school and left no sound tradition behind him." Reflections like these, interesting in themselves, also gave cultural ballast to his cricket writings: Pardon was notoriously short-sighted and watched play (according to Cardus) through "ivory-coloured opera glasses" – probably from Covent Garden – evaluating individual performances as if they were not elements of the game but interpretations of it. This habit led him to dwell on the players' sensibility as much as their skill. Thus Trumper was "the best and most brilliant" of the Australians, but also "modest and unaffected"; Blythe had "a certain imaginative quality that was peculiarly his own"; Schwartz was "quiet, almost retiring, without the least trace of 'side', and with a peculiarly attractive voice"; and of Harry Trott he remarked: "No better loser was ever seen on the cricket field." Cricketers were discussed like the heroes of plays. It was an original way to write about games, fast becoming a *Wisden* hallmark.

He did not even try to hide his brusque impatience with the post-war zest for change, and in 1920 repeated his lack of enthusiasm for all such proposals. The return of first-class cricket was leading "all the faddists in Great Britain" to come up with "fatuous suggestions" with no aim other than to keep up with the jittery nature of modern life – *Phones! Cars! Planes! Electricity!* Pardon was happy to say told-you-so after the rapid demise of the two-day experiment, which he himself had thought "doomed before half the season had run its course ... I trust we shall hear no more about the need for dramatic alterations." In applauding the public for filling county grounds ("despite a rise in the cost") he also declared himself vindicated. "Gloomy fears that the game would not retain its old popularity after such a long break proved utterly groundless," he wrote. "The season was one of great prosperity."

After the slimline war years the 1920 *Wisden* represented a return to the Almanack's tubby best, numbering 727 pages, more than double the previous year and enough to justify a price hike (to half a crown). Back to its pre-war size, it also went back to the pre-war division into two parts, so that it began with the Laws followed by Births and Deaths, pressed on through Records, Cricketers and Public Schools, and only then made room for the editor's Notes. These came at the end of the first section; part two featured the county season, MCC matches, more public-schools scores and any overseas cricket.

There were some impressive Cricketers of the Year to honour – Holmes, Hendren, Sutcliffe, Tyldesley and Ducat – and at a Lord's dinner in honour of the Australian Imperial Forces XI, glasses were raised to cricket's survival and the staying power of its loyal ally. The book was toasted like a hero. "To the compliments paid to *Wisden's Almanack* by P. F. Warner and F. S. Jackson," wrote Pardon, "I cannot – from motives of modesty – refer in detail. But I need hardly say they were keenly appreciated."

With this sort of applause ringing in its ears, perhaps it was inevitable that *Wisden* wanted to stand up for the status quo. It sought in particular to protect the game from "the menace of the Yorkshire and Lancashire leagues", with their odious tendency to offer better pay than counties. "With the busy agents of the Lancashire League always on the lookout for talent," wrote Pardon, "committees cannot hope to retain their professionals unless they ensure them a large amount." He had objected to this before – back in 1912, brooding on the fragile finances of county cricket (it was already an old story) he urged that, "any reduction in the payments to professionals would probably mean the capture by the Lancashire League of some of their more prominent players" – and now he beat the drum again. There were fine players in the Lancashire League, and in future there would be more, but Pardon was throwing the Almanack's weight behind the county game, helping to ensure that even if money was tight this would be the arena in which true cricketing prestige and acclaim would reside.

It worked so far as the young Harold Larwood was concerned. The great fast bowler was lured not by the cash on offer but by the lustre of the lovely green stages at Trent Bridge, Lord's and The Oval. But it meant that *Wisden* was being denied a chance to document in full one of the best stories of the era, which was unfolding in the awkward person of S. F. (Sydney) Barnes. Born in Smethwick, north of Birmingham, in 1873, Barnes played just one year for his home town in the Birmingham League before joining Rishton in the better-established (better-paid) Lancashire League. His wage was £3 10s a week, plus a bonus of 10s 6d for five wickets, a feat he was soon able to perform with ease, having mastered a method – in-dipping leg breaks bowled from a good height and at brisk pace – that was in some ways a mirror-image of little Johnny Wisden himself, with his snorting off-cutters. Not many accounts of his bowling style have survived, but it seems that he found a way to produce nippy leg spin with his fingers, not his wrist – what in modern times we might call a "doosra", but what was known, in the early years of the 20th century, as a "Barnes ball".

In 1899 Barnes gave a hint of what was to come when he played for the Lancashire Second XI and took eight for 38. Two years later he took six for 70 for the first team. *Wisden* was quick to take notice. The report on the Lancashire v Leicestershire fixture of 1901 ran: "A feature of the match was the successful appearance ... of Barnes, the Burnley club bowler to whom MacLaren afterwards gave a place in his team for Australia." This was indeed a choice incident. Archie MacLaren, Lancashire's captain, had invited Barnes to join England on that winter's tour (impressed, the story goes, after being hit on the thigh once or twice in the nets). It was the kind of gamble only a patrician amateur like MacLaren could have risked, and it was accompanied by the offer of a Lancashire contract for the following summer, which Barnes also accepted.

He was a novice, but didn't play like one. In Australia he dismissed the local hero Victor Trumper for his first scalp in Tests, and went on to take 13 wickets in the second match. *Wisden* felt that "he bowled finely, but was overworked in the second innings". He went on to play 17 Championship matches for Lancashire in 1902, in which he took 82 wickets at an average of 21.43 – not extraordinary, by his own high standards. The ripples of controversy from the 1901 season, in which the "unfair" bowling of Arthur Mold had so troubled *Wisden*, still lingered, but Barnes looked like a perfect replacement for the hapless chucker.

Pardon noticed. He praised Barnes for proving what honest bowling might achieve, judging that he stood "head and shoulders above his colleagues ... the only bowler in the team who could be described as first-class." It was already clear that he was remarkable – "on his good days he was the most difficult right-handed bowler in England". But he was also trouble. At the end of 1902 he refused a new contract, accepting instead a better offer in the Lancashire League. County cricket offered just £3 a week; the league offered double that just for a Saturday game. In a move that went against all that *Wisden* now stood for, Barnes waved goodbye to county cricket and, for the next four years, opted out of the first-class game altogether.

This was a heresy Pardon could not overlook. It was a "defection", an eruption of low-grade professional ethics his beloved Almanack could neither countenance nor forgive. Inevitably, perhaps, in keeping with its grieved headmaster air (*this hurts me more than it hurts you*), he saw it in moral terms. "Temperament is a great thing in a cricketer, and in this respect Barnes has always been deficient. If he had possessed the enthusiasm for the game that characterised Barlow and Johnny Briggs he might have made a great name for himself, his natural gifts as a bowler being so remarkable."

By now it was clear that Barnes did not care greatly what the likes of Hawke and Pardon thought; he was rather more (and understandably) concerned with securing a fair recognition for his own skill and labour. But *Wisden* was not set up to inspect the cricket arena in which Barnes would now be performing. In 1909 the Almanack mentioned the torrent of wickets he had taken for Staffordshire ("nothing he did was so startling as the match at Stoke against Cheshire, when in the two innings he took 14 wickets for 13 runs"). And in 1910 the Almanack stepped out of its comfort zone by naming him a *Wisden* Cricketer of the Year – the only winner of the accolade to have been picked while playing league and minor county cricket. But valiantly though *Wisden* tried, Barnes's decision to play a more lucrative, less prestigious form of cricket made him a hard act, as it were, to follow. In this sense too he was a pioneer: even today, the world's best players can occasionally be tempted away from the first-class game by the lure of bigger fees elsewhere.

Pelham Warner was quoted as saying of Barnes that "a finer bowler I never played against", but he frowned over his "disagreement" with Lancashire: Barnes had wanted "to be sure of a situation which would yield him a certain income". Being a *Wisden* Cricketer of the Year, however, was both an important badge of approval and a fair recognition of the remarkable way he had regained (at the age of 38) a place in the England team that travelled Australia in 1911–12. On that tour he once again carried all before him. At Melbourne he took five wickets before lunch (for six runs) in a burst that has never been equalled. In typical dry style *Wisden* let the facts do the talking: "Barnes led off by bowling five overs, four maidens, for one run and four wickets." Two winters later he took 49 wickets in four Tests in South Africa (still the best sequence by an English bowler, ever) and would surely have extended that record had he not refused to play in the final match after MCC declined to pay for his wife's hotel room. He downed tools to let them see how they managed without him.

England won by ten wickets, and Barnes was not forgiven. He did not play a single game for England after the war, though he was still one of the outstanding bowlers of the period. In 1920 Pardon wrote that he "can hardly be regarded now as a serious force" – a perfectly fair comment, given that Barnes was now 45 – but ten years later Bradman called him the most difficult bowler he faced on the tour of England. Barnes played 20 Tests against Australia, and took five wickets 12 times, but his face did not fit with the gentlemen-batsmen who picked the team. It was even said, in smart circles, that he had "retired". But he had not retired. He was merely wreaking havoc on a different stage, in a different world – the world of the cricket tradesman in which *Wisden*

Advertisement from Wisden *1915*

had roots, but of which it now took a sniffy view. For two decades he was paid to smash down wickets for league clubs (Burnley, Church and Rawtenstall) and for Staffordshire. For all of them he was unplayable: by the end of his career he had taken over 6,229 wickets at an average of 8.33 per wicket in all forms of cricket.* He once took five in consecutive balls, and four-in-a-row no fewer than four times. Mere hat-tricks were ten-a-penny. In 1928, aged 55, he took six wickets in each innings for Wales against the West Indies; the following year he took eight for 41 against South Africa.

It is not easy to value these efforts accurately. The great Jack Hobbs wrote that the standard in the leagues was "not very high"; another contemporary, Cecil Parkin, claimed that it was "ten times easier" to take wickets in the leagues than in county cricket. But it is also possible that Barnes was to bowling what Grace was to batting, and the unfortunate thing from *Wisden*'s point of view was that the game's great chronicler was able to deliver, given the odd shape of this career, only a partial view of it. This was not *Wisden*'s "fault" – it was a sad product of the uneven way in which English cricket (the Almanack's subject) had developed. Staffordshire seasons merited no more than a brief paragraph, so though Barnes was mentioned (in *Wisden* 1925, for example, "taking as many as 73 wickets, the England bowler, at the age of 48, wound up with the truly remarkable average of 7.17") his feats were not described in detail. For the most part, so far as the Almanack was concerned, he had, thanks to his decision to put pay ahead of glory, placed himself beyond *Wisden*'s radar. It was thus not able to record (until a round-up years later) the time a batsman tried to put Barnes off by switching from right- to left-handed, and Barnes, not fazed, switched to underarm and trapped him lbw.

---

* As always a figure like this is hard to read. In first-class cricket Barnes took 719 wickets at an average of 17.09. According to his 1967 biography (*S.F. Barnes: Master Bowler* by Leslie Duckworth) he took a further 5,510 wickets at an average of 7.2 in minor county and club cricket. This suggests, in a rough and ready way, that taking wickets in first-class cricket is more than twice as difficult, but against that we have to set the fact that many of those "lesser" overs were delivered when Barnes himself was well past the age when fiendish bowlers usually lose their zip.

Of course, it is an illusion to believe that *Wisden*, so compendious and stuffed with detail, misses nothing, but the gap where Barnes should be remains a sad one. Look in any modern *Wisden*; turn to the all-time rankings of English Test match bowlers, and there, at the top end of the lists, he stands.* In 1932 C. L. R. James, in the *Manchester Guardian*, said he was "generally admitted to be the greatest bowler cricket has yet seen". In 1963 John Arlott wrote that he "stood alone – the greatest bowler that ever lived". Yet a major part of his career was performed in the margins of the cricket world. It is a pity for the book, which would have relished more glimpses of a bowler like Barnes, but it was a shame for Barnes too – *Wisden* could have made him a name to conjure with, instead of a half-forgotten favourite loved by connoisseurs. In the bad-tempered contest between the amateur and professional strands in English cricket (the endless subject) Barnes was right on the fault-line: the most striking casualty and loss.

There isn't much doubt that he brought this fate upon himself. By all accounts he was a cussed man, quick to feel slighted – a Boycott type, we might say – and there are plenty of testimonials to his correct yet super-terse manners. As the (amateur) Yorkshire captain Lord Hawke famously said: "We don't understand you. You only play when you like." In retrospect Barnes wasn't hard to understand: he had a proud, work-to-rule sensibility very much of its time (socialist ideas and trades unions were gaining traction), and there are also warm tributes to his courtly politeness, beautiful handwriting and publicity-shunning modesty. But to the men in charge of English cricket there were overtones of class struggle in his attitude; he struck them as little less than a Bolshevik. As it happened, events in Russia really were inspiring a good deal of well-groomed nervousness about political dissidence: Kent's Lord Harris went so far as to write an article for Pelham Warner's new *Cricketer* magazine titled "Effects of Bolshevism". So while Barnes may simply have been asserting his right to a fair return for his top-class labour, some thought him a dangerous rebel.

---

* He is not the leading wicket taker (he did not play for long enough), but he comes top of Most Wickets in a Series and second to Laker in Most Wickets in a Test.

Whatever the rights and wrongs of it, no one could dispute the fact that he was a historic bowler. In different circumstances (or a different country) two decades' worth of *Wisden* might have been brimful of his achievements and style, and one can sense the Almanack's frustration that so high a figure was performing on so low a stage. *Wisden* did not bear a grudge, however. In 1963 Neville Cardus selected Barnes – on the occasion of the Almanack's own centenary – as one of his six "giant cricketers" of the last hundred years. Only then was *Wisden* able to accord Barnes the respect he deserved, and pay tribute to his genius. While noting that he was "not an easy man to handle ... a chill wind of antagonism blew from him on the sunniest day", *Wisden* added that opponents would have four men padded up when he bowled, just in case. Arthur Gilligan, President of MCC, said he was "the finest bowler there ever was"; S. C. Griffith, Secretary of MCC, agreed he was "unique"; Wilfred Rhodes, the Yorkshire and England spinner, reckoned him "the best I ever played with", while Surrey's Herbert Strudwick said he was "the greatest bowler I ever kept wicket to".

It was not before time, and another sign that *Wisden* does like to set records straight in the end. But we can also see the story of Barnes as symptomatic of Pardon's post-war hope that cricket should look to recover its lost role, not seek a new one. An out-and-out professional, unwilling to doff his cap to amateurs who were no match for him on the pitch, Barnes belonged to a future for which *Wisden* had little enthusiasm. Thus in 1921 Pardon was still urging the idea of a restoration, applauding an "exceptionally brilliant and interesting" season and declaring that the tussle against the modernisers had been emphatically decided. "Never has there been a more dismal failure than the crusade against cricket after the Armistice ... the return to the pre-war condition was equally welcome to players and spectators, and it certainly led to better cricket."

In this context it was fitting that he should have made a particular friend in Pelham Warner, a retiring giant of the Golden Age (1,000 runs in a season 14 times) and, more important, a distinguished and blue-blooded captain of Oxford, MCC and Middlesex. Now, in place of the Five Cricketers of the Year, he was given the rare distinction (not granted even to men such as Ranji or Fry) of being lauded, as only Wisden and Grace had been, on his own. "There have been many greater cricketers than Pelham Warner," wrote Pardon, his judgement only slightly clouded by sentiment, "but none more devoted to the game … It was not his batting but his skill as a captain that made his final season memorable." Warner had led Middlesex to the County Championship, a nice but not in itself historic achievement. And though a top-class player who in Pardon's eyes had "fairly won his place as a representative batsman of his day", it did not hurt that he was also, as the 1909 *Wisden* put it, "a capital after-dinner speaker". His combined attributes propelled him to a seat on the game's high table – he would go on to be a cricket writer, a knight, a Test selector and, in 1950, President of MCC.

The social dividing line that ran down the centre of English cricket remained the game's most striking feature. That was why, in 1919, *Wisden* called the Gentlemen of England v the Australians match "the most important of the whole programme". And that was why, in 1922, Pardon was still using *Wisden* to decry the purchasing power of the Lancashire League. "I object strongly to the importation of Australian players," he wrote, following news that some of the touring Australians planned to stay awhile. There was "something distasteful", he thought, about the idea of the "highest class" of player appearing for small-town cricket clubs in the north-west.

In 1923, as if seeking to defend territory on the other, more decorous side of cricket's dividing line, Pardon included a complete list of Oxbridge Blues, to which the ever-assiduous F. S. Ashley-Cooper, *Wisden*'s faithful statistician, attached the names of the schools from which these Varsity cricketers sprang. The school reports at this time were still prominently displayed at the front of the Almanack, where H. S. Altham, in his summary of the season, would assess both the overall standard and outstanding individuals. He was calling, however, for a more rational discussion of schoolboys, who needed to be "able to stand both praise and criticism" and not have their heads turned by any too-overheated judgements of their abilities.

Naturally the bread and butter in the post-war *Wisden* did not depend on Pardon's private taste – the Almanack was above all a careful record of county games, and his colleagues from the Cricket Reporting Agency performed their role with a studious sense of decorum. Some of the match summaries are bland, inevitably, but plenty are memorable, and still feel fresh. In 1920 Middlesex needed to beat Surrey to stay in the title race, and large crowds flocked into Lord's to see if they could do it – "never before has a county match proved such an attraction". On the Saturday some 25,000 watched the home team lay the foundations for what would be a 55-run victory to scoop up the title. "That wonderful Tuesday was a day in a thousand."

Such is the expressiveness of cricket's scorecards that sometimes words were barely necessary: figures told the story on their own. In 1922 Hampshire were bowled out for 15 by Warwickshire, but bounced back to amass 521 in the second innings and force a "sensational" 155-run win. For the most part, though, the reports were medium-paced – not all games were melodramatic, not all finishes were tight. In cases like these the summaries took on a dismayed tone, like end-of-term reports: "Weak batting brought about Derbyshire's defeat ... Glamorgan at last did something to justify promotion to the front rank ... Kent gave a sorry display." These deflating verdicts extended to individuals too: "Mead, it will be noted, had a terrible match ... When Tennyson did not enforce the follow-on, a draw became inevitable ... what purpose he considered would be served by taking such a course it is impossible to understand."

Bold individual efforts, however, were roundly praised: "Hammond gave the batting display of the year ... Dipper carried off the bowling honours ... the game was a triumph for Nicholls ... Wyatt's first hundred of the season was a faultless effort ... Sandham rose to the occasion in great style ... Hobbs made what was at once the highest score of his wonderful career (316) and the highest ever made at Lord's."

In continuing to hail solo achievements, *Wisden* was perpetuating the sense that cricket was a stage on which great figures could strut their stuff. And there were more routine accolades – to "a great all-round performance by Townsend" or "the splendid all-round form of Jupp". Even to be mentioned in a *Wisden* despatch was like earning a medal, or being admitted to a fraternity; to be honoured in person was like feeling the touch of a general's sword on your shoulder.

Pardon himself took great pleasure in all this "brilliant and exceptional" cricket, but was quick to sound a cautionary note, especially when change was on the menu. In letting Glamorgan join the first-class counties in 1921 the authorities had risked "sacrificing quality to quantity ... the fixture list is more overcrowded than ever". And with a prescient shudder he was distressed to think of county cricket deprived of its international stars: "It is pitiful to think of Surrey going into the field without Hobbs, or Kent without Woolley." This would turn out to be an impotent protest: home Test matches would increasingly be scheduled at the same time as county games, forcing the latter to do without their England players. It is salutary to note that this familiar argument was being voiced almost a hundred years ago.

Wisden had no actual power; it could only whistle like a shepherd when the sheep seemed fidgety. But Pardon's annual address (in his Notes) was by now a famous noticeboard, and he revelled in the fact. It mattered that he was independent, and that, though close to MCC and Lord's, *Wisden* could make up its own mind. And Pardon's decisive views – the confident ease with which he criticised the "extraordinary blundering" of the selectors – were popular (plain speaking has always gone down well with the public: rude reviews are remembered longer than kind ones). He had plenty of high horses and kept them handy. But he also loved clip-clopping down memory lane: in 1920 he echoed W. H. Knight in the way he tipped his cap to the *ancien régime*: "Nothing in the season was more gratifying than the successful revival of the university match ... watching the game at Lord's one might have imagined there had been no war."

He was happy to put himself forward as a lawmaker, too, and in 1924 argued at length in favour of alterations to the lbw rule, with a view to making batsmen more vulnerable – less likely to play the ball with their pads. As things stood, the ball had to pitch in line with the stumps, no easy task for a bowler looking to swing or spin the ball. Pardon took the bowlers' part here, though he rested his case (somewhat illogically) on a statistic that did not support his argument: back in 1870 lbw had accounted for only one in 40 dismissals; by 1923 it was responsible for one in eight. The bowlers were doing perfectly all right, as it happened.

By the time he entered his fourth decade as editor, it did not take much to make Pardon gloomy. In 1922 he delivered a now-notorious verdict when England were thrashed by the touring Australians. "During all the years I have edited *Wisden* there has never been a season so disheartening as that of 1921," he wrote, setting aside for the moment the idea that winning didn't matter. "Never before was an England side so slow and slovenly." Those post-war Australians were humbling the counties too. In Nottingham, one of English cricket's foundation stones, they scored 675 before bowling out the home side for 58. "There has perhaps never been such a deplorable match," wrote Pardon, setting impartiality to one side. The following year, planting the seeds of an idea that would flower a decade later, he again lamented the way England had wilted (as most teams do) in the face of Australia's fearful fast bowlers – "Never before have England batsmen been so demoralised by great pace." On neither occasion did he blame this weakness on the number of fine cricketers mown down in Flanders – since Australia could have said the same thing; instead he called for "systematic preparation". His advice was heeded: Test trials were soon held regularly.

In mourning the supremacy of Australia, Pardon could not help comparing the frail moderns with the glorious cricketers of olden times, and was moved to recall "the fierce spirit shown by Grace and Stoddart" in the Gents v Players match of 1895. The nostalgic note was not rare in cricket, but in this case it was interesting that the contemplation of an England v Australia match brought up memories of Gents v Players. It is almost as if, unconsciously, the old Gents v Players stereotypes were being redeployed as a way of imagining Ashes contests – with England, of course, the spirited amateurs, and Australia the upstart artisans. There was no substance to this – it was merely an echo – but it was in keeping with this impulse that a few years later (in 1930) *Wisden* would publish an article by Sir Frederick Toone, manager of the England team in Australia, which included the following statement of cricket's virtues: "It is a science, the study of a lifetime, in which you may exhaust yourself but never your subject. It is a contest, a duel or melee, calling for courage, skill, strategy and self-control. It is a contest of temper, a trial of honour, a revealer of character. It affords the chance to play the man and act the gentleman … It promotes not only physical health but mental force." The great Victorian hope for the game was rarely so well expressed. That it was inspired by an Ashes series shows how thoroughly Australia had been absorbed into cricket's cultural landscape. Australia was our brother in the southern hemisphere, and the rivalry had a fraternal (that is, a doubly keen) edge. When Jack

Hobbs, a model professional, wrote his own *Wisden* article in 1935, he admitted as much, declaring, as no more than a simple statement of fact, that "there are only two really top-class cricket countries – England and Australia".

That was the thing about *Wisden*: it could celebrate beginnings as well as endings. In the 1919 edition the young Douglas Jardine, later the captain/villain of the 1932–3 Bodyline series, gave his school, Winchester, a "capital start" by scoring 33 against Harrow and showed the "admirable judgement" that would bring him the captaincy of England. In the small print of the 1922 edition G. O. ("Gubby") Allen performed well for Eton – "undoubtedly the best school side of the year" – while Jardine, now at Oxford, was scoring 98 against the Australians. The following year he scored 997 runs at an average of 66.46, and would surely have made a thousand if a storm had not crashed in when he was 135 not out. Both these youngsters would go on to make headlines for England, as would the Yorkshire opener Herbert Sutcliffe, whose efforts in 1922 led *Wisden* to remark that "all going well, he should become one of our Test batsmen in the immediate future". If *Wisden* at times seemed anxious to be an ersatz Test selector, commending this or that player, it boasted a fair success rate: Sutcliffe was the only player to score a thousand runs each year between the wars.

Some of these young men went on to careers outside cricket (it was an important part of *Wisden*'s faith in the amateur ideal that it embraced such all-round figures). The most notable was Alec Douglas-Home, the only prime minister to play first-class cricket – he scored 66 in the Eton v Harrow match in 1922, and went on to play twice for Middlesex. There was no irony intended by *Wisden*'s note, written in 1923, that Lord Dunglass, his title at school, was useful on sticky wickets, since no one knew that this useful political skill would in time come to serve him so well. But cricket stayed with him: years later he would claim that his wife's uncle "could never walk down the nave of an abbey without wondering whether it would take spin".

The *Almanack*'s desire to notice up-and-coming talent, however, was filtered through Pardon's increasingly wistful imagination. Thus the first-wicket Yorkshire pair of Holmes and Sutcliffe, fast becoming renowned, "recalled the feats of Jupp and Tom Humphrey for Surrey in 1864". Was it a coincidence that Pardon's mind fell here on the year of *Wisden*'s own birth? It is unlikely that he had detailed personal memories of that year – he *was* taken to The Oval as a small boy, but he would only have been nine years old – so this seems primarily a rhetorical comparison.

―――――

Wisden was by now received by the outside world as a familiar friend. When Sir Edwin Lutyens was invited to create a doll's house for the Queen in 1921, John Wisden & Co contributed a miniature cricket set – bat, ball and stumps – for the playroom. There were also signs that it was becoming valuable. A review of the 1925 edition in the *Manchester Guardian* mentioned with astonishment that a "full set" of *Wisden* had recently been sold for £50 – imagine! – while *The Times* (Pardon's own paper) was more preoccupied with its sheer girth. In 1922 it even smiled at the book's increasing size – "The doctors have given a gentle pinch here and a tentative prod there" – with a tolerant sigh. "After a highly successful career a certain – er – *embonpoint* is not unbecoming; it would be a cause for alarm if you were thin."

The Times was not the only loyal supporter. Under the byline "Cricketer", Neville Cardus was giving the Almanack repeated rounds of applause in the *Manchester Guardian*. In 1921 he wrote that "the yellow cover flashes like spring sunshine" and that the new *Wisden* was "a model of compression". In 1924 he added that Pardon had a "warm, companionable mind" and "an astonishing gift for skimming the cream from a cricket season", and that he should be given "the freedom of Lord's" for rendering, each year, a service "valuable beyond reckoning".

If Cardus was hoping that these kind words might help propel him into *Wisden*'s hallowed pages, he was rewarded in time: he would go on to become one of the book's most revered regulars, and in 1989 his many contributions became a book in their own right. After his death in 1975 he was himself the subject of a friendly *Wisden* salute.

Pardon was fortunate at this time in that the business behind him was picking up too. The new directors were providing an infusion of fresh energy. In 1919 they were approached by Duke & Sons, the venerable ball-maker in Penshurst with whom Luff had tangled in court, with a view to working together, and in 1920 the companies

WISDEN'S
Rugby Football Almanack

EARLY in September Messrs. John Wisden & Co. will publish a Rugby Football Almanack. The book will aim to give a comprehensive record of the Rugby Union Game in Great Britain, Ireland, France, South Africa, New Zealand and Australia. All International matches will be dealt with at some length, as well as International Trials, Oxford and Cambridge, Inter-Service Contests, and the games in the County Championship. The records of all the leading clubs will be given, together with brief reviews of each club's season, and special attention paid to Public School Football. Full records of International Matches, the County Championship, and the 'Varsity Match will, of course, have a place in the book. It is further intended always to have a picture of players who have specially distinguished themselves in the course of the season. Coming out in September, the book will include a full list of the new season's fixtures. Special articles by prominent writers will be a regular feature of the Almanack. The book will be edited by C. Stewart Caine.

Advertisement from Wisden *1923*

merged. Ball-making was struggling in the face of competition from cheap Australian products, and John Wisden & Co men were being "enticed away" by "great promises" from rival firms, Duke's among them. In 1921 there was another strike over pay and conditions; the merger made sense. Harry Duke, who could remember the days when his father set off on horseback to deliver cricket balls to London, filling his pouch with new balls and packing a pair of pistols for the hazardous crossing of Blackheath, became a director of John Wisden & Co in 1921, but died just three years later.

The terms of the merger show that the prospects for John Wisden & Co were bright: the company bought £17,178 worth of Duke's assets for 11,452 shares, meaning that Wisden's stock was being valued at "30 shillings per share", a healthy increase on the 20 shilling issue price. It also meant that Wisden's was now rather more than an "outfitter" and batmaker – it produced the world's best cricket ball too. To celebrate, the workers at both companies were given a summer day out in Brighton. The rival firms in Kent tried to band into an association, but individual members kept reneging on the price-control agreement (not least John Wisden & Co, which admitted to supplying MCC with cut-price balls) and it soon fell apart.

Sales were expanding in Australia, Canada and South Africa, and the prospects for growth, despite the disputes over the plan to shift the Duke's ball-making facility from Penshurst into the John Wisden & Co factory in Tonbridge, seemed better than for decades (there were proposals for profit-sharing in the works). There were tennis balls too; sometimes there was a flyer for the "New Standard – the most perfect ball in existence" – in *Wisden* itself. Cricket-lovers could marvel at the information that this grand new ball "could be washed with soap and water, using a fairly hard brush".

The company was moving forward. In June 1922 the shareholders again enjoyed a dividend. A new managing director was appointed (George Gooch); the board considered a proposal to launch a rugby almanack along the lines of the cricket annual; and there were detailed talks about a new line of tennis balls. A rights issue – existing shareholders were offered new shares for a pound – raised £5,000 in new capital, and in 1924 John Wisden & Co acquired the Taylor-Rolph Company, which specialised in billiards and bowls. A year later it opened another new factory in Fitzgerald Road, Mortlake, off what is now the Upper Richmond Road – along with the Tonbridge works it was now a two-centre operation. In 1927 Pelham Warner joined the board, cementing the company's connections with elite cricket, and a year later the Cranbourn Street shop was wound up in favour of the premises in Great Newport Street. Occupying numbers 9, 15, 16 and 19, John Wisden & Co was a lordly presence in a row of small outlets: film agent, wine purveyor, drum-maker, dance teacher, bookmaker, tobacconist and the Société Culinaire Française.

The company tried to cash in on the spreading weight of the Wisden name by going ahead with the *Rugby Almanack*. The first edition, edited by Pardon's deputy Stewart Caine, was published in 1923. Caine stated that it was a "hazardous" enterprise thanks to the costs involved, and he was soon proved right. *The Times* welcomed it as "a little brother to a tome that need not be further specified", and hoped it would be the first of many. It praised the 1924 book as "the equal of the famous Cricketer's Bible ... a remarkable achievement". But rugby was not like cricket – it did not invite the same level of mazy recollection. And Caine made an error of both tactics and tact by devoting little more than a page (out of 500-odd) to the game in New Zealand, of all places. It did not go down well. "If the compilers desired to kill the game in New Zealand," retorted the *Auckland Star*, "they could hardly have gone about it in a more likely way."

The second volume admitted that sales of the first had been less than exhilarating, and the third wailed that an increase in readership was "imperative" if the project were to survive. Such an increase was not forthcoming, and the final whistle blew.

But it turned out that the post-war Empire, combined with Britain's huge fondness for sport, had created conditions in which a company like John Wisden could thrive, even though there were rivals on the scene, like Slazenger and Dunlop. It meant, apart from anything else, that Pardon was left largely to his own devices, and he expanded the introductory prose until the Almanack was a small compendium of topical writing. If the match reports had the wet-ink flavour of eyewitness accounts, the other pieces had ambitions to be final rather than first drafts of history. It was no surprise when in 1922 Alec Waugh, brother of the novelist Evelyn, minted a cliché in averring that *Wisden* was "the cricketer's bible ... in the same way that the letters x and y possess a significance for mathematicians, so for the cricketer the bare figures are a symbol and a story." He was writing in the London *Mercury,* in one of English literature's most famous years, when modernist texts like Joyce's *Ulysses* and Eliot's *The Waste Land* barged on to the world stage – but also the year before Lord's acquired its new Grace Gates – and he could not resist echoing Pardon's famous sentiment about the Almanack as a winter consolation: "Towards Christmas there came, as there must always come, an evening when we sat over the fire and remembered suddenly that it was four months since we had held a cricket bat, that May was still a long way off, and the procession of Saturdays seemed endless. On such an evening we take down *Wisden* ..."

It was one of Pardon's achievements that he made this maxim obsolete. As *Wisden* grew (it was nudging the 1,000-page barrier), it ceased to be possible to publish it as a Christmas treat in the depths of winter, as a diversion for those long dark nights. It now appeared in March, and automatically seemed fresher and more forward-looking, acting as a gong for the season about to start. As if by magic, a venerable collection of facts and figures acquired the bright whiff of spring.

In 1924 the book ran over 1,000 pages for the first time, and its happy editor sighed: "The only real difficulty in producing *Wisden* these days is to keep the book within reasonable limits." But the following edition would be Pardon's last. He did not know it, but the world was changing, and the post-war recovery he had sought, in his own way, to resist, was starting to curdle into something more poisonous. In Germany, two years after his failed Munich putsch, Adolf Hitler was publishing *Mein Kampf.* In Italy, Benito Mussolini was declaring himself dictator. In America and Britain strikes, mass unemployment and financial collapse loomed. Pardon simply bemoaned the fact that the previous summer had been "dismally wet" and noted that many counties had been "driven to desperation". Nor was he anxious to express a view on an argument that had disfigured the match between Yorkshire and Middlesex the previous year, beyond saying that the Sheffield crowd had behaved in an "unseemly" fashion. But part of the function of *Wisden* was to stand apart from the quarrels of the day (though at times it unconsciously reflected them) and fix its gaze, instead, on the bigger picture. Thus the standout essay in 1925 was Bosanquet's article on the googly, which described how he came to invent it after spinning a tennis ball.

That November, with the 1926 edition only beginning to take shape, Pardon, in his 70th year, hosted a lunch and then went to an orchestral concert at the Queen's Hall. Afterwards he dropped into the office and was chatting to his colleague Stewart Caine when he suffered a "sudden illness" (usually taken to be a stroke). He was taken to St Bartholomew's hospital where, the following morning, he died. The funeral procession wound past Lord's on its way to Golders Green cemetery; wreaths were laid by his old colleagues Stewart Caine, Sydney Southerton and Hubert Preston, but also by the whole staff of the Cricket Reporting Agency. Pelham Warner sent flowers, as did MCC, Surrey and Middlesex Cricket Clubs, Reuters and the Queen's Hall Orchestra.

He had been associated with *Wisden* for four decades, three and a half as editor. He had seen it turn from a sketchy cricket annual into the unquestioned authority on the game, and was a major figure both in cricket and in the circles where it was loved. *The Times* said that though Pardon always tended towards a "dignified conservatism" he managed to retain the "trust of all parties", an important skill in a field which was not just the national sport but a significant proving ground in England's divided social scenery. "He leaves behind no enemies and many friends," wrote the *Sporting News*.

"He had a genius for making his exact meaning clear," wrote the *Observer*. "He had, by natural astuteness and an unsurpassed experience, a sense of cricket values that was almost uncanny in its accuracy, not merely for the promise and achievement of the individual, but for great questions of policy and ethics."

This was above-average praise by any standards. At least he lived to hear, if not witness, one of the outstanding moments of his tenure as *Wisden* editor. In the summer of 1925, in Taunton, the great Jack Hobbs ("the wonder and delight of all cricketers" said *Wisden* in 1926, singling him out as the one and only man of the year), first matched and then went past W. G. Grace's record of 126 first-class centuries. It was part of a run that seemed, to anyone who had not watched Grace himself, unimaginable – in this single summer he scored 3,024 runs with 16 centuries at an average of over 70, all in the calm, controlled, modest yet magisterial style for which he was famous. It was "masterly cricket", wrote *Wisden* the following year. "Tremendous cheering greeted the accomplishment of the feat." It seemed typical of Hobbs that, having made the public wait a jittery few weeks for him to achieve the record, he should celebrate by scoring another century in the second innings. "Less than thirty hours after equalling W. G. Grace's record, he surpassed it."

The Almanack marked the occasion by printing, in place of any Cricketers of the Year, a full survey of Hobbs's career (pointing out that he was "the most talked-of man in England") along with a full photograph. It made for a memorable issue, what with the obituary of Pardon and an amazing bowling performance by one Parker of Gloucestershire, who took 17 Essex wickets in one two-innings match before taking nine against Surrey in his next outing.

The new editor for this 1926 edition, the biggest so far (1,031 pages) was Stewart Caine, a Hampshire-born CRA loyalist, editor of the short-lived *Rugby Almanack* and a long-time *Wisden* associate (in 1893 he had dared call the press facilities at Lord's "far from adequate"). He was already a popular and revered figure in journalism, one of the leaders of the Press Club. His first instinct was to declare that the show must go on. His Notes dwelt on England's chances in the forthcoming Ashes (not good), on the need for improved hotel arrangements for England players, and on the reported use of resin (an early form of ball-tampering) by bowlers ("quite foreign to the spirit of cricket"). Caine also related a story from Tasmania concerning a bail that flew more than 83 yards after a fast bowler had hit the stumps. In Caine's view this was a world record, and even the passing of *Wisden*'s greatest editor could not check the airing of so grave a matter.

But his primary duty, in putting the book to bed, was to lay a wreath on his friend's memory by praising the breadth of his interests: "he was a mine of information, and used to charm his friends with descriptions, always illuminating, of happenings in bygone days". Of his theatrical know-how Caine wrote that he "hardly missed seeing anything in the way of serious drama during a period of fifty years ... of plays and players his knowledge was encyclopaedic". But Pardon's true legacy, he suggested, lay in the "ever-increasing popularity" of the book he had assembled for so long.

This was published along with other tributes that were generous even by the kindly standards of obituary etiquette. "He was a power in

the cricket world and all for good," wrote A. J. Webbe, an ex-captain of
both Oxford and Middlesex. "A more kind-hearted man I never knew,"
said Lord Hawke. "There will be many who miss him much," wrote
Lord Harris, "but none more than I." Few farewells were warmer than
Pelham Warner's. "He had seen all the great singers and actors," he
wrote in his autobiography, *Long Innings*, "and he knew the pedigree
of the great horses, even to their grandsons and great grandsons ...
Committees and individuals were glad to have his opinions on the
burning questions of the day, and he had courage in expressing those
opinions. I can see him now with a cigarette, which he invariably
smoked to the bitter end, talking in the most animated way. He was the
soul of *Wisden* ..."

He was more than that: he was the foundation stone. Through his
work as editor he laid down the manners, structure and attitude of the
Almanack; and by making it a province of the CRA he placed it at the
heart of English sports journalism. So he bequeathed not just an ethos,
but a system, a mode of production – an achievement few journalists
can claim. If it proved insufficient to earn him an entry in the *Dictionary
of National Biography* (to this day) then that was the *DNB*'s loss.

He also did much to shape the intellectual backdrop of English
cricket. Of course, we cannot attribute to him alone the persistence of
the professional/amateur divide (or its equivalent, the gulf between
north and south), but his Almanack did play at least a part in
maintaining it. Whether this was something to be proud of is another
matter, but in working so tirelessly to keep it alive Pardon was being
truthful to an unmistakeable quality of English life, however ambiguous
its ramifications.

The only pity (as some contemporaries observed) is that he wrote no
memoir, for what an age he spanned – from Grace to Hobbs – and what
an unrivalled view he had of it. There were 420 pages in the first volume
he edited; by the time of his death there were more than twice that.
There were 753 entries in the first Births and Deaths (in 1891) and 6,274
in his last. When he inherited the Almanack from his brother it hung in
the balance; when he died it was the unquestioned and greatly loved
voice of the game.

Even in his heyday cricket writing was not a noisy job – "I doubt if
Sydney Pardon would have allowed anybody to use a typewriter at

Lord's or any other cricket ground," wrote Neville Cardus, many years later. At that time reporters at Lord's had to use the telegraph office at the Nursery End, but even in these pen-and-paper times, Pardon was fathering a press dynasty. Stewart Caine, his successor, was only the first in a long line of CRA men to pilot the Almanack: Sydney Southerton, Wilfrid Brookes, Hubert Preston and his son Norman would all maintain the link for another half century. And since institutions develop and transmit specific cultures of their own, it became the norm for *Wisden* to be run by men who were neither fish nor fowl; they had not played cricket at a high level, nor had they sprung from the cradle of the amateur game in a famous public school. They stood apart from the events they described, serious-minded artisans who loved cricket and were happy to spend their lives watching, discussing and reporting it. The world would soon suffer a terrible buffeting, but *Wisden* had deep roots by now, and would not be easy to dislodge.

Advertisement from Wisden *1937*

7

Summer Bottled

The Times gave a friendly welcome to Caine's first *Wisden*: "Let me embrace thee, good old chronicle," it cried. But it could not forget that his predecessor saw cricket as a matter of character, not numbers – records were not everything. "He knew that what made a record worth recording was not magnitude; he regarded it as an artist rather than a curio-hunter." In praising Caine for the "hereditary sanity" of his observations, *The Times* was above all praising his fidelity to his master's voice.

The *Observer* declared, as a matter of "melancholy interest", that though Caine was to be "congratulated", *Wisden* could not be the same without Pardon. "It is in the nature of things that the loss of Sydney Pardon should for a year or two at least leave the cricket world wondering how far *Wisden* can sustain its extraordinary level of excellence ... in athletic journalism Pardon occupied a solitary and lofty niche." Even on the other side of the world the news was noted with regret. "Sport is the loser," wrote the *Evening Post* in New Zealand, "in the passing of a great exponent."

It was a tribute to the Almanack that the loss of its figurehead should inspire such remarks. And there were other reasons to be cheerful, not least the fact that the "old country" had – after a "wonderfully interesting struggle" – won back "the mythical Ashes" that Australia had held since 1920–21 (the series that had so shaken Pardon). At The Oval, thanks to "superb batting on a difficult pitch" by Hobbs and Sutcliffe, England prevailed by 289 runs, and "the crowd was so large that the gates had to be closed shortly after noon". Pardon himself could hardly have complained.

But even without this popular triumph the sense of continuity was strong. Caine used his new platform to express familiar misgivings about the swell of international cricket, which was starting to threaten the good old county game. "Is there not a danger," he asked, "of this Test match cricket becoming rather a fetish?" It was true that the Ashes had, since the debacle of 1920–21, become increasingly torrid, but Caine was grim. "Cricket must not be made subservient to these hectic struggles."

It was a Pardonesque reflex. Just as amateur cricket had once needed protection from professional circuses, and just as "fair" bowling had been impelled to resist the rise of "dubious" new methods, so now county cricket needed allies to help it survive the advance of the international game. Yet not so long ago (1910) Pardon himself had stated: "I am strongly of the opinion that there is too much county cricket." It was spreading the paying audience too thin, he felt, leading to financial stress all round, and was in danger of drowning the even more glorious peaks of the amateur game.

A theme was emerging: the elite cricket favoured by MCC and *Wisden* was inclined to oppose anything that resembled a more popular or successful version of itself. Caine had taken the wheel at a time when the international game was rising up like a fawn struggling gawkily to its feet. The West Indies were becoming a force (though not always: they were bowled out for 80 by Lord Harris's XI in 1923), and South Africa were keen (though they too collapsed to Gilligan and Tate for 30 at Edgbaston in 1924). Cricket was on the rise in these lands, and in New Zealand and India too. In far-off climates, where palm trees swayed in warm tropical breezes, on hot pitches deluged by squalls, a new form of the game was taking shape.

In keeping with the sense that the barricades needed manning, Caine also followed Pardon in disparaging the arrival of overseas players in the Lancashire leagues … what was to stop them appearing for a county too? Gloucestershire had permitted just that, and in 1927 Caine protested that two "very prominent" Australians, Ponsford and Richardson, had been given contracts by Lancashire clubs; he felt sure he was not alone in finding "something objectionable" in the idea, predicted "a general and very proper outcry", and begged Lancashire to impose a "self-denying ordinance".

Those damned Lancashire leagues: in 1929 the great West Indian all-rounder Learie Constantine was signed by Nelson for £500 a year, plus a return ticket to Trinidad – a prince's ransom at a time when even the finest county professionals earned only a few pounds a week. So when one of the great match-ups of the era took place it was in league cricket, in 1931, when Constantine faced the still-remarkable 58-year-old Sydney Barnes. He later prized the 96 he scored that day as among the finest innings he ever played, while Barnes had to settle for a routine haul by his standards: seven for 68.

There were other signs in Caine's work of the "hereditary sanity" noted by *The Times*: in 1928 he again echoed Pardon by swearing that "the summer of 1927 will probably be regarded as one of the worst in the history of cricket". This was chiefly to do with the weather – "practically all the big games were either interfered with or ruined" – but it also touched on the effect this had on the game's finances. *Wisden* was increasingly alert to such matters, fussing over gate receipts like a tut-tutting accountant. It was not always gripping reading: "It is no exaggeration to suggest that last summer the up-keep of competition cricket suffered in diminished receipts to the extent of £20,000 while, as a matter of fact, the amount may well have exceeded that sum by a considerable figure." But it drove nails into the idea that *Wisden* was more than a mere spectator; it was an associate member as well.

There were other grounds for dismay in 1927 (how rapidly the mood had changed). That year's County Championship had been a dud, the pitches were unreliable, and various experiments with hours of play and other regulations had been in vain. Finally, there was a storm over the invitation extended to Herbert Sutcliffe to captain Yorkshire. No one could dispute his eminence as a batsman, but heavens above, the man was a professional! Caine had imbibed the house style when it came to such things, so he reported that Yorkshire cricket circles were "greatly perturbed" by the idea and stressed "the undesirability of having a professional captain". Even a cricketer as eminent as Sutcliffe (second only to Hobbs in the pantheon of contemporary batsmen) was bound to lack "qualities of leadership", he felt. *Wisden*'s feelings here were well known – one of that season's Cricketers of the Year was one Douglas Jardine, "the soundest of present day amateur batsmen", having been "in a class by himself" as a schoolboy, as well as the scorer of a stylish century for Gents v Players. Some, even then, would have seen Jardine as almost the emblem of the toff-cricketer, but it was still hard for *Wisden* to accept the concept of a professional captain. Did amateur captaincy have advantages, asked Caine, over the leadership of a more gifted professional? "Personally I think it does." Luckily, Sutcliffe punctured the argument by declining the post, and Caine was happy to pronounce the matter "settled". Captain Worsley had been asked instead, and "that gentleman stepped into the breach".

The following year, at long last, Caine could wave his hat above his head. "Not for 17 years has the reputation of English cricket stood as high as at the present moment," he wrote. It would be nice to say that this was down to some noble act of fair play, but sadly it meant nothing more than that England had beaten Australia – in the end it has always been winning that counts. And since there was, in any Ashes victory, an echo of the relief the Gents felt when they put the Players in their place, it was a doubly rewarding year. We might notice, though, that in harking back to the happy season of 1911–12, Caine was remembering the season in which S. F. Barnes had proved so unplayable. Two decades later, Caine admitted that if only Barnes had been entrusted with the new ball in the first Test of that series (the one they did not win) then England "would have been successful in all five". But even this uneasy memory was not sufficient to spoil the "prowess" of the team behind such "great work" down under.

The Times, equally infected with the triumphant mood, was delighted. "*Wisden* is as ever a perfect record of contemporary cricket," it wrote, "indispensable and inimitable." By now this latter quality was no more than the truth. There was no great secret to *Wisden*'s success – all it took was thoroughness and care – and modern communications methods were in theory making it easier to produce similar works. But no newcomer could ever acquire the history that had accumulated behind the 1929 Almanack; nor could the gravitas this generated be easily mimicked.

One side-effect of *Wisden*'s historic pedigree was that its reflexes did tend to look back rather than forward; it was natural that Caine, a *Wisden* man since the 1890s, should see the amateur world of Bligh, Ranji, Jessop and Warner as the noblest form of the game. And since champions like these had attended the two great universities, it was inevitable that the status of the Varsity remained supreme. The quadrangles of Oxbridge had been a cricket nursery since *Wisden*'s birth, and would remain one for many decades yet. It gave their matches a solemn prominence. In 1930 Oxford "threw away by mistakes in the field" a good chance of winning, but prevailed the following year thanks to the remarkable Nawab of Pataudi, whose 231 not out provided lustrous echoes of Ranji. While lavishing praise on the innings ("Pataudi made runs all round the wicket in masterly fashion") the report also, in a way that was becoming typical, took a moment to record a factual oddity: "neither side included a left-handed player".

Etched onto the factual substance of such matches we find names that in due course appear in lights. In 1930 Ian Peebles, later an England player and *Sunday Times* cricket writer, took six wickets; in 1933 the Edinburgh-born bowler, Raymond Robertson-Glasgow, made 48 at No. 10 for MCC v Cambridge before falling lbw to a bowler named J. H. Human (whose nickname, had he played in modern times, must surely have been "Only"). The history of the event – the repeated re-enactment of a rivalry – mattered almost more than the game itself. Thus 1927, the centenary of the Varsity match (the oldest first-class fixture in existence) was marked in *Wisden* by an account of the dinner held in memory of that historic game, which seemed like only yesterday. Lord Harris contributed a memoir of Oxford in which he let slip that it was not just a sporting joust, but a gambling medium ("my father-in-law having asked me to put something on Oxford for him, I was haggling about the odds"); the 1929 edition featured more memories of the 1870s; and in 1936 Leveson-Gower wrote about other long-lost struggles ("I may perhaps be excused for going rather fully into the match of 1896"). While admitting that the Varsity match was "not what it used to be", he ended with a toast: "Long may the universities continue to be the stepping stone of Cricket."

This was cricket with a capital C. Among the list of names at the Savoy Hotel dinner the hereditary principle was plain to see: Douglas Jardine sat beside his father, who had scored his own century for Oxford back in 1892. And not many details were too minor when it came to Varsity cricket. It was assumed that clubbable *Wisden* types would want to know that "the Parks [the Oxford University playing field] is the only first-class ground in England where it is impossible to get a bath in the pavilion".

Schools cricket also remained a high priority, appearing ahead of the county scores. It was vividly recalled in the Obituaries section, too, always keen to summon old glories. "The story of the Eton v Harrow match of 1910 has been told over and over again," ran the notice on Captain Robert Fowler, who had famously dominated the game with 85 runs and 12 wickets, "but it can never grow stale." We can scoff, but thanks to *Wisden* here we are, more than a century later, retelling the tale once more.

In retrospect it seems forlorn, this faith in the amateur path, especially since Caine's editorship began, as we have seen, with the apotheosis of Hobbs, and was about to be illuminated by the exploits of three all-time great cricketers – Walter Hammond, Herbert Sutcliffe and Don Bradman. In truth, all editors should be so lucky in the players at their disposal; but the vexed question of whether professionals could also be taken seriously as captains was always nagging at *Wisden*'s reflexes.

Hammond was dogged by controversy from the start. Born in Kent, he went to school in Gloucestershire (where the Army sent his father) for whom he rose, like cream, to the top of the county game. But Kent, under the crusty leadership of Lord Harris, objected to the fact that Gloucestershire was not the county of his birth, and succeeded in having one of the country's brightest talents suspended for a year while his residential qualifications were debated. Hammond soon proved himself a jewel, however, and *Wisden* bowed before him. In 1923, when he scored 174 "in rather less than four hours", it was "the batting display of the year". A few years later *Wisden* took great pleasure in seeing him score 139 and 143 at Cheltenham against Surrey (along with ten catches) before, on the following day, taking nine for 23 against Worcestershire.

The Almanack's favourite word for Hammond was "masterly". But the class divide meant that he could captain neither his county nor his country until he retired as a professional in 1938, took a managerial job with a tyre company, and made himself available as an unpaid cricket-lover. No such delicacies interfered with the giddy rise of Don Bradman, however; the Australian system was none of our business. *Wisden* by now included reports on Australia's domestic game, so was able to record Bradman's first game for New South Wales in 1927 and his Test debut in 1928. Thereafter it was simply a matter of listing his gargantuan totals. In 1930, in England, he took 236 off Worcestershire in great style – "Batting for just over four hours and a half, he drove, hit to leg and hooked with wonderful power"; against England at Lord's he made a 254 which "will assuredly live long in the minds of those who saw it"; and at Leeds he made 334 in six hours and a quarter, almost exactly a day's play ("as usual he rarely lifted the ball ... his footwork was admirable"). *Wisden*'s attention to detail means we can marvel not just at the scale but also at the pace of these efforts. Thus Bradman's 334 came in *just over six hours* – one day's play. Many modern teams fail to achieve in an entire day what Bradman achieved alone.

Perhaps since he was Australian, *Wisden* felt that Bradman's financial affairs were beyond its jurisdiction, but his career also raised one or two questions about the credibility of amateur status. Though technically an amateur, Bradman found plenty of ways to earn a living from the game. In 1931 he actually turned down a handsome offer (£1,000 per year) from a Lancashire League club, Accrington, and later admitted that he was "greatly tempted ... I don't think anyone could have blamed me". After his 334 at Headingley he was happy to accept a gift of £1,000 from a delighted Australian soap magnate; he earned large sums from endorsements and media work, and when, after 1934, he was "employed" by an Adelaide stockbroker, the South Australian Cricket Association paid the major portion of his annual salary.

So far as *Wisden* was concerned, this was a footling matter in the context of his fabled batting achievements. Between 1927 and 1948 he came to dominate the Almanack's match reports and rankings. Year after year, like a bell tolling, his name rang out through its pages. "Bradman put together a delightful innings ... Everything else in this game paled before the phenomenal performance of Bradman ... Bradman played exceptionally brilliant cricket ... Bradman, seizing upon the occasion to register his eighth hundred, gave a brilliant display... " By the time he finished he stood on a lonely perch at the top of the all-time batting list (with that famous, unmatchable Test average of 99.94). He contributed two articles of his own (one on 1939 and the other nearly half a century later, in 1986), was a Cricketer of the Year, a Cricketer of the Century and the subject of many tributes and appreciations. After Grace there was Hobbs, so Bradman was the third great character in the story of cricket, and therefore the third great hero of the book, inspiring Raymond Robertson-Glasgow to write, when the Don hung up his bat in 1948: "So must ancient Italy have felt when she heard of the death of Hannibal." It is possible that he was also the last: the modern world, with its intrusive media and wider cast of characters, was not so conducive to the production of such giants. The fact that he was not English changed the book too: his enormous and constant presence obliged *Wisden* to look beyond its own shores and become an Almanack of world, not just domestic, cricket.

But in 1931, when Stewart Caine nominated Bradman as a Cricketer of the Year, he tried not to go overboard. And Sydney Southerton, in his account of the 1930 tour, also felt that he had "limitations ... when he met a bowler either left-hand or right who could make the ball go away, he never seemed quite such a master". We have already seen how, with respect to Grace and Barnes, *Wisden* could be hard to please, and with Bradman too it was not willing to lower its guard: "This young batsman has something to learn in the matter of playing a correct offensive stroke." It is true that in 1931 Bradman had not yet developed into the incontestable maestro he would later become (even though he had scored a record 974 Test runs the previous summer), but while this highlights a significant aspect of the award itself – players can win it only once, so it does not always coincide with their greatest year – this was faint praise. Or maybe it was a cunning calculation: the ostentatious reluctance to be over-impressed added polish to *Wisden*'s reputation for austerity by suggesting that, like some sage deity that had seen everything a hundred times, it had learned to be sparing with praise.

Throughout this period the Almanack remained close to Lord's, publishing MCC proceedings in detail even to the extent, in 1930, of listing the various DIY initiatives at Lord's. These involved the moving of the tennis court – "many mourned the loss of the old ivy-mantled wall" – and the creation of new "luncheon arbours". It did not question MCC's historic right to be "the parliament of cricket", on the grounds that it had done so ("free from any serious attack") for a hundred years already, and that it had "never failed to aim at securing the best interests of the game as a whole and to preserve the spirit in which it should be played". A subsequent article in 1931 enlarged on the same topic; in 1932 Lord Hawke, the aristocrat of Yorkshire cricket, was invited to dilate on the subject of "discipline and fellowship"; and in 1933 there was a similar homily on umpiring. At times like this *Wisden* sounded like a deputy head reciting the school motto. But in reminding England that cricket was a moral as well as physical exercise, it was as if it sensed there was a storm approaching.

Caine's Notes were never as clarion-like as Pardon's; he rarely seemed to be etching utterances from on high. He worried away at the lbw law without expressing any very trenchant view on the matter. He fussed over the "destination" of the Championship and the absences foisted on county cricket by England calls. At times he was ponderous: "Twelve months ago I ventured the opinion that there could not be a third consecutive wet summer. I based that conclusion upon recollections covering a period of more than fifty years, but precedent went by the board ..." He did show an acute sixth sense, however, when he debated the likelihood that Douglas Jardine would be appointed captain of the winter tour of Australia in 1932. While recognising that "the old Oxonian" was an "exceptionally sound watchful batsman", he added that he "does not seem to have impressed people with his ability as a leader on the field".

This was not the orthodox view, and Jardine was indeed destined to be a controversial captain. But Caine's faltering eyes were fixed more on the past than the future. In that same edition he thanked F. S. Ashley-Cooper, who was retiring after a lifetime spent overseeing the Almanack's Births, Deaths, Obituaries and Cricket Records. Ashley-Cooper was a remarkable contributor: born in 1877, he had been polishing facts for *Wisden* since 1901, had produced 103 books (some of which were published by John Wisden & Co – a tribute to W. G. Grace in 1916, and guides to Surrey and Nottinghamshire cricket in 1922) and also been secretary of Nottinghamshire. His hallmark was "phenomenal accuracy" but now, due to "ill health and failing sight" he was calling it a day. It was a touching reminder of the vast labour involved in the annual production of the Almanack, by a growing platoon of devoted servants; but it was also an indication that the good ship *Wisden* once more had an ageing crew. Caine had been working on the Almanack for 40 years, as had his "colleague and partner" Hubert Preston, another member of

Advertisement in The Times, *April 28 1929*

the CRA who had been helping out since the heyday of Ranjitsinhji. In 1933 Preston's son Norman joined the team too, but the leadership remained grey-haired. As a gift to his successors Caine began to clear out Births and Deaths, which was threatening to burst its banks. In 1929 he "eliminated" the less memorable names and got it down from 111 to 82 pages. In the years ahead this would be an annual and Sisyphean task; the list grew like a beanstalk, and it was simply impossible to include all the notable players who ever lived. In taking a hatchet to it, Caine was actually helping it to survive.

Despite the loss of Pardon, the 1920s were a time of optimism for the Almanack and the sports company behind it. Retail sales of cricket gear were rising. In the latter years of the decade shareholders were rewarded with a dividend and bonuses were paid to staff. Various advertising schemes were considered, and money was set aside to promote *Wisden* on the London Underground, on buses and in the press. "Here a whizz, there a whizz, everywhere a whizz-wizz," shouted one display in the *Sunday Times*. "It's Wisdom to buy *Wisden's*," ran another. The board even considered (in the spring of 1930) opening a factory in Australia, and approved a scheme to give away a copy of the Almanack free to anyone who bought one of the new "Exceller Extra Special" bats. The following year they put a four-page "supplement" on "The House of Wisden and Sport" into the *Evening Standard*. Board meetings were spent discussing new patents, new techniques for manufacturing tennis racquets and new markets (such as a tennis ball called the "Springbok", created for South Africa). The company was looking ahead with optimism, and even in this area it continued to emphasise the old Victorian hopes about sport. Its sales catalogues urged customers to read Sir Henry Newbolt's "Vita Lampada" and added: "To 'play the game' one must have the right spirit as well as the right equipment."

The enlarged premises at Great Newport Street had room to house a notable collection of bats, ranging from the "oldest bat in existence" – a crude club dating from 1750 – to the modern "Exceller" range (once made by Crawford's, but now manufactured by John Wisden & Co). In all there were 132, marked and numbered. Here was the one MacLaren used for his 424 at Taunton, and here was Giffen's with which he made

2,000 for Australia. Lohmann amassed nearly 6,000 with this one, while that patched-up thing got an Ashes century for F. S. Jackson in 1893. This bat belonged to the Prince of Wales, here was Learie Constantine's; over there were the weapons of Grace and Fry, Ranji and Jessop, each with an autographed note. "This," wrote Trumper, "is the best I ever used. I never want a better." The place was at once a hoard and a hall of fame, and the company actually compiled and published a series of books about it all (*The Past and Present of Wisden's, with Some Interesting Sporting Notabilia*). There were neat drawing of the bats, and then a sequence of articles and "odds and ends", most of which recorded the use of Wisden equipment in top-class tennis, hockey, squash, boxing and cricket. There were explanations of bat- and racquet-making, photographs of Grace and Hobbs, and various Wisden-like "curiosities" – the time in Sydney when a bail dislodged by a fielder at one end flew up the wicket and knocked a bail off at the other end, too; the gentleman spectator who yawned so widely at a dull passage of play that he dislocated his jaw; the fielder in New South Wales who was chased by a tiger snake – and when the batsman went over to thump it with his bat, the heartless wicketkeeper ran him out. Here we can see glimpses of the kind of impish miscellany that would, 60 years later, become a regular feature of any modern *Wisden*.

There was nothing unusual about this celebration of virtuoso performances – they were a central part of cricket culture – but in other respects the company was held back by a dislike of individualism, which it saw as an affront to the team ethos. Thus in 1931 John Wisden & Co announced, as if to demonstrate its own probity, that "we do not pay commission or pecuniary consideration of any kind to famous players whose names may appear in connection with a brand of article marketed by us". This may have struck a high-minded note, but it might not have been far-sighted. Even then, celebrity backing was a hugely important sales weapon – budding cricketers of the 1930s wanted to copy their heroes, just as they do today, and no cricket supplier was better placed to satisfy them. Had John Wisden & Co not felt above such things, it could have taken its pick. Imagine: Hobbs or Bradman posing with a Wisden bat!

Bat-making by now had become an elaborate procedure, and John Wisden was a market leader. The willow was grown in East Anglia, where flat ground and damp soil provided ideal growing conditions. Company "willow-readers" would tour the fields – trees were usually planted by arrangement with farmers on the margins of existing agricultural land – and inspect the calibre and age (12–15 years was about right) of the wood. A moth, a dry summer, a rusty nail or too much frost … any of these could compromise the wood. Once felled, the tree would be split into rough "clefts", yard-long planks that were stacked in a barn to mature for two years or so. Then the real work would begin. The clefts would be sculpted – by saws, then knives – into blades, and pressed. Handles were forged out of rubber-strengthened cane that was grown, chopped and shipped home from Malaya before being glued into place. Each handle was fabricated from 16 cane strips, elaborately layered and bound into a springy whole. Finished off with string and a rubber grip, and given a final planing by hand to achieve the desired weight and balance, the bat would be ready to go.

If that seemed complicated, it was child's play compared to the intricate crafts required to make a cricket ball. It was by no means the work of a moment. A piece of oxhide ("the hides of four-year-old oxen are thought best", according to one of the reminiscences in *Wisden Past and Present*) were soaked in lime-water for a week. The hair was then scraped off with a knife, and the hide returned to a water bath to rinse out the lime. The leather was cut into an eight-piece spherical jigsaw before being soaked again, this time in water and oats, and hung out to dry. It was dyed, stretched with pincers, shaped, gauged and pricked with a toothed wheel to make holes for the stitchers. Finally it would be sewn together and shaped into cups – the two hemispheres of the finished ball. While all this was going on, the interior would be sculpted from cork and twine, hammered and wound into shape and then baked to "strengthen it by contraction". The ball would be pressed, weighed and measured until it conformed to the accepted limits, stitched together with silk, flax or cat-gut, and polished. And there – hey presto – was a brand-new cricket ball.

The procedures of cricket bat manufacture may not seem relevant to the Almanack, but there is a resemblance. As with the creation of a blade, the book fused a wide range of crafts into a single artefact: writing, editing, photography, design, statistics, printing, paper-making and bookbinding. The chief subject of *Wisden* was cricket, of course, but the book itself was a compressed blend of art, literature, design, maths and engineering. Craftsmanship informed it every bit as much as it informed the bats, and even became, in a few decades' time, one of the pillars of its enduring appeal.

It is easy to say so now, but it might have been better if John Wisden & Co had concentrated its firepower on cricket, the area of its expertise and contacts. But since the end of the war the firm had been keen to expand the variety of its products, with a view to becoming a major all-round sporting supplier. The 1931 catalogue claimed prowess across an ambitious range of sports – "Athletics, badminton, basketball, baseball, bandy-sticks, boxing, cricket, croquet, fives, football, golf, hockey, lawn tennis, lacrosse, netball, polo, quoits, racquets, squash racquets, stoolball, table tennis, water polo." There were boots, gloves, goal posts, presses, bags, knee supports, bats, dartboards, all available on generous terms (2.5% monthly). In his early days John Wisden manufactured nothing himself – he was merely a salesman for other people's products, such as Crawford's Exceller bat. John Wisden & Co was no longer a purveyor of fine tobacco, but by now the Fitzgerald Road factory and the workshops in Kent were turning out everything from shove ha'penny boards to tennis nets.

All of these products required a distribution system, and the company was lucky to have the British Post Office, one of the managerial wonders of the world, at its disposal. Back in 1923 John Wisden & Co had exhibited many of these products at the British Empire Exhibition at Wembley Park (which aimed to "bind Mother Country to her Sister States and Daughters", and left as its legacy a cavernous football stadium). In the years that followed the firm would press into the larger imperial arena. According to one visitor, the postroom at Mortlake was like Christmas Day – stacks of parcels bound for romantic destinations. Most were large consignments destined for shops and agents overseas. Badminton racquets bound for Melbourne and Bulawayo, squash balls for Trincomalee and Singapore, cricket bats and hockey sticks to Barbados and Lahore. Riding crops, walking boots, fishing rods and tennis gear … they criss-crossed the domain on which the sun never set, from the Indian Ocean, where whales dived in equatorial streams, to the polar-bear regions of Hudson Bay. In the years preceding the Second World War, about a third of

John Wisden & Co's products were exported. The British love affair with games was sailing into the hottest and most distant corners of the earth. This box of tennis balls was going to Rabat, in Morocco; that one was en route to the Cape Verde Islands. This parcel was for Ashanti, that one for Cape Town. Hockey sticks in Cawnpore, squash balls in Kabul, hip flasks for Tehran and Madras ... there seemed no end to it. Somehow, an ordinary factory full of ordinary men in an ordinary road in south-west London looked out over a vast empire. It did seem, quite literally, to be going places.

The Almanack was growing too: it now regularly topped 1,000 pages. Pardon had worried about space since the 1890s, and Caine had the same problem. He continued to prune Births and Deaths while reminding readers that during his own association with *Wisden* (by his death he had worked on 45 editions), the book had almost tripled in size.

When a firm called Hazell, Watson and Viney Ltd offered to buy the Almanack in 1929, the directors emphasised, in formal words that indicated their awareness that the Almanack had traditions to which even the owner should defer, that "no proposals for sale of the Almanack be entertained if such proposals should involve the alteration of the Almanack in any way". They knew it was precious, and agreed, with a view to celebrating that fact, to stiffen the back cover, bind it with a smart red ribbon, and attach bookmarks in the shape of bats to each copy. While they were about it, they instructed Caine to move advertisements from rival businesses from the front to the back.

But the Almanack was no gold mine – in business as well as on the cricket pitch it leaned towards the amateur approach, counting on the goodwill of many contributors. More important, perhaps, John Wisden & Co was, like everyone else, beginning to flounder in the financial ripples from the 1929 Wall Street Crash and the depression that followed. In 1932 the managing director (George Gooch) reported to the board that trading conditions were "extremely difficult" in the home market, and impossible in Europe thanks to the high exchange rate. Faraway markets looked more promising, and an agent had been signed in Argentina, but in India, it seemed, "a large percentage of the population are still averse to buying British goods". There had been "serious complaints" about the company's tennis balls too, and it transpired that the cores, which were made by the Avon India Rubber

Company, were defective. "The whole of the balls sent out to India and to South Africa all lost their inflation and the seams opened." It was a major setback. Orders stalled, and difficult times were predicted in the "home, foreign and colonial markets". Sir Herbert Blaine of the Avon India Rubber Company actually attended a John Wisden & Co board meeting in London, at which he conceded that the mishaps were due to the "disorganisation" of his own firm. After a long discussion, it was agreed to renew the arrangement, but it would only run for a few more years, and in 1936 it was "terminated".

Neville Cardus was still giving the Almanack very warm notices in the *Manchester Guardian*. In 1931 he said that *Wisden* was "summer bottled … you only have to turn a page and some magic casement in the memory is opened". In 1932 he added that despite topping a thousand pages the editors had achieved "wonders of compression", and declared that Caine was "more than an editor – he is a good host". He also thought highly of Sydney Southerton, recalling the affable triumvirate he formed with Caine and Pardon as *Wisden*'s three wise men: "they shared the old-world charm of manner, the old unselfconscious dignity of appearance, combined with wit and poise".

At moments such as this Cardus, as so often, was not speaking of cricketing matters alone: he was putting cricket at the heart of a varied cultural menu. In Pardon he saw a music-loving kindred spirit who, like Cardus himself, liked nothing better, after a day at Lord's, than to go and see *Tristan and Isolde* at Covent Garden. Sometimes they would go together, allowing Cardus to demonstrate that he understood *Wisden* perfectly, the way it held cricket to be part of cultivated life. He meant it when he called it, in 1934, "the most English book in existence".

Chief among the ways it achieved this, to Cardus, was through its reliance on the bare facts rather than dizzy descriptive passages. This was indeed a trademark. When Middlesex met Essex in 1929, for instance, *Wisden* wrote merely: "An overthrow to the boundary and three byes gave Middlesex the lead." It was up to the reader to sense the shout of dismay from the bowler as the overthrow levelled the scores, the rage with which he rushed in to deliver the next ball, and the way it raced away for byes.

Other sensational happenings lay hidden in this dry-as-dust prose. "After the interval," *Wisden* told us, "Parker took the remaining five wickets in ten balls without having a run hit", while Fender "at one point scored 52 runs off 14 consecutive balls". There were thousands of such instances. *Wisden* was too calm and experienced to make a song and dance about the game; it simply provided the tools with which an informed reader could bring them to life. So when Holmes and Sutcliffe set a record partnership of 555 for Yorkshire against Essex, *Wisden* was terse – "the partnership was a magnificent feat in every way and especially of endurance" – though it was also captivated by the way it all ended: "Sutcliffe – very naturally, since it was Yorkshire's policy to declare as soon as possible – threw away his wicket, playing-on with a rather casual stroke, and all the players at once left the field. Then, to everyone's amazement, the total on the scoreboard was altered to read 554 …"

There is a pleasing irony in Cardus's identification of this quality, since his own style was the opposite of this: flowery, with classical allusions, Latin phrases, musical analogies and adjectival rushes. Of Hobbs he wrote (in *Wisden*) that he arrived "full armed, like Jove". He described Charles Macartney as "the Figaro of cricket – not Mozart's, but the drier-minded one of Rossini", and felt that his own great hero A. C. MacLaren "played cricket as some proud Roman might have played it" and expressed "the meaning of epic romance". He loved saying of any favoured cricketer that he represented cricket "in excelsis". Perhaps it was the wordiness of his own style that sharpened his fondness for the plainer *Wisden* voice, which presumed it was enough to relay the fact that Grace took seven wickets for no runs in 17 balls without trying to ramp up the drama by adding that he threw himself at the enemy like Achilles before Troy, singing anthems to storm-conquering Zeus before vanquishing the shattered turrets and scything a path through his God-abandoned foes. Sometimes the plain facts were enough: readers could conjure for themselves the great silhouette shuffling to the stumps, the round-arm heave that sent the ball skidding down, the succession of oaths, the giant waistband hitched, the famous beard split by a grin.

Similarly, there was no need to expand on the news that W. Hyman, for Bath against Thornbury, scored 359 in "one hundred minutes" and "punished E. M. Grace for 32 in one over and 30 in the next". No amount of excited chatter about such numbers could enhance them. The rest – the shouts, the laughs, the bemused fielders, the spilled beer and the sage heads shaking in the scorers' tent – lay through the "magic casement".

This belief that actions speak louder than words has been an important part of the *Wisden* recipe for a long time – it grew out of and supported an idea of Englishness as something restrained and wondrous, adventurous yet well mannered. The fabled politeness of that encounter between Victorian explorers in central Africa ("Dr Livingstone, I presume"), with its suggestion that the codes of Pall Mall could operate even in the darkest heart of the Dark Continent, had been resonating down the generations. Though it described a meeting between a Welsh journalist (working for an American newspaper – he emigrated to New Orleans when he was 18) and a Scot, it came to epitomise a distinctly English quality. So did the unvarnished style evolved by *Wisden*. Outlandish events could be narrated in the tones of a station announcer, lending them grandeur, humour, piquancy or anything else the occasion demanded.

Not that it was yet the serious volume of prose it would later become. Despite the fame of Pardon's Notes, the editorial excursions were secondary to the factual material: it was a reference work, not a journal. It was a repository for the Laws, in true mosaic fashion, and a curator of Births and Deaths. The records section still had the flavour of a highest-mountain-longest-river collection of astounding facts: Great Individual Scores ... a Century on Debut ... Long Partnerships ... Sixteen or More Wickets in a Day ... Most Hundreds in a Season ... Great Totals ... the silhouette of cricket itself could be seen in this range of majestic peaks. There were lists of Oxbridge Blues, summaries of Public School seasons and, of course, the Cricketers of the Year. The Editor's Notes were in the middle, on page 300 or so; in fact they came at the end of the Almanack's first part – the second would present full scorecards and match summaries from county cricket, schools and "other cricket".

It was a slightly ramshackle arrangement that was becoming, as the book continued to grow, somewhat unwieldy. Not the least awkward of its traditions was the way that counties appeared according to their position in the previous year's Championship. Yorkshire and Surrey might come near the front, Essex and Hampshire towards the rear. It did not make *Wisden* the easiest book to use.

———

Caine was fortunate in that his reign was relatively placid. He was not called upon to respond to a major controversy. But in 1933 he died, from what the obituary in the *Manchester Guardian* called "serious heart trouble", at the age of 71. In the course of a long career in journalism (he joined the CRA in 1885, and wrote about both the Ashes and Chelsea FC for the *Observer* as well as working on *Wisden*) he had been "a true gentleman and a perfect sportsman". The *Observer* called him "one of the most lovable of men". As chairman of the Newspaper Press Fund he had long occupied a senior position in the industry, and there was a strong turnout at his memorial service in St Bride's, the journalists' church behind Fleet Street. In his will he left £100 to be distributed among his old colleagues at the CRA.

The new editor, Sydney Southerton, faced one of the most incendiary subjects ever to land in the Almanack's lap. In describing England v Australia matches as "hectic struggles" in his first editorial, Caine can claim to have seen the uproar coming. And in his final *Wisden* (in 1933) he was able to mention the controversy ("The public in Australia appear to be getting very excited about the fast bowling of some of the Englishmen") while emphasising that it would be dealt with fully the following year. He put up an unmissable signpost, however, regarding the way *Wisden* might respond to the subject by saying that, if the reports were accurate, the English bowling strategy was "altogether wrong" and "against the spirit of cricket". Having said that, he added that the thought of Jardine instructing his bowlers to pursue this tactic was "inconceivable", and suspected that the Australians' batting technique might be to blame. It was left to his successor to inspect the affair more closely.

Fortunately, Southerton had been born for such a role. His father, James Southerton, had played in the first Test match, and he himself had been recruited by the CRA in 1894, having impressed them when acting as a scorer for the Australian touring team – he was known as the "figure fiend" for his dexterity with a number. A "useful all-round player" himself (according to his colleague Hubert Preston, who wrote his *Wisden* obituary) he was "reared in cricket air" on Mitcham Green and once, in the Press v Authors game at Lord's in 1895, had actually taken a hat-trick. He was a friend of Ranjitsinhji, writing in his obituary that "I count myself fortunate to have been a witness" to such a man. Ranji, he felt, was "all that a cricketer should be – generous in defeat, modest in success and genuinely enthusiastic regarding the achievement of his colleagues or opponents". He was an "ardent freemason" and a good enough golfer to win press competitions. History ran in his veins: his grandfather had been press-ganged into Nelson's navy. He was well suited, in other words, to keep a classical view of cricket at the front of *Wisden*'s mind.

This was just as well, since fate decreed that his first edition (1934) required him to address the issue of Bodyline. It was more than a year (in the winter of 1932–3) since Jardine and Larwood had so controversially battered the Australians with their famous barrage of short-pitched bowling, but the wounds from the episode were deep, and not yet healed. Devised primarily to thwart Bradman, by far the best batsman on either side, Bodyline aimed to deliver short-pitched bowling (sometimes from round the wicket) to a leg-side field, making it all but impossible to score on the off side and bringing the batsman's body into the line of fire. But it wasn't the theory in itself that unsettled the Australians (it had been used in English county cricket before) so much as the strange, icy hauteur that England's captain, Douglas Jardine, brought to the task. Things came to a noisy head in the Third Test at Adelaide when Larwood first fractured Bert Oldfield's skull with a lifter, but still carried on the assault. It suggested a merciless streak not always linked with the old idea of fair play.

What would be *Wisden*'s final verdict? Caine had put down a strong marker while reserving the right to back either side, so it was a delicate matter: national pride was involved. But while it went against the grain to diverge too far from the MCC line, which had been reluctant to see any merit in Australia's protests, neither was it tenable, with the benefit of a year in which to brood on the subject – including a summer in which the West Indies tried to give Jardine a taste of his own medicine – to depict Australia's anger as mere sore-loser whingeing.

In the event, Southerton began quietly, confident that *Wisden*'s measured style could soothe raw nerves. The death of his "distinguished" predecessor was announced before the contents of the Almanack were outlined – "notices of the counties, reviews of the tours of the West Indies team in England and that of the MCC in Australasia". He thanked those who had made the issue possible – his colleagues at the CRA and his "partner" Mr Hubert Preston: "without his invaluable aid I doubt if the book could have been got ready so soon". And he promised readers an "appreciation" of Ranjitsinhji and a summary of Public School Cricket. The Cricketers of the Year were also named.

There was nothing at this stage to alert even careful readers that there was anything unusual to report: Southerton might as well have been announcing that the library would shortly be closing. It was an expressive gambit: not even a topic as hot as Bodyline, his attitude implied, could disrupt the usual routine. When it came to the topic itself he clung to the same undemonstrative style by publishing the full text of the various cables that flashed between Sydney and London.

He might have been setting out the boat departure times from Harwich and Tilbury, but the cables themselves quivered with strong feelings. Australia began by protesting ("From the Australian Board of Control to MCC") that England's "Bodyline" attack had "assumed such proportions as to menace the best interests of the game". It had provoked "intensely bitter feeling between the players" and was, not to mince words, "unsportsmanlike". No allegation could have been better calculated to unsettle MCC. If it prided itself on anything it was on its addiction to good conduct; to stand accused of punching below the belt was more than it could accept. Its reply, stiffened by the need to defend English dignity, was cold. "We, Marylebone Cricket Club, deplore your cable," it began. "We deprecate your opinion that there has been unsportsmanlike play. We have the fullest confidence in captain, team and managers and are convinced that they would do nothing to infringe either the Laws of Cricket or the spirit of the game." It regretted the injuries to Woodfull and Oldfield but wished to point out that "in neither case was the bowler to blame".

Australia's response was unapologetic. "We, Australian Board of Control," it began, mimicking the sniffy tone, "appreciate your difficulty in dealing with the matter raised in our cable without having seen the actual play." It went on to mention "the ideals of the game". A haughty MCC reply noted "with pleasure" that Australia did not propose to cancel the tour, and asked, with no little pomposity: "May we accept this as a clear indication that the good sportsmanship of our team is not in question?"

This was the kind of tone – pedantic, puffed-up and supercilious – that gave British governance a bad name. But Australia adopted a mild stance at this point, cabling that it did "not regard the sportsmanship of your team" as being in doubt, thus allowing MCC at least the technical satisfaction of having had the allegation withdrawn.

There followed an exchange directly on the point of dangerous bowling. Australia felt it "not in the best interests of cricket" and wanted the Laws to reflect this – it proposed that umpires be empowered to step in if they felt a bowler was seeking to "intimidate or injure". MCC spent four months digesting this before stating that "Bodyline" was a "misleading and improper" description of "leg-theory" – a distinct and "legitimate" line of attack. It took the chance to deplore the "barracking" handed out by local crowds: "cricket played under such conditions is robbed of its value".

On and on the cables rumbled and spat, with both sides trying to gain the upper hand. Australia expressed pleasure that MCC considered intimidating bowling to be against the spirit of the game. MCC was pleased to hear that Australia had promised to address the problem of barracking. As the messages flew back and forth, repeating themselves, they slowly grew briefer, like tyres going flat. Eventually they petered out in a sort of agreement, and the show, it was agreed, would go on. Australia sought a "guarantee" that Bodyline would not be practised on their tour of England in 1934. MCC hemmed and hawed and half-promised that it would think about it. Eventually, almost a year after the first cable, it announced, as if struck by a noble brainwave: "Any form of bowling which is obviously a direct attack by the bowler upon the batsman would be an offence against the spirit of the game."

Southerton's decision to let the cables speak for themselves was firmly in line with Cardus's comments on the Almanack's cool narrative style. But Southerton added an elegant statement of his own – and his publication's – position. While hoping that the cablegrams charted "almost the whole course of the disturbance", he promised (in a shrewd bow to MCC) that he would henceforth use the term "fast leg-theory" rather than "Bodyline", which was a phrase "calculated to stir up strife". By now it hardly mattered what people called it – everyone knew what it meant – and Southerton folded this into an appeal to the game's common sense. "Every cricketer knows at once, or rather feels at once," he wrote, "the difference between hard and rough play." Sketching the context – "one could not fail to detect a subtle change taking place in the conduct of Test matches" – he stood up to be counted: "I deplore its introduction."

Sifting through the debris of the dispute Southerton noticed that Jardine and Larwood – as captain and fast bowler – had repeatedly denied targeting batsmen; but also that there were "numerous statements by responsible Australians" who felt that something of this nature really *had* been the case, and that these were honourable men too. "I cling to the opinion," he wrote – rather bravely, we must say: a few MCC members must have glowered at him next time he passed them by – "that they cannot all be wrong." The idea that the Australians were moaning about nothing was "not quite correct". He had seen the West Indians Constantine and Martindale try the same thing at Old Trafford, and while neither had the "deadliness" of Larwood, the sight was more than enough to convince "people with open minds" that this was a "noxious form of attack not to be encouraged in any way".

Southerton ended by taking the opportunity to remind *Wisden* readers that "the game is of far greater importance than the result". This was, by tradition, what the "spirit of the game" amounted to – a refusal to let winning take precedence over fair play. The events in Australia on that fateful tour, he asserted, were "a disgrace to cricket".

This was strongly put, and impressive, given that the match coverage in the very same *Wisden*, composed as it was in the embattled heat of the moment, was rather less sympathetic to the Australian view. In saying, for instance, that the Third Test at Adelaide would "go down in history as probably the most unpleasant ever played", it could not but take the Englishmen's part. "So hostile was the feeling of the Australian public against Jardine," it said, "that on the days before the game started people were excluded from the ground when the Englishmen were practising." Jardine himself was on the receiving end of "insulting" comments, while Larwood was handed "a storm of abuse ... not to put too fine a point on it, pandemonium reigned". Jardine was praised for his pluck in fielding on the boundary, where he was "an easy target for offensive and sometimes filthy remarks" from the stands. And he captained the side "like a genius". Whatever the rights and wrongs of his tactics, *Wisden*'s reporter was proud of him: "Much as they disliked the method of attack he controlled, all the leading Australian critics were unanimous in their praise of his skill as a leader."

It was, all in all, an eloquent response, capturing enough discordant voices to show that this was a significant quarrel, while pouring oil on the whole troublesome affair. By distancing itself from MCC – not a thing to be undertaken lightly – *Wisden* earned an even more Olympian reputation than before. While MCC could not disguise the extent to which it felt obliged to speak in the national interest, *Wisden* could occupy the high ground by having only the *game*'s cause at heart. Southerton did some small amount of scraping to Lord's sensitivities – he called the original Australian cablegram "petulant" and MCC's "placatory", when he might easily have seen the first as indignant and the reply as hostile. But this was a surface courtesy. The 1934 *Wisden* appointed itself the guardian of cricket's proudest idea, that the end does *not* justify the means; if anything, the means *were* the end – the game was merely a forum in which the so-called English notion of fair play could be acted out.

There was a degree of conservatism behind this emollient tone. In seeming to urge compromise – Southerton praised quick bowling ("the faster the better") so long as it was "of good length and directed at the stumps" – his Almanack was restating the founding precepts of the Victorian amateur game. Bodyline was fraught because it was double-edged. At first it looked like yet another blow to the gentlemanly myths surrounding the "spirit of the game", and as such was easy to condemn: it seemed to embody the relentless advance of the ugly, take-no-prisoners professional approach. But this simple proposition – the reclamation of the amateur ideal – was complicated by the fact that the offence was committed by *England*, the thoroughbred upholders of that fair myth, and by its most favoured sons to boot – Warner (the tour manager) and Jardine. When all the dust settled it appeared that Warner, the epitome of English cricketing nobility, had more than mere qualms about the tactic – in his memoirs he wrote unequivocally that Jardine was "a great captain" who had "encroached on the ethics of the game". But given the upstairs-downstairs sociology of English cricket it was all too easy for people to see it as an establishment plot. As late as 1980 Benny Green was writing, in his *Wisden Anthology 1900–1940*, that: "It is at least interesting that the Bodyline fracas was brought about by those two paragons of the Gentlemen tradition."

Bodyline hit a nerve in another sense. Cricket really was one of the ways in which Britain transmitted its values through the Empire – in those endless games under far-off skies, cricket sought to carry Britain's feelings about fair play, courtesy and class distinction from the school cloisters to the wider world. It is easy enough now to see this as hypocritical nonsense, and true that such ideas were more often parroted than upheld. But that does not mean they were wholly ignoble or entirely shallow. *Wisden*, torn between the urge to condemn unsporting behaviour and a reflex to support any Englishman under fire from uppity colonials, chose the former, thus bolstering its reputation as an impartial judge. It might have earned a few sour looks in the corridors of Lord's, but it is equally possible that had it opted for a brash defence of Jardine the Almanack might not have lasted till its 100th birthday, let alone its 150th.

Cardus said, in the *Manchester Guardian*, that this 1934 *Wisden* was "the ideal bed book – only it is so fascinating that it absolutely keeps sleep at a distance". Was it this dense mesh of divided loyalties that kept him awake? Very possibly. He saw the Bodyline coverage as "a palpable hit", though he felt that Australia had made a "sad error" in diplomacy by feeling that a protest was necessary: "The Australian objection to Larwood was nothing like so comprehensive," he wrote, a trifle optimistically, "as the objection of the majority of English cricketers."

The general readership reacted warmly too – *Wisden* was always at its best when it had an exceptional story to tell – inspiring Southerton to write in the 1935 Preface that "the Almanack serves a great purpose". But, of course, the 1934 edition had not been a single-issue volume; it continued to range its gaze over the rest of cricket too. Like the patriarch of an extended family, *Wisden* in these years was treating the game's most distinguished performers like relatives at a Christmas lunch. It celebrated the 333 scored by K. S. Duleepsinhji in 1930 by saying that it "brought the great distinction of beating the Sussex record made by his uncle, K. S. Ranjitsinhji"; at other times it treasured both the famous – impeccable triple centuries by Bradman and Hammond – and the less well-known: like the 28-year-old member of the Trinidad inter-colonial team who died when he contracted "blood poisoning caused by a nail in his cricket boot".

In 1935 it published an essay by the Master himself, called "The Hobbs Era". The great batsman agreed that Bodyline had done "great harm", but defended the game against the endlessly popular notion that it was sliding inexorably downhill. He also addressed cricket's class divide by proposing the unification of professional and amateur dressing rooms – a still-radical suggestion which he tactfully couched in ultra-deferential terms, not insisting on equality as a point of principle but simply observing that professionals had better manners these days. There had, he felt, been a "pronounced improvement in the bearing of professional cricketers", to such an extent that "the average professional can, I think, hold his own as a man in any company".

Wisden was always happy, like some great school or college, to spare a thought for its favoured old boys. In 1937, when Patsy Hendren hung up his boots, *Wisden* was happy to give space to his diffident reminiscences ("I thought it as well to give up while I was doing well"). Hendren's memory stretched back far enough to include a game with Grace ("I well remember him clapping me on the back and saying in that high-pitched voice of his, 'You'll play for England one day, young 'un'."). But now he was off, like the Little Wonder before him, to coach at Harrow. A couple of years later (in 1939) it would be Frank Woolley's turn to say his fond farewells. "It is a severe wrench," he wrote, "leaving the game which I have enjoyed so much."

Wisden continued to enjoy such musings, and though its prime concern was to note outstanding efforts with bat and ball, it liked incidents of a humbler sort too: "The second day's attendance of 7,000 was the largest ever seen on the ground … It is safe to say that no better wicket had ever been prepared … the match was remarkable for the fact that five men were unable to play on the Thursday."

In a nod to the old ideas regarding cricket's manly qualities, it also knew how to bring a macabre smile to its readership. When Gloucestershire played Yorkshire in 1927 it had narrated the tale of a luckless official called Parry – "an umpire whose leg had been amputated below the knee, fell in getting out of the way of a ball, and fractured the maimed limb". And in 1935 it soberly told the story of Maurice Nichol, a Worcestershire batsman who was "found dead in his bed" on the morning of the 1934 Whit-Monday match in Chelmsford. It was, *Wisden* observed "a sad event that marred the enjoyment of the match but did not prevent Worcestershire gaining a first-innings lead". In 1939 the Almanack deployed an even more straight-faced tone to describe a fatal car crash: "Bull was killed and Buller injured. Defeat in such circumstances was not surprising."

In March 1935 Sydney Southerton died – like his predecessors, in harness. After a dinner of the Ferrets Cricket Club at The Oval he made a short speech and proposed a toast to "Cricket" before sinking back in his chair, his heart giving out. He was the third *Wisden* editor to die in a decade – the policy of giving very senior men the chair was proving rather fraught. This time the board sought out a younger man, and the choice fell on Wilfrid H. Brookes, age 40, ahead of the more experienced Hubert Preston (who was then 66). It sounded, from his Preface the following year, in which he spoke of "other heavy calls upon my time", as if he was ambivalent about the task, and he had a sizeable list of 17 colleagues to thank, on whom he depended "very considerably". He was also "greatly indebted" to the counties for their statistical help. He didn't sound exactly delighted to be in charge.

By now the twenties had long since stopped roaring. Depression-era economics and German rearmament was giving Britain, the so-called "workshop of the world", the jitters. In 1933 unemployment reached 2.5 million – a quarter of the workforce. In some towns (such as Jarrow) almost everyone was out of work. John Wisden & Co was buffeted by these storms as painfully as everyone else: the 1935 minutes spoke of a "steady falling off" and "the unsatisfactory position of sales", and a management consultancy firm (Messrs Whitehead and Staff) was invited to review the structure of the firm. George Gooch, the present

managing director, was not best pleased. He took exception to
"numerous points" in the subsequent report, and did not go out of his
way to help the Whitehead representative, co-operating "in the letter,
but no way in the spirit" of the law. A new sales manager was appointed,
so that more energy could be put into exports, but at this time John
Wisden & Co was not a happy ship. By 1937 the company's results
were "disastrous", and Gooch was reporting that the sports trade was
in "a very bad way". He had tried hard to crack the tennis market, with
a promising seamless ball, but with little success. Henley's Tyre and
Rubber Company was engaged to produce the ball cores, but a large
investment in racquet-making machinery was not yet producing results,
a joint venture with a tennis court firm (anyone for a "Wisden Deny's
Hard Court"?) was foundering, and John Wisden & Co was being
firmly nudged out of the Indian market by Slazenger. When two
directors volunteered the thought that the only options were "a change
of management or liquidation", the chairman said he was "forced to
share that view". Opting for the former, he asked Gooch if he was
willing to tender his resignation. When Gooch declined he was given
three months' notice.

This time the Almanack was suffering too. By 1937 only 8,000
copies were being printed, and the board was even expressing concern
(noted in the minutes) regarding the structure of the book. It turned to
Whitaker's, a well-established publishing company, to investigate
matters and, in time, to assume control. And in 1938 the two companies
each bought a half share in a Whitaker's imprint called Sporting
Handbooks, which had been producing a *Rugby Football Annual*
(referred to in *The Times* as the *Wisden* of rugby in 1934) since 1913.
The terms of the agreement were unusual. Each company put £100
into Sporting Handbooks in return for a half share in which, the board
minutes emphasised, "the interests and powers of the two owners"
were "identical in every respect". It was an interesting arrangement:
although, from Whitaker's point of view, there was little point in their
using the imprint to publish titles of their own (since half the profits
would go to John Wisden & Co) the equipment company was bringing
good sporting connections to the party, which might produce a flow
of books. Indeed, in the decade to come Sporting Handbooks
published many works, including *The Book of Cricket* by Pelham

Warner, *Denis Compton: a Cricket Sketch* by E. W. Swanton, and *How to Watch Cricket* by John Arlott.* There were titles on tennis too (including *Wimbledon Story* by Norah Gordon Gleather). The last book to roll off the presses (*England Down Under* by John Kay) was an account of the 1958–9 tour to Australia. The 1939–40 edition of the rugby annual was the twentieth and last, and though the next four editions of *Wisden* were published under the Whitaker name, from 1944 onwards it would be a Sporting Handbooks product.

Whitaker's was run by Lieutenant Colonel Sir Cuthbert Whitaker, and, though its own famous Almanack – an encyclopaedic directory of astronomical information and general knowledge – was four years younger than *Wisden* (founded in 1868), it was a more dynamic commercial force. Its first edition had been a "resounding success" and sold some 60,000 copies: the revolutions of the moon were more popular than cricket.

Sir Cuthbert Whitaker entrusted *Wisden* to his son Haddon Whitaker, who had just missed out on a Cambridge rowing Blue before joining the family business in 1932. Now, with Brookes, he planned a transformation. With the 75th issue approaching and circulation sinking fast, it was time for a thorough overhaul.

The 1938 *Wisden* broke with the past in numerous ways which, taken together, made it a watershed edition. Instead of running county reports according to their place in the previous year's Championship, it put them in alphabetical order. The ancient division of the book into two sections, each with its own page numbering (which Brookes called a "quaint Victorian survival") was torn down. Births, Deaths and Obituaries were moved to the back; the Laws were shunted to the middle; the old Cricketers of the Year portraits were replaced by more ambitious photography; and the Contents page was replaced by a

---

* Arlott's book included a canny assessment of the wickets at England's grounds: Taunton was "plumb, but often green before lunch", Lord's "plumb to fair, occasional tendency to crumble on second day". It ended with an ardent declaration: "Cricket needs no defence and no excuse; its glorious justification is in the eyes of small boys watching their country's star players and the eyes of old men looking beyond today's match to another whose players are dead and gone these twenty years."

Advertisement in the 1938 Australian tour of England programme detailed Index (though the Contents page returned in 1939 alongside the Index). There was even women's cricket, in honour of the first match between England and Australia in England (they had already met in Brisbane three years earlier, in 1934).

Brookes's introductory remarks were hopeful: "Cricket in England proved keener and more interesting than in several years", thanks to a zestful approach by the counties that had produced "more spirit and adventure in their play". Even the sky was "comparatively fine". He urged reform, suggesting that some counties merge or fuse; he applauded the proposal to update the points system and encouraged positive captaincy, and set his head against "purposeless drawn games". In advancing the merits of both Hutton ("should be an automatic choice") and Yardley (the Cambridge captain) he was honouring both the professional and the amateur way. He dropped Caine's hostility to overseas stars and advised clubs to hire charismatic players at all costs. "In few counties is there a commanding personality about whom everyone talks and wants to see. A fresh registration scheme ought to be framed so that counties at present unable to enjoy the assistance of talented players may obtain, quickly, the services of good cricketers who do not possess a birth qualification."

His keenest wish was that the game be played with vigour. In 1936, commenting on the dreariness of the England team, he declined to blame the selectors and bemoaned the more general absence of stars on the county scene who were a "turnstile asset". He was scornful of the Eton side which, set a target of 156 to win in 105 minutes, did not even try to win: "they preferred instead to play for safety". As it happened this match did produce an arresting moment: an Etonian batsman blocked the ball and helpfully tapped it back towards the wicketkeeper, but when the keeper missed it and the ball hit the stumps he was inevitably, on appeal, given out.

Brookes continued to oppose defensive tactics. His Notes dwelled enthusiastically on the MCC-backed plan to promote attacking cricket. And selecting young Hutton as a Cricketer of the Year in 1938, he stressed that though "his off-drive is beautifully made" and he was "blessed with the right temperament for the big occasion" he could also be a bit dull: "It must be said that he often carries caution to the extreme."

He apologised if the refashioned book felt "rather strange" but insisted that "nothing, I hope, of real interest to cricketers has been

omitted". Indeed, he had made a special effort with the contents, too.
There were features by Gubby Allen (the England captain in 1936–7)
and Patsy Hendren. There was a solemn tribute to the ever-amazing
Don Bradman. And the match reports struck the usual much-loved
note. One player "spun the ball appreciably", while another "drove
powerfully"; one "hit merrily" while his team-mate "turned the game
in favour of Australia".

It all came wrapped in a distinctive new look. Robert Harling, who
years later would be editor of *House and Garden* (and a friend of Ian
Fleming) but who at this time ran a small design journal called
Typography, was asked to develop a new style, and he did. "I thought
little needed to be done," he wrote; *Wisden* seemed to him one of those
"traditional publications" which "got their format right first time". He
did, however, replace the old paper cover with "strong linen",
recommend a new typeface (Times New Roman), create an eccentric,
Wild West typeface he called Playbill for the name on the cover (Wisden)
and suggest to Whitaker's that the artist Eric Ravilious be asked to
provide a new jacket illustration. The result – a playful woodcut of two
top-hatted cricketers in period costume, set in a forest-fringed vignette
redolent of England's ancient countryside – has been *Wisden*'s emblem
ever since. In one sense it pushed against the modernising premise of the
makeover, but the Victorian image showed that the lineage of the game
still filled *Wisden*'s arteries. It was appropriate that Ravilious was, like
the founder, a Sussex man (he trained in Eastbourne) and that his
woodcut looked like a pub sign, echoing as it did the image hanging
outside The Cricketers at Petworth in the South Downs, where Wisden
himself had gone shooting with Jemmy Dean. As it happened, Ravilious's
daughter later learned that her father did not earn a fee for his work, on
the grounds that he may have copied an existing pub image (a charge
that she found difficult to believe).* Four years later, in 1942, Ravilious,
by then a war artist, was "presumed dead" when his plane did not return
from a flight over the Atlantic, but in the swirl of other losses *Wisden*
uncharacteristically failed to give him an obituary (until 1994).

---

* The most likely source was The Bat and Ball at Hambledon, which depicted
two antique players in a very similar pose.

The 1938 edition was well received – the *Manchester Guardian* noticed "certain improvements" – and seems to have been a success, but it came too late to save a company that was spiralling down, smoke streaming behind it like the trail from a wounded Spitfire. The Almanack, however widely it was revered, was no one's idea of a breadwinner: it could not support a failing sports goods business on which the descent into war was having a catastrophic effect. The departure of Gooch (he was replaced by Thomas Horabin) generated a brief burst of energy: in 1937 the company bought new premises at Penshurst in Kent with a view to building a new tennis racquet factory there. And by the end of 1938 the numbers were in slightly better order – sales for the four-month period August–November were £22,276, higher than in the same months of the previous year (£19,276). The company, said the managing director with obvious pleasure, was running on "oiled wheels". But things were turning down fast. The entire tennis strategy continued to be an embarrassing mistake. The new factory (Henleys) contracted to supply the ball cores was, like its predecessor, producing a "bad ball" which did "considerable harm" to the company's image when it failed to win LTA approval. Slazenger and Dunlop, meanwhile, were busy acquiring rights to a patented vacuum-canister to keep tennis balls fresh. At the end of January it emerged that there had been an export collapse and a sharp decline in sales over Christmas, resulting in six-month revenues worth only £29,598, a grave undershoot on the £46,000 required to break even. The cash position was "serious"; suppliers were limiting credit; and the bank overdraft was at the limit. Put simply, John Wisden & Co could not pay its bills, and the fact that the Almanack was looking distinctly smart these days was no consolation. In December 1938, when the disgruntled former managing director, George Gooch, tried to sell his shareholding, the board informed him that they knew of "no likely purchaser". He reacted by coming to the Annual General Meeting as a shareholder and criticising "at length" the company's approach.

They were powerless to stop the slide. Oh, there were resolutions to replace adverts in the Almanack from rival firms with own-brand promotions, but that was merely tinkering at the edges. Wally Hardinge had left the firm in 1934, and in 1938 John Wisden & Co reversed its policy of not paying star players to use its products by agreeing terms with Denis Compton (£50 per year – not exactly a king's ransom) to endorse *Wisden* bats. Meanwhile, the head office moved into an expanded office at the new Penshurst factory. It was hardly the ideal time for such a move, but who could have guessed that *Wisden* was now right on the flight path of the German bombers that would soon be lifting away from the conquered airfields in France.

When the company failed to win a War Office contract to make 5,000 handles for bomb cases, the chairman called a meeting to discuss the "serious cash position": it had "changed vitally" in the last few weeks, and suppliers were restricting credit. He announced that the only honourable course was to appoint a receiver. It was amicably done. P. J. (Percy) Chaplin, an executive from the firm of accountants (Singleton, Fabian & Co) that had been presiding over Wisden's since 1914, was named both receiver and manager in February 1939, and the famous old sports business, nearly a hundred years after John Wisden's first cricket shop opened at Leamington, was declared bankrupt.

Wisden had picked a dire time for a relaunch. German rearmament, and Hitler's violent ambitions in Austria and Czechoslovakia, were putting Britain on a war footing once again, just when cricket was stepping into the modern era. In 1938, for the first time in its history, Worcestershire fielded a team composed of professionals and, in another development that would ordinarily have signalled the arrival of the future, the Lord's Test was televised. Fears that it might deter the crowd proved groundless. The Saturday attendance (33,800) was the largest ever assembled at the ground, and the overall match figure (100,933) was also an all-time best.

It was The Oval Test match, however, which inspired an even richer slice of cricket history. Len Hutton ("this batsman of only 22 years") walked out on the first morning, faced the first ball and proceeded to rewrite *Wisden*'s record by scoring 364 runs in a colossal England total of 903 for 7 declared. In so doing he passed the existing mark held by Don Bradman, who was playing for Australia in this match but who injured his ankle badly enough to be absent hurt in both innings. It was "phenomenal", wrote Brookes, and "may stand for all time". This was a reckless prediction to find in a publication that knew more clearly than most that records rarely went unbroken, but the sober match report saved the day. "No more remarkable exhibition of concentration and endurance has ever been seen on a cricket field." An enormous crowd (30,000) filed into The Oval to see him clinch the record with "a perfect cut off Fleetwood-Smith".

It was a sporting high point, a flash of brilliant light against ominous clouds, the longest as well as the largest innings ever played ("lasting from half-past eleven on the Saturday until half past two on the Tuesday"). But in *Wisden*'s eyes it was a triumph of resolve as much as skill. Hutton "never altered his cautious style" and "his defence never faltered". It was, the report concluded, an innings of "grim, determined dominance". It was as if *Wisden* knew in its bones that these were the qualities that would most be needed when the skies over England went dark.

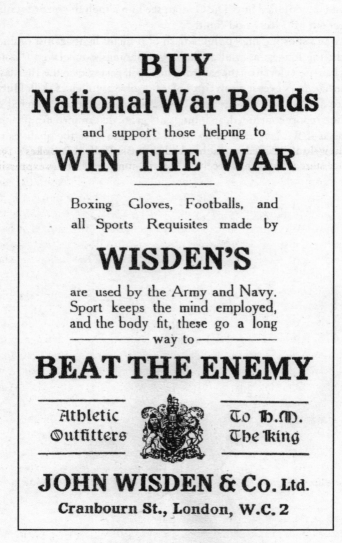
Advertisement from Wisden 1918

8

Brothers in Arms

The new-look *Wisden* was a marked success. Wilfrid Brookes's 1939 Preface stated that he had received "a large number of letters expressing strong approval of the changes" and that sales had increased by "over seventy-five per cent" – a sharp and confidence-boosting rise. Given that sales had in recent years sagged to low levels this may not have been quite so resounding as it appears – it may have amounted to no more than a few thousand copies. And it is even possible that Brookes himself might have exaggerated a little – good news was in short supply in 1939.

What happened next was surprising: Brookes walked out. Unlike his predecessors he was no elderly CRA loyalist, stuck in his ways, but he did not leave to pursue some prominent role elsewhere – indeed he faded from public life and did not trouble the cricket world again until he died, in 1955, in a nursing home in Putney.[*] There was a clue, in his first Preface, that he was a reluctant editor in the first place, and the war may have had something to do with it as well. Years later, the *Wisden* editor Graeme Wright would be told by Leslie ("Tiger") Smith, a tireless Almanack contributor, that Brookes had taken fright at the prospect of bombing and done "a runner" – the cruel scuttlebutt in the CRA office was that he was not keen to see what war was like.

Either way, Haddon Whitaker felt no need to appoint a successor: overlooking Hubert Preston again he took the chair himself, and would

---

[*] *Wisden* (of all places) contrived to get Brookes' name wrong (Wil*fred* for Wilfrid) in its brief 1956 obituary.

not pass it on until the end of the war was in sight.[*] In a sign that he and Brookes had not seen eye-to-eye, when he did hand over to Hubert Preston in 1944, he failed even to mention Brookes in declaring himself proud to be "re-establishing the august tradition of the Pardons, Stewart Caine and Sydney Southerton".

It is one of a few ironies in the *Wisden* story that Brookes, whose bold new 1938 Almanack made him one of the more influential editors in its life, only edited four editions. In an indirect way he may have been a casualty of war, since his resignation was part of a reorganisation imposed by the crisis in which *Wisden* found itself. The agreement with Whitaker's was one of the first items on the agenda of Percy Chaplin, official receiver to the bankrupt John Wisden & Co. Haddon Whitaker had assured him that sales of the Almanack might "reach" 7,000 (at five shillings apiece) – enough to generate a minor profit – so Chaplin agreed to continue the arrangement. In effect, the receiver-run company was agreeing to give away half the Almanack's profit in the hope that Whitaker's would take a more vigorous role in marketing it. It was not an especially favourable deal for John Wisden & Co, but it is possible that Chaplin was motivated partly by a desire to park *Wisden* somewhere safe while its owner lay broke and vulnerable – under the terms of the receivership he was obliged to "convert into money" as many of the company's assets as he could. It gave Whitaker's power over editorial matters: John Wisden & Co was no longer the boss.

Whitaker did not usually describe himself as the editor – his first Preface informed readers that he would be "co-ordinating the contributions" in the constrained times that lay ahead. But though the 1940 edition was published late, in June, no one was going to complain, what with England still coming to terms with the shattering events at Dunkirk, and bracing itself for a do-or-die struggle in the skies. *The Times* declared itself grateful for "at least one more edition of a book which is very dear to most Englishmen", but in truth, cricket almanacks were no one's prime concern.

---

[*] Whitaker himself claimed, with pleasing modesty, that whenever he saw himself named as a *Wisden* editor it made him feel an "interloper" in the list of "distinguished reporters" who had presided over the Almanack. Had he not steered the book safely through the war years, however, there may well have been nothing left to edit.

In 1939, as part of the new arrangement, *Wisden* moved out of the St Bride's offices of the CRA and into the Whitaker's building at 12 Warwick Lane, EC4, near St Paul's. It was a move of only a few hundred yards, but it would prove a momentous one. A few months later, Neville Chamberlain announced in his famous radio broadcast that the "final note" had been handed over, and that the nation was at war; by the following winter of 1940 France, Holland and Belgium had fallen, Greece and Egypt teetered on the brink, and Italy and Japan had linked arms with Germany. London was being blitzed, and while the gloom of Dunkirk had been lifted by the success of the Few in the Battle of Britain, the war news was grim. The North Atlantic was full of U-boats and larger predators, and rationing was the order of the day. But when *Wisden* moved to the Whitaker's offices, no one imagined what it was letting itself in for.

The timing was almost comically unlucky, but on 29 December 1940, as the cricket world wondered what the New Year would bring, the old one brought a murderous surprise: the worst wave of German bombers yet seen. In what would later be known as the Second Great Fire of London, the northern swathe of the City of London was blitzed even more violently than it had been in 1666. This was the night when the northern environs of St Paul's Cathedral were pulverised and lost in a plume of billowing smoke, as 120 tons of explosive and over 20,000 incendiary devices hailed down on the City. While the residents cowered in underground shelters, a *Daily Mail* photographer called Herbert Mason watched the scene from the roof of his newspaper office in Fleet Street; and when the wind blew the clouds away from the glowing roof of the cathedral he "lowered his shutter" on one of the most famous images of the war – the queenly dome of St Paul's floating untouched, as if protected by angels from the engulfing firestorm.

The cathedral was saved thanks to fire wardens on the roof, who kicked off the incendiaries; but the Whitaker's office in nearby Warwick Lane was not so lucky: it was "obliterated". The company records of John Wisden & Co were elsewhere (in Mortlake, Penshurst and the offices of the receiver in Staples Inn). But next time you see that image, pregnant with the heroic sense of an indomitable spirit rising above misfortune, look at it one more time: somewhere in that cloud of swirling ash, drifting skywards along with the burnt remnants of eight

Christopher Wren churches, much of the documentary history of *Wisden* – including most likely, the woodblock on which Ravilious carved his famous illustration – is, quite literally, going up in smoke.

At this point, *Wisden* became a child of the spirit of the Blitz. There was nothing for it but to grit one's teeth and carry on. Haddon Whitaker, in the broken remnants of his family company, resolved to get *Wisden* out somehow. The bombing of the office had left the *Wisden* material, in the safe, "charred beyond recognition", and in a separate accident the schools section was also hit by the Luftwaffe while in the post – both the posted copy and the original manuscript went up in flames. Some of the burned editorial material from the New Year's Eve bombing was slowly re-compiled, and four pages of house advertisements were inserted in place of the missing schools report. One, a page asking "What did the *Wisden* Almanack say in 18–?" invited readers to fill gaps in their collections while stocks lasted: "The volume you want may still be available." This was more than a waste-not-want-not bit of wartime housekeeping: it was an attempt to carry on as normal. Prices ranged from a crown to five guineas, a sign – though few cared just now – that a real market was developing.

A defiant story in the *Manchester Guardian* noted that "the former premises were burnt out and the balance of stock and all records of sales were lost", but the 1941 Almanack *would* come out as planned, even if it was not quite itself. In the event, despite its brevity and a tiny print run (4,000 copies) it did not appear until almost Christmas – but better late than never. For this alone Haddon Whitaker counts as one of the heroes in *Wisden*, if only for the grit he showed in keeping it alive. The contents hardly mattered: it was keeping up appearances that counted at a time like this.

By that time Brookes had long gone. But a copy of his final edition (the 1939 Almanack) turned out, despite everything, to become perhaps the most celebrated of them all. He may not have been solely responsible for it (he credited Hubert Preston with "much of the book"), but the 1939 *Wisden* would, thanks to events beyond anyone's control, have an extraordinary life. When the cricket writer and broadcaster (for the *Evening Standard* and the fledgling BBC) E. W. Swanton was captured following the rout of Singapore he was flung, with thousands of others, into a Japanese prisoner-of-war camp, first at Changi and then at Wampo and elsewhere, on the Burma-Thailand railway made notorious by David Lean's film, *Bridge on the River Kwai*. Even here, cricket was a morale-boosting diversion: Swanton would, in the first post-war *Wisden* (1946), recall witnessing, in that unhappy winter of 1942, the fastest century he had ever seen – "scored in about five overs by a very promising young Eurasian cricketer called Thoy, who, with graceful ease, kept hitting the tennis ball clear over the huts!"

It was Swanton's own copy of the 1939 Almanack that made history, however. A group of soldiers in the camps formed a library of "several thousand" books scraped together from the leftovers and the rubble. Mostly it comprised the kind of worthy titles a casual browser might find in any second-hand bookshop of the time – piles of Priestley, Waugh, Galsworthy and Maugham. But none turned out to be so popular or so well thumbed as Swanton's precious Almanack. He used it to give broadcasts on an improvised camp radio station. And just as cricket filled the homesick hearts of the trench-bound troops in the previous war, so the long-suffering victims of the railway prison camps found sweet calm, it seems, in these familiar echoes of a vanished English summer. Marked by the Japanese censor as "non-subversive", the book was a crowd-pleasing hit, borrowed so frequently that it began to fall apart.* Patched up with strips of torn tape, and bound with glue made from boiled rice paste, it "could be lent out only for periods of six hours". Yet somehow, in a story that seems to exemplify the bruised career of *Wisden* as a whole, it scraped through.

At the end of the war Swanton himself, safely home, shared memories of the cricket games he had seen while he and his comrades were "guests of the Japanese"; but his famous copy of the book, well known in cricket circles, became a proper celebrity after his death in 2000. His executors gave it to the Lord's Museum where it remains to this day, alongside the Ashes, the sparrow that was killed by a ball (bowled by

---

* In his autobiography, *Sort of a Cricket Person*, Swanton would speculate that his own 1939 Almanack may have been "the most-read copy of *Wisden* ever published".

Jahangir Khan) in 1936, and a thousand other treasures. Swanton's book had, commented the former curator, Stephen Green, been "one of the prisoners' lifelines to sanity", and since then hordes of cricket enthusiasts have seen this battered wartime artefact, now rebound, as a resonant emblem of English culture. In its long history *Wisden* has been many things to many people; it is hardly out of character that it should itself, for a while, have been a defiant prisoner of war.

Even without this, it was a memorable volume. It had a dashing summer of Ashes cricket (a "marked revival" barely spoiled by Australia winning) in which Bradman scored a century in each Test in which he batted en route to amassing a season's total of 2,429 runs at an average of 115.6. "One did not detect any waning of his powers," commented Brookes with dry admiration, before inviting Bradman to write for the Almanack.* "The Editor of *Wisden* has honoured me by asking for a contribution …" Bradman began, with his usual politeness, before discussing "the quickening of the modern tempo". He chided England's lovable fondness for "hastening slowly", and urged cricket to keep in step with the times: "We cannot arrest nor impede the tenor of everyday life." As an Australian he was permitted to say such things – even to argue that no could "reasonably object" to eight-ball overs except fast bowlers. Pardon would have twitched in his grave.

The 1939 edition also of course featured the full story of Len Hutton's tireless innings at The Oval, in which he passed both Bradman's record Ashes total (334) and Hammond's all-comer's record (336 v New Zealand). Brookes said that this had done "much to restore our self-respect" and felt vindicated, having resisted the lure of pessimism in 1938. He was generous in his appreciation of Bradman's Australians ("the happy spirit pervading the team was very evident") though he countered suggestions that Bradman was a match for W. G. Grace by pointing out that Grace had not embarked upon Test cricket until he was 32, so no true comparison was possible. The previous year he had himself expressed reservations about the "ticklish question surrounding the captaincy of Hammond" (he became eligible only by becoming an

---

* Brookes loved the Ashes, and in 1937 had written, for *The Times*, a full-page history of the rivalry.

amateur), but had the decency to confess that "events proved that opinion wrong". There were memoirs by two elderly stars – Lord Hawke of Yorkshire and Kent's Frank Woolley – balanced by news of an exciting new hero in Denis Compton. The pen-portrait of him to mark his selection as a Cricketer of the Year – an annual ceremony which was now building itself into something resembling a dictionary of national biography for cricketers – claimed that even at the age of ten he had showed ability "far above that of most lads" and that he had become the most exhilarating batsman of the day: "there is no one better worth watching".

It is easy to see how this mix of record-breaking feats and sheer novelty entranced prisoners as hungry for consolation as they were for food (Swanton lost five stone in the camps). In helping to make *Wisden* part of the British fondness for eccentricity, the 1939 Almanack also encapsulated what Cardus meant by his "magic casement" to a cricketing dreamscape. A book that seemed like a bland trove of information had an exhilarating tendency to waylay readers by throwing threads to and fro in time. Each of its incidents echoed or anticipated similar events at other times and in other places. Opening any *Wisden* might lead us, via Bradman's run of six consecutive centuries, back to this 1939 edition, and there in turn we might be waylaid by reports on Denis Compton's bravura displays, or glimpse in the Obituaries a 13-year-old called Ken Goldie who scored 239 for his school in 1896 – and before long we would be drifting in a web of connections with links to games and people in both the past and future.

In the same 1939 book we might read about a big-hitting all-rounder called Arthur Wellard, and if we rolled forward to the following year's Almanack we see him being "missed four times in the course of five balls" playing for Somerset against Kent. Glancing at the scoreboard, we can see that he was batting No. 10 and scored 48 – not bad for a tailender. These are facts; the furniture or scenery we must conjure for ourselves, imagining the top-edge into the gully dropped, say, followed by the failed swish and the missed stumping, then the hard nick to a ham-fisted slip and the high slog to the man on the midwicket boundary – who spilled it, red-faced and cursing.

We might have a feeling that Wellard hit a lot of sixes, and be sent back through the years (51 in 1933, 57 in 1938 and 66 in 1935, records that were not beaten until Ian Botham hit 80 in 1985). Harold Pinter enthusiasts might recall the glowing tribute he wrote about Wellard (a Cricketer of the Year in 1936) who years later turned out for Pinter's own weekend team. "What was Hammond like, Arthur?" the actors would ask, and in a flash a different world springs before us – of eager weekenders with only fragile links to their idols. "Hammond? Nobody could stop him. Never anybody to touch old Wally on the off side … What about Larwood, Arthur? How fast was he? Larwood? He was a bit quick, Larwood. Quickest thing I ever saw …"

There was much along these lines to stir the emotions of Swanton's fellow prisoners. They could also have read about military personnel they might have met, such as C. P. Hamilton, who scored 205 for the Royal Artillery against the Royal Engineers, or Lt Harbottle of the 43rd Light Infantry, who made 109 against the Navy. In the Obituaries they could imagine the "exceptional promise" shown by that high-scoring schoolboy, later Major Kenneth Goldie, who had gone on to play for Sussex with Ranji; or they could raise a glass to Charles Grace, the last surviving son of old W. G. himself, who had died while playing in a cricket match in Hawkhurst. And how sad to read about the passing of John Sharp, who played in two FA Cup finals for Everton and scored a century against Australia at The Oval (in 1909) but walked out of cricket in dismay when he was jeered at for dropping a catch at short leg in 1925.

There was a ten-page list of new books to dream about (biographies of Grace and Barnes, memoirs by Warner, Jessop, Jardine, Hobbs, Sutcliffe and Fry; history by H. S. Altham, reportage by Cardus and refined comedy by Robertson-Glasgow and Wodehouse). For a prisoner of war even to imagine a world in which a man might curl up in a chair by a fire with a book – what luxury! It was wonderfully refreshing, as Cardus noticed in a review for the *Manchester Guardian*, that there was "no mention anywhere of Hitler". Any inmates from Cambridge could smile to read the news that Oxford had failed to win a single match – "a record never before known". And if they felt envious of the flannelled parade they only had to glance at the ill luck that dogged Notts in the pre-war season: "Rheumatism attacked Larwood, sciatica incapacitated Staples, appendicitis terminated Butler's activities, synovitis held up Voce, and an injured ankle prevented Woodhead from showing his full possibilities." Maybe war wasn't so rough after all, eh lads? After you with the *Wisden*.

One of the chief attractions of the 1939 *Wisden*, of course, was that it described a season unshadowed by war. Even the advertisements seemed like innocent fun: here was Len Hutton, no less, celebrating his historic 364 at The Oval by promoting boot-cleaning fluid – "You can rely on Meltonian Liquid White for long, brilliant innings every time." And there was a playful description of cricket "conundrums" – unlikely events that suggested it remained a field of rich possibilities. *Wisden* readers could learn how it was possible to lose five wickets in a single ball (absent, run-out off a no-ball, retired hurt, caught and timed out), how a man might be "half-caught" (when the ball breaks in two pieces) and what to do with a batsman who holds on to the bails with his hands, preventing them from tumbling to the ground.

The 1940 edition could not be so carefree. Haddon Whitaker's Preface warned that it would henceforth "conform with the smaller issues of the Great War", but in fact this one was (at 875 pages) still quite plump. Wisely, he did not attempt the editor's Notes himself; instead he invited Raymond Robertson-Glasgow, the Oxford cricket Blue and a notably brilliant cricket writer, to summarise the season in his place. In the circumstances it was not a run-of-the-mill assignment, and Robertson-Glasgow began with a sober recognition of the fact: "So great was the thing which started, for us, on 3 September last year, so pervasive of our thoughts, homes, even of our pastimes and sports, that to look back on the English cricket season of 1939 is like peeping curiously through the wrong end of a telescope at a very small but very happy world. It is a short six months since Constantine gave the England bowlers such a cracking at The Oval, like a strong man suddenly gone mad in a fielding-practice, but it might be six years, or sixteen; for we have jumped a dimension or two since then."

If this grand, affecting tone had been maintained – if Robertson-Glasgow had continued to see the game in this compressed, unreal form – he might have written a superb essay. After the initial formalities were over, however, he adopted a much more breezy manner: he criticised the timeless Test in Durban as "laboured and tedious", tut-tutted over the poor level of modern play ("the standard of bowling is low"), applauded the "virility and gaiety" of the South Africans, railed against the impact of "ludicrously docile" pitches, and begged county members to keep up with their subscriptions. His first Notes ended up being nearly twice as long as Brookes's the previous year, and though the *Manchester Guardian* called them "sapid and sapient" (meaning tasty and wise) the rococo tone sounded like faint praise.

Naturally we must note that Robertson-Glasgow's Notes were written in the phoney preamble to war, when nothing violent had yet erupted; and the fact that he was a guest writer rather than the editor of an august publication might have hampered his authority somewhat. But the decision to be jaunty – "Optimism is the thing ... I can see no reason or gain in wearing mental sackcloth in advance" – turned out to be a fraction indelicate, and the nostalgic flourish with which he recalled the good old days – "Many would delight to see again a few Edwardian drives and a late Victorian pull or two" – seemed mere picture-book flippancy. Aiming for cheery insouciance, he ended up striking the kind of pose that encourages people to think of cricket as small-minded. *The Times* reviewer frowned, noting that in replacing "pontifical judgement" with a "pleasantly composed essay" *Wisden* was abandoning the idea that it was, even in a small way, required reading. And in the years to come this once-loyal friend would continue to hand out brickbats. When Births and Deaths was omitted in 1942 the paper sighed over its "rather naked appearance", and in 1943 added that *Wisden* had "the character of an illustrated magazine rather than a book of reference".

If Robertson-Glasgow's musings seemed to take the edge off the Almanack's usual gravitas, Whitaker sought to balance things by also including an extensive essay on "Cricket in Wartime" by Major H. S. (Harry) Altham. This took a more sober and tactful view – "Today the horizon is again dark, and it is idle to try to look far ahead" – before delivering a panoramic survey of the militarised game. Altham, a schoolmaster at Winchester and cricket historian, ran through games played in the War of the Austrian Succession, the War of American Independence, the Napoleonic wars, the Crimean campaign, the Boer War (noting that this conflict was barely mentioned by *Wisden* at the time) and the First World War. It was a timely history lesson, echoing the first volume of 1864, with its list of potted dates. But something had changed. Previous wars had been conducted by professional troops in faraway places; news was slow to travel, so there was no such thing as a home front, and cricket was not greatly ruffled. In the age of the aerial bombardment – as *Wisden* would soon find out – this was no longer the case. By promoting cricket as British sangfroid in action ("Six days before Waterloo the Duke of Richmond was playing near Brussels") Altham echoed Wellington's dictum about the playing fields of Eton and bolstered the idea of the game as a central figure in the imperial project. He even recalled a visit to Lord's – "sandbags everywhere" – in order to doff his cap to the resolve he sensed. "It would take more than totalitarian war to put an end to cricket."

This 1940 *Wisden* had almost a full season of real cricket to describe, so was a substantial work. And if it felt odd, given the state of play in the wider world, to be reliving sporting ups and downs, it was perhaps appropriate that the most startling event of 1939 had been a surreal non-event. It took place in Durban and was a supposedly "timeless" Test, which was truncated by bad weather and a shipping schedule after ten batsman-friendly days. Hutton's triumph at The Oval had given England a taste for big scores, it seemed, but at Durban, when South Africa set England 696 to win, "few people imagined the team had a ghost of a chance of averting victory". Centuries from Gibb and Hammond, backed by a grand 219 from Bill Edrich, made victory seem certain until, with 42 needed (and five wickets standing) the "threatened downpour" arrived and washed away all hopes of a conclusion. As *Wisden* put it: "the England team had to catch the five minutes past eight train that night (Tuesday) from Durban in order to reach Cape Town in time to make the necessary arrangements for their departure on the *Athlone Castle* on Friday." There were "no limits to the possibilities of what may occur in cricket", but it was also a farce, since "insufficient time remained to finish the 'timeless' Test".

There was not, at this early stage, a long queue of wartime deaths to report, so the Obituaries section continued to pick out cricketers such as James Baker, "one of the best forcing batsmen Otago and New Zealand have produced", and William Wells, who "performed the hat-trick" for Northants against Notts in 1910. There were players of substance to honour, like Tom Hayward (44,000 runs for Surrey), but since they also serve who only stand and wait, there was space too for the county treasurer who "earned no special recognition on the pitch" but who used to take visiting teams on boat trips along the Manchester Ship Canal. In between came the usual gallimaufry of cricket-lovers: the Oxford Blue who "could not devote much time to county cricket owing to scholastic duties"; the Middlesex player who won £600 in winning bets at Newmarket by walking one mile, running another and riding a third on horseback, all in under 18 minutes; the Bristolian contemporary of Grace who "sheep-farmed extensively in Western Australia"; and the ecclesiastical architect (an Old Etonian batsman) who was "credited with the idea of placing candle holders on pianos".

In 1941 the promised paper shortage did kick in, halving the print run down to 4,000 and shrinking the book by a similar ratio, from 875 to 426 pages, and there were no portraits of Cricketers of the Year. *The Times* called it "very attenuated". It was also – as we have seen – very late. Robertson-Glasgow once more adopted a tone perhaps intended as courageous insouciance. "The military crisis wiped out several matches due to have been played at Lord's," he wrote, as if filing a complaint, while "enemy action has caused occasional disturbance on well-known cricket grounds". In a twist on *Wisden*'s earlier stance he was troubled by the fact that many professionals had left the Lancashire leagues – an inevitable development that "sadly diminished the gates". In the old days, the Burnley v Nelson match might have brought in £250, thanks to the presence of Constantine; in 1940 it raised only £14. Robertson-Glasgow, meanwhile, could not resist a sarcastic cavil at the quality of cricket in the leagues – "the crowd is better pleased, and so more likely to fill the hat, if a bowler can knock stumps out rather than merely knock them back … which is foreign to the temperament and the habit of the average county cricketer."

In his defence, he was hampered by the fact that there was no first-class cricket to report, but there were various scratch teams in frequent action – including a London County team chaired by Jack Hobbs, and a British Empire XI led by Sir Pelham Warner – whose games provided a stage on which the top players could perform. And though the Lancashire League might have suffered, the Yorkshire and Birmingham leagues were full of famous professionals. This might in itself have formed the basis for a major essay on Britain's ability to keep calm and carry on – indeed there were signs that the appetite for cricket remained strong: 15,000 watched a hybrid match between Kent/Surrey and Essex/Middlesex. Robertson-Glasgow contented himself with the thought that the teams were doing "major work for war charities". He was pleased to report, in passing, that Bradman had turned out for an Army School team in Adelaide and been bowled first ball ("we have not found that secret"). He was not keen to ruminate on the jarring fact that, even as the little ships were juddering their way back from Dunkirk, a British Empire XI was beating the London Fire Service at Lord's; but he was tickled by the notice on one south-coast ground, which responded to overnight bomb damage with a stoical message: "Local cricketers are as pleased as you. Each peardrop which fell on this ground saved lives and property. We shall carry on. Nothing which falls from the skies will deter us, except RAIN."

The newspapers rallied round. The *Observer* felt that "a better five shillings worth could not have arrived at a more timely moment", and the *Manchester Guardian* noted that there had been "complications" but found "much in it to enjoy". It added, cleverly, that the edition was bound to be of interest to collectors – "for its contents and its rarity". It did, however, frown on the schools editor for upbraiding a leg-spinner who "nearly always bowled long hops". There was a war on; worse things were happening at sea.*

The 1942 *Wisden* began with a rash of breast-beating. Like its predecessor it was published late (in August) in a still-small print run (5,000) and Whitaker apologised to readers unable to obtain copies the previous year. As always, he thanked "Mr Hubert and Mr Norman Preston" for their "kind help and wise advice"; it is clear that they were now the engine room of the Almanack. Even at this dismaying time, with the war going badly, they came up with an innovation, replacing Births and Deaths with a compact yet "full list" of all the international players since 1876.

---

* Some advertisers rallied round too. Edwards Ltd, who made cricket nets, continued to take space in the Almanack even though they were not actually allowed to manufacture them. "A net regret," ran their notice, alongside a picture of a cricket ball, "Government regulations prevent Edwards from supplying nets for this ..."

Once again the most notable games that year were got-up versions of the real thing. Perhaps the biggest, at Lord's, saw the Army take on the RAF, both sides bolstered by stars: Sergeant-Instructor D. Compton (Middlesex), Captain H. Verity (Yorkshire), Sergeant C. Washbrook (Lancashire) and Flight Lieutenant L. Ames (Kent).

This time Robertson-Glasgow found a fitting subject for his introductory words – the resilience of cricket. Recognising now that "it would be an error to rate our wartime cricket on technical values", he was happy simply to celebrate the fact that it existed at all. "It has been cricket without competition, a snack, not a meal," he wrote, but who cared? The game now served a much larger purpose: "It reminds us of what has been and what soon will be again." Not that he was about to let standards slip. One of the diverting by-products of wartime cricket was the blossoming of one-day cricket, an improvised response to wartime needs. Even the Varsity match was a one-day affair, a compromise so bracing that Cambridge produced a new, semi-blue cap (with white stripes) for the occasion. Robertson-Glasgow, borrowing *Wisden*'s haughtiest robes, could accept one-day cricket as a wartime necessity but denounced the idea that it had a future. It was "a new clockwork monkey in the nursery" which "waves its arms and waggles its head". It "delights for a few short hours" but had no lasting appeal. Real cricket, he insisted, was a "three-act play" not a "slapstick turn".

He must have thought he was being high-minded and outspoken; in fact he was merely repeating a *Wisden* formula that had been established over many decades. In this context, cricket was a rare art that needed protection against cruder, less patient impulses. A well-bred conviction that there were distinctions of class that must be upheld led him to see a man who wanted more adventurous cricket (and who knows, he might have been a frostbitten veteran of an Arctic convoy, or a burned pilot) in haughty terms, as a "senseless glutton" who "dislikes a finesse which he cannot understand" and would choke on his sleazy diet of slogs and sixes. This was a cousin of the attitude that to the Almanack's sorrow relegated S. F. Barnes, perhaps the greatest bowler the country had ever produced, to the margins of *Wisden*'s worldview. The new must not be allowed to displace the old; the young could not be allowed to unseat the old guard.

Perhaps that is why this edition also contained one of *Wisden*'s oddest entries: a full account of an imaginary birthday party. In June 1941 an

MCC team led by luminaries such as Pelham Warner, Gubby Allen and
R. E. S. Wyatt went north to Rugby (Warner as an Old Boy) to play
against the school on the "centenary" of "the Tom Brown match" – the
game made famous by Thomas Hughes's novel, where the great idea of
cricket as a character-forming crucible of Englishness had been born. This
was, it needs hardly be pointed out, the centenary of a match that had
never happened – a fictional game – but the players dutifully assembled
for a group photograph that appeared in the following year's Almanack.
At the bottom, after all the players had been named, a bracket informed
readers that there was one omission: "Absent from group: L. S. H.
Hingley (who arrived late after bombing German factories till 5 a.m.)."

It is nice to imagine the scene when he finally arrived. Hurry up,
Hingers old man, we're fielding! From the scorecard it seems that the
poor man did not bat or bowl; maybe he snoozed on the boundary.
MCC thrashed the school, bowling the boys out for 31, but it didn't
matter, because it wasn't a game ... it was an institution.

The fact that so many first-class players played in the leagues gave
Wisden a chance to give them more space, and it tried – but it went
against the grain. In 1942 it gave just eight pages to league cricket, even
though there were "39 men of county calibre" in the Bradford League
alone, 13 of them Test players. The public schools, on the other hand,
hogged 83 pages – this was still the arena that made *Wisden*'s heart beat
faster. In a way there was a logic to it, because for the next four years
the Obituaries were again swollen by young cricketers-in-arms, many
of whom (the officer class) had passed through these same schools. The
veneration was emotional and reflexive; a fondness for cricket exploits
merged with a reverence for Remembrance Day poetry.

Some of the casualties were first-rate players. Pilot Officer Kenneth
Farnes, who died in a plane crash, was a fast bowler for Cambridge,
then Essex and England – 17 wickets against Australia in 1938. Flight
Lieutenant Donald Walker, meanwhile, scored over a thousand runs
for Hampshire in 1939 and captained both Dorset and the RAF at
rugby. Pilot Officer Anthony Baerlein was a more than useful
wicketkeeper for Eton for three seasons – and a tennis player who won
the Amateur Championship 13 times. And Major Ronald Gerrard
headed the averages at Taunton School but also played wing three-
quarter 14 times for England, was a fives champion and "a first-class

rifle shot". Sub-Lt. Adams played five years for Bishop's Stortford and scored a ton against MCC in 1937 before dying at sea, while Lt. Col. Godfrey Bertram headed the Eton batting averages before being killed in Libya. One plane crash accounted for Squadron Leader Ashton, a triple Cambridge Blue, and Squadron Leader Winlaw, an Old Wykehamist who had played for the university twice.

There are waves of such men in these stark columns, pouring through the boarding houses of Aldenham, Hurstpierpoint, Harrow, Rugby, Repton, Lancing, Haileybury, Shrewsbury and many others, before climbing into uniform and heading off to die in some distant fray. Fallen cricketers of more routine pedigree were also mentioned. Montagu Bennett was capable of no more than "useful things with the ball" for Lincolnshire before being listed as "missing, believed drowned at sea"; while Gunner David Shaw, who fell in North Africa, was included out of family feeling: his chief connection to cricket was that he kept the first-class averages for the CRA. But on the whole the Almanack commemorated the well-born dead, honouring them above all for gallantry, as if each had been in death a self-effacing member of Dr Arnold's ideal XI. "Few could resist his handsome presence and charm of manner," ran one, while others "set a splendid example in the field ... possessed the ideal temperament ... an inspiring leader ... gave every indication of a successful career ... played racquets very well."

This was playing up, playing up and playing the game all right. "After skilfully leading his platoon," ran the obituary of one officer, "he personally put guns out of action and, though wounded, advanced alone to within a few feet of the enemy before being killed." Not for the first time, the dauntless character forged on a bumping pitch and in a blinding light was proving its mettle on the most epic field of all. And as always there were large stories hidden in the smallest print, sometimes even in parenthesis. The fact that the London schools were evacuated to tranquil areas of the countryside was registered by brackets detailing their new homes – a typically *Wisden* respect for minutiae. City of London went to Marlborough; Westminster went to Herefordshire; and Mill Hill to Cumberland. The Leys went to Pitlochry in Scotland, where they built a concrete cricket pitch on a golf course, while both King's Canterbury and Clifton (Bristol was also a target) went to Cornwall. *Wisden* tried to keep track of their abridged seasons, noting that St Paul's, bivouacked in Berkshire, were hampered by the "dislocated thumb" suffered by their captain.

The *Manchester Guardian* was enthusiastic, praising Robertson-Glasgow's assessment of Hammond and admiring Hubert Preston's history of the County Championship, which came with a detailed breakdown of the various changes to the scoring system since the 19th century. This was serious and original cricket history. The suspension of normal service had provided a space, and Preston had risen to the challenge.

The 1943 *Wisden* was again not published until August, and this time was more expensive. Robertson-Glasgow by now had his eye firmly in, and produced a forceful set of Notes, combining his usual easy manner with some stern opinion forming. While acknowledging that cricket chatter was "trivial in the face of the one great issue", he thought the time "ripe, indeed over-ripe" for a thorough consideration of the split between amateurs and professionals in English cricket. He called for "plain speaking and honest thinking ... the sweeping away of anachronisms and the exploding of humbug". It was his contention that both professionals and amateurs loved cricket and made it central to their livelihoods, and that both, if the world was honest, were paid to play it: "The only difference is that the professional's pay is direct, and the amateur's indirect." To distinguish between the two was no longer tenable. Those grand old amateurs who never asked for a shilling in expenses but offered themselves to the game purely for the joy of it ... "they are survivors of a lost society, of an age that is nearly gone." In summary he pressed for "the total deletion of all distinction between professional and amateur", not least because the consequences of the distinction were so silly: "To me at least such questions as the position of a cricketer's initials and the precise gate from which he is to enter the field have long seemed vastly absurd."

This was, as promised, clear thinking (the *Manchester Guardian* called it "a gust of life-giving fresh air") and it chimed with the most prominent obituary in the volume. Of course there were many deaths to record, mostly involving brave soldiers overseas, but none seemed so emblematic as the demise of Andy Ducat, who keeled over at Lord's while batting for the Surrey Home Guard. Ducat had been a high-profile professional, representing England at both cricket and football – he was also captain of Aston Villa when they won the FA Cup in 1920. A man of humble origins, he grew up in Brixton, joined Surrey as a youth and rose through the ranks to make 52 centuries for the First XI (including 306 against Oxford University back in 1919) and went on to spend five years as the cricket coach at Eton. No one could better have dramatised Robertson-Glasgow's point about the futility of the split between professional and amateur. He had batted against Australia in an Ashes Test and been manager of Fulham FC. He had spent time at the crease with Hobbs. Now, at the age of 56, he was gone. With his score on 29 he "expired directly after playing a stroke ... he was dead when carried to the pavilion". As a man he was invariably "gentle and kind, but strong and clear. Nothing showy, insincere, or envious came near his nature." His sudden death was, in a time of so much death, a "shock to countless friends and admirers".

As if determined not to look exclusively backwards, the 1943 *Wisden* also featured a report on the Advisory County Cricket Committee meeting in December 1942 (the first such gathering since the war began) in which the future of the game was debated. The end of the conflict was not yet in sight, but the "end of the beginning" had long since been declared – it was time to look forward and plan the post-war game. Many counties were keen to install a championship of two-day matches (as happened in 1919), on the grounds that the three-day cricket before the war had been high scoring but often tedious, and that the third day was financially weak. But two of cricket's "great men", Sir Stanley Jackson and Sir Pelham Warner, urged members to resist the lure of "brighter" cricket in terms borrowed from Sydney Pardon himself. Jackson was troubled by plans to alter the "very implements" of cricket – stumps – while Warner wanted cricket to remain "a leisurely, intricate game of skill ... I do not wish to see anything better than two fine batsmen opposed to two first-class bowlers, backed up by good fielding; the number of runs scored in an hour is unimportant". He referred to the Findlay Report, published in the 1938 *Wisden*, which was "splendid and so up to date". There could hardly have been a clearer reminder of the sense in which the Almanack, though not formally connected to MCC, was eager to stand alongside it to the extent of being its secretary or minute keeper.

In most ways the 1943 volume was an achievement: arresting and modest. It was a victory that it appeared at all. Yet there was another put-down in *The Times*, which repeated its charge that *Wisden* "bears the character of an illustrated magazine rather than of a book of reference". It was as if the newspaper had a grudge, as if Wilfrid Brookes himself had taken up residence there to fire barbs at his old home.

In his role as the publisher Haddon Whitaker announced, in the Preface to the 1944 edition, that "prices have had to be increased" (to six shillings and six for the limp edition; two shillings extra for the cloth) and apologised for the fact that the paper quota meant that once again "there will not be enough copies to go round". But as part of the restructuring he stepped down as editor and handed *Wisden* over to Hubert Preston, now aged 74 and who had worked on every edition of *Wisden* since 1896. Born in south London, Preston had been to a prep school overlooking The Oval, and then City of London School in Blackfriars. He began work as a journalist in the London office of the *Manchester Guardian* and "farmed for some time" in Canada (a sort of Victorian gap year) before joining the CRA, first as a reporter and then, in 1919, as a partner. A keen footballer, he played for Clapham Rovers and was a knowledgeable student of tactics; his articles for the *Manchester Guardian* dwelt at length on the difference between the "machine-like combination" of the professionals and the "long passes and rushes" of amateurs. He urged the best Corinthian teams to deploy their greater "brain power" by developing subtle combination play.

In his early days he wrote a number of reports on the great professional/amateur split that rocked football in the years before World War One, when the Old Boys teams formally withdrew from the Football Association. One article in particular, on the "Principles of Amateurism", revealed an attitude that would later inform his cricket writing too. The amateur, he believed, had a greater "zest for the game". He believed too in "the chivalry of Harrow's playing fields", with its "scrupulous fairness" on the field; he even voiced the fear that football had been annexed by people "possessed of very rudimentary ideas of sport". Arguing that Corinthian amateurs could happily go their own way, he failed to see how any "professional" match could be more keenly fought than "the glorious struggle between the Westminsters and Malvernians at Vincent Square". Such arguments seem dated now,

not least because it is hard even to imagine football – a game whose
players almost universally treat the referee as an opponent – being
played in the kind of spirit Preston wished to see upheld by cricket.
Like the Pardons, Caine and Southerton, his cricket sensibility had
been largely formed by Grace – indeed it could be said that it was partly
by moulding the mental furniture of at least seven *Wisden* editors (with
61 Almanacks between them) that Grace had imposed himself so
colossally into cricket's history. Preston played a bit himself, for
Brixton Wanderers, and also took part in the famous Press v Authors
match at Lord's in 1895 (a pleasant day out with writers such as Arthur
Conan Doyle and J. M. Barrie) during which Southerton took his
famous hat-trick. He knew the sporting ropes, in other words, and by
the time he became editor he was a journalist of wide experience. He
"did not hesitate to accept" the post, trusting that he had the support of
colleagues, including his own son Norman. *The Times* applauded his
arrival, thanking Whitaker for keeping the Almanack alive but happy
to report that "the august tradition of the Pardons" was back in its
rightful place.

Preston hit the ground running. His first Notes, "Cricket in Wartime",
were forceful – almost a rebuke to the more verbose Robertson-
Glasgow. In 1948 Robertson-Glasgow would write (not in *Wisden*) that
cricket was "not an imitation of, but a refreshment from, the worldly
struggle" – a pleasant but mild angle of attack. Preston begged to differ.
Rather than seeing cricket as a secret bat-and-ball hideaway, a diversion
from unhappy events, he tackled the notion of war head-on and urged
all clubs, even the smallest, to imitate the Lord's habit of hoisting the
flag over the pavilion every day. Suddenly, instead of seeing cricket as a
refuge, a playful escape, *Wisden* offered it as a patriotic, morale-boosting
contribution to the war effort. Cricket, it noted, had been encouraged
"in every way" by Ernest Bevin, Minister of Labour, and by the
adjutant-general. Far from being a truant pleasure, it was a sacred duty
– even a form of resistance. Borrowing from Altham's history of cricket
and war, printed in the 1940 edition, Preston recalled the Rev. Pycroft's
view that the efforts of Napoleon were insufficient to prevent "balls
from flying over the tented field". He mentioned a match played in
Stalag Luft in East Prussia, in which an Australian XI beat England by
three runs, "the last wicket falling to a wonderful catch off the last ball".

And he praised the war memorials in Yorkshire, Surrey and Kent, where cows could idle across the pitch as a bovine tribute to the game's bucolic roots. That, he thought, was the spirit.

It was a simple yet inspired gambit. At a stroke, *Wisden* was restoring cricket to its central place in English life while appointing itself as the game's spokesman. Perhaps *The Times* was right all along; perhaps Whitaker's *Wisden*, in allowing itself to adopt a mild sense of cricket as a heedless pastime, had rendered the game too dainty and marginal. At any rate, Preston was able to put the game back where it belonged simply by assuming, and acting, as if it meant something, as if it mattered.

Even the more whimsical moments in the 1944 *Wisden* seemed somewhat stiffened by this bracing approach. Sir Stanley Jackson contributed an essay on fast bowlers he had faced since 1893, which was a gentle potter down memory lane. But it did dispel one longstanding myth. It had long been said that a ball from Ernest Jones had once passed clean through W. G. Grace's beard; Jackson, who was batting with Grace at the time, denied it. How could he not? *Wisden* was a truthteller, not a mythmaker.

Another way in which *Wisden* seemed more sober was in its attitude to the game's financial facts. The 1945 edition carefully printed the breakdown of the charitable revenues raised at Lord's – some £11,557, allocated to various military funds and committees. It recorded the fact that 167,429 members of the public had bought tickets to watch cricket at Lord's in 1944, despite the "difficulties" caused by flying bombs, only a small decline from the 232,390 who paid their way in 1943. Altogether there were 41 matches at Lord's that year, including three school games, and so far as *Wisden* was concerned the cricket "gave enjoyment to all concerned". This was not soft-hearted cheerleading; in performing the secretarial function with such deference, the Almanack was cementing the idea of itself as a neutral, factual authority.

All of which allowed Preston to be unfazed by the absence of first-class cricket: he did not need Hutton centuries to feel that cricket was alive and kicking. One segment of his 1944 Notes was a reverie suggested by a trip to a Surrey village, Tilford, home of "the immortal William Beldham", whose nickname, "Silver Billy", now reminded Preston of how people used to call old Sydney Pardon "Lumpy". It was a "delightful age-old setting" where cricketers, on Sundays, still hit sixes over the road and where a hen might peck its way to the wicket. Beldham himself died in a cottage there at the age of 96, so this village green was a field of "hallowed memories".

This was whimsy with a purpose, reminding readers that cricket was more than a bit of fun on the side; it was a keen part of England's genetic inheritance and complexion. It was no great leap from here to move on to an RAF v Navy match in Iceland, since this too showed how easy it was for "the King of Games" to move into foreign fields, even frozen ones. Naturally it did not hurt that "those matches in a neutral country on a football stadium lent by the authorities at Reykjavik gave recreation to our fighting forces when free from duty for brief spells." Cricket was part of military training.

Once again, with the end of the war in sight, he gave added coverage to *Wisden*'s one-time foe – league cricket – since this was now the place where famous names could be glimpsed. Otherwise, in recalling the domestic season, it was a question of reliving what we would now call "champagne moments" – Leslie Compton plucking the ball out of the air with one hand while leaning on the pavilion rail, Gimblett diving to grab the ball in front of the sightscreen, or the last-gasp four with which United Hospitals beat the London Fire Force – a taut finish echoed when a British Empire team beat the RAF by one run thanks to a wicket off the final delivery. These victories clutched from the jaws of defeat reminded Preston, ransacking his own memory, of the Varsity match of 1870 or Fowler's in 1910, famous close shaves and allegories of Britain's wartime pride: "Truly a match is never lost until it is won!"

Wisden had found a stirring new voice. By the simple device of seeing cricket not as a bouncy contrast to the war but as one of its strident and patriotic tributaries, Preston gave the Almanack back a sense of its own importance. It no longer seemed out of place to debate the merits of winning the toss and saying "you bat first", or to insist on fast, well-rolled wickets, or on changes to the follow-on law. The odd schoolmasterly reminder of what was "not cricket" seemed just the thing. When in 1944 a flying bomb exploded 200 yards from Lord's during a match between a Lord's XI and the Schools, it was an excuse to notice that the break lasted only "a little over a minute" and that "the spectators, some of whom had thrown themselves flat under seats for protection, showed their appreciation of the boys' pluck with hearty hand claps".

He also urged a rule change concerning the way matches finished. As things stood, a match ended exactly when the time elapsed, so if a wicket fell within two minutes of the close the umpires would pull out the stumps on the grounds that there was no time for a new batsman to continue the innings. Preston was scornful: "Surely either side should be allowed the opportunity of victory until that last over is finished."

It was through opinionated arguments such as this that cricket had always evolved, after a hundred detours, amendments and debates. In a way it resembled the principles of English common law: progress was achieved not through sweeping or authoritarian movements, but by small incremental steps and a vigilant respect for precedent. In finding the confidence to reclaim this voice, Preston's *Wisden* was once again a forum for such discussions and a conservative lobbyist in the never-ending debate.

Given all this, it barely seemed an overstatement when the editor's Notes ended with a plea by the Bishop of Leicester: "Cricket will always have a stable place in this nation." Preston took charge of *Wisden* like a field marshal conducting a review, leaning forward to share a joke here or brush off a speck of dust there, adjusting a gun barrel by an inch or two and straightening the odd cap. It was a solid beginning.

Of course, he still had to produce a formidable Obituaries section. The 1944 edition paid tribute to Lieutenant Crawford Boult ("a fast bowler with a good action"), who was the fourth captain of Oxford to die in the war when he fell in combat in Tunisia. Colonel Victor Cazalet was a "determined player" for Eton who was also amateur squash champion four times before perishing in the plane crash that accounted for Poland's prime minister, General Sikorski. There were too many such brief lives to mention. Some tell of gifted sportsmen, such as Lieutenant Henry Cholmondely, who captained Harrow and, though he seldom bowled, once took four wickets for nine against Eton as well as dismissing Gubby Allen in an MCC game with what Patsy Hendren described as "one of the best catches I have ever seen". Another notable name from *Wisden*'s past was Flight Sergeant Lancelot Hingley, who had been late for the photograph at the Tom Brown centenary match at Rugby in 1942. A former captain of the school, he topped both the batting and the bowling averages, and scored three centuries, one of them against the RAF. Back in 1941 he had missed playing for a Lord's XI against the Public Schools,

John Wisden at the end of a long career as a professional purveyor of "fast and ripping" off-cutters.

The first Wisden emporium in New Coventry Street, London, where Victorian sporting enthusiasts could buy "brass-ferruled stumps" or a "treble whalebone handle bat". This 1862 price list had much the same design as the Almanack itself, two years later.

John Wisden (*seated, far left*) and his England team-mates crossing the Atlantic on the pioneering 1859 tour of America. Wisden himself remarked, in a patch of rough weather, that the ocean would benefit from "the immediate use of the heavy roller".

The Cranbourn Street shop, near Leicester Square, over which John Wisden himself would preside, "radiant with watch and chain".

21 Cranbourn Street today. Above a fast-food kiosk, the original tile-work of the Leicester Square underground station still carries a reminder of nineteenth-century cricket.

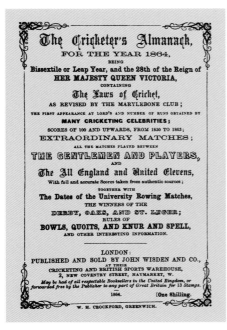

The first Almanack, in 1864, was hailed by *The Sporting Gazette* as "a neat, well got up, unpretending little affair".

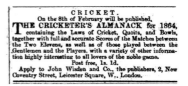

The birth of *Wisden* was announced quietly, in the columns of the *Bradford Observer*, on February 4, 1864.

Sydney Pardon, the father of the modern Almanack and "the soul of *Wisden*", according to Sir Pelham Warner.

A new annual accolade, the *Wisden* Cricketers of the Year, was introduced by Charles Pardon in 1889. The most famous cricketer of the day, WG Grace, would not be honoured until 1896.

The 1905 Australian tourists visiting the Wisden factory in 1905. John Wisden was providing sports equipment to all of Britain's far-flung empire.

Messr John Wisden & Co.

You are hereby appointed

Athletic Outfitters

to

The King.

Given under my hand and seal
at Buckingham Palace,
this first day of February 1911 in the
first year of His Majesty's Reign.

W. Carington

Keeper of His Majesty's Privy Purse.

In 1911 John Wisden & Co became the sports shop of kings when it was honoured with a royal warrant.

Haddon Whitaker, the publisher who became *Wisden*'s editor to shepherd the Almanack through the Second World War.

In 1938 the artist Eric Ravilious produced an antiquarian woodcut, based on this rough sketch. It immediately became the time-honoured emblem of *Wisden* (*below*).

On 29 December 1940, after heavy wartime bombing sparked the "second great fire of London", *Wisden*'s own records went up in the smoke above St Paul's.

Hubert Preston, who grew up watching WG Grace, took over the editor's chair in 1944, aged 74, and launched the second great *Wisden* dynasty. He worked on over 50 editions between 1896 and 1951.

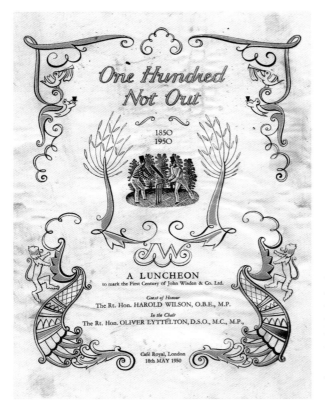

One Hundred Not Out

1850
1950

A LUNCHEON
to mark the First Century of John Wisden & Co. Ltd.

Guest of Honour
The Rt. Hon. HAROLD WILSON, O.B.E., M.P.

In the Chair
The Rt. Hon. OLIVER LYTTELTON, D.S.O., M.C., M.P.,

Café Royal, London
18th MAY 1950

Guests at the company's centenary dinner in 1950 could chew over both classical cuisine and a hundred years of cricket memories.

(*From the left*) Wisden's editor Norman Preston, a "cricketing Mr Pickwick", Learie Constantine and Ken Medlock in 1963. Preston is holding the new Wisden Trophy for England vs West Indies contests.

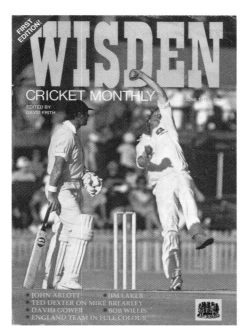

The first issue of the Wisden magazine launched in 1979.

In 1984, the 100th anniversary of John Wisden's death, a new commemorative stone was placed in London's Brompton Cemetery, where Charles Pardon had also been buried. William Gray (*on the left*) and David Frith look on.

"Cricketers are heroes to me." The philanthropist Paul Getty, who bought Wisden in 1993, watches a Lord's Test alongside Prime Minister John Major in 1994. Getty's Mound Stand box was fronted by a *Wisden* advertisement board.

Founts of *Wisden*: between them, the editors John Woodcock (*centre*), Matthew Engel (*left*) and Graeme Wright presided over 26 Almanacks.

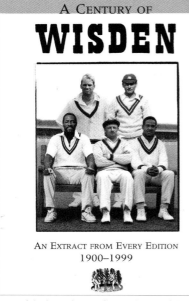

Five of the best: the *Wisden* Cricketers of the Century in a mock team picture on the cover of a book which accompanied the Millennium Edition.

The more it has changed, the more it has stayed the same: *Wisden* notches up its own 150 (not out) in the spring of 2013.

having been wounded in a bomber flight over Essen. Now, three years later, he was "missing ... presumed killed". Others were less athletic. Lt. Williward Clarke earned a posthumous Victoria Cross for his assault on an enemy position in North Africa, pressing on through his wounds before dying "gloriously" a few feet from the enemy. He was the fifth member of his family to win a VC, but the quality that got him into this distinguished company was more specific: in his day he had been a "useful bowler" for the Uppingham Second XI.

Once again the pages shiver with wasted life. The most famous cricketer among the fallen was Hedley Verity, the England and Yorkshire left-armer who died of wounds while a prisoner in Italy. Robertson-Glasgow wrote the obsequies, describing how Verity was captured after showing "rare courage" in pushing forward across a burning cornfield. There followed a survey of his career: nearly 2,000 wickets (ten in an innings twice, nine seven times) and seven title wins in his decade-long Yorkshire career. Without Verity's bowling, Robertson-Glasgow thought, Bradman's average would have been 150. Bradman himself supported this by contributing a signed statement (*Wisden* printed his signature) to the effect that Verity was "one of the greatest if not THE greatest left-arm bowlers of all time ... His life, his skill, his service, all merited the highest honour."

This was a proper *Wisden* burial, done with due ceremony. It chimed with Preston's attempt to make cricket a central ritual of English life – more than a game, indeed. And there was more in this vein. Maurice Turnbull, "such a grand person ... the best of his generation never to captain England", had been shot in the head by a sniper in France; while Archibald (A. C.) MacLaren, who "will always be remembered for his 424 for Lancashire against Somerset" (not to mention his patronage of Barnes) and had led various England teams overseas, died in more peaceful circumstances, at home. Flight Lieutenant Gerry Chalk, an Oxford captain, Kent batsman, DFC-winning rear gunner and Spitfire flight commander, had met a "tragic and uncertain" end after a year of being merely missing in action. The list, as before, went on and on.

The war had been more than hard on John Wisden & Co. The Tonbridge factory was requisitioned first by the Civil Defence Service, and then by the RAF. Although the new works in Penshurst was now up and running, there was very little trade. In the summer of 1943 the bankrupt company, John Wisden & Co, was bought by the Co-operative Wholesale Society, a nationwide retail chain based in Manchester. The transfer of shares was arranged by Percy Chaplin and his colleagues in London, and the Little Wonder's old sports shop had a new owner. Chaplin was invited to stay on as chairman and manager, a proposal to which he was "very pleased" to agree. He had spoken to Haddon Whitaker and was happy to report that Sporting Handbooks, which published *Wisden*, looked like showing a small net profit. The board meetings were now being held in Penshurst, but the mood was relatively upbeat: they spoke of the "enhanced prosperity" that lay in the future, and began to explore the possibility of expanding the West End "showroom" at Great Newport Street.

But on the night of 18 February 1944 another blow fell. The John Wisden & Co factory in Fitzgerald Road, Mortlake was hit by German bombs and entirely wrecked. There was no great discussion of the catastrophe, for it was hardly an isolated case. The chairman, Percy Chaplin, informed the board that the factory had been "destroyed by enemy action". There was no mention of any casualties; instead there was talk of entering a claim for loss to the War Damage Commission while the firm negotiated for temporary premises nearby. It was a major blow. This was where the famous bats were made, and where bowls were tested on the enormous Taylor-Rolph table. "No doubt the Cabinet was unmoved," wrote Major Altham, "but cricketers felt it as an almost personal outrage." It meant that the 1944 Almanack came out "despite the attentions of the enemy". The Almanack was not produced out of Mortlake – Preston was based at the CRA in Fleet Street – but it was still a calamity. The 1944 *Wisden* was almost ready when the factory was bombed. And though the tide had turned, there was still no sign of an end to all this.

The book had in any case been prepared with the resumption of cricket in mind. In the spring of 1945 it looked as though the game might be able to brush itself down and start again, and *Wisden* wanted to help. Citing the "disastrous" 5-0 defeat by Australia in 1921 (which had so upset Pardon) Preston urged cricket not to rush too fast into international contests; instead it should put the county championship back together in the right way. It was sound advice, and in delivering it Preston allowed himself a sip of the bubbly mood, exalting the "wonderful hold" the game still had on the public mind, even with "the menace of fly-bombs" buzzing overhead as he wrote.

It wasn't that he had anything against Anglo-Australian cricket. On the contrary, this 1945 Almanack began with a detailed tribute to it. Australia was depicted more or less as an extension or outcrop of the English cricket world. Perhaps this was why the Ashes were so intense; it was a fraternal wrangle, a civil war. The West Indies under Constantine were splendid, and South Africa were tough, but the rest of the world did not yet provide exacting opposition. *Wisden* was pleased to endorse the tribute to Lord's by Australia's prime minister, John Curtin, in London. "Lord's is to Australia what it is to this country … While we may argue about whether or not the game is played according to the rules, we most certainly decline to permit some intruder to decide what the rules should be. We are defending those 22 yards of turf, which we hope will be used time and time again." Preston couldn't have put it better himself.

It suited *Wisden* to be assured that cricket was still an English game, and that MCC was its rightful ruler. And it emboldened Preston to echo Robertson-Glasgow's dismissive attitude to one-day cricket. A few scratch games in wartime were all very well, but they could not be allowed to put down roots in the peacetime world. "A game of skill was being diverted into a vaudeville exhibition," he argued. "Though cricket must be entertaining, it can achieve that without sacrificing the dignity of craftsmanship." He rejoiced over the fact that there had been a "rout" of the "hustlers" who had been seeking to embrace the shorter, more boisterous form, calling it a "triumph of conservatism over the heresy that progress and speed are synonymous".

This was no mere pose; it was a heartfelt plea that cricket remain loyal to its past. Some of it was informed by a distaste for professional football. Though no aristocrat himself, Preston, like many *Wisden* writers, had absorbed cricket's class distinctions and found it natural to look down on less intricate games. He cherished it not just as a game, but as a part of the social scenery, part of life. So he also included an essay by Robertson-Glasgow called "Views and Values", which sought to restate the traditional charm and merit of the summer game. "Cricket reformers should be more honest about their aims," he said. "They talk much about improving cricket, but what they are really talking about is money ... They believe that one-day cricket would mean more spectators. I believe it would empty the grounds as surely as the rain."

Robertson-Glasgow went on to defend three-day cricket both as a sporting contest ("a thing of hope ... it gives time for recovery and surprise") and as a cultural milieu. "Without the three-evening match," he mused, "I should never have seen Yorkshire's Arthur Dolphin, with his rufous face set off by a whitish apron, selling fried flat-fish in the twilight, at a whacking profit, to the citizens of Taunton; I might never have listened to Sam Woods' nightly conversation on cricket and the world, compared with which all books that have ever been written on sport are like cocoa and hot water; I should never have asked Jack Hobbs how he felt on the Monday morning after sitting out the weekend with six runs wanted to equal W. G. Grace's 126 centuries, and he would never have answered by hooking my third ball to the boundary."

In the absence of any Cricketers of the Year Preston provided a detailed essay on the history of that feature – a nice instance of *Wisden* celebrating itself. We can hardly help noticing, in its 102 batsmen and 57 bowlers, signs of a preference for the gentleman batsmen over the burly labourers who pounded in on blistered feet.

Finally, E. M. Wellings, the Surrey all-rounder soon to become the *Evening News* correspondent, contributed an article on his own "return to cricket". Aside from airing what seemed long-held views on running between the wickets ("Another common fault is that of watching the ball and the fielder at the back of a batsman while he is running. The batsman's pace is inevitably reduced ..."), he too frowned with dismay at one-day cricket – a "sprint race" with "no lasting values". The quick-quick modern TV game had not even been born, but this was already a *Wisden* house whine.

The 1945 edition still did not include Births and Deaths – this would not return until the following year – but *The Times* still called it "a splendid volume in every respect". It hadn't taken Preston long to make his mark, and as *Wisden* moved into the post-war era Haddon Whitaker reported that sales were set to reach 7,000 again (double what they had been in the paperless days of the war) raising the real possibility of a profit and reassuring the board that keeping a skeletal *Wisden* going had been worthwhile. "You know," Sydney Pardon told the young Cardus when he was a new boy at Lord's, "Hubert is quite sensationally deaf." It was true: he carried a famous ear trumpet and to some his nickname was "Deafy".* But it didn't stop him becoming a father figure in the press box, just as his ancestors had been.

Things were looking up. And Denis Compton hadn't even taken his uniform off yet.

---

* E. W. Swanton confessed, in *Sort of a Cricket Person*, that he and a colleague would sometimes laugh at Preston's deafness. It sounds as though Preston did not see the funny side. He was, according to Swanton, "a sober chap of formal dress and rigid principles who struggled to combat acute deafness". They may not have been friends.

one hundred years of...

Ever since 1850 Wisden's have made cricket equipment. Their name has become famous throughout the world, wherever cricket is played.
And today, combining traditional craftsmanship with newly-invented processes, Wisden's maintain the reputation for perfection which began 100 years ago.

...WISDEN
CRICKET EQUIPMENT

Advertisement from Wisden *1950*

9

Father and Son

The 1946 edition was still ration-book skinny, thanks to limited paper, but the Preface hoped that it would be the last to be thus "curtailed". Preston's Notes were brightened, though, by the fact that the end of the European war the previous May had been celebrated with a series of impromptu "Victory matches" between scratch England and Australia teams. He made allowance for the fact that some of the participants had come "straight from the battlefields" and saw the games primarily as "a reunion". But once again he found a way to place cricket not on the fringe of historic events, let alone as a pleasant alternative to them, but as bound into their spine. It helped that the first of these three-day games came up with an exciting finish for the 17,000 spectators who pushed into Lord's: Australia struck the winning run off the fourth ball of the final over after an adventurous run chase full of the old cavalier spirit.

The world was coming back to life, and so was the game. In the 30 matches played at Lord's in the summer months (while Britain was voting Winston Churchill out of office) the average attendance was 8,000. Change was in the air. Australia were asking MCC to send a team south as soon as possible, while India, the West Indies and New Zealand were also putting teams "in the field". Of course, it struck *Wisden* as a fine thing that cricket should be playing its part in the tremendous process of demobilisation and disarmament: "the whole British Commonwealth of Nations became identified actively with cricket almost before the joyous shouts for peace, raised on the collapse of Japan, ceased to echo".

Enlarging on the cricket side of the story, Preston could not resist writing as if the Victory matches really were Ashes Tests – one player "had a beautiful square cut and hooked well"; another "gave promise of developing into a dependable all-rounder". He was most impressed by a young all-rounder, Flight Officer Keith Miller ("I firmly believe he is destined to become one of the great men of Australian cricket") and printed the averages as if they were first-class: Squadron Leader Bill Edrich made 331 at 47.28, just ahead of Flight Sergeant Cyril Washbrook, who scored 329 at an average of 47.

But though the teams were captained by famous names – Hammond and Hassett – this was not quite an Ashes battle: the sound of gunfire was still ringing in everyone's ears, and the presence of two prisoners of war in the Australian team made it hard to forget recent tragedies. Preston didn't try: he simply folded war into the game. "Despite spending nearly four years in a German prison camp after being shot down in a Maryland aircraft during the Libyan campaign," he wrote, "Williams soon found his form." Carmody, on the other hand, though "released by the Russians after one year in Germany, failed to produce the form he showed before his capture".

The matches were not wholly light-hearted. One member of the Australian Board of Control, Flight Lieutenant Keith Johnson, flew over to manage Hassett's team. He had never been to Britain before, but when he left he delivered an eloquent speech, which Preston quoted at length. "Many of our team have been in your country for many years, and all have been away from home a long time, but it is with feelings of regret that we are saying goodbye to a land where we have been received with so much kindness, hospitality, and co-operation. The matches of the 1945 season will always be a pleasant memory to us, and if we have in any way contributed to the rehabilitation of English cricket, then it was our honour and our pleasure."

He ended on an even warmer note. "You are putting your bats away here now, and in other parts of the world they are taking them out. The village greens of other countries are ringing with the joyous shouting of youth at play, for the grand game is always being played in some part of our Cricket empire. We look back with pride and pleasure to the grand country where the game was born and nurtured."

It is not hard to see why *Wisden* wished to frame this warm-hearted eulogy and put it on the wall: it suggested that cricket might yet come through the storm of war with its spirits intact. And they allowed Preston's Notes to adopt a tone, as far as possible, of business as usual.

In practice this meant a slightly stiff insistence on the letter of the law. *Wisden* had never liked the tendency of batsmen to pick up the ball and toss it to the bowler, and had mentioned it in previous editors' Notes. Now he was pleased to see a former England captain, G. O. Allen, given out for handling the ball in this way ("an obvious infringement of law 29") in a match at Lord's between South of England and Australian Services XI. Nor did he sympathise with the South African who made as if to pick up a ball and, even though he did not touch it, was given out. This was "a still stronger warning for a batsman always to leave the ball to the fieldsmen". Kicking the ball was "an equal or even greater offence", and Preston did not hesitate to cite even his game's bright new star, Keith Miller, as guilty of this "ugly gesture".

Since there was not a great deal more cricket to report, Preston gave further thought to cricket's finances which, paradoxically, had not been greatly harmed – the war had actually reduced county wage bills, while an impressive core of members continued to pay their subscriptions as part of the home-front spirit of rallying round. In admiring this stalwart attitude Preston did object, however, to the government's imposition of an "entertainment tax" on gate receipts, given that so many counties were having to find a way to replace their "blitzed pavilions". It seemed an especially flint-hearted policy since many of these matches were charitable fund-raisers: the £957 10s 10d lost to this tax through the Lord's "Victory" game was destined for good causes in any case (it still raised almost £2,000 for English and Australian service charities). But these were only minor blots on an essentially delightful view. Preston ended on a high note by describing a recent visit to Lord's, where the green turf glistened in the spring sunshine, the stands flashed brilliantly with new white paint, and the famous weathervane, Old Father Time, had been restored to his perch above the grandstand – "a resplendent golden figure looking down with benign expectancy". There were those, in the altered political climate that followed the war, who wanted to look to the future, not the past, but *Wisden* sought only to see cricket restored to its rightful place.

———

The new owner of John Wisden & Co, the Co-operative Wholesale Society (CWS), was soon expressing "satisfaction" with the way things were going. The defeat of Germany was releasing England's games-playing spirit once again, and business was returning to life. In February 1946 the CWS put an additional £50,000 at John Wisden & Co's disposal through the issue of new shares to themselves, the sole shareholder. The new capital was needed primarily to expand the premises at Penshurst in Kent and turn them into the John Wisden & Co head-quarters (the total cost of which would in the end come to more than £72,000). The board anticipated that the move from the temporary premises in Richmond would take place in June.

The Almanack was by now being produced by Sporting Handbooks under the terms of the coyright agreement with Whitaker's: Haddon Whitaker continued to preside over the Almanack, but he was soon joined by Tom Tatham, who would replace Sir Cuthbert Whitaker at the head of *Whitaker's Almanack* in 1950 and worked on *Wisden* as well. A keen MCC member and cricket-lover, he was hands-on – editing, reading over proofs and (according to his obituaries in 2002) preparing the Index too.

In the years to come Sporting Handbooks would become little more than the publishing equivalent of a brass plate, the name under which Whitaker's published *Wisden*. It was based in Whitaker's new offices at 13 Bedford Square, London and many years later, when Sporting Handbooks sent a representative to a *Wisden* lunch in 1971 it was none other than Tom Tatham, the long-serving editor of *Whitaker's Almanack*. In October 1946 it could report a net profit of £2,440. The half share of the profit flowing from *Wisden*, meanwhile, was only a token £148.

But the following year the Almanack regained its former bulk, printed 20,000 copies and earned £4,645. A slight delay in printing and binding, not to mention a spate of "heavy blizzards and a shortage of coal", meant the book came out late, but these were still "record figures". The sum accruing to John Wisden & Co from its profit share also improved, to £690. The arrangement cooked up before the war and under the shadow of receivership still suited Whitaker's rather well, since it could offset some of its overheads against the Almanack's fragile income. Still, the board was sufficiently impressed to toy, at least for a while, with the idea of a junior or "pocket" edition the following year, in time for the spring market. It would, they insisted, be "a forerunner to, but not in place of, the Almanack".

In the event this idea came to nothing. Hubert Preston did not have to stoop to gimmicks; the traditional format could serve very well. Even the "execrable weather" that spoiled the 1946 summer was not enough to dampen the editor's spirits: his 1947 Notes admired the "zest" shown by the players and the "splendid support" from the public, which produced record-breaking attendances up and down the country. He was even able to deploy *Wisden*'s historical weight to put the rain into context: "Was the weather worse than that in 1888?" he asked, recalling the year Charles Pardon had described as "detestable" and "indescribable". Could it truly match the "lamentable" summer of 1912? Even in meteorology, it seems, *Wisden* had the soul of an archivist.

It may have been this keen sense of the past that took Wisden to Lord's, at the end of July 1946, to see Clifton play Tonbridge. But it was the future that was on show that day. Tonbridge seemed to have unearthed a new star, and sure enough, when the 13-year-old Michael Colin Cowdrey (given his famous initials by a cricket-loving father) came in at No. 3, he went on to score 119 runs, almost half the 331 scored by his team. *Wisden* was restrained in its praise, observing merely that he was "reputed to be" the youngest player ever to appear at Lord's while conceding that he was "deadly" with his leg-spin, taking eight wickets in the match.

Preston's connection with the Almanack went back over half a century, so it was inevitable that his preferences were framed on traditional lines. And he was well-enough schooled in *Wisden*'s ways to assert them in the calm manner of a parent admonishing a wayward child. He opposed "freak declarations" – attempts to manipulate first innings scores in order to create a spectator-friendly run-chase – he preferred "real cricket", played out in the best way possible, and if that meant a draw, so be it. He also campaigned against "pad play" and "sitting on the splice" – ultra-defensive methods that he described, in familiar terms, as "contrary to the spirit of the game". He didn't like the fact that Australia persisted with eight-ball overs when the English game had settled on six, and he wanted the two countries to observe the same routines when it came to the rolling of pitches. In England they were automatically rolled before play each morning and between innings; in Australia they were not, which at times encouraged captains to bat on overnight, especially before a rest day, leaving the opposition to bat on a whole weekend's growth of grass.

Finally, he repeated his plea for an alteration in the close-of-play regulations, so that the last over would be completed no matter what. Eventually his argument prevailed; the law was amended, and Preston gave himself a pat on the back. "I first urged this in my notes in the 1944 edition of *Wisden*," he wrote, several years later, when the laws had been adjusted. "I may take some credit for bringing about this alteration."

On other matters *Wisden* was ignored, however. Preston had urged England not be too hasty in sending a team to Australia, but the lure of the Ashes was too tempting, and MCC did venture south in the winter of 1946. It was not a happy tour. Since it was still under way as the 1947 edition was receiving its finishing touches, Preston could do no more than mention that some of the old Ashes rancour had resurfaced in a series of spats about umpiring: Edrich had been given out lbw despite a snick loud enough to be heard at Lord's. "Desire for victory can be carried too far," he wrote, adding, with a hint of *I-told-you-so*: "I would sum up the situation in these words: This Test series has not recaptured the spirit of cricket."

The home series against India, on the other hand, had produced cricket of a far more pleasing and chivalrous sort. Tempers had not frayed even at The Oval, where the Indian tailenders, Sarwate and Banerjee, both scored centuries against Surrey to set up a bravura nine-wicket win over their astonished hosts. "They were not separated for three hours ten minutes," ran *Wisden*'s match report. "Never before in history had Nos. 10 and 11 in the batting order each scored a century in the same innings."

It was not just the handshakes and smiles that delighted *Wisden*. It was evident from games like this that cricket remained a stage on which wonders could be performed, fresh ground broken. Not that this led the Almanack to neglect the past. The wartime one-day games were echoed at The Oval when the King himself, along with 15,000 members of the public, attended a Surrey centenary match featuring many former stars, and *Wisden* revelled in the memories. The King joked with Percy Fender, Maurice Tate and Patsy Hendren, while Frank Woolley, at the age of 59, "drove with the same ease that had delighted crowds" in the good old days; Douglas Jardine appeared to be "as polished as ever" in his famous – or infamous – Harlequin cap.

It was not a coincidence that Preston published attendance figures even for a game like this. *Wisden* was by nature a faithful collator of facts, but from the beginning it had also been preoccupied with the game's fragile finances. There was rarely much to celebrate on this front, but these post-war years were unusual, and the summer of 1947, in particular, was a high point in the game's popularity. In his Notes Preston quoted Colonel Rowan Rait Kerr, the Secretary of MCC, who told a meeting of county secretaries that the involvement in recreational cricket was "computed to approach three millions". It meant the endearing notion of cricket as a form of social cohesion was not completely imaginary – and something similar was visible in the numbers passing through first-class turnstiles. More than a quarter of a million paid to watch Yorkshire, while nearly 200,000 watched Kent, an increase of almost a third on the 1946 total. County memberships were on the rise too, which made benefit matches for retiring or popular players increasingly lucrative. Bill Bowes raised over £8,000 – a semi-fortune in those still-austere days (bacon, sugar, eggs and butter were still rationed) and a similar sum was raised by a Hedley Verity memorial match. Long before Live Aid and Comic Relief, cricket was doing its bit to help its veterans – Herbert Sutcliffe raised £7,000 for England all-rounder Leonard Braund, who had lost both his legs, and Hampshire's C. P. Mead, who was blind. *Wisden* wrote it all down.

Preston, himself hard of hearing, dealt with matters such as this with the same care he gave to double-centuries or hat-tricks, and was happy to support the MCC proposal that a similar testimonial be arranged for Frank Chester (an umpire "regarded as the best") who made three hundreds for Worcestershire before losing an arm to gangrene following a shrapnel wound in Salonika in 1914. It was, said Preston in his 1948 Notes, "a catastrophe not only for his county but for his country". He also took the trouble to find a flattering reference in the 1914 *Wisden* to Chester's "high, easy action", which produced "plenty of spin". The following year he had the "pleasant" duty of announcing that Chester's testimonial had earned £3,200, more than quite a few players though not a match for the £12,200 pot scooped by Denis Compton. But in backing the appeal on Chester's behalf *Wisden* was not just standing up for umpires; it was echoing the military ideal of going back for your wounded, and implying that cricket too could inhabit this noble realm. And for neither the first time nor the last it was affirming its own special role as the guardian of cricket's past.

Preston reinforced this in *Wisden* 1949 by announcing the centenary of W. G. Grace's birth (a year late) with the air of someone attending a friend's birthday party. He quoted Sydney Pardon's eulogy on Grace's death, and agreed: "one may assert confidently that no one has risen to equal fame in the world of cricket ... he remains supreme". It helped that he had memories of his own to draw on. He had seen W. G. play at The Oval in 1884 (the year of John Wisden's death); had watched the "bearded giant" score 170 a couple of years later, and was actually introduced to the great man in the tent at Gravesend, when Grace scored 257. He could still see, in his mind's eye, how Grace "trotted from the dressing room in his tweed tail suit and his hard felt hat, carrying his heavy cricket bag to a four-wheeled cab".

This long memory also came in handy when Glamorgan won the Championship in 1948. Preston was able to recall the day, decades earlier, when he and his brother had been enjoying a knockabout game at The Oval and were told to clear the way for a proper match: Surrey v the Eighteen of Glamorgan. "From such a humble start, about seventy years ago, the Welsh county have become champions." By concentrating on a single, personal incident Preston was able to suggest a loftiness in *Wisden*'s purpose, a sense that nothing could escape its gaze. In his 1948 Notes he actually apologised for having failed to point out, in mentioning the appearance of five Surrey players in England colours, that Yorkshire had achieved the same feat back in 1938. This sort of grimace almost amounted to a boast: who but the most gracious giant would think to apologise for forgetting something only a superhuman memory might have recalled.

———

Preston was fortunate in that he had a pleasing resurgence in cricket's popularity to report; this was a vibrant moment not just in the English game but across the cricket world. No sooner were the post-war formalities over than cricket seemed to snap into life. If 1947 was the year of Compton and Edrich, 1948 was illuminated by the glories of Bradman's famous "Invincibles", and in 1950 the West Indies brought something new to the world. For almost the first time since the days of Fry and Ranji, there was barely a cloud in *Wisden*'s sky. The game it so treasured seemed reborn.

It wasn't easy to know what to say about what Preston called (in his 1948 Notes) the "marvellous doings of Compton and Edrich". The

Middlesex and England pair set so many new records that they "almost leave one bewildered". In that single summer Edrich scored 3,539 runs (at an average of over 80) while Compton went even better, piling up 3,816 (with 18 centuries) at an average of over 90. Both eased past the previous best-aggregate record, lifting their county to the Championship and England to a rare new realm. As luck would have it, the relaxation of paper rationing meant that *Wisden* could print 21,000 copies, a dramatic jump from the 8,000 published in 1945, and sell them all. Preston wrote that the season "bears favourable comparison with any year within living memory", adding that the Test match opponents, South Africa, gave "indications of real quality" without troubling either batsman for long. He left the more lyrical stuff to Robertson-Glasgow, who declared of Compton and Edrich that "they go together in English cricket as Gilbert and Sullivan go together in English opera". Not everyone loved Gilbert and Sullivan, perhaps, so Robertson-Glasgow added that they were "kings … champions in the fight against dullness". This was Robertson-Glasgow at his charming best. When some contemporary cricket maestro needed a fulsome "pen-portrait", he rose to the task with relish.

Compton "has the habit of batting", he wrote, "as the sun has the habit of journeying from east to west." He had genius "and, if he knows it, he doesn't care". His partner Edrich, on the other hand, had "started with a number of talents and has turned them into riches". They made a contrasting pair: "Compton is poetry; Edrich is prose". A gallery of other cricketers were sketched in similar terms. Lancashire's Eddie Paynter was "workman and artist invisibly blended", while Alec Bedser was a "giant" among bowlers: "We do not picture an England attack without him. Since 1946 he has been its spearhead and its stay, its start, middle and finish." Bradman was "a business cricketer. There was no style for style's sake. His aim was the making of runs, and he made them in staggering and ceaseless profusion." Robertson-Glasgow did not hide the fact that, however mighty the numbers, Bradman could chill the blood; but he graciously turned this into a compliment: "There are no funny stories about the Don," he wrote. "No one ever laughed about Bradman. He was no laughing matter."

Sentences like these confirmed that *Wisden* was not just a reference book, a vault of facts and figures. It was a literary construction too. This was not new – Pardon and Cardus both had lavish prose styles

– but the provision of memorable writing was an increasingly important part of the *Wisden* recipe; radio microphones and television cameras were beginning to take viewers into cricket grounds, changing the nature of the public's relationship with a book.[*] The Almanack needed to recognise that readers would have seen or heard about the games (especially international matches) for themselves: they needed more from *Wisden* than mere news; they needed lively eyewitness literature. As cricket became an international game the longstanding relationship with the CRA became more important than ever. The Almanack could not afford to send special correspondents around the world, but Preston, with both hats on, was able to send his "son and partner" Norman to Australia in the winter of 1946–7, even though he would not be able to publish his reports until the 1948 edition.

He was able to extend the Almanack's range closer to home as well, still responding to this sense that *Wisden* needed to offer something more than mere scores. Preparing the 1950 edition, he asked the broadcaster and writer John Arlott to review the year's cricket books. As the years passed this would grow into an authoritative annual survey that had the useful side effect of attracting publisher advertisements. At this early stage he was willing to inspect books of all types, from the memoirs of famous cricketers to slightly more specialised works: *The Official Souvenir Brochure of the Kenya-Asian Cricket Tour of South Africa* ("brief but valuable") or *A Short History of Camberley Cricket Club*. There was a sense, even here, that no contribution was too minor and that nothing could be allowed to escape *Wisden*'s steady gaze.

But, of course, *Wisden* could still be relied upon to narrate the game in greater detail than a casual observer could manage. It saw, for instance, that behind the headlines a Charterhouse schoolboy called Peter May was scoring 651 runs at an average of 81.37 (in a team that included the novelist Simon Raven and a "diligent scorer" called William Rees-Mogg), giving a premonition of great things to come. There was a sense of fun

---

[*] The first cricket broadcast in England was in 1927. Only weeks later Cardus was satirising the new rhetoric ("As I speak an aeroplane is flying over the field"). Pelham Warner was tried out as a commentator in the early days, but his voice was too "melancholy". John Arlott's famous tones would begin to pour over the airwaves in 1946.

in the obituaries: when K. E. Burn (for a while the "oldest living Test cricketer") was selected as a wicketkeeper for Australia's tour of England back in 1890, he was forced to admit when he joined the ship in Adelaide that he had, alas, "never kept wicket in his life". And there were dozens of close matches between counties, studded with remarkable individual feats and exciting finishes (two of them actually finished in ties). The 1947 season was played out beneath blue skies, in front of "ever-increasing multitudes". Honestly, what was there not to like?

In October 1947, in recognition of Denis Compton's unbelievable season, John Wisden & Co gave him a one-off reward of £100 – he was their poster-boy, after all. It was a nice gesture, and no less than he deserved. The most exciting batsman in the country (and after 1947 only Bradman could rival him as the best in the world) was representing the firm's bats – he was cheap at the price! But when Compton and his representatives began to talk about interest from "another manufacturer" and suggest that his annual fee (still only £50) be increased, the board dallied and opted out. The long-standing sense that professional demands should be regarded as a form of low-grade blackmail led the company to look cricket's most dashing gift horse in the mouth and shy away. Understandably, perhaps (the war years had not been the best time to be selling cricket bats) it was not common knowledge that the decisive element in sports sales was the calibre of the player who endorsed them.* John Wisden could not have wished

---

* Despite the agreement with John Wisden & Co, the bat in the Lord's Museum with which Compton scored his runs in 1947 is a Warsop's. According to Godfrey Evans, quoted in *Denis Compton: The Untold Stories* by Norman Giller (1997) there was an anecdote behind this. "It was crafted by the Middlesex batmaker Harry Warsop," he said. "But because Denis had a contract to play exclusively with a Wisden bat Harry replaced his logo with that of Wisden. But I can tell you that all Compo's runs in 1947 were made with a Warsop." Compton himself, however, gave a Wisden bat to the Great Newport Street museum with the note: "With this bat I scored 163 runs and also 208 in the First and Second Tests against South Africa in 1947." Even in 1947, it seems, there was sometimes more – or less – to the maker's name than met the eye.

for a hotter property than Compton, but he slipped away. His contract was due to expire at the end of May 1951, but the board "could not meet his demands".

Compton signed for Slazenger. For the want of a nail, the shoe, the horse, the battle and the war were all in jeopardy. In time the company would go on to discuss or sign deals with other players, but none in the same class as Compton. It was a strategic error, and, as if to rub it in, the same board meeting that declined to meet Compton's terms waved through a proposal to buy a new car for the Scottish salesman, a grey Wolseley 450 saloon, for £716. A lovely car, no doubt – but the company could have had the most dazzling cricketer in the land for the price of the wheels.

The bat he used to score 163 and 208 against South Africa was mounted in the Great Newport Street museum along with 169 other bats dating from 1750 onwards. One of Grace's was there, alongside the old blades used by Jessop, Ranji, Trumper, Worrell, Constantine and many others. Some had whalebone in the splice; others had cane in the handle. But it was still a sad day: Compton did not yet belong in a museum.

The full implications of his departure would not be clear for a while. And though, not surprisingly, Compton was not able to repeat his 1947 heroics in 1948, someone else could. The 1948 summer brought Bradman's Australians to England, and while it was no great surprise to see him on majestic form (that was no more than expected) no one was quite prepared for what happened. The summer took on a baggy green colour as Bradman's team went through the season unbeaten. For the first time, all five of *Wisden*'s Cricketers of the Year were Australian, and their captain (not in that number, having been anointed back in 1931) was rewarded instead with a knighthood ("a distinction never before awarded to a cricketer while still active in the game") and a trip to Balmoral to meet the King and Queen. There had been plenty of occasions in the past when an Ashes defeat such as this would have made England's cricket world (and its recording angel, the Almanack) tremble with shame, but on this occasion there was no ill-feeling. The relentless march of Bradman's "Invincibles" was like a royal progress, and the "lamentable lowering of England's colours" (as Preston put it in his Notes) was accepted with "the best humour possible". Australia themselves had suffered "rough treatment" in bygone days, and *Wisden* consoled itself by recalling some of them – in particular Hutton's great triumph at The Oval ten years earlier ("a display marked by perfect mastery in the stylish manner peculiar to himself").

Preston had always considered Victor Trumper the greatest of batsmen, and kept a large print of the famous photograph – showing the Australian striding down the wicket, bat raised high behind him – on his office wall. But he was now on good terms with an even mightier figure. When Don Bradman was awarded his knighthood Preston wrote congratulating him on the honour and hoping that it affirmed cricket's role as a bond between the two countries. Bradman agreed. "It is a great tribute to the importance which the Mother Country places upon the goodwill which can be engendered by international cricket," he replied, adding: "I trust that nothing will happen in the future to disturb this happy state of affairs." He did his best to maintain this by sending, in the heat of the Australian summer, a handwritten Christmas card ("All the Joys of the Christmas Season") to Preston's house in Bromley; the following year he sent his own goodwill message on the occasion of John Wisden & Co's centenary – few knew better than the Don the symbolic pleasure of notching up a hundred.

This centenary was celebrated in 1950, a hundred years after Wisden and Parr had set up as fledgling sports outfitters in Leamington, and the company was keen to celebrate the centenary of that first step with a pop. In truth it is possible that 1955 – a hundred years since John Wisden and Fred Lillywhite opened the shop in New Coventry Street – would have been a more appropriate anniversary; but this was a good promotional opportunity, and the new owners did not want to wait any longer than they had to.

The year began with a burst of optimism. For the second time in a decade the CWS invested new capital (in the form of 50,000 new shares to itself) and set in motion ambitious plans to expand the factory in Penshurst. Two months later there was a lavish centenary lunch, organised by the chairman, Percy Chaplin, at London's Café Royal, in Piccadilly, where Oscar Wilde used to hold witty court. The guests included cricketers such as Hobbs, Sutcliffe and Warner, but the master of ceremonies was an MP, the Rt Hon. Oliver Lyttelton. And though it was a noticeably cold day there was a warm message from Prime Minister Clement Attlee. "It is a great pleasure to see that your centenary finds cricket and its chronicler, *Wisden*, both flourishing as a national institution," he wrote. "I send you my very best congratulations in the confidence that this is not the last century you will score." Another political leader, Sir Robert Menzies of Australia, sent a friendly communiqué of his own ("I send greetings not only as Prime Minister but as one of your ardent readers").

The menu was a decorative affair, with the Ravilious illustration on the front cover and a four-page history of John Wisden and his famous book. Guests could tuck into the *Delice de Sole Waleska* while reading about the "set of brass-ferruled stumps" the company were selling in 1881; they could enjoy the *Blanc de Volaille Senateur* while pondering the "pliancy and driving power" of the famous Exceller bat, and boning up on the merger with Duke's between spoonfuls of *Poire Glace Melba*. Everyone was presented with a copy of a specially commissioned hardback, *A Wisden Century*, which contained a more detailed history of the company and its founder. A note on the menu promised that if bats were still being made in a hundred years, they would be made by Wisden's (a vain boast, as it turned out). No one could doubt, however, that of all the company's products, the Almanack was the star. The menu went on to suggest that John Wisden had surpassed himself in fame through his own publication: "The Little Wonder is forgotten in the greater wonder he created for the entertainment of the steadily growing number of cricketers all over England." It is often remarked that *Wisden* declines as a matter of principle ever to refer to itself as the good book, but this 1950 menu proudly boasted that it was "internationally recognised as The Cricketer's Bible". It went on to compare itself to *Who's Who*, *The Times* and the Bank of England as – what else? – not just a book but an "institution".

The guest of honour was Harold Wilson, President of the Board of Trade and a future prime minister. Despite having no cricket in his own background he was a Yorkshireman who had grown up with cricket in the air he breathed, and he gave a well-pitched speech, the highlight of which was an anecdote about a match behind the Iron Curtain on a trade visit. The game – in a woodland clearing – had only just begun, and Wilson was about to bowl, when two mounted Soviet riflemen rode their horses on to the "wicket" and tried to halt these "orgies and strange pirouettes". Wilson persuaded them, "after some negotiation", to drop back out of the way, and inevitably the ball was soon hoisted in their direction. Neither made the smallest attempt at the catch. "After that," Wilson smiled, "my opinion of the Russian secret service fell even lower." He ended by suggesting that this anecdote be logged by the Almanack as "the only case of a catch being missed at square leg by a member of the NKVD off an off-spinner by a visiting British minister." It duly was, in *Wisden* 1951.

A few weeks later the *Illustrated London News* borrowed this corny assumption that foreigners did not understand cricket when it reviewed the Almanack. "Looking through its expanded and gently exciting pages," it wrote, "one feels with Colonel Blimp, 'Gad, Sir! If only these confounded foreigners would learn to play cricket, our problems would be solved.'" After two world wars, and after Bradman, the idea that cricket was a peculiarly English pursuit still had traction.

The occasion was also marked by a match, held at Lewes, in John Wisden's own beloved Sussex hills, between a company team and a well-known literary eleven called The Invalids that included the poet-cricketer Edmund Blunden. The team had been formed originally from wounded veterans of the Great War – club badge: crossed crutches – and is held to have been the model for the archetypal gaggle of enthusiasts in A. G. Macdonell's *England, Their England*. The event was attended by the mayors of Brighton and Westminster, and Denis Compton sent a supportive message to the White Hart Hotel, Lewes, where the teams toasted "cricket and the Little Wonder". The Invalids' founder, Sir John Squire, said: "I do not mind admitting that I knew my Bible before I knew *Wisden*, but I knew *Wisden* before I knew Shakespeare." The word was out: the Almanack was a desert island book. The Invalids won the day, bowling the Wisden XI out for just 89, but a return match was arranged in Penshurst the following year, and this time the reference book turned the tables, winning a low-scoring encounter by 36 runs.

The Times marked the centenary with a leading article that swam with emotion. *Wisden* used to be "the best of Christmas presents", it wrote (a nice idea, though only older readers could recall the time when it appeared in time to be wrapped and placed under a tree) but then grew "fatter and fatter and later and later" until the present day, when it began to come in spring. The anonymous leader-writer was a keen but clear-headed fan: he knew there was more to the book than cricket data: "Statistics, stories, stories of matches long ago, and style, all are there, and in the long row of volumes the history of the game tells itself in a manner that has proved inimitable." He ended by reminding readers that 1950 was the centenary only of the company – the hundredth birthday of the book would be even more glorious. "Nineteen hundred and fifty is a good year for *Wisden*," it concluded. "1964 will be a better one." No one minded that he got the year wrong (the hundredth edition would come out in 1963).

Preston's Almanack enjoyed the fuss. His 1951 edition published a summary of the company's life by Lord de L'Isle that ended with the ringing claim: "*Wisden* and cricket are synonymous". It wasn't far from the truth.

———

The future, that summer, looked well aspected. In some ways the season of 1950 was a vintage one, and the 1951 Almanack was cheered by the sunny new dimension that the touring West Indies team seemed to have brought to the game. The three Ws were the headline act – Worrell ("for beauty of stroke no one in the history of the game can have excelled him"), Walcott ("a sheet anchor") and Weekes, with his five double-centuries – but there were also those two "little friends of mine", Ramadhin and Valentine. Before coming to England they had been "unknown in first-class cricket", but they bamboozled the domestic cricketers to the tune of 258 wickets in the 31-match tour.

But though all very splendid, this brought a subdued frown to the *Wisden* countenance. The weather had been unpleasant, and the "triumphant march" of the West Indies was hard to swallow for the average England supporter. *Wisden* felt that the national game was at a "low ebb" and found it hard to congratulate the touring side without gritting its teeth with an uncharacteristically patronising shudder: "Nothing can fathom the fact that the pupils visiting their teachers gained ten victories without having to bat a second time." Oxford bowled them out for 127, restoring at least a fragment of English pride, but against Cambridge the West Indies scored 730 runs for the loss of only three wickets. Was this a sign of the times? Could English cricket respond to this buccaneering new force? Given the geopolitical commotions juddering the old empire – the emergence of independent India and Pakistan, the founding of Israel, the first frost of the Cold War over Berlin – another question loomed in the background. Did the world have to change quite so fast?

The Almanack was correct to sense that this was part of a fundamental change in the hierarchy of world cricket. For a hundred years England had only rarely (and only with respect to Australia) needed to consider anyone else as a serious rival. And there were other changes on the horizon. Television coverage was still a novelty, but the cinema newsreels were starting to make their presence felt. In 1948 Preston had commented on the "remarkable film pictures" showing Ray Lindwall's back foot sliding or "dragging" past the crease at the stumps (the laws insisted that the bowler's back foot land behind the line, but some players were dragging their back foot across the line before delivering the ball with their front foot closer to the batsman). This was only the first tremor of the revolution in which the camera would have a better view than the umpire (whereas today the footage is on YouTube). The implications of *that* would take many years to become plain; for now, *Wisden* conceded merely that it was necessary to update the existing no-ball law. "If the law insisted that the front foot must be grounded between the two creases the trouble would be removed."

But the ground was shifting. The many-splendoured doings of Denis Compton and his friends could not last for ever, and *Wisden* knew it.

It didn't help that the sports equipment business was also floundering. By 1951 some of Wisden's football makers were being stood down, and their cricket ball-making was struggling in the face of stiff competition from Australia. Gray-Nicolls was close to winding up its ball-manufacturing altogether, and approached John Wisden to see if it might take over the Gray-Nicolls factory in Hildenborough, Kent. Wisden's declined, but did hire one of its young craftsmen in an attempt to rejuvenate its own ageing workforce.

Bolstered by the Co-operative Wholesale Society's backing, the company prepared, like a First World War general, for one more big push. The attempt to become a major producer of tennis balls had failed in the years before the war, but the new company was willing to give it another try. The Lawn Tennis Association (LTA) insisted that new balls must be manufactured at least in part by the company whose name they would carry, so once again a cumbersome arrangement was put in place whereby a partner (first Spencer, Moulton and Co in Bradford-on-Avon, and then Dunlop) would supply the rubber cores, leaving Wisden's to wrap them in its own-brand cloth. The enlarged factory in Kent was ready at last, but this was still a complicated venture. In a bizarre departure John Wisden & Co also started to manufacture toys and fireworks, products even its own salesmen knew little about. The manager in charge of the Penshurst factory was Harold Tipper, who had been with the company for years now (in 1922 he was given £15 as a wedding present), but who was still determined to make a success of the tennis-ball business. It would prove to be uphill work.

In the summer of 1951 the accounts for the year ending at the end of May showed a loss of £2,236; and there was an outstanding bill of £20,388 for work on the Penshurst factory. The CWS agreed to provide the funds, but in the autumn of 1951 the CWS encouraged Percy Chaplin to resign as managing director, though he remained in the chair. No successor was appointed: Harold Tipper was manager of the Kent factory, and the CWS saw no need for another senior executive. After many delays, tennis-ball production finally began in April 1952, and the all-important LTA approval came through two months later, but it was too late. In 1952 the company reported a net loss of £16,815, and worse was to come. Sales for July and August, important months for a firm specialising in summer games, were well down. As for the new product lines, firework sales amounted to less than a thousand pounds, and the revenue from toys was little better: £1,673. When the LTA turned about and refused authorisation for the 1953 tennis ball, at a time when the company was fighting a legal battle in Sweden to recover a relatively modest debt, it looked as though the ship was sinking all over again.

Chaplin launched a "complete review of the company's position". He wanted both "immediate economies" and "fundamental changes". Sales staff were sacked, and there was talk of putting the bat-makers on a three-day week. Cricket ball prices were cut by 5%, and Tipper was urged to rent part of the expensive new Penshurst premises to a bowling club; in the end they were leased to a plastics company.

Sales of the Almanack were affected, too. The post-war, Compton-inspired euphoria had produced a surge of affection for the old book.

The 1949 print run was 31,500, and in 1952 25,000 were sold within a week (for 12 shillings and sixpence). This produced a return to John Wisden & Co of only £523, however, and the following year the net profit sank again, to £85. By 1955 the print run had dipped to 26,500. This time the board reacted, but it no longer had the confidence to claw back its rights in the book; after long board-level discussions about a "revised" agreement it opted out altogether in 1957, selling its shareholding in Sporting Handbooks to Whitaker's for £3,329. On one level it was a logical move – the stake seemed of little benefit – but it was a significant surrender of control over the Almanack's fortunes. The new arrangement (under which Sporting Handbooks would publish *Wisden* under licence, earning John Wisden & Co a simple royalty) was pleasant enough in the short term – but Whitaker's was now the sole guiding hand. It was also given a strikingly generous guarantee that seven years' notice would be required to break the arrangement. If owning a national monument (under a copyright licence) was not enough, it now had an unusual degree of protection too. Given that the Almanack was within sight of its own centenary, and was by far the most prestigious product in the company portfolio, it was not the most confident state of affairs.

Hubert Preston's health was weakening – he was in his eighties, after all. In the summer of 1951 he informed the directors that he was retiring: a heroic 57-year association with *Wisden* was at an end. The board merely noted his retirement in passing: the painful saga of the tennis ball remained the dominant theme. No one saluted a career that went back to the Grace era, and the editorship passed, without much fuss, to the next in line, who was also the next of kin. But though Norman Preston's appointment did chime with *Wisden*'s taste for the dynastic, it was a natural succession. He had been working on the Almanack under his father's guidance since 1933, so he was no newcomer. He was a keen writer – the volume of Sir Walter Scott's poems he won as a history prize at school stood proudly on his shelf all his life. And he was a popular figure, a cricketing Mr Pickwick to his pals in the press box. No great player himself (though the clock he won as a schoolboy sprinter was a family heirloom), he maintained the *Wisden* affection for music: he was a keen singer round the piano both at home and on the ships that carried cricket teams overseas.

He was famously wobbly behind the wheel of a car, and could be quick-tempered when things went wrong; he didn't like it if someone cut the scores out of *The Times* before he got to them himself. At cricket matches he would by all accounts enjoy a decent lunch but be sure to return to the press box in time for the tea trolley, dictating letters "between bites of jam doughnut". He enjoyed a snooze in the afternoon. But according to those who worked with him he was a "lovely" man, bursting with pride in his father's legacy and devoted to the idea of *Wisden* as a form of holy writ.

The Preface to *Wisden* 1952, his first edition as editor, said that he was "sensible of the great responsibility" conferred by the editorship, and apologised for its length – it had "continually fought a losing battle against obesity" and was now consistently over a thousand pages long. Eager to get off the mark with a boundary by demonstrating his belief in adventurous cricket, he asked Neville Cardus and Colonel Rait Kerr, the retiring MCC Secretary, to rail against "slow play". The former claimed that "safety first can ruin cricket", adding that even a batsman as great as Hutton would profit from a bit more zip – he was "not certain in an innings of three hours not to bore us". Rait Kerr called for "more enterprise" and a "dynamic attitude", with teams aiming for victory "from the first ball". The problem was straightforward, he thought: in 1938 a quarter of county games ended in a draw; in 1951 it was almost half. There was a clear correlation with falling attendances: the gigantic post-war crowd had already begun to melt away. "Can the game in this country really survive the emphasis on security first and last?"

It did little to allay this sad observation that among the gifts Rait Kerr received when he retired from MCC in 1952 was "an antique bookcase to house his set of *Wisden*".

In the years ahead Preston wrestled with the Almanack's deadlines and began to deliver it earlier and earlier, pulling the publication date back from summer to spring. The 1958 edition came out on 27 April, the earliest it had managed since the end of the war. And he was fortunate in having a magical barrage of cricket to present.

In his debut edition, for instance, he could name England's brightest new star, Peter May, as a Cricketer of the Year. "Schoolboy prodigies do not always justify predictions," began the profile, but May, still at Cambridge, was "the most promising batting prospect of English post-war cricket". He was top of the first-class averages and had scored a century in the Leeds Test against South Africa (one of nine he made that summer) – not bad going for an undergraduate. In the Gentlemen v Players match of 1951 he even restored some amateur pride by scoring 119 not out to secure a rare win. It was almost like the old days: Preston was glad to be able to thank Charterhouse for instilling "the importance of concentration" in the youngster, though he could not resist giving a tip of his own: "his back lift is not as straight as the purists would wish".

That same year, Len Hutton made his hundredth hundred. Barrington, Cowdrey and Graveney were hovering in the wings. And in his 1953 Notes Preston could hail the arrival of a tough new fast bowler, Fred Trueman. In the years to come a number of other players rose through *Wisden*'s school lists: Ted Dexter at Radley, Micky Stewart at Alleyns, Raman Subba Row at Whitgift and M. J. K. Smith at Stamford.

There was history in the offing during this decade, too. At the end of 1951 the West Indies met Australia in Melbourne and produced one of the most stirring games ever played ("No more exciting finish could be imagined"). In the end a "gallant" last wicket stand of 38 allowed Australia to squeak home by one wicket – the definition of a close-run thing. When, five years later, back in England, Surrey's barely playable spin duo (Tony Lock and Jim Laker) each took ten wickets (against Kent and Australia respectively) no one suspected that it might be only a sign of greater things to come, but in the Test match at Old Trafford Laker went further, taking 19 Australian wickets – beating Barnes's 17 against South Africa – a sensational achievement that defied existing cricket logic. Leslie Smith reviewed the match for *Wisden* and did not forget, in honouring this "wonderful bowling ... it is doubtful whether he bowled more than six bad length balls", to pick out extraneous details as well. It was the first time that "lignum bails" had been tried, he noted, and they were "most successful, not once being blown off". The weather played its part, too, staying fine just long enough for Laker to complete his rout. That night the rain returned and the following day not a single ball was bowled in any of the county matches, allowing Smith to conclude with a powerful homily. "It can be seen how close was England's time margin, and how the greatest bowling feat of all time nearly did not happen."

This was *Wisden* at its most confident and relaxed, and there was plenty more to celebrate. But in spite of these highlights the early years of Preston's editorship were marked by a contradiction. Even with all this to enjoy – a successful England team, new characters on the scene and dramatic cricket all round the world – he felt himself to be looking at a gloomy and uncertain landscape. If those heady years after the war, when his father was editing the Almanack, had felt like the beginning of something marvellous, he now seemed to fear that they were, if anything, a flamboyant last gasp.

Perhaps his sense of foreboding was strengthened by the fact that the most vivid cricket was being played by foreign teams on the far side of the world. And there were other signs that this might be the case. In 1958 Garry Sobers struck his 365 against Pakistan, knocking Hutton into second place in the Test standings, and in 1959 Hanif Mohammad almost did the impossible before being run out for 499 (in a Quaid-e-Azam game against Bahawalpur – first-class though not quite the same as a Test match). New milestones were being reached, and new flags planted. But it was not Englishmen attaining these peaks (just as Everest, which London's newspapers were proud to celebrate as a British triumph, was conquered by a New Zealander and a Nepalese).

It all led Preston to brood unhappily on "the causes of listless cricket", and it did not help that attendances were falling "to an alarming degree". In 1954 he wrote, "a horrible new term has crept into cricket – Occupation of the Crease". He was acutely depressed by the negative ploy of safeguarding wickets before intervals ("even half-volleys and full tosses are treated with respect"), calculating that this produced nearly an hour of wasted cricket each day, at "the ideal time to punish tired bowlers". He commissioned one article called "Batsmen Must be Bold" (in 1955) and another by Lord Cobham (in 1956) that sighed: "I do not think people will follow cricket much longer unless the game is reborn." Could we not, he asked, "get rid of these awful bores who prod doubtfully at half-volleys and let every long-hop pass by".

Preston echoed these sentiments in his own Notes. "Complacency could certainly lead to disaster," he fretted, though "perhaps the West Indies will lead a revival in the art of batting". It was a constant refrain.

"Time and again over the past eight years," he wrote in 1959, "I have drawn attention to the decline of professional batsmanship." You had to read between the lines to notice that, somehow or other, England did not lose a single Test series between 1951 and 1958. A less anxious editor might have seen this as a golden age, what with May ("a born leader", wrote Preston in 1957) sweeping all before him and Compton still going strong (and still wearing, as Cardus put it, "the ironside breastplate as well as the cavalier plume"). But Preston seemed content merely to hope that, thanks to May, the amateur cause might yet not be lost. When Hutton became the first professional to lead England in 1952, *Wisden* supported the appointment, happy that history was being made – "in future no man will be picked as leader unless he is worth a place in the side". But Preston also touched on the old idea that a professional was likely to be too cautious. "He must be ready to snap up the golden opportunities and be fearless," he wrote. "I do not wish to see a repetition of his tactics at Lord's last summer."

This was a reference to Hutton's failure the previous season, when, faced with a target of only 77 to win in 80 minutes on the fourth day of the Test match, he dawdled his way to just 40, leaving the last rites to the following morning and depriving a restless crowd of a result. Preston had reported on that game himself, and called it "a pathetic display". Out in Barbados that winter, also under Hutton, England idled their way to just 128 runs in five hours, again causing spectators to "seethe with indignation".

When Hutton won the Ashes in 1953 and retained them in 1954–5 Preston threw his hat into the air. "Rarely has any series of matches produced such interesting and exciting cricket ... there were times when industry almost stood still." It was a "great triumph" and, as if that wasn't enough, a "great thing". But not the least of the pleasures was the fact that "two young amateurs" (Cowdrey and May) had "carried off the batting honours" and raised once more the hope that "the time may not be too far distant when England will have an amateur in charge again".

Was it really possible that, with cricket firing on all cylinders, *Wisden* was still impaled on the old amateur/professional dilemma? It seemed that it was. But it was an ambiguous matter, and Preston actually got himself into warm water with MCC by leaping to Hutton's defence in asserting, in 1955, that he had been "only a single vote" away from losing the captaincy. MCC denied this charge – in a letter to *The Times*, no less. The decision to keep him as captain, it declared, was "unanimous". Preston had to publish a blushing retraction the following year, in which he ruefully admitted that he had been "misinformed" and had indeed failed to "verify the facts" before going into print. He tried to save face by insisting that "at one stage" Hutton's selection as captain of the team was in the balance, but it was a jittery moment. For almost a century *Wisden* had been diplomacy itself with respect to MCC. Throughout that time, the divide between Gentlemen and Players hovered like a sarcastic star over the cricket world, and this accident revealed that it was still a raw subject.

It is possible that the sources of Preston's pessimism were broader. Britain might have won the war, but the effort seemed to have half-killed us: the country had barely begun to rebuild itself. The humiliation of Suez, the bewildering new popular culture, the shattered town centres and bombed-out remains of a grand past ... it didn't taste much like victory. And Preston was an all-round sports reporter whose national self-esteem took a blow when Hungary (even further off than the faraway country for which we had gone to war) exposed the myth of English soccer power at Wembley in 1953. And the Munich air disaster of 1958 just made sport seem cruel. The fact that England had a decent cricket team was not enough in itself to dispel the gloom.

In 1955, on the centenary of Sydney Pardon's birth, *The Times* printed a substantial front-page tribute praising the old editor as one of the great figures of his time. "His name is remembered with affection and gratitude wherever cricket is played," ran the article. He had made the Almanack something cricket lovers looked on "with awe"; it was everywhere recognised as "one of the most complete reference books ever placed on the market". We should not be surprised to find *The Times* so eager a friend. The publications had been connected since Pardon himself (and would remain so). In 1949 it welcomed the return of Births and Deaths ("always a valuable source"); on the centenary it remembered John Wisden as "the smallest fast bowler who ever made history";

and in 1951 it hailed "an essential volume". The two publications shared something of the same DNA as well. As the relentless publisher of legal proceedings and official reports, *The Times* knew what it was to be a paper of record. Thus in May 1956 it ran a major piece taking up the points aired in that year's Almanack, a sign that *Wisden* was not just following debates, but leading them.

The finances of the book were another matter. In 1955 the Almanack produced a net profit of only £639, and the company as a whole was losing its grip. Chaplin's attempt at an overhaul did not work: in 1953 the loss was £11,482, and in 1954 it was £8,412. It refused to come round. In 1957 the CWS, having asked Chaplin to stand down as managing director back in 1951, now asked him to stand down as chairman too. A CWS executive, R. G. Gosling, was installed in his place, and a dismayed Chaplin took the opportunity to remind the board that, while of course he accepted its wish to "re-organise and instil new blood", he felt harshly dealt with, having taken a "lively interest" in *Wisden*'s affairs for two decades. The centenary lunch in 1950 had fallen "almost entirely on me personally", and in a slightly peeved tone he expressed dismay at the Co-operative Society's failure to provide the pledged retail support. It was "common ground", he stated, that John Wisden needed another £30,000 of turnover to be viable, but most CWS outlets had not been interested in John Wisden products, while independent retailers were not happy to see their famous supplier giving discounts to a rival chain. Chaplin thanked his colleague Harold Tipper, head of the Penshurst factory, for his "sterling qualities and reliable work … shareholders past and present owe a lot to him". For his part, Gosling admitted that the CWS had indeed not been able to "provide additional turnover" in the way they had originally hoped.

Harold Tipper, who rarely addressed these meetings, loyally took the opportunity to air the same grievance, listing the lukewarm response his representatives encountered at CWS stores. Birmingham was "not buying … small sports department"; the Bolton manager was "away in London"; the York and Cambridge buyers were also absent, and at Royal Arsenal the store was "too busy to grant our travellers an interview". It was, he said, uphill work obtaining orders from these supposedly friendly outlets, and since he was also being shunned by *rivals* of the CWS, he was trapped.

None of this affected the Almanack directly, and Preston was sensibly left free to plough his own furrow. But having sold its own half-share in Sporting Handbooks to Whitaker's, John Wisden was now only what the minutes called a "copyright owner"; the famous old Almanack was no longer of any commercial significance to the company that created it. In 1955 it received royalties of £904, and though this rose to £1,380 in 1956 and £1,655 in 1957, it was now an arm's length franchise. The board seemed happy enough, however, and stated that the new arrangement was a "marked advantage".

In the years ahead, the royalties evaporated: sales were falling, and the price was rising. In 1956 24,000 copies were sold (at 15 shillings apiece), but there were a thousand unsold copies, so in 1957 a thousand fewer copies were sold for a shilling more. Carry on at that rate, and a surreal future beckoned in which *Wisden* would have been printed in an annual edition of just one copy for a rare-book auction. As it was, the book was still a major voice in the cricket world, with devoted readers all over the country.

Preston was certainly equal to the task of producing an authoritative record of the cricket year. As the game's senior pundit he took a detailed interest in its playing conditions, and he was pleased by the fact that in 1955 the counties would have finished in exactly the same order "if the number of matches won was the only factor taken into account". He disliked what he saw as the overcomplicated nature of the contemporary season, and berated captains for timewasting, for bowling wide of the leg stump and for slow over-rates – the usual suspects. He sneered at the decision to ban Sunday cricket – a move he saw as a sign that the game was being run by myopic managers on behalf of children and the retired, not the working population.

As he watched the ascent of the game in other parts of the world he opened *Wisden* up not just to new achievements, but to new voices. In 1952 Vijay Merchant, tracing the history of Indian cricket, voiced the inconvenient idea that "partition has deprived India of future fast bowlers". And Learie Constantine reversed the racial cliché by admitting that when West Indies first came to England "we could not tell one white man from another". When a Hobbs or a Tyldesley was dismissed it was as if the batsman marched off, turned round and came out again. "It was many years after," he wrote, "that I learnt that some English players shared the same thoughts and anguish about us."

Preston could smile, too, at the occasion when Bruce Pairaudeau kindly acted as a runner for two West Indian team-mates, only to find that both of them played rather well: he had to spend eight hours in the middle without facing a ball. *Wisden* still collected oddities and novelties of this sort. Cricket could still be a lucky-dip box.

In his first edition as editor, Norman Preston had returned to the subject that dogged *Wisden* in its early days: unfair bowling. In 1952, a new generation of bowlers stood in the dock and it was time to call a halt. He addressed the topic after Surrey's Tony Lock was accused of having a kink in his arm. Citing the arguments advanced by Sydney Pardon himself (readers were referred to the 1895, 1898 and 1899 editions) he condemned the practice all over again, calling for firm umpiring. In 1960 he commissioned a lengthy analysis of recent developments, written by Harold Gee, which hoped this might be the year when the endless row over "suspect actions" would finally be settled. In his 1961 Notes he recalled the bold work of James Phillips, who had no-balled Mold out of the game at the turn of the century. Indeed, he added, when going through the papers of his late father he had come across a pamphlet in which Phillips had spelt out his feeling that it was simply a question of there being "perceptible movement in the elbow joint" at the moment of delivery.

MCC had also been campaigning to check "throwing or jerking", and was urging umpires to take a firm line with transgressors, but by 1958 no bowlers had been hauled up, and MCC was reduced to repeating its call for action. Australia, meanwhile, was brooding on the same topic (diverted somewhat by a proposal to take the term "jerked" out of the laws) and had at last come up with a lucid definition of the problem – "A ball shall be deemed to have been thrown if immediately prior to the delivery of the ball the elbow is bent, with the wrist backward of the elbow, and the arm is then suddenly straightened." In the winter of 1959 MCC followed suit, distilling the Australian construction such that throwing was judged to be nothing more than "a sudden straightening of the bowling arm".

In his 1960 Notes Preston applauded the "legislators" for at least confronting the issue and seeking to define the rights and wrongs of it. "Never before," he stated, "had this been attempted." But while it was an important step forward, this was becoming a pernickety and frankly repetitive story. *Wisden* had, as Preston reminded his readers, been busy in this area for years – it didn't say much for its power that so little had been done. One of the obstacles, it had often been said, was the attitude of professional cricketers, who disliked the idea of ruining a fellow-player's career. In 1960 he printed a full-page photograph of Australia's Gordon Rorke (who was notorious in his four-Test career for "excessive dragging", and was at the centre of another bowling controversy when England toured Australia in 1958–9) above a caption that drew attention to "the elbow suspiciously bent". By today's relaxed standards it looks almost straight, but the following year Preston took a deep breath, referred to the previous summer as "the sad season", and carefully went through the whole business all over again.

There was nothing wrong with any of this. But it didn't feel – how to put it – very original. *Wisden* had been here many times; it was sounding like a stuck record. And one or two other aspects of the Almanack were also looking a touch congealed: the run of team photographs at the beginning, which recorded the previous year's best performing elevens, did nothing to suggest that cricket wasn't a stiff, formal pursuit. Back in 1950 Preston's own father had introduced spidery diagrams of county grounds to help radio listeners imagine the venues in greater detail; and in 1954 his son added passport photographs of top players beside the county badge. As a visual effect it was not quite awe-inspiring. Somehow, despite the excellence of the writing and record-keeping, *Wisden* was beginning to have the slightly crumpled air of an annual report.

The mood in the CRA offices remained buoyant. One member of the team would later remember it as a "wonderful, wonderful time".* High up in the fifth-floor office overlooking Fleet Street, waiting for the cricket scores to come in, the reporters would play improvised

---

* Norman Preston's secretary, Pat Voller. She joined as a 16-year-old and later married Michael Gee, whose father Harold was a regular *Wisden* contributor. The CRA, and by extension *Wisden* itself, was always a family-minded business.

games: cricket with a miniature bat ("probably signed by one of the touring teams") and a brown-paper ball – "four if it hit the far wall". Sometimes the ball would fly out the window and the youngest player would have to run down after it. There was also a slip-catching device made out of a stool and elastic bands.

It wasn't a party, however: the collection of data was methodical. The reporters would collate the scores, each day, keeping track by cutting them out of *The Times* the following morning. The growing file was kept by Leslie Smith, the senior reporter. If the odd mistake crept in it was usually a minor one. There were plenty of cricket-mad fusspots keen to point out errors, but they weren't always right. "The general feeling about *Wisden*," recalled Terry Cooper, a young reporter at the time, "was that it was the Bible."

But if the writers were cheerful, the CWS executives were frowning. The decline of the sports business behind the Almanack was inescapable. Home sales were weak and the overseas market was plummeting fast. It was like watching the depth meter spinning on a stricken submarine. In the year to September 1956, exports amounted to £8,121; by 1958 they were generating only £3,845. The net loss, in 1957, was £6,000, with no hint that it might improve. When the northern sales representative had a heart attack, it felt like a sign that the game was up. As the 1960s dawned, Harold Tipper wrote to the board suggesting in all honesty that he felt the company should be liquidated.

The sense that a great institution was being eclipsed was intensified when, around midnight on 8 August 1960, the editor's father, Hubert Preston, breathed his last in a Surrey hospital. In a memoir published the following year Cardus waxed lyrical about his former editor: "He was naturally a man of few words because of his deafness, but his sparkling eyes could talk ... He was loved as a man and a gentleman. And he was respected by his colleagues as a craftsman." Another ex-colleague remembered "HP" as a man who "wrote what he meant and meant what he wrote", while Jack Hobbs, no less (the two men shared a birthday) contributed the final word when he said that "players looked up to him as a genuine reporter who knew the game".

He left his beloved book in good hands, and good shape. But his death felt like an epitaph as well: after 110 years, John Wisden & Co was expiring.

Advertisement from Wisden 1964

10

Across the Boundary

Harold Tipper's suggestion that John Wisden & Co be liquidated was duly placed on the agenda for the next CWS board meeting in Balloon Street, Manchester (in the autumn of 1960) and was odds-on to be approved without objection, since it was clear that the business was failing. The CWS stores had not proved keen to stock John Wisden goods, recognising that cricketers preferred to buy from specialist outlets. Running a sports shop was still a conventional career path for retiring players: just like Wisden and Lillywhite a century earlier, players such as Jack Hobbs (in London) and Herbert Sutcliffe (in Leeds) were now running shops – much more fun for fathers and sons to try out bats in their venues rather than in some budget department store.

Fortunately, that CWS board meeting was interrupted by a new and dissenting voice. It belonged to Ken Medlock, a specialist in bottle packaging, meat refrigeration and other "non-food" aspects of the industry who had been chief engineer in Newcastle, but had now been invited to join the board (a promotion involving a salary cut – this was in the stolid days before the glitzy bonus culture). The day before the meeting he had been startled to see, buried near the end of the 200-page agenda for his first board meeting, the proposal to dissolve John Wisden & Co – an asset he did not, until that moment, even know the company owned.

As chance would have it he was a lifelong cricketer. In Newcastle he had played club matches with Colin Milburn's father ("big strapping man – typical miner") who brought his six-year-old son (a future England batsman) to games; and all his life he had played for Birch Vale CC on the edge of the Peak District, a lofted drive from the first slopes of the Pennine Way. He was the proud holder of a club batting record (an innings of 118, in the days when the local rules did not recognise sixes) and by now was club president, a position to which he would proudly cling for 60 years. He was a real cricket lover, in other words, and unlike his fellow directors ("it was just a sideline to them") he knew *Wisden*. And though he was the new boy he was quick to raise his voice. "I think we must be out of our minds," he said. "Don't you realise we are talking about liquidating the most famous name in cricket here?"

After a brief murmur of consternation he was invited to continue. He acknowledged that the sports goods company was not thriving, but stressed that the Almanack was part of cricket heritage, the last word on the national game. Something must be done.

The chairman suggested that the proposal to liquidate be set aside for the moment, and that young Mr Medlock be sent south to see how things stood. Medlock wasted no time. The following Thursday he climbed into his car and drove to Penshurst to meet Harold Tipper, and it didn't take long to see that the long-time Wisden manager had more or less given up. "He was deeply negative and dispirited," said Medlock. "Everything I suggested, he said 'Oh, we've tried that'. He couldn't see any way forward. After a while I asked if he could get the production manager to show me round – I didn't want him to take me, I knew he would be too down about it all."

The production manager turned out to be Harold's stepbrother John, and he was in for a surprise. He had no idea that Harold had actually proposed liquidation.

When they went into the factory itself it was Medlock's turn to be taken aback. The famous "Wisden" name did not square with this untidy workshop, where a row of distinctly aged men sat on tall stools hand-stitching cricket balls. It turned out that their average age was 73, and while this was partly a side effect of some obstinate trade union habits – a cricket ball involved many crafts, all vigilantly protected – it also suggested a horse-and-cart operation with its feet planted in the very distant past.

Medlock had seen enough. He returned to Harold Tipper's office and with some bluntness told him that there were going to be some changes at the top. "He protested a little bit. I think he thought the place couldn't run without him. But I said it wasn't running very well *with* him. Then I wrote him out a cheque for six months wages and said thank you. It felt harsh, but if anything I think he was relieved."

A few moments later he called in John Tipper, asked *him* to become the manager, and began to pick his brains. It turned out that Tipper knew Stuart Surridge, the ultra-successful captain of Surrey, who had won five consecutive Championships and who also ran a sports company. Medlock met him for dinner in a Tunbridge Wells hotel. "Cards on the table," he said. "We are doing badly. In fact we are on the brink of closing. Is there anything we can do to help each other?"

Surridge admitted that things were going badly for him too. Like John Wisden & Co he was losing ground to the Kookaburra ball, which was running the local manufacturers – half a dozen small companies all jostling for the same market – off their weary feet.

By the end of dinner it was clear to both men that the only sensible way forward was to join forces. Duke's had continued to trade in its own name even though it had long been owned by John Wisden & Co, and Surridge urged that they bring in the other Kent firms: Gray-Nicolls and Ives. John Wisden & Co detached its own ball-making arm and within weeks a new cricket-ball co-operative was created: Tonbridge Sports Industries. Each of the participants took a 25% share. It was housed in the factory once owned by Duke's, now by John Wisden & Co, on Chiddingstone Causeway, Penshurst, and it soon began to deliver balls on a greater economy of scale. Although the joint venture produced only one kind of ball, each of the partners wanted to retain their own brand name, so an identically made ball could appear under four different names. "It used to make us laugh," said Medlock. "You'd hear people talking about this or that one being better than the other. People would sometimes bring out boxes of balls and toss them up as if they were different. But they were all the same."

Medlock's next move was to scale back the John Wisden & Co range to a couple of core areas: cricket bats and – since the beautiful black *lignum vitae* stones crafted by Taylor-Rolph were still the market leader – bowls. Everything else – especially the long dalliance with tennis balls – was wound down.[*] In February 1961 the board confirmed the departure of Harold Tipper, and Medlock was sworn in as chairman.

---

[*] The Great Newport Street showroom also closed in 1961, ending more than a hundred years of Wisden retailing in central London.

The Almanack was the least of his worries. Initially Medlock was surprised that Whitaker's, which as sole owner of Sporting Handbooks was the publisher of *Wisden*, had not been a more energetic flag-waver for the Almanack, but when he met Haddon Whitaker he found him happy that the copyright holder looked set to have more purposeful ownership. In 1961 the company licensed Billings & Sons to produce facsimile reprints of the first 15 *Wisden* editions (1864–78) in a limited set of 150 copies – a sign that *Wisden* appreciated its own historic importance, and saw this not just as a pleasant fact, but as a commercial opportunity.

The vigorous post-war circulation had ebbed – down to an average of 21,000 – but the 1960 volume (published on 14 April) had at least generated £1,490 for the copyright holder. The following summer, Whitaker took the opportunity to share with Medlock his concern about sales of the 1961 edition. In recent times the John Wisden board had spent more time discussing the canteen arrangements in Penshurst than they had on the Almanack. There had been no attempt to promote it, and Whitaker saw the change of ownership as a chance to secure some extra backing. He asked that *Wisden* be treated as a trust and urged the board to do "everything possible to ensure its survival as the repository of the English cricket record". He hoped too that "early consideration" would be given to the 1963 book, which would be the hundredth. Medlock released £500 for publicity, and also agreed to a price rise; but what really got his attention was the Almanack's 100th edition. The most effective promoter of *Wisden* would be ... itself.

The 1961 edition achieved gross sales of £11,818 – £1,555 of which was paid as a royalty to John Wisden & Co; in 1962 an even smaller sum, £248, was forthcoming. Despite an improved sales figure, £12,165, there had been a sharp increase in the printing costs. All the talk about holding *Wisden* in trust was partly an argument by which Whitaker's hoped to enlist the full support of John Wisden & Co, which still had a strong vested interest in the book's success even though Whitaker's was the publisher. Haddon Whitaker even argued that the book was a "diminishing asset", and that his task was to hold off the rate of decline for as long as possible.

In one sense there was some truth in this. Television coverage was turning cricket-followers into viewers, not readers, and since one of *Wisden*'s historic advantages lay simply in the fact that it was there at the grounds, a privileged eyewitness, it was now rather vulnerable – its unique vantage point was being supplanted by all-seeing cameras. Worse, while a man sitting at Scarborough or Canterbury could do little more, in a dull patch of play, than turn to the crossword in his newpaper, the armchair cricket fan could switch channels, or turn it off altogether.

Medlock was determined to enjoy his new toy, however, and he could see that the Almanack, while no gold mine, was a unique and precious accessory. One day, in the press box at Lord's with Norman Preston, he met Learie Constantine, the West Indies all-rounder who was now High Commissioner for Trinidad. They shared a passion for Lancashire League cricket, and between them cooked up a neat idea – a centenary-inspired Wisden Trophy – to be awarded as a prize for the 1963 Test series between England and the West Indies (a Caribbean version of the Ashes).

Medlock wrote to Lord's and was at first rebuffed (MCC still saw itself as a gentleman's club, above such things), but after Constantine persuaded the West Indies Board of Control to support the idea, there was a change of heart. In November 1962 MCC agreed to the suggestion without any great discussion – it was more strenuously involved in detailed talks about the creation of a new one-day competition to be sponsored by Gillette. Medlock commissioned a silversmith in Birmingham to craft the trophy, which was topped by three figurines (of Wisden, Hobbs and Larwood – none of them, surprisingly, West Indian). The board noted that the project was a great "honour" since MCC had "in the past set their face against any commercial sponsorship".

At the end of the 1963 series Medlock and Constantine presented the trophy to Frank Worrell, captain of a victorious West Indies team that seemed to represent all that was buoyant and exciting about cricket (Preston was given a "suitably engraved" replica in recognition of his work on the centenary edition). Constantine was already a friend of *Wisden* – a Cricketer of the Year, in 1939, he had written for both the 1956 and 1957 editions. In truth, the West Indies had become the standard bearers for a more cavalier approach – a liberated colony was showing the Mother Country a thing or two about the game. Back in 1960 they had taken part in the famous tied game in Brisbane which *Wisden* itself described as the "greatest match ever played". Australia, needing seven to win off the final over, lost three dramatic wickets (two of them run-outs) to leave the match all square.

It was a triumph for positive cricket – both teams straining to win until the last ball; but it was also, in a small way, a victory for *Wisden*. In the old days, when the fall of a wicket would lead the umpires to pull out the stumps, since there was not time for a new batsman to walk out before close of play, the tie would not have been possible. Noting that the game "ended four minutes after the appointed time", *Wisden*'s reporter, E. M. Wellings, emphasised that "but for a recent law amendment" the entire drama would have been stillborn. He reminded readers of Hubert Preston's argument that the final over should always be completed even if it meant running into overtime. Now, he suggested, *Wisden* was vindicated by a finale that lasted nine heart-stopping minutes. "I was there," wrote Wellings. "I saw it all." It was a "Homeric" tussle, with "both sides set on winning or perishing in the attempt". He went on to urge that the lesson be taken to heart in England, where "tight, restrictive tactics" so often prevailed. Australia and the West Indies were offering a "new lead, which England can neglect to follow only at the risk of a great loss of prestige".

Norman Preston backed him up, asking Jack Fingleton, an Australian Test player turned journalist, to drum out the same message. "There is as much virtue in losing as in winning," wrote Fingleton, "if the game has been played honourably." The great leap forward, it seemed, was really a great leap back to the ancient ideals of the game.

———

By the time the Almanack's hundredth birthday came around *Wisden* was ready. Norman Preston said in his Preface that he hoped the 1963 edition would prove to be "the best ever", and he did his best to make it so. In addition to the customary material – the season summarised and collated, the Records and Laws, Cricketers of the Year, Notes and Obituaries – the book bristled with special features. There was a full-page image of the founder (John Wisden himself) and Neville Cardus was invited to select and describe the century's six "giants". He produced textured portraits of Hobbs ("the more his years increased, the more he harvested"), Trumper ("the embodiment of gallantry"), S. F. Barnes ("the unsmiling destroyer"), along with Grace, Bradman and Tom Richardson.

The new Wisden Trophy was pictured, and there was a history of the Almanack by Leslie Gutteridge. There were reports on a hundred years of school cricket, university cricket, county cricket and the international game, as well as a survey (by John Arlott) of cricket books in the *Wisden* century. It was a wide-ranging series that explored not just the game but also *Wisden* itself, and it found space – by reviving the Calendar – for eccentric details such as the fact that 1 August was the day, in 1737, when Essex beat London by "seven notches", that 20 May was the day when the first Australian team arrived in England in 1878, or that 4 December was the day, in 1948, when Denis Compton made a cracking 300 in three hours against Transvaal. Its 1,131 pages (a record) contained a barrage of memorable cameos including an article by the Australian Prime Minister Robert Menzies, confirmation that *Wisden* moved in elevated circles. And in his history of Test match cricket E. M. Wellings enjoyed pointing out that "there was no anxious wait for the first Test century ... the man who received the first ball, C. Bannerman [in 1877] scored it at the first attempt."

Preston, not always keen on the whimsical strain, even included a vision of cricket's future by John Solan, who scanned the tumbling attendances like a gardener watching frost form on his thermometer and wrote that "a county cricket ground used solely for cricket will soon be an insupportable luxury". Robertson-Glasgow, let off the leash to put his finger on "the joy of cricket", compared it to "eating *paté de fois gras* to the sound of trumpets" – a distinctly Glyndebourne-picnic idea of bliss. He also indulged himself with a fantasy in which he bowled Trumper for nought – a happier thought even than the actual fact that he once bowled Hobbs for a duck – "I didn't believe it at the time and, in spite of the printed word, I don't believe it yet."

It was an admirable collection of cricket writing. Preston's Notes, however, found it hard to maintain the party mood, for a very specific reason. The long fight to defend the position of the amateur at the head of cricket's affairs had come under renewed assault, and this time the line had given way. In November of 1962 the Advisory County Cricket Committee met at Lord's and voted (eleven against seven) to sweep away the distinction that had shaped English cricket for the whole of *Wisden*'s life. From now on there were no gentlemen, and no players – there were simply cricketers, and all would be paid. No longer would amateurs be given fake "jobs" in the back office at the county ground – a recent ruling had agreed that "any cricketer carrying out full-time administrative duties

with a county club should continue to be regarded as an amateur." Trevor
Bailey, the England all-rounder, was theoretically Essex's "Secretary" – a
position sufficiently undemanding to let him remain an amateur and
captain the county. That was all over; the modern game was here.

Wisden could not bring itself to cheer; if anything, the news was
ruining the birthday party. It was a "big surprise", Preston wrote in his
Notes, and a "strange" decision that ran counter to the MCC statement
in 1958 that "the distinctive status of the amateur cricketer was not
obsolete, was of great value to the game and should be preserved". In
the 1960 Almanack Preston applauded this decision; brooding on the
fact that even Yorkshire had now appointed a professional captain (J. V.
Wilson) he reminded readers of Lord Hawke's famous declaration of
1924 ("Pray God no professional will ever captain England") and
wondered what the old Eton and Cambridge man would have made of
the fact that this truly did seem "the twilight of the amateur". Much
was at risk, he felt. "English cricket cannot afford to lose" its distinctive
character. He concluded: "I would not like to see the amateur disappear",
though by this time there were of course plenty of cricketers unlikely
to applaud Hawke's sentiment.*

Just two years later, in 1962, the towel had been tossed into the ring,
and *Wisden* – perhaps stung that its support for the amateur cause had
not been heeded – was still not persuaded that it was the right way
forward. The reality of the situation was that English society really had
changed: there was no longer a large class of leisured blue-bloods with no
need to earn money and plenty of time for cricket. In many ways this was
a sign of progress and a cause for celebration, but Preston was plaintive.
"Is it wise to throw everything overboard?" he asked. "I do not believe
that cricket, as we know it today, would be such a popular attraction, or
so remunerative to the professional, without the contribution which Dr
Grace and his contemporaries made as amateurs. By doing away with the
amateur, cricket is in danger of losing the spirit of freedom and gaiety
which the best amateur players brought to the game."

---

* Hubert Preston himelf, in his obituary of Lord Hawke in the 1939 *Wisden*,
noted that, "he was more famous as captain and president than he ever was as
a batsman".

W. G. Grace was a surprising figure to cite as an example of the amateur spirit; his own infringements of the code were well known. We might notice too that *Wisden* had spent decades bemoaning the erosion of the qualities that Preston now saw as threatened; it was not as if the existing arrangement was working well. But he could not prevent himself from predicting that the new rule would have a "detrimental effect". Nor could he disguise the sorrow he felt at the passing of the old way. "We live in a changing world," he wrote, like a mourner at the funeral of a chum.

All years are years of change, of course, but retrospect allows us to see that 1963 really was unusual. It was the year of Martin Luther King's civil rights confrontations and the year of John Kennedy's *Ich bin ein Berliner* speech – not to mention his assassination. It was the year the Vietnam War began to escalate, the year Charles de Gaulle shocked Britain by countering its request to join the Common Market with a thunderous "Non!", the year of the Aldermaston march against nuclear bombs, the year Kim Philby became an asylum-seeker in Moscow and the year Kenya gained independence from Britain. Betty Friedan's *The Feminine Mystique* was published, igniting a wave of egalitarian energy in Western women, and this was also, famously, the year of the Beatles' first LP (and their second, come to that). In 1963 Dr Beeching began to close Britain's railway network, and children squirmed in front of the inaugural episode of *Dr Who*. Newspaper readers could gasp at the Profumo affair, the Great Train Robbery and dolly birds in miniskirts. It was, more or less, the launch party of the swinging sixties: traditions were cast aside like old-fashioned collars, and Austerity Britain was quite forgotten. Life was a party.

The final dissolution of the distinction between amateur and professional in English cricket might seem, in this context, small beer. But the game was being swayed by the same "winds of change" that were blowing through every other aspect of life, and every other part of the world. The ancient gap between the chivalrous amateur and the skilled yet dour professional no longer made sense; the only wonder is that it took so long to bridge it. As we know, *Wisden* itself had roots in the professional jamborees of mid-Victorian England. But these had long withered, and it had been in a tacit huddle with MCC for decades by now. Though independent, its heart was with the establishment, and it felt threatened. Having said which, before we agree that cricket must have been a hidebound sport run by unworldly greybeards in St John's Wood, we need to remember that another sport, tennis, would not permit professionals (such as the Australians Rod Laver and Ken Rosewall) in Grand Slam events for five years yet, and that the division in rugby would survive for three more decades.

This long love affair with the distinction between amateur and professional may seem merely an administrative matter, or a trivial and anachronistic preference. But the class divide perpetuated by English cricket had been a powerful cultural fact for the entire *Wisden* century. The Almanack had absorbed England's class predilections and then disseminated them, in an innocent-seeming form, as an essential part of the way the game was played. In so doing, it laid down a paradigm or template for many other related dichotomies, in ways that were at once subtle and far-reaching.

Sport is escapist, but it is also embedded in our instincts – baby animals play games without hesitation or encouragement. Cricket in particular evolved in accordance with, and as a response to, the needs, fears, hopes and dreams of the place in which it first took root (which is why its language has rustic echoes). But even by the time of the first *Wisden* this bucolic mindset, along with cock-baiting and prize-fighting, was giving way to a more metropolitan psychology, and cricket was absorbing a fresh top-dressing of conservative ideology – not least to secure the patronage it needed. In the subsequent years, as we have seen, a set of very precise assumptions had threaded their way into the fabric of the game. The fundamental contest between bat and ball, which came to seem a negotiation rather than a dispute, a *pas-de-deux* rather than a duel, was expressed through a range of other distinctions. Since batting was the preferred field of the well-born amateur, bowling became the "province" of the professional. This division was then echoed in the annual joust between Gentlemen and Players.

In this way the realities of class difference first reflected the outside world, and then informed it. A gap opened up between "first-class" cricket and "inferior" forms. In two world wars the division between Gentleman and Player was echoed in the gap between officers and rank-and-file, while the same up-down hierarchy coloured the rivalry between north and south, or between England and Australia. In each case the established elite was attempting (and often failing) to put an upstart rival in its place. Sport being sport, the senior body did not always prevail, but as the years passed, this range of tussles came to resemble shadowy boxers, circling one another in a calm green field as they sparred for supremacy. And there, in a ringside seat, was *Wisden*.

It could hardly have been more appropriate. *Wisden* had begun life as a chronicle of professional cricket before turning into a standard-bearer for the amateur code. The crackle of energy between these two poles had shaped the book's long life. Now, on its hundredth birthday, the old dream of a union between the two was coming true.

The team that put the 1963 Almanack together (all professional journalists) were invited to a grand hundredth edition dinner on 14 January in Piccadilly. The menu called it "The Pardon dinner", and it was a feast: *Crème d'Asperges, Truite de Rivière Meunière* and *Contrefilet de Boeuf,* washed down with a nice Gevrey-Chambertin.

Leslie Smith, the senior pro, asked that the staff be also given the afternoon off, and the CRA agreed; so it was a leisurely occasion. Everyone signed the menu and the men were given a special, limited edition *Wisden* tie, with a radiant little silhouette of the Little Wonder himself stitched on to the midnight-blue background.

With the backing of the £500 budget provided by Medlock, a publicity firm called Everetts was engaged to promote the edition, and it helped. An initial run of 24,000 copies were printed; by July they had sold out and two reprints followed, leading to a record sale that earned the firm "considerable prestige". "The newspapers, television and sound radio were lavish in their praise," wrote Preston the following year. The corporate image was boosted further by the televised contest for the new Wisden Trophy, a gripping series whose highlight came at Lord's, where England achieved a draw thanks to the poignant courage of Colin Cowdrey, who shuffled to the wicket in the final over with a broken arm. In the event he was not required to face a single ball, but it was an act of decorous, *Boy's Own* courage, a symbolic gesture in keeping with England's post-war image of itself. "He intended," *Wisden* wrote, "to turn round and bat left-handed to protect his left arm." This was heroism; this was cricket.

The royalty that came back to John Wisden & Co from the 1963 book sales was shrunk by the decision to set the costs of the trophy, including the provision of miniature replicas for each player, against the proceeds from the book; this amounted to more than £1,300, and ate up most of the additional revenue. But the following year 25,000 copies were printed and distributed, and though Wisden's royalty was again modest, it did seem that the book had found its audience again. More to the point, *Wisden* had managed to attach its name to one of the great new rivalries in cricket. Until this time, the Ashes were by far the dominant duel in the world game, but the Wisden Trophy was a formal recognition that cricket had expanded, and in an explosive Caribbean form. The West Indies played the game with an exhilarating and refreshing quality of flair, vigour and pride. In Sobers they had a man who could fill stadiums on his own. No one knew that before long they would be as invincible and charismatic as Bradman's Australians; at this stage it was enough that cricket had new character.

It seemed to jolt the general mood, even in England's domestic cricket. In the year of the centenary an equally remarkable match took place at Old Trafford, where Jim Laker had taken all those Australian wickets not so long ago. Lancashire played Leicestershire in the first game of a brand new knockout competition to be sponsored by the Gillette Razor Company. The Wisden Trophy was not alone in breaking down the taboo against commercial sponsorship: cricket's new patron was a shaving conglomerate. From MCC's point of view it was as momentous a change as the dissolution of the amateur, but the game's wallet was empty; the post-war crowd had melted away into a social lifestyle based around television, and the old networks of patronage were growing weaker. The Gillette Cup (the name it acquired in its second year) was designed to lure people back, and it worked: crowds streamed through the turnstiles. A success in itself, it also paved the way for the introduction, in 1969, of a new 40-over Sunday League (sponsored by the cigarette firm, John Player). Between them these competitions inspired a fresh audience of couch potatoes (many of them young!) and even if the attendance at three-day cricket continued to dwindle, county cricketers were once more household names. The one-day fiestas seemed to produce exciting finishes of a sort the longer version of the game inspired all too seldom.

Wisden did not fire many rockets for the new competition, though Preston's 1964 Notes admitted that the year was "notable" for the "successful introduction" of the new format. The brief match review was relieved to report that Lancashire batted "without undue recklessness" and that the "steady medium pace" of Marner (along with 121 runs) was enough to clinch "a gold medal as Man of the Match" – a concept that at one time would have been deemed not quite the done thing. *Wisden* did not foresee (how could it?) that one of Leicestershire's opening batsmen, H. D. Bird, looked to be better suited to umpiring than to facing Brian Statham. Nor did it mention the irony by which this, the groundbreaking start of one-day cricket in England, actually ran into the second day thanks to rain on the first morning. But though it threw no tickertape over the new game, it was on hand to record the first expressions of this game-changing new format. One-day cricket was clearly not so refined and elevated a brand of the game as three-day or five-day cricket; it was a compressed, party-sized adaptation of the real thing. But it chimed with the public, not least because this was the only length of the game that most people – at school, in villages or for clubs – had actually played. *Wisden* did not erupt with applause, but neither was it scornful. It looked on with interest. And several years later (in 1971) it could only gasp when Lancashire somehow beat Gloucestershire after an improbable Gillette Cup semi-final run-chase led by the tailender David Hughes, who hit 24 off the 56th over in near darkness. It was not quite cricket as *Wisden* knew it ... but it was certainly something: "It was well past ten o'clock before the big crowd dispersed."

Buried in the small print of the book, meanwhile, less glamorous deeds were being carefully set down, as always. A notice in the 1965 *Wisden*, for example, described one of the most modest careers ever enjoyed by a cricketer. Frederick Hyland played once (as a professional) for Hampshire in 1924. As chance would have it the game – away against Northants – was washed out by rain after only two overs, during which the home side batted and made one run. Yet this, it turned out, was the summit of his cricket life – he was never selected again, and retired to Cheshire where he became a nursery gardener. It is nice to imagine him, trembling with nervous pride having been selected (he was 29), fielding for those two damp overs. Perhaps he was even at fault for the single – a wet ball that slid through cold hands, a red-faced curse, a mumbled apology ... anything that would make a more telling anecdote than failing to do a single thing of note. But then it was back to the pavilion and the oblivion from which he had sprung. Who knows: with a bit more luck he might have clung on to a snorting catch, been picked to play the following week, cobbled together a brave half-century on a bad wicket in Southampton, and been a first-class player for years. As it was, he had this one miniature heyday with which to console himself when frost laid siege to his camellias – a ten-minute career in which he made no impact whatsoever.

And here is the funny part: by playing just once, and so briefly, he achieved more than most cricket-lovers manage in their dreams.

———

One of the features of the Almanack during these years was John Arlott's annual book review. He had been writing this since 1950, so his centenary-edition *tour d'horizon* in 1963, "Literature in the *Wisden* century", was a natural extension of his regular column. Since there were usually around 60 books to consider, he had read almost a thousand by now, and though he rarely said an unkind word about any of them (to an extent that it seemed a rather uncritical survey) he was beginning to grow word-weary. Back in 1949, he noted, there might have been half a dozen "substantial books" in a year's crop; these days there was often only one. The rest was a pile of "star" autobiographies of only passing interest.

He inspected them with care, however, applauding the sheer size of the cricket library, which he put at 8,000 volumes, adding that "no other game can remotely approach that figure".* Whatever the reasons, *Wisden* was both a cause and a symptom: Arlott's annual review attracted publishing advertisements while the man himself pored over endless histories, biographies, statistical and reference works, descriptive musings, memoirs,

---

* It has often been said that cricket is unusually productive of literature – *Wisden* itself grew from an enthusiastic union of sport and books. Many reasons have been suggested: it is a long, subtle game, with individual and team aspects, a high degree of technical skill and plenty of time for conversation, which makes it susceptible to slow analysis and discussion. More important, perhaps, is the social milieu it inhabits – it is the game of the book-reading class, which inevitably enjoys reading about … itself.

tour diaries, how-to manuals – even some fiction and poetry. He did not even flinch when faced by '*Studien zum Verbum in Englischen Fachsprachen* (Cricket)', a 517-page PhD thesis by a Linguistics graduate at the University of Erlangen. He admitted that "it was not within the province or capacity of this notice to pronounce judgement" but was happy to confirm that it was "wide-ranging" and "meticulous", and that "the phraseology of a single sport has never before been examined on such a scale". It was, at least, "an immense compliment to the game".

Otherwise he was both patient and loyal. In 1962 he praised the Billings & Sons reprints of the early editions of *Wisden* as an "ambitious and costly publishing venture", and when the time came he was happy to praise the hundredth *Wisden* as "the largest volume ever … a landmark in cricket publishing". Elsewhere he ranged across the field with a sympathetic eye. *The Problem of Soil Salinity in Turf Wicket Management* was "extremely informative"; *A Look at the Leg Before Wicket Law* was "careful, lucid and valuably illustrated"; the *Scottish Cricket Guide* was "well printed on good paper"; even *I-Spy Cricket*, a while-away-time-in-the-car book for children, was "remarkably clear and wide-ranging". One of the few efforts he frowned at was a bad-tempered history of league cricket fuelled by resentment. "The League and its cricket are done no favours by a book as ungenerous as this," he wrote. "One cannot imagine it making many friends." He wondered, given the indiscretions recorded in Denis Compton's *End of an Innings*, whether even this illustrious figure might in time "doubt or even regret" some of the blotchy laundry he had aired.

Every now and then his wine-writing alter ego crept in, as when he pronounced the 1970 crop "one of the three best years since the Second World War". And in 1964 he had to catch his breath when a genuine masterpiece fell on his desk. He had been glad to call Don Bradman's *The Art of Cricket* "a classic", but needed new words to describe C. L. R. James's *Beyond a Boundary*, a deep meditation on cricket, the West Indies, the Empire, Englishness and his own life. Perhaps it helped that James had "devoured *Wisden*" as a young man, but Arlott was in any case moved to declare that here was a book "so outstanding as to compel any reviewer to check his adjectives". He studied his own before concluding that *Beyond a Boundary* was "the finest book written about the game of cricket". In so doing he made *Wisden* into something new. In a hundred years of continuous publication it had been a reference book, a historical anthology, a sermonising pulpit, an honours board, a lawgiver, a home for sports reports and an archive. Now, thanks to Arlott, it was a literary journal too.

In some unknowable, subterranean way James's book also heralded the arrival of a new force in cricket: dissident geopolitics. The Bodyline row had been inflamed by colonial sensitivities, but it stopped short of being part of an independence movement. In expressing the West Indian love of the English game, however, James was very much claiming it as a Caribbean fact: "Eton and Harrow had nothing on us". This was apt, because though no one knew it, a great post-imperial controversy was poised to burst on the cricket world. In the summer of 1968 MCC was preparing a winter tour of South Africa in the shadow of a statement by South Africa's prime minister, John Vorster, to the effect that he would not accept a team including Basil D'Oliveira, the Cape-born all-rounder who could not, because of his colour, represent the country of his birth. D'Oliveira was now, after playing in the Central Lancashire League and for Worcestershire, qualified to play for England; and despite an unremarkable tour of the West Indies in the winter of 1967–8 he had already excelled at Test level.[*] *Wisden* made him a Cricketer of the Year in 1967 and called him "a fairy tale come true".

What happened next has become one of cricket's best-known stories. The fairy tale went sour. In the final Ashes Test of 1968 a recalled D'Oliveira scored 158, making it near certain that he would be selected for the winter tour. When he was omitted there was an outcry among those who believed (no matter how stout the denials) that MCC had been swayed by careful pressure from Pretoria and had, in effect, let South Africa's government pick an England team. Few believed the

---

[*] John Arlott himself played a part in D'Oliveira's Lancashire League career, when he responded to a famous out-of-the-blue letter and introduced the South African-born all-rounder to Middleton CC in 1960. As coincidence would have it, another helping hand was extended by Wisden's chairman, Ken Medlock, who gave D'Oliveira a "job" in the electricals division of the CWS in Manchester. He lasted less than a week: after a few days D'Oliveira went to Medlock and said he couldn't continue – his new colleagues just wanted to talk about cricket all the time.

selectors held D'Oliveira's race against him – it was merely that the
desire for a quiet life, an unrocked boat, proved too strong an impulse.
Had a different batsman – Colin Milburn, for instance – struck 158 in
that Oval Test it was very hard to imagine him being ignored.

The quandary developed a new twist three weeks later when one of
the players who *had* been selected, Tom Cartwright, pulled out of the
squad (citing an injury that was seen by some as a discreet protest – he
later said that he "went cold" when he read that D'Oliveira's exclusion
had inspired a standing ovation in South Africa's all-white parliament).
This time MCC did select D'Oliveira as his replacement, and, to no
one's surprise, South Africa's prime minister cancelled the tour,
declaring that he would not accept a team chosen "by our political
enemies". But by then MCC had already lost the high ground, and a
group of members called for a debate about the committee for its
fumbling of the affair. A four-hour meeting attended by a thousand
cricket-lovers was held in Church House, Westminster. The motion of
no confidence (led by David Sheppard, an ex-captain of Sussex and
England and now Bishop of Woolwich, and the young Mike Brearley,
not long out of Cambridge) was defeated by a postal vote that made the
debate somewhat redundant, and left MCC's friends free to depict the
whole event as an unpleasant and frankly needless fuss.

All of this is well known now. At the time it was, in *Wisden*'s view,
still clouded. Preston tried in his Notes to imply that it was merely
"exasperating". But in regretting that "the name of cricket and the
name of MCC have been besmirched", he seemed to favour the idea
that it had been soiled primarily by the protesters, not by the weak-
willed initial selection. "At a time when we admire the American
astronauts who encircled the moon on Christmas Day," he wrote, "we
have to record in this 106th edition of *Wisden* the petty squabbles of
men on earth." It was a studied attempt to belittle the controversy, and
it allowed him to align the Almanack with MCC: "I was pleased that
the majority of members rallied to their support," he wrote. He asked
Michael Melford of the *Sunday Telegraph* to summarise the dispute
and, though Melford did a faithful job (including details such as the fact
that the *News of the World* cheekily hired D'Oliveira to report on the
tour if it *did* go ahead) he toed the MCC line that D'Oliveira was "far
from an automatic choice" and presented the protest as blinkered ("It

was easy for many to assume political motives"). He nodded at MCC's desire to "foster cricket wherever it is played" and respected its plea that it could not be the "inquisitor-general" into the affairs of foreign countries. (He did not point out that no one was actually asking this; the dissidents merely felt that MCC had been pushed around by an apartheid state and might have been made of sterner stuff.) The whole thing, he concluded, citing as evidence the fact that the rebellion was repelled by 4,357 votes to 1,570, had been "sad and unnecessary".

The story was fated to roll into the New Year, however, since South Africa were due to visit England again in the summer of 1970. Anti-apartheid protesters warned, with added vehemence, that they would disrupt the tour as much as they could – there was talk of ruined pitches and barbed wire – and the row became ever more heated. Some politicians begged MCC to cancel; others felt that cricket was being unjustly persecuted, and joined the fund-raising effort to help finance the cost of police and security arrangements. It was whispered from Buckingham Palace that a touring South African team would not be invited to a reception by the Queen.

Through it all, the ruling body clung to the line that an "open bridges" policy was preferable to a severing of links. "More good is achieved," said S. C. "Billy" Griffith, Secretary of MCC, "by maintaining sporting links with South Africa than by cutting them off." On 18 May 1970, after a long meeting at Lord's, Griffith gave a press conference in the Long Room in which he stated that the Cricket Council – the new body, formed only a year earlier, to preside over strategic matters – had resolved "by a substantial majority" that the tour "should proceed as arranged". There was a nationwide howl of disbelief. Four days later MCC was summoned to a meeting with the Home Secretary James Callaghan, at which it agreed to bow to a request from its own government to cancel the tour. It was a change of policy, if not a change of heart. The decision was made, and announced, "with deep regret".

Later histories would add substance to the theory that MCC colluded with apartheid South Africa in maintaining the status quo to a greater extent than was imagined at the time; but we cannot blame *Wisden* for not knowing more about these machinations. It was, nevertheless, not the Almanack at its best. In his 1971 Preface Preston said that "for the sake of history I considered it necessary" to publish a summary of the events (in fact he ran a lengthy article by Irving Rosenwater); but his own Notes skirted the subject, registering only that the South Africans would surely have been a great success had they been allowed to tour, not least thanks to the "excellent weather". In truth he was more preoccupied with the new lbw law, the first-class status of the Rest of the World matches that took place instead of the South African series, and the dire state of the game's finances. "None of the seventeen counties made a profit in 1970", he wrote, listing their losses, which ranged from the inconsequential (£500 – Essex) to the "alarming" (£10,000 – Warwickshire). In this context he enjoyed reporting the coincidence that 33,000 people had squeezed into Old Trafford to see Lancashire beat Yorkshire on the very day that a "quality newspaper" declared "in its boldest type" that cricket was dead. He did not even regret the fact that the fightback was being led by a limited-overs game in the new, tobacco-sponsored John Player League. On the contrary, he was grateful to the game's new backers. "Very few counties have ever made cricket pay," he wrote. "Wealthy individuals used to help out, and now cricket, like many other sports, has to thank sponsors such as Rothmans, John Player, Gillette, Ford, Guinness and the Wrigley Foundation for coming to the rescue."

In hindsight (which offers a luxurious view) we can see this as a missed opportunity for *Wisden* to sound an independent note. The Almanack had not exactly supported MCC during the Bodyline row, but on this occasion it did fall in with the official view. Various private representations were made: in the spring of 1970 Bishop David Sheppard, with uncommon moral authority, wrote to Preston: "I don't see how it can be anything but an unhappy time ... I wish that MCC was aware of the damage that can be done to race relations in this country." But there were lots of contrary opinions as well, and Preston tried to pick a path between the rival camps. "Personally," he wrote in 1970, "I have never condoned apartheid in sport." He stressed that D'Oliveira was "something out of the ordinary" as a cricketer, and would have been "a great success" in South Africa. And he was able, in his reports on the meetings of 1969, to print many intriguing details from the proceedings of MCC. These revealed, among other things, that the president, secretary and treasurer of the club all knew, six months before the fateful day when D'Oliveira was not selected, that

South Africa would refuse to admit an England team that included him ("anyone else, but not D'Oliveira"). They acknowledged that the secretary, Griffith, had offered to resign "for the good of cricket" but that his offer had been rejected; and added that D'Oliveira himself had turned down the offer of a fat contract (£4,000 per year) to coach in South Africa if he "did not make himself available" for England.

But this was one of those cases where the impulse to see both sides was in fact a covert decision in favour of MCC. While reporting the MCC's "aversion to racial discrimination of any kind", Preston could not suppress his wish that the tour go ahead. There was "no question" of accepting money from South Africa to defray the cost of police protection. All of these pronouncements were dutifully recorded in the following year's *Wisden*, and the small print noted that a hundred MPs had written "in the hope of stopping" the tour.

While logging these details, however, Preston could not resist championing South African cricket in other ways. In 1969 he chose the Durban-born Barry Richards as a Cricketer of the Year, and though the achievements were unarguable (2,395 runs for Hampshire at 47.9) this was a telling selection in the circumstances – especially when, in 1970, he picked another South African, Mike Procter, on the grounds that he "represents what the ancient game needs everywhere – a real personality". The 1970 volume calmly praised the all-white team that Wilfred Isaacs brought to England as "popular and worthy ambassadors of South African cricket" while, elsewhere, another article by Michael Melford narrated the "Ups and Downs of the Springboks" (which celebrated the way the "English game" had colonised the Afrikaner imagination) as well as delivering a list of Notable Events in South African Cricket. No one could doubt where *Wisden*'s sympathies lay – with the congenial cricketers who had been press-ganged into isolation by political hotheads.

It was not *Wisden*'s finest hour. "With hindsight," wrote Stephen Moss, summing up the episode in the *Wisden Anthology 1978–2006*, "we can see that *Wisden* was on the wrong side for much of this period." Perhaps it was all too vexatious. Far from seeing it as an exciting editorial challenge, Preston preferred to wind the clock back to a less troubled time. The cricket devotee in him won out over the journalist. That summer he wrote to the elderly Cardus inviting him to write something as usual. Cardus's reply was warm. "I woke in bed at 4.30 a.m. (I always do) thinking that this year Norman Preston hadn't asked me for a contribution to the next *Wisden*, and I would not like not to be in it! Then, at 8 a.m., came your letter..." Crisis? What crisis?

Revisiting the relevant volumes today one is struck chiefly by a forceful ghost at the feast – the absence of a major article on the affair by John Arlott, *Wisden*'s annual book reviewer. He was supremely well informed and had a close personal knowledge of the D'Oliveira story. And there is no doubt what he would have said on this issue. Some years back, on the BBC's *Any Questions?* (he was a founder-member) he had denounced apartheid, calling the government of Dr Malan "predominantly Nazi" and regaling the audience with the tale of how, when required by intimidating South African border agents to state his "race", he and his party had defiantly put "Human". South Africa reacted angrily to Arlott's broadcast and the BBC took a similar view, suspending Arlott for his "outburst" on the grounds that it broke the Corporation's vow on partisanship (a vow it was hard *not* to break in a forum like *Any Questions*).

His views on the matter were very well known, in other words. So far as he was concerned it wasn't the protesters who were seeking to press politics into sport – it was the government of South Africa, a country that claimed to revere sport and yet treated its native population in the most unsporting manner imaginable. In December 1969, at the Cambridge Union, he opposed the MCC line that "politics" should not be allowed to mix with games to the point of taking issue with an old friend, Wilfred Wooller: "I have known the honourable third speaker with great admiration for some 37 years," he said, bringing his best rhetoric to the party, "during which time we have dined, wined and argued together, and in that entire period I have been completely amazed at the political naivety of one so shrewd in other matters." It became a famous put-down, not least because it was so exquisitely polite. The following spring, in the *Guardian* ("Why I am off the air") he outlined why he would not commentate on the forthcoming South African series (which in the event was cancelled). "MCC have never made a sadder, more dramatic or potentially more damaging decision," he wrote. "Apartheid is detestable to me, and I shall always oppose it."

We do not know whether Preston (knowing what Arlott would say) declined to ask him to address the subject, or whether Arlott himself avoided doing so, feeling too personally implicated. The fact remains: in 1969 and 1970 *Wisden* missed a rare chance to publish what would probably have been one of the great pieces of its life. It might have raised a few hackles in the more old-fashioned corners of the game (some of which could still be found at Lord's), but it would have cemented *Wisden*'s moral authority around the world. As it was, it put a question mark over the idea that cricket even knew the meaning of the "fair play" culture it so keenly espoused. Arlott read the 1969 *Wisden* for his own review, and called Melford's account "a moving story ... notably careful and objective" without mentioning his own part in the saga or his well-known views on such topics. Bickering with the umpire was not his style.

11

End of an Era

In April 1965 the Cricket Reporting Agency merged with the Press Association (PA), but it continued to be known as "Pardon's" and stayed in the same familiar offices at 85 Fleet Street. Ken Medlock did nothing to alter the structure by which the Almanack was assembled – it was an effective partnership, and he had enough on his plate, what with completing the cricket-ball merger, closing down tennis-ball production and winding up product lines that existed "solely to provide variety". There were other problems: owing to illness, the northern sales manager had been off work for nearly a hundred days the previous year, leaving Wisden barely represented in the heartlands of Yorkshire and Lancashire. It had even lost its standing in the northern league clubs, a circuit close to Medlock's heart. In 1964 the company's new "name", John Hampshire, was joined by his Yorkshire team-mate Phil Sharpe to represent Wisden, for the modest sum of £50 a year (plus a shilling a bat royalty).* But though an England batsman and a famous slip, Sharpe was no Denis Compton.

It was hard to believe the great days could ever return. The company was still trading at a loss: £8,259 in 1962, £7,015 in 1963, and £9,286 in 1964. And there was a further dip in 1966 when England went football mad. It was no more than a sign of the times when, in the October

---

* Hampshire and Sharpe gave John Wisden & Co exclusive rights to use their names as signatures on their bats. They were given six bats to use themselves, and were also required to do "everything" in their power to advance the sale of such bats.

following the World Cup, the factory in Penshurst was leased to Subbuteo, the table-football game, for seven years.

Despite the absence of any real investment, however, the Almanack trundled along fine, selling around 22,000 copies a year. The reporters at the PA spent the winter primarily involved with soccer or rugby (sport was still seasonal in those days), but the Almanack was a big part of their daily routine. A special set, bound in green leather and with "CRA" gold-tooled on to the spine, took pride of place on the bookshelf in the head office. A big sign on the wall said "Check Your Facts". But there were no complex instructions regarding the house style; the contributors were steeped in it already. One of them, Terry Cooper, recalled: "we were told to be as timeless as we could. No journalese." But paradoxically the best way to be timeless was to write as if the match were unfolding day by day, as if the result were not known. Every now and then – as when E. M. Wellings described the great tied Test of 1960 – it felt silly to begin with the bland statement that one or other side had won the toss and decided to bat. But for the most part the idea was to permit posterity to re-read the reports without knowing (since they had long forgotten) what was about to happen. It was like the improved, corrected and steady-eyed first draft of history – not the final word.

The formula had been tried and tested over a long period, but things were about to change at John Wisden & Co. In 1968 sales recovered a little, rising by 10% and producing a loss of only £1,849, an improvement over the previous year's loss of £6,624. But as these figures show, John Wisden & Co was a very small company, and at the following spring's board meeting in Manchester – at which only Medlock and John Tipper were present – it was decided that the CWS could do no more, and that it was time to sell. The balance of losses carried forward was now up to £21,614, but the hint of a turnaround was enough to make a deal possible. As it happened, the CWS was also changing its structure, and it was clear to Medlock that, though he personally enjoyed it ("it opened doors for me I never would have got near") owning John Wisden & Co "wasn't serving any useful purpose" any more. He took pride in the fact that he had reorganised the company to the point where it could at least be sold, not dissolved ("It was going to live – that was the thing") so he sought out William Gray, who through Gray-Nicolls had been a fellow director of Tonbridge Sports Industries. The takeover was swiftly agreed and completed in October 1970. Very little money was involved; from Grays' point of view it was a question of keeping a minor rival out of the hands of the competition. The Cambridge-based, family-run sports company bought 100,000 shares from the CWS, William Gray became chairman, and Ken Medlock marched back to his former life to become, in time, deputy chief executive of the CWS.

Medlock has been described as the man who "saved" *Wisden*. In truth, if John Wisden & Co *had* gone into liquidation again in 1960 it would have passed through the hands of a receiver who would almost certainly have found a buyer for the copyright, if nothing else. Nor is it likely that Whitaker's, for instance, would have been happy to let it vanish. Indeed they had a licence to publish it, with a seven-year notice clause. Medlock himself knew as much. "Of course, when it became public that the company was being disposed of, then yes, there could have been buyers for individual assets, such as the Almanack." But this is not what happened, and there is no knowing what might have befallen *Wisden* had that been its destiny: it might have been changed or "modernised" beyond recognition.

So Medlock did, at the very least, decisively influence the course of *Wisden*'s life. It was facing a fork in the road, and he steered it up the path that led to eventual safety. Wisden repaid the favour: chairing it was one of the highlights of his life; it was thanks to the Wisden connection that Learie Constantine sponsored Medlock's son when he became a barrister. As he withdrew from the company Medlock remembered the old collection of bats. The Great Newport Street showroom had closed, and the bats were stacked in a corner of the factory in Kent, gathering dust. "They were lying about like leftovers," he said. A busy-minded man, he planned to donate them to county clubs – some are in the Old Trafford Museum – and he once took a bat signed by Victor Trumper on a flight to Australia, explaining to uncertain customs officials that it was not an offensive weapon (which, as a few England bowlers could have told him, was not quite true).

On the business side there was, Grays found, little to excite them. For a while they wondered what had happened to the cricket bat collection, but they didn't make a fuss about it. It wasn't the most pressing issue, because the ball-making business was once more struggling to compete with overseas manufacturers. And Britain's accession to the Common Market was about to make things even tougher; the company depended on imports from Commonwealth countries such as India and Pakistan, and these would soon cease to be duty-free. Grays closed down some product lines and merged others until John Wisden & Co, as a manufacturer, effectively ceased to exist.[*] But the Almanack was a modest jewel in anyone's crown, and Grays took swift action by reversing the terms of the publishing deal so that the company, instead of receiving a royalty (for its name, effectively) would now pay a flat fee to the book's publisher and take on the publishing risk. For the first time in years, *Wisden*'s owner had a stake in its own success. The price was increased, and Grays also hoped to invigorate the marketing of the old tome.

Even as it altered the terms of the publishing arrangement, Grays found itself less than impressed by Whitaker's. The *Bookseller* (itself a Whitaker's publication) went so far as to compare relations between the two to the ill-feeling that had sprung up between the notorious Yorkshire rivals, Boycott and Illingworth. But in 1971, when Grays sought to have *Wisden* published elsewhere, Whitaker's reminded them of their notice clause. "Right," said Grays, "we give you seven years' notice."

From Norman Preston's point of view, the new arrangements meant that for the bulk of his final decade there was a less-than-ideal structure behind the book's production. At the beginning of the apartheid crisis, in 1968, Norman Preston actually retired from the PA and prepared to edit the Almanack from the front room of his family house in a suburban cul-de-sac in Kent. His address – Mapperley, Romanhurst Avenue, Bromley – was printed each year at the foot of his Preface and became quietly famous in the cricket world as the modest hub of a web of contributors, each of them signed up in the world's press boxes over many years, who continued to send scores, records and reports to south-east London. He

---

[*] Grays did manage to revive the firm's financial position, however. In 1970 John Wisden & Co made a loss of £6,963. In 1971 the loss was nearly halved, and in 1972 there were pre-tax profits of £6,189. In 1972 this rose to £14,095. The show, even as the name itself was dissolving, was to some extent back on the road.

would still commute to matches at Lord's and The Oval and meet old pals in the press box – in those days people didn't whinge about commuting; but he had no back office, no team of reporters to help him, and of course there were no snazzy electronic methods of processing data. His front room was piled high with stacks of paper, a couple of historic cricket pictures and – of course – a full set of *Wisden*.

It was a demanding task to keep the project on track, but outwardly the Almanack remained a calm voice in stormy times. The reflex to find fault, indeed, may have prevented it from appreciating the fact (clear now) that the 1970s were another golden age for county cricket. The presence of overseas stars – Garry Sobers in Nottingham, Zaheer Abbas and Mike Procter in Bristol, Barry Richards and Gordon Greenidge in Southampton, Rohan Kanhai and Alvin Kallicharran at Edgbaston, Clive Lloyd in Manchester, Glenn Turner in Worcester, Asif Iqbal in Kent and many others – was transforming. And they did not seem like mercenaries: they were adopted by their counties as favourite sons and returned year after year, where they beguiled the new armchair audience with flashing exploits in the John Player League. How could anyone doubt that England was the home of cricket, when so many great players were here?

It mattered because county cricket, of course, was still the true heart of *Wisden*'s universe. It had first crystallised in the years following the Almanack's birth in 1864, and the centenaries were falling thick and fast, inspiring anniversary articles on all parts of the great old cricket map. *Wisden* had inserted itself into the geographical pattern of English life at a time when someone from Kent might well regard someone from Lancashire as a damned foreigner, and had stolidly recorded the doings of such teams ever since, capturing every last detail about Leicestershire's annual tussle with Glamorgan, or Sussex's rivalry with Kent. Over the years, of course, as the population gathered in cities, the old allegiances began to fray, so though the 1970s were not quite a last hurrah, they were a time in which county colours were fading. The one-day finals of this period, in which thousands came to Lord's to cheer on their local heroes, were a modern equivalent of the social whirl at the old amateur match-ups. They had a revivalist feeling. And it remained a palpable and important fact (from the marketing point of view) that many county members and followers, even if they did not collect *Wisden*, would buy it in a year when their own team was the champion.

The international game was glowing, too. In the early 1970s England (under Illingworth, with Greig, Snow, Underwood, Boycott and Knott to the fore) were competitive, while Australia, with Lillee, Thomson and the Chappell brothers, were a powerhouse. And as the decade wore on the West Indies became a cricket superpower, with a seemingly endless supply of fast bowlers and superlative batting as well – Fredericks, Greenidge, Lloyd and Richards were a match for anyone on earth. India and Pakistan were starting to flex their muscles too, so that when India won the one-day World Cup in 1983 it was a surprise, but not unbelievable.

Wisden made no special allowance for these commotions. The familiar features rolled on as they had always done. Births and Deaths was compressed (or restrained) by raising the entry requirement. To be included a man needed to have played at least ten first-class games, then 50, until finally it would become a list of players who had played at Test level. There were plenty (Arlott notable among them) who mourned the trimming of this unique directory, but *Wisden* could only have preserved it by adding a second volume.

Wisden also continued to be cricket's chief mourner; it had long acted as head of the cricket "family" at the funerals of its friends. In the 1960s it had said farewell to Patsy Hendren, Sir Pelham Warner, Sir Jack Hobbs, Walter Hammond, Bill Woodfull, S. F. Barnes and Sir Frank Worrell – a mighty group of players. But there was also space, in 1965, for a brief notice about Peter the cat, a "well-known cricket watcher at Lord's". Sir Len Hutton wrote that it was "hard to think of a greater Australian batsman" than Stan McCabe, a cheeky thing to say with Bradman still around, and Edward Alletson was recalled as the holder of the record off a single over (34, for Notts v Sussex in 1911) even though this would not last much longer (Sobers was warming up to go two better). As usual, the obituaries also touched on those for whom cricket was not their only claim to fame. Earl Alexander of Tunis had played in "Fowler's Match" at Lord's in 1910, but earned more honour by becoming one of the most prominent Allied commanders of the Second World War. Canon "Tishy" Browne was given a place despite having a bowling action that "defies description".

The Preston era lasted for so long (from 1952 to 1980), and the game changed so markedly in these years, that it is not easy to detect a consistent thread in the editor's thoughts. But since Preston was neither an iconoclast nor a crusader, the contents and outlook of his Almanack were at least relatively stable. He always kept a close eye on the new generation of cricketers in the well-established nursery of the private schools: Chris Tavaré at Sevenoaks, the young Cowdreys at Tonbridge, John Barclay at Eton, Roger Tolchard at Malvern and a great many others. Alastair Hignell was impressing at Denstone College (he would go on to win rugby caps for England) and Vic Marks was thriving at Blundells. Worcester Royal Grammar School, meanwhile, was strengthened by an "unusual schoolboy", Imran Khan – he had already toured England with Pakistan, so it was no surprise when he "monopolised" the bowling and the batting for his school, taking a hat-trick against King Edward's Birmingham.

Wrapped around these staples was a reliable garland of beguiling material. Preston consistently favoured attacking cricket, and criticised the "boring" nature of the Ashes Test at Old Trafford in 1964, when Australia batted into day three, killing any chance of a result. Bobby Simpson made 311 out of 656, and Ken Barrington replied with 256 out of 611, which was good record-breaking grist to the mill, but also a grinding waste of time that echoed, in some minds, the Cold War stand-off between the nuclear powers. *Wisden* felt that "both sides were to blame" for "needlessly tiresome batting". The famous dry tone was still in evidence seven years later, when Boycott was run out for 88 against Middlesex. *Wisden* stated that it was "one of the very few occasions this entry is made against him in the scorebook, although he frequently figures in run out errors". It was a notably civilised way of drawing attention to Boycott's reputation for running out team-mates while keeping his own bat safely grounded.

The small print in these years was constantly humming with minor points of order. Tom Graveney was fined £1,000, "severely reprimanded" and banned for three games for playing in a benefit match on the rest day of a Test; Boycott's request to tour South Africa with a Derrick Robins' XI was turned down (not surprisingly, since he had declined to tour Australia – Lillee, Thomson and all – with England); the new sponsor, Commercial Union, promised a "videotape recorder" for the best young player of each month; underarm bowling was banned to "eliminate sharp practice".

Some of the more exciting cricket in this period came in one-day form: in 1969 the touring West Indians were beaten by Ireland, of all people, in Londonderry – bowled out for 25 on what *Wisden* called "a damp and definitely emerald green pitch". Yet *Wisden* had mixed feelings about the one-day game. Of course it was grateful for the fact that one-day cricket was luring crowds back into county grounds, but it clearly did so by promoting a brand of cricket that a purist could construe only as a vulgar cousin of the real thing. * When the world's first one-day international was staged – an impromptu affair to give the crowd something to watch when an Ashes Test match was rained off in 1971 – *Wisden* all but ignored it, rather poetically repeating its error of almost a hundred years earlier, when it missed the very first Test match in 1877. And when the first World Cup was staged in the summer of 1975, devised in part to take the place of yet another cancelled South African tour, *Wisden* covered the tournament in a dutiful but hardly enthusiastic way.

There were some embarrassing mistakes, too: the photograph of East Africa's team got the names wrong for an entire row of players, and there was an even more striking lapse in the report on the final, a game that became famous around the cricket world partly for a ravishing century from Clive Lloyd, who swatted Australia's bowlers around Lord's like a mild-tempered bear, and partly thanks to the hawk-eyed fielding of a newcomer called Vivian Richards, who prowled the covers like a circus knife-thrower, sprinting and swooping his way to a hat-trick of run-outs which announced him, long before it was known that he was one of the all-time great batsmen, as a world-class performer. *Wisden*, not quite giving the game its full attention, casually gave his hat-trick to the "amazing Kallicharran" and concluded that, though entertaining, the game "might not be termed first-class cricket".

But *Wisden* took care not to set its face too resolutely against the one-day game. Apart from its welcome effect on gate receipts, it also

---

* In the 1974 *Wisden* Gordon Ross pointed out that attendances at first-class county games had fallen from over 2.2 million in 1947 to 719,661 in 1963. The effects of the one-day boom were "miraculous", but he stressed that while one-day cricket might rescue the game's economy, it should not be mistaken for the real thing. "This type of cricket has become a family occasion," he wrote. "It is certainly not a connoisseur's day."

promoted bold cricket, a long-standing *Wisden* ideal. The 1976 Almanack had little time for the work-to-rule attitude of India's Sunil Gavaskar, who, faced with a daunting England total of 334 in the first World Cup at Lord's, came out and "sat on his splice" for the whole innings, poking his work-to-rule way to 36 not out (in 60 overs). Nothing could have so damaged his "cause" – cricket's traditions – than this boorish display: thousands of cricket fans suddenly conceived a sharp dislike for the so-called traditions Gavaskar imagined he was upholding, and *Wisden* rightly took the spectators' part: "even their own large contingent of supporters showed their disapproval".

Preston's *Wisden* was certainly popular. The print run in 1976 was 35,000, and the following year's edition was reprinted for the first time since 1963. It was not an accident: in Preston's view stability mattered. "Our regular readers know their way around the book," he told an interviewer from the *Sun* (then a broadsheet) in 1971. "They don't want to be monkeyed around. Look, it's got a preface, a list of contents, an index. That's all that's wanted." The public seemed to agree. Year after year the Almanack headed the *Sunday Times* hardback bestseller list: in 1975 it was number one (ahead of *The Good Food Guide*) and stayed in the top ten for eight weeks; it did the same in 1976 and 1977. In 1978 it was used to illustrate Britain's inbuilt frivolity in an article by Jill Norman, editorial director of Penguin Books, who railed that while Germans bought Günter Grass, we bought cricket books – "typical of our concern with pleasure". This was not a like-for-like comparison, and we need to recall that bestseller lists back then were not scientific; but neither were they meaningless. And Wisden appeared on them year after year – in 1982 it rose to number one ahead of Robert Lacey's *Princess*, a portrait of the new royal bride, Diana Spencer.

"We don't set out to be bright," Preston wrote modestly. "But we don't set out to be dull either. Our readers like hard facts." By now he was one of the game's elder statesmen, the man the newspapers would go to for a swift quote. Who else could they count on to express a scornful view, for instance, of a scheme to redevelop The Oval in 1973 that would reduce the playing area from six to three and a half acres. "They will have problems," said Preston, understating the case, "meeting

the requirements of first-class cricket." In 1977 he was awarded the
MBE and a lunch was held in his honour at Lord's, where William Gray
was in the chair, Hutton and Edrich on the guest list, and Denis
Compton was the guest speaker (Gray was a good host: he had held a
similar lunch in 1972 to celebrate two decades of Preston's editorship).
A few months earlier Preston had been enjoying the Centenary Test in
Melbourne between England and Australia – a perfect *Wisden* day out.
It was a jolly gathering of top players, and it generated one of cricket's
best stories: after five grand days Australia won the game by the exact
same margin (45 runs) as that first such encounter in 1877. It was, ran
the report, "an occasion of warmest reunion and nostalgia ... an event
which none fortunate enough to be present could forget". There was
"much champagne", a specially minted gold coin for the toss, and a
merry cavalcade of old friends. Denis Compton even brought back
memories of the good old days by leaving his passport in Cardiff; he
only made the flight from London after a high-speed dash along the M4.

In February 1975 Neville Cardus died, and two other Wisden contributors, Ebenezer Eden and Harold Gee, were soon to pass away too.
Preston lauded them in his 1976 Preface, but it felt like a changing of
the guard. In the second half of his third decade he permitted himself
some increasingly whimsical commissions. The 1977 Almanack, for
example, included a long article by Basil Easterbrook, with painful
slugs of bad verse, about the "Surrey Poet", Albert Craig – "a
phenomenon of his time as in their different ways were W. G. Grace,
D. G. Bradman and Neville Cardus". This was a heavy-handed joke;
Craig was the McGonagall of the Home Counties, only more boring.

> Most hearty plaudits seem to rend the air
> You might have heard it at Trafalgar Square.

Bad literature can be a good joke, but it does not require nine pages to
share it. Even Easterbrook admitted that Craig's prose showed "a
complete absence of style", as in his "thumbnail sketch" of the 1893
Australians: "We feel fairly safe in opining that no Colonial batsman
can lay on the wood with more power than this big six footer."

This wasn't the only sign of a certain loss of editorial pressure in this and other late-Preston volumes. There were roomy reflections on other legends of yesteryear, such as Gubby Allen, Arthur Gilligan and W. A. Oldfield, and further reminiscences about W. G. Grace. There was a piece on "A Hundred Years of the Scarborough Festival", and a tribute to Warwickshire's long-standing and popular West Indian coach, Derief Taylor. There were fond-hearted pieces about Cardus, about a hundred years of cricket in Leicestershire, and about Bert Lock – "King of Groundsmen". *Wisden* was still a byword for cricketing respectability, but even its most nostalgic readers could have been forgiven for finding this too much of a good thing. In 1974 the only article (of nine) that addressed the present day was Gordon Ross's analysis of the Gillette Cup, which in the decade since its launch had changed the way the world thought about cricket – the competition had now spread to Australia, South Africa, New Zealand and the West Indies and had also inspired the first World Cup. In 1977 the Notes dwelt on the previous summer's freak hot weather ("most outfields resembled the Sahara") and chided the West Indies fast bowling as "unsavoury", but did not so much as mention Viv Richards's magisterial 291 at The Oval, the highlight of an almost Bradmanesque summer from the Antiguan even though, as the tour report put it: "Mere figures cannot convey his perfect style and stroke play."

It was almost as if *Wisden* were deliberately looking the other way (backwards) from the freight train that was flying down the tracks towards it. In that same year cricket erupted in a way that really would change everything. An Australian television magnate called Kerry Packer, irked by his failure to land the contract to broadcast Test match cricket on his own channel, decided to set up a rival cricket tournament of his own. Everyone knew cricketers were not well paid, so it wasn't hard to sign 35 leading stars (who were threatened with bans by their national associations from appearing in official first-class cricket – a move that led to a convoluted court case in London) with a view to staging a brash new event called World Series Cricket. It would involve half a dozen "Tests", a sequence of one-day matches and various other clashes. It would involve floodlights, coloured clothing and a white ball. It would be a radical new spectacle, and if the cricket world didn't like it, it would have to lump it.

It was a challenge to almost everything *Wisden* stood for, and in his 1978 Preface Preston (pausing only to express the forlorn wish that the season just passed "will be remembered by most people for the Queen's Silver Jubilee") called it "the greatest upheaval and division the first-class game has ever known". His Notes merely warned that "no solution appeared to be in sight", and that "it is possible that night cricket has come to stay", and he then handed space to Gordon Ross to narrate the saga up to this point. Ross did a thorough job, setting out the way the players were recruited (many during the Centenary Test), the influence of Richie Benaud (who acted as an agent), the expensive court case when players such as Tony Greig, Mike Procter and John Snow sued the cricket authorities over restraint of trade (Greig had been sacked as England captain) and all other issues surrounding the breakaway tour.

In 1979 Ross had a second bite at the topic, noting with pleasure that the Packer games "had not met with the resounding success" that was envisaged, and that crowds "were considerably smaller" than planned. It was clear that "this long drawn-out saga rolls relentlessly on" and that it would keep doing so "for a long time to come". He did not mention the fact that the Packer initiative, however brash, was in its way a simple re-enactment of the cricket caravans founded by William Clarke (and featuring John Wisden himself) over a hundred years earlier. As we know, it was the "doings" of exactly this sort of team that *Wisden* had first set out to celebrate.

Preston's Notes took a less fatalistic line, scorning the "jet-age razzamatazz cricket" that Packer stood for, and which seemed more "masquerade" than sport. He could no longer tell if cricketers were players or mercenaries. The divide between honourable sportsmen and grasping vulgarians, echoing as it did the historic rift between amateurs and professionals, was still a sore point – it was not easy to accept that a man might be both. Many years later, in 2006, traces of the same reflex would continue to shake the Almanack. The obituary of Kerry Packer duly recognised his importance – Tony Greig called him "a truly great Australian" and Christopher Martin-Jenkins was simply stating the fact of the matter when he wrote: "With the possible exception of W. G. Grace, there has been no more influential figure in the history of cricket." The editor at that time, Matthew Engel, was happy to register a less rosy view as well. "If cricket ever erects a statue," ran the end of

the Packer obituary, "there will be plenty of passers-by who will have
an irresistible urge to spit on it."

━━━━━━

By now Preston was no longer the "short, thick-set, merry man ... a fit,
golfing 74-year-old" he had been when the *Sun* interviewed him back
in 1971. A modest man, he added the MBE he won in 1977 to his name
on the cover of the 1979 edition, but left it off in 1980. He continued to
plead for better behaviour on the pitch, and still did not see this as a
matter for the authorities. "It's up to the players, not the rules, to
brighten the game." But producing *Wisden* from home was not easy,
and the succession of recent controversies, none of which appealed to
his sense of cricket's traditions, was denting his appetite for the task.
He was starting to resemble, perhaps, a once-great fast bowler who had
lost that crucial bit of nip. And now, at the end of the decade, he was
obliged to adapt himself to another change of regime – or at any rate a
change of publisher. In 1971 Grays had put Whitaker's on seven years'
notice that they intended to seek a new publishing partner, so in 1978
the long association with Sporting Handbooks came to an end. Queen
Anne Press, an imprint of Macdonald and Jane's, was given the job. The
brainchild of Lord Kemsley, owner of the *Sunday Times*, it had once
been run by Ian Fleming, the paper's foreign editor and the creator of
James Bond; since his death in 1964 his widow, Ann Fleming, became
involved in it, once famously asking her friend Evelyn Waugh to "write
me 10,000 words on some saint".

Queen Anne Press won the contract by pledging to print more
copies, get them into the shops sooner (its habit was to emerge in May,
missing the first few weeks of the cricket season) and publish more
books under Wisden's name. A year later Grays did just that themselves
by consenting to lend the name to a new magazine, *Wisden Cricket
Monthly*, the invention of the noted historian and author David Frith.
It was set up with a view to competing with the one existing magazine,
The Cricketer.

Queen Anne Press also brought Graeme Wright into the *Wisden*
fold. A New Zealand-born publisher and author, he had lived in Britain
since 1968, working on numerous sports books (such as Rothman's
Football Yearbook) and with cricket personages such as Michael Melford

and Irving Rosenwater, the historian and sometime *Wisden* record-keeper. He himself had admired *Wisden* since, as a schoolboy in 1959, he leafed through it in a local bookshop and found that John Reid, who had once coached Wright himself, was a Cricketer of the Year. His selection was a big news story in New Zealand, and that day Wright read how Reid had learned the game with his grandfather in "a paddock beside a house in the Hutt Valley". Now, 20 years later, he was about to become the book's guiding hand.

Drafted in alongside Gordon Ross, the new associate editor and book reviewer, to support Preston, both as production editor and assistant editor, he brought a new level of book-trade expertise, an impressive (and much-needed) appetite for hard graft ("I never dared work out what the hourly rate was") and a patient affection for both sport and literature to the task. Preston wrote generously in his Preface that he "could not praise too highly" Wright's efforts on his first (and Preston's 27th) book. The 1979 *Wisden* was published in the middle of March and sold 30,000 copies.

Preston's spirits were flagging, however, and it showed. When Frank Keating interviewed him for the *Guardian* in 1979 he expected a "grave and biblical" figure, but found an outgoing Mr Pickwick, proud of the words with which he had answered the Queen when, presenting him with his MBE in 1977, she asked what he did: "I am a general and sporting reporter, your Majesty." But it was clear from his own writing that he was becoming deflated, even intemperate. In 1978 he berated as "dubious" the growing frequency with which Pakistan claimed new cricket records. "In a list of 103 players since 1859 whose maiden century was 200 or more, nine of the last 11 were scored in Pakistan," he wrote, unwilling to suspend his disbelief. "Since 1964, three totals over 800 have been amassed, and all in Pakistan." Were these really first-class scores? He had his doubts. He even queried Hanif Mohammad's famous 499 which was, he felt, achieved against "second-class bowling". He predicted that "each and every world record will be broken sooner or later in Pakistan".

There was bewilderment as well as injury in these lines. Records mattered, and so did accuracy – and in the expanded cricket world it was becoming hard to count on either. And all-professional cricket was starting to produce some grave anomalies, too, as captains pushed the rules to the limit in search of an edge. Was there value in a batting record achieved against help-yourself declaration bowling? It was a shame, in this context, that Preston was mistaken in saying that Hanif Mohammad was "not out" – as *Wisden* itself showed, he was *run* out, attempting to bring up his 500.

Preston's 1980 Notes were even more dejected. "The game of cricket has long been known to epitomise the highest levels of sportsmanship," he wrote. But "bad behaviour" was now the norm – "ridiculous appeals … disparaging remarks … banging the bat on the ground … kissing and cuddling". It was "nauseating". Of course he was entitled to his dismay, but the tone of baffled sorrow sounded merely grouchy. "Is the advent of big prize money," he asked, "causing the spread of bad manners?" It was a good question, and he must have thought he knew the answer.

It is no easy matter to grasp quite how much cricket changed in the course of Norman Preston's 29-volume career as *Wisden*'s editor. He picked up the reins in the courteous world of Peter May, David Sheppard and amateur captaincy, when radio and television were novelties and England held easy sway over the non-Australian cricket world (beating South Africa 3-1 in his first edition, and India 3-0 in his second). Professionals were paid £75 per Test match, umpires just £50, and although there had been a "frightening" drop in attendances cricket remained, without question, the national game. Winston Churchill was poised to return as prime minister and King George VI was on the throne. Tea was rationed, Charlie Chaplin was still in the cinemas, and the futuristic Comet was only just starting to propel air travel into the jet age. Nor was South Africa yet a pariah: at Trent Bridge Preston had seen a "lion-hearted" Dudley Nourse spend the best part of two days accumulating 208 runs on a "placid" pitch, and had enjoyed every minute. Touring sides in those days travelled by ship: Preston himself had been part of the tour party to Australia in 1946, singing tunes from his own school book, *Gaudeamus*, around the piano. Indeed he returned via America in the company of Len Hutton – introducing him as the English Babe Ruth – and also formed a lifelong friendship with Compton, helping him write his *Daily Express* column.

It is possible that Preston sensed, at the start of his reign, that he was entering a period of tremendous upheaval. In his very first Notes (in

1952) he identified, as if they were smoke signals from an approaching army, the rival attractions that were threatening to push cricket into the margins of the national life: the 5.2 million cars (as against 4,300 in 1901) or the 5,700 cinemas (compared to only 12 at the turn of the century). He didn't mention that Britain had just developed its own atom bomb, or that the first images of the Earth from space were being taken. His own childhood had been spent in a very different age, but by the time of his last book, 28 years later, cricket was a hectic pageant, live on television, with domestic one-day trophies and a World Cup of its own. Preston was at Lord's in the summer of 1979 to see the World Cup final in which Collis King scored 86 in an hour, and could see that the methods of a Boycott, who opened for England that day and spent 17 overs reaching double figures, belonged to the pony-and-cart era. Touring teams were travelling by air, watching in-flight movies and downing trays of beer in mid-flight. Mrs Thatcher was preparing to fight the trade unions at British Leyland, British Steel and the National Coal Board. The first hatchbacks were zipping along new motorways; the Yorkshire Ripper was on the loose, and John Lennon was being stalked by a murderer.

These events may seem like so much mood music, but they also signalled a profound shift in Britain's place in the world. When Preston worked on his father's *Wisden*, in the years immediately after the war, the pound was worth four dollars, and Barbados, India, Kenya, Malaya, Nigeria, Palestine and Rhodesia were colonial possessions: London held sway over 458 million souls. By the time he took over himself, India was independent and the rest of the Empire was heading that way, but the pound was still worth two and a half dollars; Britain could still see itself as a hero that had, not so long ago, seen off Hitler. By the end of his stewardship, however, the Cold War, the nuclear arms race and Suez had chilled the imperial blood, and the IMF had been asked to bail out an insolvent UK whose currency was worth a dollar and a half, and which was now in receipt of loans from Germany, of all countries. The land of hope and glory, Mrs Thatcher was crying, had become a land of beg and borrow.

It was some sort of achievement that *Wisden* managed to pass through so many far-reaching convulsions not just unscathed but barely changed. So though it is tempting (and has been common), from our easy vantage point in the 21st century, to see Norman Preston as a cautious editor, he may have been exactly what this bruising period most needed. He might not have been an innovator, but that was a conscious decision, not a failure of nerve or creativity. He disliked the end of the amateur/professional distinction, the hint of mob rule in the quarrel over South Africa, and the Packer revolution. He was rarely thrilled by the crazy whirl of modern times. But once again *Wisden* seemed to have called forth in its editor what it most required: a sure hand on the tiller and a clear sense of duty to its traditions. Preston had inherited the editorship from his father, and saw it as a personal as well as a national heirloom. In any case he belonged to that generation – barely imaginable now – that had seen two global bloodlettings and had a fixed urge to cherish and restore. A more fidgety or fashion-conscious editor might well have led *Wisden* into choppy waters, but Preston pointed the ship into the wind, held it to the appointed course and never let go. His achievement was that *Wisden* continued to be a calm voice in a noisy world.

He never ceased to campaign on behalf of vibrant cricket, however; when it came to the game itself he prized vitality above mere victory. In his 1967 Notes he lamented the spiritless approach of so much first-class play and made a point, when selecting his Cricketers of the Year, to pick out "those whose performances in this time of mediocrity do most to draw in the crowds" (among others he chose the big-hitting Colin Milburn, and – a poignant selection – Basil D'Oliveira). Nor did he ever fail to commend the merits of young players; he was a keen advocate of youth. In his 1978 Notes, praising the forceful style of the youthful Ian Botham, he recalled how in 1975 he had admired the man's "upright style" and urged that he be capped "while still young and enthusiastic". He promoted the merits of players like David Gower, Mike Gatting and Chris Tavaré, and in 1980 even noticed that Jonathan Agnew had "undergone a winter of tree felling to build up his young muscles".

One of his final acts was a concession of defeat. In 1971 he (along with his new chief record-keeper, Bill Frindall, the "bearded wonder" of the commentary box) followed the TCCB stipulation and treated the England v Rest of the World matches of the previous summer (sponsored by Guinness and arranged in place of the cancelled South

African tour) as Test matches, with a right to be included as such in
cricket's records. In a way it was a last, forlorn attempt to place cricket
above politics as an eternal rather than fashionable pastime. The players
were all Test match class, ran the argument (and the matches conformed
to the Test format), so their efforts should be part of the historical
record. At the time *Wisden* had called it "a magnificent series", though
not everyone had been so thrilled to see four South Africans – Barlow,
Pollock, Procter and Richards – gambolling about on England's
greenest stages after all that had so recently happened. And while the
standard of cricket was certainly top-notch, the series did not fit the
rough-and-ready sense that a Test match was a tussle between two
countries. Now, a decade later and with a baleful sigh ("much against
my will") Preston confessed that he had been asked to change his tune.
"It has been decided by the publishers of *Wisden*," he wrote, "to strike
those games from the record books."

Deleting records is no easy task, and has some cruel knock-on effects.
One player, Glamorgan's Alan Jones, won his first and only England
cap in that series; rewriting the past made him, after nearly a decade of
dining out on his achievement, someone who had never won a Test cap
but would become the heaviest run-scorer never (officially) to play in
Tests. It meant, too, that Derek Underwood, Preston's near neighbour
in Bromley, Kent, would be destined not to be in the select band of
bowlers to have taken 300 Test wickets after all.* But Wright, in
consultation with Frindall, was aware that other cricket record-keepers
did not regard the 1970 games as Test matches, and felt that *Wisden* was
out on an uncomfortable limb. He took Preston for a slap-up lunch at
Simpson's in the Strand – noted for its fine roast meat – and made his
case. "Norman had a good argument," he recalled. "He felt that he had
followed TCCB advice at the time and it would not be honourable to
disregard it now. But in the end I think he saw that it was inevitable."

---

* This became especially poignant in 2005 when the ICC ruled that an
experimental Australia v World XI series be included in Test records, though
it was not a success and was not repeated. There may have been more politics
than logic to the decision. There were many objections at the time, but if the
series *had* been relegated to the second tier, then Muttiah Muralitharan would
not, alas, have taken 800 Test wickets.

In one sense this was only another ripple from the Kerry Packer convulsion. No one, least of all Preston, wanted to treat the recent World Series as Test matches, but what, in retrospect, was the 1970 summer but a decorous, white-flannel version of a modern Packer circus? Either way, not long after Preston wrote this final set of Notes, and a few weeks after looking over the proofs of his 29th and final Almanack, he died following what the *Guardian* called "a short illness".

"We have lost Mr Pickwick," wrote John Woodcock in *The Times*. "In every press box in England Norman Preston had his own seat, from which emanated good cheer, great warmth, a quizzical assertion and conscientious reporting in the old-fashioned style." There were plenty to echo those words. "The primrose is edged with black," wrote Frank Keating in the *Guardian*, a florid tribute, though the same paper also noted Preston's passing in "Sport in Brief", between news of Mark Thatcher's motor-racing ambitions and a straight-sets defeat for "Britain's Sue Barker" in Texas.

The memorial was held at St Bride's, the Fleet Street church; Denis Compton gave the address, calling the old editor "one of my best friends". Preston had once confided that singing in Sydney Cathedral one Sunday morning had been the "greatest thrill" of that particular trip. "Throughout my cricketing career," Compton began, "his jovial face, lively sense of humour and infectious laugh endeared him to all cricketers." In case this made him sound foolish, Compton added that "He was a definite man: definite in appearance, definite in his opinions, and definite in his likes and dislikes."

In the *Wisden* obituary his colleague Harold Abel said that his old friend "sang better than he played cricket" but that he would be greatly missed. "His parting leaves a deep chasm." It was the end of a famous era. He and his father might have fallen short of the Pardons' record – Charles and Sydney led *Wisden* for 39 editions; the Prestons managed "only" 37, but between them worked on an astonishing 86. Somehow they steered the ship through the wreckage of war and lifted the circulation as it raced down the years, while always waving a flag for old values. Their *Wisden* remained a byword for cricket's traditions. If it seemed as if it could use new blood, it was only because it had sucked the last drop from Hubert and Norman.

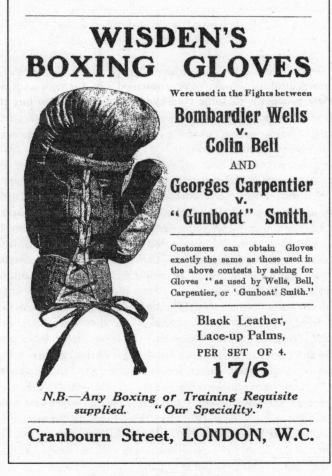

WISDEN'S
BOXING GLOVES

Were used in the Fights between

Bombardier Wells
v.
Colin Bell

AND

Georges Carpentier
v.
"Gunboat" Smith.

Customers can obtain Gloves
exactly the same as those used in
the above contests by asking for
Gloves " as used by Wells, Bell,
Carpentier, or ' Gunboat' Smith."

Black Leather,
Lace-up Palms,
PER SET OF 4.

17/6

*N.B.—Any Boxing or Training Requisite
supplied.   "Our Speciality."*

Cranbourn Street, LONDON, W.C.

Advertisement from Wisden *1916*

12

Nothing Must Go

The new editor of *Wisden* was unearthed not through a draining interview process with some cold-eyed headhunting firm but at the wedding party for Brian Johnston's daughter Clare – a ceremony that was held, after a service at St John's Wood church, in the Long Room at Lord's. John Woodcock, cricket correspondent of *The Times*, had just returned from England's tour of Australia (stopping in Bombay to watch one more Test match) and at the reception he found himself chatting to Kirsty Ennever, a friend of the bride who also happened to be the managing editor at Queen Anne Press. Woodcock was, of course, aware of Norman Preston's recent death, and asked, with his reporter's hat on, how they were getting on with the search for a replacement. He added that he wished someone would ask *him* to take on the job. It was something to say at a party. But Ennever passed on his interest to the managing director of Queen Anne Press, Alan Smith, who was excited by the idea and, the following Monday morning, rang Woodcock to dangle the prospect in front of him.*

He was pushing at an open door: Woodcock had been a *Wisden* disciple since early boyhood – indeed his end-of-term reports from the Dragon School, in Oxford, said that as long as he treated *Wisden* as his

---

* It was not widely known at the time, but Christopher Martin-Jenkins, the *Test Match Special* commentator who was then editing *The Cricketer*, had already been sounded out by William Gray. He was flattered, but declined, and did not make the offer public until he mentioned it in his autobiography, *CMJ: A Cricketing Life*, in 2012. "Woodcock," he wrote generously, now that all the water was safely under the bridge, "was worthier than I."

only set text he wasn't going to make much progress in his studies. His interest did not wane at St Edward's, Oxford, where he featured in the first XI in 1944 and 1945 before getting a hockey Blue at Oxford. When he joined *The Times* a few years later, and became its cricket correspondent, he had not lost his affection for the Almanack. "I just loved it," he said. "And it became a hobby. I collected every one from 1933."

He had, apart from anything else, the perfect initials for the job. And as *The Times* man for more than a quarter of a century, he was restoring a connection with the newspaper that went back to Sydney Pardon and George West. So it was by no means the hardest decision of his life. "I came home to think about it," he said, "and just thought, yes, it would be fine."

He was fortunate in that Graeme Wright had already familiarised himself with the swarming cat's cradle of ropes required to steer the publication. And Wright was not alone. In his first year, having just moved house and dazed by the enormous pile of scorecards to check, he had turned to a neighbour for help. Christine Forrest had, with two growing children at home, just started to think that she herself should be looking out for a bit of part-time work when Wright (literally) came knocking.

In *Wisden*'s case, of course, part-time work is not a very meaningful concept, and a neighbourly bit of reading scores aloud soon turned into a formidable list of "tasks" that filled two pages, and ran to six months worth of 11-hour days. Forrest had never been a cricket fan ("I didn't know a leg-bye from a wide, or a short leg from a silly mid-off") and her idea of fun was "a weekend at Stratford cramming in three plays". But she soon assumed the role of production editor, taking responsibility for the entire *Wisden* timetable, from the fountain of words and numbers gushing from the world's cricket pitches to procedural details for the final typesetting. For 20 years she checked proofs, collected records from schools, chased advertisers, flagged dates and deadlines, organised photographs, calculated pagination and paper quantity and whatever else was required. In return she was allowed to help with the coats and umbrellas at the annual *Wisden* dinner, which remained an all-male gathering until the mid-1990s. She did not object – "I respected it from the point of view of tradition" – and soon became an integral part of the *Wisden* engine-room.

Even after speaking to Wright and Forrest about the volume of work involved, Woodcock was taken aback by the scale of it. "Graeme and Christine were indispensable," he said. "Without them there's no question: the 1981 edition wouldn't even have come out." They soon fell into a pleasant routine. Wright and Forrest would drive down the M3 from London to Hampshire, to meet at Woodcock's idyllic thatched cottage near Andover, with a trout stream babbling across the meadow, and bright MCC and I Zingari umbrellas parked inside the front door. Woodcock's long dining-room table became, for a decade, the editorial headquarters of what was, quite literally, a cottage industry.* "I like to think we were a happy team," he said. "They used to come down and sit here for the whole day, popping to the pub for lunch. It was totally and utterly informal. They were wonderful, those two, and a marvellous girl, that Christine. With her and Graeme, I didn't worry at all. I never worried, until it became too much."

"We only ever had one argument," said Wright. "It was about how to abbreviate Middlesex, I think. I can't remember now who wanted what, but neither John nor I would budge. At one point he even suggested ringing Swanton for a ruling. We went back and forth for about ten minutes. Christine just sat back and tried not to laugh."

When Forrest retired, in 1998, the *Observer* called her *Wisden*'s "unsung guardian angel" and Matthew Engel, who by then had taken over as editor, agreed, adding that without her the "sequence of 135 years' continuous publication would have been broken". The fact that she was not driven by an addiction to the game itself never struck her as odd. "You don't have to like cricket to enjoy the statistics," she said. "There is a culture that just enjoys the figures." In her own way – a perfectionist urge to get things right crossed with a traditionalist urge to maintain standards – she was as keen a purist as any of the starry-eyed cricket-lovers who had run *Wisden* down the years. The rebel tours to South Africa saddened her not (or not only) because they vexed a liberal conscience, but because they messed up the averages. Could real runs be

---

* During Woodcock's last year as editor, a BBC documentary about *Wisden* filmed the three of them sitting around that very table, leafing through letters. It did indeed seem an enviable and civilised office.

ignored, however controversial the context? She took a similar position over one of Woodcock's first decisions, in 1981, to drop the formal nicety by which amateur players were given the prefix Mr in Births and Deaths. Again, her objection was historical – the formal distinction was a concise and informative way of communicating a long-standing cricket fact. "It told you something about a player – but it's lost for ever now."

Early in 1981 Wright wrote an airmail letter to Woodcock, who was following England in the West Indies. "Between streaming noses, head-aches and poor facilities at the printer's," he wrote, "we managed to get *Wisden* off safely." England was in the grip of freezing fog, and it can't have helped his mood that the flimsy envelope had to be sent to Woodcock care of the "Paradise Beach" in Barbados. It was a built-in hazard of the new structure that the editor would often be away reporting cricket for *The Times*. But his elevated position in the press box hierarchy – he was already the "Sage of Longparish" – and the elegance of his writing added a cultivated twist to the Almanack's already deep conversation with cricket. His earth-spanning travels with the newspaper, meanwhile, gave him fine contacts within the game; he was friendly with Don Bradman (who once gave him a lift back to the hotel from a Test match, chatting about fast bowling all the way) and Richie Benaud; Australian tourists would visit him to try their luck fly-fishing on the River Test. "I loved the overseas tours," he said. "I used to look forward to them. In those days there was time to get to know the players. It's all very different now."*

In his six-book period in charge Woodcock (with Wright and Forrest's energetic help) would enhance and modernise the Almanack not by remodelling it but by pushing here and nudging there. The Index was compressed by nearly 20 pages, and the Schools section was condensed. This allowed him to expand the coverage of international

---

* Bradman himself had actually written to congratulate Woodcock on his appointment. "Dear Johnny," he wrote, after seeing a "small snippet" in the paper, "they are fortunate to obtain an editor of your calibre." He added that he was himself very fond of the Almanack: "I have been privileged to be a personal friend of previous editors," he said, and was "proud to be the possessor of a complete set since 1900".

cricket: he introduced scorecards for the domestic tournaments in West Indies, South Africa, India, Pakistan and New Zealand. He gave the book reviews back to John Arlott (for the last two Preston years they had fallen to Gordon Ross) and welcomed E. W. Swanton back into a fold from which he had long been absent.* He also gave first outings to two *Wisden* editors of the future, echoing the procedures of England selectors: promising up-and-comers were given a try-out in the middle order before going on to higher things. Matthew Engel of the *Guardian* was asked to narrate another chapter of the South African saga for the 1984 volume, after yet another ill-judged plot to send an MCC team to South Africa was rebuffed; while in *Wisden* 1981 Scyld Berry of the *Observer* explored the faraway cricket fields of Fiji and Papua New Guinea, where he found a pastor who "leads the flock by opening the batting and the bowling, a monopoly which no one is going to challenge as long as he keeps the kit in his house".

Woodcock's *Wisden* began by noticing that most of his predecessors had started in a sour mood. "English cricket needs an injection of culture and enterprise," Norman Preston wrote in 1952, echoing what Brookes had written in 1936: "The happiest man in the country must have been the born pessimist." So in sounding a "cautionary note, even a sombre one", Woodcock was only showing how well he had absorbed the *Wisden* mindset. He condemned the bolshy behaviour of players like Dennis Lillee, Michael Holding and Colin Croft, all of whom had thrown tantrums when decisions did not go their way. And he glowered at the number of overseas cricketers who were "impeding England's cause" by playing county cricket. In true *Wisden* style he was also horrified by the way the increased use of helmets – "an objectionable trend" – were imposing a "wretched anonymity on players". As the years passed these would remain major themes: he was a loud opponent of intimidatory bowling (a menace for which helmets were also partly to blame – they encouraged bowlers to target tailenders). And he clung to

---

* Norman Preston was certainly well acquainted with E. W. Swanton: they went on three overseas tours together, to Australia, West Indies and South Africa. So his absence from *Wisden*'s pages for the 29 years of his editorship is quite pointed.

the idea that cricketers should be sportsmanlike, especially when it came
to respecting the decisions of the umpires (even if they were wrong).

Naturally he found room for a brief but disapproving lecture about
the "scuffle" in the Lord's pavilion that marred the Saturday of the
centenary "jamboree" in 1980 – when some MCC members made a
noisy scene in protest against the fact that rain had stopped play. But he
could not bring himself to be too indignant. "It seems laughable to be
able to land a man on the moon," he sighed in his Notes, "yet to have
discovered no adequate way of protecting the square at Lord's."

One of his keenest wishes – and in this he had the wholehearted support
of Wright and Forrest – was to restore the Almanack's reputation for semi-
Papal infallibility. On the whole it remained a minor miracle of detailed
fact-checking, but no one could deny that the Errata box was becoming a
bit too crowded these days. "It was a highly professional product," said
Woodcock. "How they did it I don't know. But in the period after the war
there *were* quite a lot of mistakes – if I picked out a *Wisden* from the 1940s
I could find a dozen just like that, mainly to do with initials."

The fabled authority of *Wisden* in such matters would be publicly
contested in 1995 when the Association of Cricket Statisticians, a
research body founded in 1973, discovered, in the course of creating a
digital archive of first-class scorecards, that the Almanack was in fact
far from error-free. This was reported in the newspapers with glee – it
was a pleasant feet-of-clay story claiming that cricket's "so-called
Bible" had, in fact, a spotty record, and that as many as 70% of the
scorecards contained mistakes.* "The venerable pillar has been shown
to have cracks," said a leader in *The Times*. Matthew Engel, by then the
editor, declared that any such mistakes would have been minuscule – a
miscounting of no-balls or leg-byes. And Norman Preston's
ex-secretary, Vivian Gladman, also wrote to *The Times* to defend her
old colleagues against the slur. She described the careful procedures by
which results and scores were transmitted, logged and entered into
Wisden's lists. Scores would be phoned in by reporters and checked
when they arrived; if they did not balance they would be run by the

---

* Though since the story appeared in the *Sunday Times* on 1 April, of all days,
it was itself taken by some to be perhaps less than 100% reliable.

reporter again until they were correct. There were "innumerable" further checks. The safety net involved the interrogation of scorers, umpires and even players. While admitting that scores were occasionally balanced by adding a dot here or a leg-bye there, she remembered the editor himself as tigerish. "If Norman Preston ever had his attention drawn to an error, it was always thoroughly investigated."

Even so, mistakes did sneak through: in *Wisden* 1950 the young Fred Trueman was described on his debut as a "spin" bowler. But for the most part they were indeed minor – leg-byes treated as byes, totals that didn't exactly tally with bowling figures. A match might have been played at Kettering, not Northampton; a batsman may have scored 103, not 105. And sometimes they were simply spelling slips: Sydney Barnes as "Sidney"; Samuel Beckett with the initials S. V. instead of S. B.; and Bradman himself, in his first appearance, as "D" rather than "D. G.". Some mishaps suggest an era when reporters phoned in scores, and a crackle on the line might lead a Boycott century to be scored at Leeds, not Lord's. But this couldn't explain why Tom Graveney was left off the list of century makers in 1954, and, despite an apology, left out again the following year. In 1946 Frank Evershed was surprised to read an obituary of himself, and ten years later the wrong Frederick Fane was treated to the same odd experience.

Ah well. What is cricket but a game of mistakes? If batsmen never erred they would never be out. And the surprising thing is not the odd fumble but that significant errors truly are rare. Attempting to correct the slip in its report on the 1975 World Cup final, when *Wisden* congratulated "the amazing Kallicharran" rather than Viv Richards on the hat-trick of brilliant run-outs that propelled the West Indies to a scintillating victory, the Almanack only dug itself into a deeper hole. The Errata box the following year got it wrong again, but the record was not amended until 2008, when *Wisden* tried to straighten things out ... even then it said that the mistake was in "*Wisden* 1975", rather than the 1976 volume.* This is, of course, one of the most common

---

* In stating that the hat-trick belonged to Richards, *Wisden* 2008 added that Kallicharran "had a hand" in two other dismissals. Alas, Kallicharran had nothing to do with those either. *Wisden* 2009 finally put the record right – a rare case of three errata entries relating to the same blunder.

Wisden errors, since it is always one year behind the events it records. In *Wisden* years, Compton's *annus mirabilis* was 1948, and Botham's Ashes were in 1982.

As we have seen, owning up to mistakes was good public relations: the act of coming clean was a way of emphasising *Wisden*'s commitment to accuracy. Getting the record straight was one of the Almanack's solemn duties – it never thought that such things didn't matter. In *Wisden* 1934 it reported on the "unfortunate oversight ... a serious blunder" by which the Yorkshire Second XI had been wrongly credited with points for a win against Staffordshire, when in fact they won no more than a first-innings lead in a washout draw. It wasn't *Wisden*'s mistake, but it was an error of some consequence since Yorkshire were thus judged to have come second in the final table before going on to defeat Norfolk in a play-off. Now, in retrospect, it appeared that Wiltshire should have contested that play-off in Yorkshire's place. Too late now.

If nothing else, mistakes were a way of triggering letters from readers. For every one who wrote with a word of praise or gratitude there were dozens who relished the challenge of finding a misprint. Indeed it was often children, in this age before daytime TV and laptop games, who took the trouble to calculate averages and locate discrepancies in *Wisden*. One of the most charming came from a ten-year-old girl in Manchester who wrote that she had been looking at "my Daddy's 1982 *Wisden*" and was shocked to find, in Births and Deaths, that Lancashire's Barry Wood had died four decades earlier, on 26 December 1942 – odd, since she had seen him at Old Trafford only weeks ago. "Am I," she wondered, putting it in the record-breaking terms *Wisden* would respect, "the first person to see a ghost playing cricket?"

Not all the letters were so good-natured. A 13-year-old boy from Ballarat, Australia sent in a list of suggestions – more international cricket, fewer schools – along with various other quibbles. Woodcock replied generously, urging the boy to feel free to carry on the good work, but might have regretted it when, the following year, an even more detailed and self-confident critique arrived, pointing out assorted "inconsistencies of style" and many other areas of "disorder".

But the question of accuracy took on a more serious significance when it came to the tricky matter of W. G. Grace's career record. In

1980, not long after Norman Preston's death, *Wisden*'s statistician Michael Fordham brooded on a vexed issue: how many first-class centuries had W. G. Grace scored? According to the figures in the 1916 *Wisden* (the standard source set out by Ashley-Cooper) Grace made 126, and this had been the orthodox number ever since. But recent research, again by the Association of Cricket Statisticians, argued that two of those hundreds – against a "scratch" Somerset team and on a tour of Canada – were not truly first-class and should be subtracted.

The revised figures were entered in the 1981 *Wisden*, and letters duly thumped on Woodcock's doormat. "The implications are too awful to contemplate," wrote David Frith. A collector wrote: "I do NOT understand what you have done," and a *Wisden* regular, E. M. Wellings, added: "What has happened? At first I thought the change from 126 to 124 might be a printing error ... Damn it, the man must be a lunatic."

Woodcock was not best pleased himself. The changes had been "smuggled in without reference to me", he told Frith, promising to reverse the amendment. He did so in fine style, asking Fordham to write an article justifying the change, publicly disagreeing with it himself, and restoring the traditional figures to the record section.

Fordham's argument was that the Association had been more than thorough, cross-checking records in 17 different ways, consulting MCC minute books, old scorebooks and newspapers. It had been the opposite of hasty: it had spent three years discussing the matter before declaring its support for the change, which had since been embraced by most other publications, including Bill Frindall's *Wisden Book of Cricket Records*.

Woodcock was firm. "It is my intention to return W. G.'s record to what it was," he told the Association, and in *Wisden* 1982 he was clear: "No amount of research could, to my mind, justify changing a record so honoured by time and custom ... then, as now, contemporary opinion was the best criterion." There would, he promised, be a "relevant note" to indicate that the record was now in doubt, but the past – the word according to *Wisden* – would not be rewritten. Tampering with history was no simple matter, he argued, since the ripples from those original figures had gone on to shape other legendary moments in the game. The famous day when Grace scored his hundredth century, or the one when Hobbs equalled and then surpassed Grace ... that was a "national ceremony". Was *Wisden* supposed to rewrite *that* story too?

Woodcock and Wright were not quite of one mind on this issue. Wright's reflexes favoured publishing the most precise figure available, not merely the one sanctified by time and tradition, and he wrote to Woodcock in support of Fordham's proposed amendment. "As the acknowledged reference work on cricket," he reasoned, "*Wisden* must be as accurate as is humanly possible ... Reverting to the original figures will inevitably leave *Wisden* at variance with most record books." This mild demurral never became a quarrel, however, and the editor's decision stood.

Woodcock and Wright also differed with respect to David Frith's magazine, *Wisden Cricket Monthly*. Woodcock, weary of being quizzed about it, proposed a clarifying footnote to the effect that there was "no connection" between the Almanack and the magazine, nor with Bill Frindall's *Wisden Book of Cricket Records* and the *Wisden Book of Test Cricket*. But the suggestion that only the Almanack was truly "Wisden" sounded a bit haughty to Wright. He wrote to Woodcock suggesting that the footnote "smacks a little too heavily of a rebuke", and urged him to insert no such remark.

There was a similar conversation regarding the arcane matter of players' initials. This was no small thing: many cricketers were remembered only by these initials – and plenty of cricket-lovers did not even know what the W. G. or C. B. stood for when they prefixed Grace and Fry. But a determined search of birth records was finding anomalies: A. A. Lilley should have been A. F. A. Lilley; J. D. Robertson was really J. D. B. Robertson; J. Gunn was J. R.; A. C. Russell was C. A. F. Once again Woodcock resisted change and vowed to "use those by which a cricketer has always been known". If accuracy could be achieved only at the expense of clarity, it was a will o' the wisp, not worth pursuing for its own sake. Imagine if Fry had been christened Julian, and then dropped it in adult life – would anyone seriously want to rename him J. C. B.? One might as well insist on calling Coco the Clown by his true name – Nicolai Poliakoff.

The conversation was conducted in public and above board, and the Association did not bear a grudge. Two years later, reviewing the 1984 edition in its journal, it wrote that for "many years" *Wisden* had been in a "rut" but that Woodcock had revived it: "there have been a number of changes, most of them not before time, all of them improvements".

It even proposed a two-*Wisden* solution (a domestic edition in the spring and an overseas version in November) that would allow the Almanack to supply "world cricket coverage second to none". It remains an enticing idea, though with the volume of cricket in the 21st century even two might not be enough.

The 1982 *Wisden* was fortunate in that, aside from this prickly matter, there was some grand cricket to celebrate: Ian Botham's performances the previous year had brought England to a halt like nothing since Compton's amazing form in 1947. Woodcock praised him in terms that wouldn't have meant much to Botham's younger fans, calling him "the reincarnation of Jessop", but in linking him to a great name from the past he was rescuing him from the attentions of those who saw him as a rebel hero. To emphasise that it had not *quite* been a one-man show, Woodcock also invited Mike Brearley to air his thoughts on leadership, his own brand of which had proved so magical.

But it was the match reports that told the real story. By now everyone knew that the most important *Wisden* reader was posterity, and Botham's feats were narrated with a solemn lucidity that had one eye on the future. The Third Test in Leeds opened under "familiar slate-grey clouds", with the new electronic scoreboard enjoying "a mixed reception"; the second day was "pedestrian in the extreme"; and the third ended with "unhappy scenes" when the umpires stopped for bad light and, though the sun came out, never resumed. Readers were invited to imagine a tedious game that was merely going through the motions. Only then did Botham tear up that script and replace it with a comic-book ending, hammering 149 to set up the amazing finale in which Bob Willis hurtled in to take eight wickets and pull off one of the game's most shocking turnarounds. It was "something unique", said *Wisden*, refusing to get over-excited. "This was Willis's hour, watched or listened to by a vast invisible audience." It feels as though *Wisden* was imagining not just the fans who were following events on radio and television, but the even greater crowd waiting to read these words in the future.

Unusually (though not uniquely) the Five Cricketers of the Year in the 1982 Almanack were all overseas players – Allan Border, Richard Hadlee, Javed Miandad, Rodney Marsh and Terry Alderman, and while this reflected Woodcock's well-travelled sense of cricket's international nature, it also said something about the award – players such as Botham, Brearley and Willis were ineligible, having been honoured before. But, by now, being named in *Wisden* was a popular honour. When the young Boycott was named in 1965 he wrote a respectful letter to Norman Preston, and when, 20 years later, Larry Gomes was picked by Woodcock (partly, in truth, because so many of his fellow West Indians – Richards, Lloyd, Greenidge and Holding – had already been singled out) he received "a million thanks" from the young West Indian. Gomes's friend Hugh Henderson wrote to recall that Gomes, as a 16-year-old, said it was one of his lifetime "goals" to be in the *Wisden* Five. The player was "delighted beyond words".

The sad thing about the 1982 *Wisden* was that, for Woodcock, even the splendid story of Botham's Ashes was overshadowed by "politics". The issue of South Africa was again filling the horizon. The West Indies had refused to play New Zealand, following an All Blacks rugby series against South Africa, and England's tour of India had also been imperilled by the selection of players (Geoffrey Boycott chief among them) who had played in South Africa. Only the intervention of India's prime minister, Mrs Gandhi, saved the day, which made the announcement, shortly before going to press, of a "rebel" tour (orchestrated in part by Boycott himself) even more embarrassing. The rebel players were condemned and banned for three years.

Woodcock, like many MCC members, thought this excessive ("I sincerely think cricket has been set back") and declared his preference for an open-door policy. "I believe in the bridge with South Africa," he was quoted in *The Times* as saying in 1983, "though there is no doubt that isolation has forced them into making changes they would not otherwise have made." He sympathised with players who were thus deprived of international recognition, and thought that the South African Cricket Association had made at least some strides towards multi-racial cricket. He drew polite attention to the irony by which Allan Lamb, a South African, was permitted to play for England, while Graham Gooch, who had merely taken a temporary job there, was not. So he asked Walter Hadlee, the former Kiwi captain, selector and father of Richard Hadlee, to address the issue in the 1982 Almanack. He did so in terms that created some heated headlines in his home country, where he was accused of speaking out against the national policy.

Even *The Times*, Woodcock's own paper, could not quite support the *Wisden* line in this area. The standard view (as indicated by an MCC vote in 1983 which resolved *not* to send a team to Johannesburg) was that the boycott, while not enjoyable, and bad luck on some talented cricketers, was effective. Bridge-building was all very well, wrote the sports editor, Nicholas Keith, "but it is not possible when the river is in full flood".

Partly because of this, and partly because of the increasingly garish atmospherics of the modern game, Woodcock's *Wisden* often wore the same grim frown that had characterised so many volumes in the past. Once more we can't help noticing that a book motivated by a love of cricket spent an awful lot of time complaining or beating its breast – as if its love were unrequited. "In purely technical terms the standard of English batsmanship can never have been so low," wrote Woodcock, adding a new line to the historic claim that cricket was going downhill. And in *Wisden* 1983 he wrote: "There were times when Trent Bridge and Edgbaston sounded like football grounds." When Trevor Chappell, in collusion with his brother Greg, bowled an underarm daisy cutter to prevent New Zealand hitting the six they needed from the last ball, it was "disreputable", a sign that sportsmanship was dead. Cricket was still "an incomparable pastime" but it was surely endangered by these lapses of taste.

His most biting criticism was reserved for the kind of dangerous bowling of which the West Indies (having been battered by Australia's pace attack in their time) were now the prime exponents. In his 1984 Notes Woodcock wrote of "the thuggery of the bouncer", adding that "the viciousness of much of today's fast bowling is changing the very nature of the game". And the following year he repeated the charge, calling it a new and "chilling dimension" in cricket. In some quarters this was taken as mildly anti-West Indian in tone, though Woodcock took care to extend his rebuke to other nations too. But there was an aggrieved, Canuteish tone to the complaint, and the world's fast men were not about to start pitching it up just to please *Wisden*.

A lot of energy went into these and other debates. But the editor's usual lot was often more routine. Should the season's averages be arranged in alphabetical order to make it easier to look up a player? Should something be done about the weight of bats (Bradman's had weighed only 2lbs 2oz, whereas the thudding modern clubs were 3lbs or more)? And when it came to contributors it was a case of some you win, some you don't. Alec Douglas-Home turned down Woodcock's invitation to contribute an article ("I don't seem to be able to get myself into the mood"), but Bradman, an old acquaintance, accepted. Back in 1939 he had urged cricket's administrators to adjust to the "quickening tempo" of contemporary life, and now, in 1986, he repeated the homily, asking people to accept that one-day cricket was "here to stay" and that, while not to be compared to Test matches, it did have merit: "It rids the game of the unutterable bore who thinks occupancy of the crease and his own personal aggrandisement are all that matter."

Woodcock himself had applauded the unlikely victory of India in the World Cup final of 1983, when they surprised the all-conquering West Indies and ignited a giddy new enthusiasm for cricket in the vast population of the Indian subcontinent. "They brought warmth and excitement in the place of dampness and depression," he wrote. And in his Notes the previous year he drew his readers' attention to the amazing fact that, in the space of a third-wicket partnership of 455 in the 1981-2 Madras Test, roughly 75,000 Indian babies had been born. He called this a "random thought" but in fact it was shrewdly aimed. In this one number he was glimpsing the future of the game.

It was not easy to glimpse the future of John Wisden & Co at this time, though: in the mid-1980s it was being tossed about in choppy commercial waters like a cork on a stormy sea. This was the buzzing dawn of deregulated markets, the steep first wave of predatory boardroom feasting and plundering, the age of junk bonds and Wall Street deal-making, a time when men in suits stumbled upon a way of living like Renaissance princes and when all sorts of hungry beasts roared out of the financial jungle: corporate-finance gurus, asset-strippers, greenmailers and white knights.

Wisden felt the first flare of this brash new world in 1981, when Robert Maxwell acquired the British Printing Corporation (BPC – though he soon changed its name to the British Printing and

Communication Corporation, or BPCC). This was the parent company of Macdonald's, which in turn was the home of Queen Anne Press, so thus Maxwell was now the owner of *Wisden*'s publisher. He was a mysterious figure: a Czech émigré, a British Army Captain who had won a Military Cross, a one-time MP, a businessman and a wheeler-dealer. He had money and swagger, but also something that might not – how to put it – be quite cricket. Back in 1969 he had been formally declared, following a complaint to the Department of Trade and Industry about his takeover tactics, to be "not in our opinion a person who can be relied upon to exercise proper stewardship of a publicly quoted company". One way or another, he made *Wisden* nervous.

"Oh yes," wrote Wright at the end of one his chatty airmails to Woodcock, sending news from the home front to the tropics. "Not only have you been saddled with Murdoch [*The Times* had recently been taken over by the Australian magnate] but you are also indirectly working for Robert Maxwell. He has taken over a large share of BPCC and is now the chief executive and deputy chairman." As it happened there would soon be an exodus from Macdonald's. Alan Smith, who had been looking after the Almanack, went to Collins, confiding to Woodcock as he left that he would dearly love, when the agreement with Queen Anne Press ran out, to take *Wisden* with him.

At the 1983 *Wisden* dinner Robert Maxwell, who was seated between Gubby Allen and William Gray, started promising, off the cuff, to modernise this clearly out-of-date little number, making it bigger, more legible and altogether spiffier. If he expected a whoop of applause for his dynamism and chutzpah he was sadly mistaken. "It was obvious he didn't know anything about it," said Woodcock. The cognoscenti in the room could only shudder, and William Gray put a polite hand on his arm and said it was his duty to point out that Maxwell did not actually own *Wisden* – he merely owned the publisher that had the contract to produce it.

Arlott wrote to Woodcock: "I feel if Maxwell tried violently to change *Wisden* the Cricket Society would march on him and trample him to death." And a review in *The Times* agreed. "Heaven forbid," it thundered. "Nothing must go." Actually it wasn't altogether illogical of Maxwell – a larger-format book would not have needed to be 1,298 pages. But changing *Wisden*'s shape and style would have wrecked its value as a consistent link to the past, and therefore as a collectable antique. It was trapped in its small-page format, like it or not. But this was no joking matter, and Grays began to look for alternative publishing arrangements. In early 1984 it was announced that *Wisden* would return to being published by John Wisden & Co (now a subsidiary of Grays), but that it would be marketed and distributed by a new partner, Gollancz. Graeme Wright was appointed publishing director in an unusual structure by which John Wisden & Co would present a complete book to the Gollancz back office. When a young diarist at *The Times* called Simon Barnes wondered whether this meant there were "vast changes afoot", Wright was quick to reassure him: "The news is that there is no news."

Grays, meanwhile, was running into a different sort of trouble. Anxious to protect its market-leading position in metal-shafted squash racquets, it had been slow to see the importance of the new graphite models. It was a costly mistake. At the beginning of 1984 the Squash Racquets Association gave its blessing to graphite, and within six months it was barely possible to sell a racquet made from any other material. Grays had staked its future on an old-school racquet that was now defunct. This major business mistake led to frosty relations between the two brothers at the top of the firm, William and John Gray. It also led to 74 redundancies across the business, an acute cash flow problem and severe pressure from Barclays Bank.

No one at the Almanack knew it, but *Wisden* had effectively been mortgaged – put up as surety for £400,000 worth of Grays' bank loans. Fearful that Barclays might take possession and seek to "monetise" a saleable asset – the bank *was* making stern noises about the need for Grays to reduce its £1 million overdraft without delay – William Gray approached Wright and urged him to seek a buyer. He wanted to sell the firm in its entirety while, in a novel twist, retaining the right to get some or all of it back 12 months later – an option he had "every intention" of exercising. In effect he was looking for an ally, a haven, a safe place to park *Wisden* while the wind raged.

Wright sounded out a few connections in the City before offering the Almanack to McCorquodale, a venerable printing company with solid sports credentials in its own right. One of the directors, Alastair McCorquodale, had opened the bowling for Harrow in the 1944 Eton match (scoring 27 and taking three wickets, according to *Wisden*). He had also taken part in the 100 metres final in the London Olympics in 1948, missing out on bronze in one of the first-ever photo finishes, but winning silver in the relay before giving up sprinting for good. He went on to play three times for Middlesex before joining the family firm, which had been set up in Liverpool (printing railway tickets) by George McCorquodale back in 1878. In 1946 the company had bought William Clowes, the printer for whom Charles Dickens had once worked as a "blacking boy", so it had its roots in the same steam-powered era as *Wisden* itself. He knew *Wisden* partly because he had been in it, but chiefly because a McCorquodale subsidiary, Spottiswood Ballantyne, had been typesetting *Wisden* for Sporting Handbooks since 1964. Spottiswood Ballantyne had a proud heritage of its own: founded in 1739, it had printed Dr Johnson's dictionary and moved from London to Colchester before being acquired by McCorquodale in 1955. It was partly this, indeed, that had led Wright to favour McCorquodale as a purchaser – having a new owner might be interesting, but finding a new printer could be a nightmare.

The deal was announced in January 1985. McCorquodale (aware that if *Wisden* went elsewhere a substantial print contract was at risk) bought out the entire Grays holding. The equipment side was ordered to "cease trading with effect from 1 January 1985", meaning that the Wisden "double-groover" bat, as advertised in recent Almanacks, would be the last of its kind. But few mourned the loss of this once-famous bat. Indeed such was *Wisden*'s prestige that McCorquodale's share price actually rose (by more than 10%) on the news. Nicholas Heroys, finance director of McCorquodale and later President of Kent County Cricket Club, was made chairman.

The firm was well known in social circles. The notorious romantic novelist Barbara Cartland had married *two* members of the family, and Alastair's son would go on to wed Diana Spencer's sister. They were surprised when Grays exercised their option to buy back 50% of Wisden a year later, and it left Wisden with a fragile ownership, at a time when the murkier alleys of the stock market were alive with corporate raiders, circling like sharks.

One of the most rapacious was the man behind *Wisden*'s former publisher, Robert Maxwell. After his failure to buy Waddington's (the board-game concern behind Monopoly and Cluedo) he was using his base at BPCC and the Mirror Group (bought in 1984) to lay siege to rival print companies. So when Norton Opax announced a bid for McCorquodale he bought himself a seat in the game by buying a large block of Norton Opax shares. As it happened, McCorquodale itself was trying to ward off the Norton Opax bid by looking for a "white knight", Extel (the Exchange and Telegraph Company), not knowing that Extel was itself being stalked by Maxwell. When the dust settled on the flurry of subsequent trades (and following a Monopolies and Mergers Commission inquiry into the probity of the deal), Norton Opax won the day; but it emerged that Maxwell himself now had a 24% shareholding in Norton Opax. Maxwell, who went on to buy the *New York Daily News*, sold his stake in Norton Opax to Bowater, thus helping Bowater to take over Norton Opax in 1990 (for £382 million – a number far over the Almanack's head). Somehow or other, without lifting a finger, *Wisden* found itself with its fourth owner in as many years.

Throughout this hectic see-sawing, Grays had faithfully retained its own half share, but since Bowater wasn't much interested in the Almanack, it remained a precarious ownership arrangement. *Wisden* was now an extremely small fish in a deep and intimidating pond. It was both revered and modestly profitable, but it wasn't going to have much impact on the bottom line of a company that, not long ago, had been the largest paper-producer in the world.

John Woodcock, meanwhile, was continuing to man the barricades against the threats to his game. Violent bowling was still the "unacceptable face of cricket" – the time when Malcolm Marshall made "so inept a batsman" as Pat Pocock jump about at The Oval was "woeful ... entirely lacking in chivalry". The rise of short-form cricket was also perilous. "Unless we are very careful, the one-day international will drive out the Test ... as inexorably as the grey squirrel drove out the red."

Whatever his reservations, his Almanack was thriving. In 1985 Grays claimed that the circulation was 55,000, and while this is no ironclad figure (it may refer to the print run; it may not include returns; and it was certainly a nice number to put before a prospective buyer) it is clear that the book was doing well. At the time of the takeover by

McCorquodale in 1985 the *Financial Times* estimated that it sold "55,000-60,000 copies" per year. The 1982 edition, which told the story of Botham's Ashes, had been especially popular: it was reprinted and rode high in the bestseller lists for nearly four months, even with a busy set of Charles-and-Diana wedding souvenirs as competition.

There was also a pleasing little occasion in 1984 when William Gray backed an initiative by David Frith, editor of *Wisden Cricket Monthly*, to unveil a new headstone for John Wisden in Brompton Cemetery, where he had been laid a hundred years previously. John Barclay, captain of Sussex, was invited to unveil the new monument, but when he was tied up in pre-season training in Brighton, the Archdeacon of Middlesex led the ceremony, praying that the Lord would "lead us to avoid all that is not cricket".

The Willows Publishing Company had joined the party in 1983 by reproducing the 1885 edition in a limited edition of a thousand copies, in brown cloth with gilt lettering. Now, to mark the centenary of the Little Wonder's death, they reproduced the 1884 edition. In announcing the publication they were pleased to note that the editor back then, George West, had been on the staff of *The Times*, like the present editor himself. And as if reprinting its antique editions were not sufficient sign of its own historic weight, *Wisden* was also anthologising itself with an imposing set of best-of compilations edited by Benny Green. Green had suggested the idea himself when reviewing the Almanack for the *Spectator*, and was by far the best man for the job: a jazz-loving, cricket-mad historian with no airs and graces and a keen feeling for *Wisden*'s oddball charm as well as its sterling qualities. John Arlott, reviewing the third anthology, said it "would keep an addict quiet for a week", while the *Telegraph* called it "a golden book". Green saw one-day cricket as a form of prostitution. In place of amateur patronage it had made a pact with a diminished version of itself, to attract paying customers. It meant survival, he conceded, "but survival at a cost so great as to transform the technique, morality and social significance" of the game. He proposed that cricket be funded like Covent Garden, as culture – a vain hope that only showed how well he had internalised *Wisden*'s own worldview. In time Green would produce an illustrated *Concise Wisden* rendering of the entire collection, a Russian-doll tribute to the sheer scale of the Almanack's memory. But he could not quell, in his final anthology, the sorrowful feeling that he, and we, were now staring at the game's death-rattle.

If Woodcock ever hoped that his *Wisden* life would be quiet, he was disappointed, because these were not calm years. Even the annual dinner in 1984 was noisily disrupted after a policewoman, Yvonne Fletcher, had been killed by a bullet fired from the Libyan Embassy in St James's Square, diagonally opposite the venue for the cricket occasion, the East India Club. Fletcher had been supervising a clutch of anti-Gaddafi protestors outside the embassy when she was hit by a burst of automatic fire. The square was cordoned off, but it was too late to cancel the dinner: the guests were already en route and, in this age before mobile phones, there was no way to warn people off. The police laid siege to the Libyan Embassy for more than a week, but at this early stage of the drama they were willing, while Libyan Radio declared that its loyal staff had merely fired at an unruly mob in "self-defence", to direct the cricketing men in dinner jackets down hidden alleyways to the club's back door. The show went on.

But Woodcock was beginning to reach the end of his tether. In his final Notes, in 1986, he began by revealing that even the players were "disenchanted" by the weight of the modern game – in 1985 there were 94 Test matches, double the number played in 1980. He was also compelled, by the fact that an Australian rebel team had been to South Africa, to return to the same old sore point once again. Following objections from Bangladesh and Zimbabwe (on the grounds that the team contained cricketers who had played in "the forbidden land"), the planned England B tour was cancelled.

Even with the help of Wright and Forrest, Woodcock was finding his dual role too much. The *Wisden* workload was so great that it had to be spread through the year, so there was always a deadline pressing: a letter to Zimbabwe asking for a breakdown of extras; commissioning match reports from Australia; an inquiry about bonus points in the West Indies; the need to find a new "man in Lancashire"; and the typing of a New Zealand contributor – "*I can seen from the forgoing xxxx that I will have to imporve my typing before I sand off my copy --pneumonia is a very draining afflictionI have discovered*". There was a large team of other contributors to look out for, too. One sign of how dependent the Almanack was on the old amateur ideal came when Bob Arrowsmith, the principal obituary writer from 1976 to 1988, wrote a plaintive note to Woodcock regarding his fee – £125 per year. Arrowsmith had been a classics teacher at Lancing and Charterhouse, and a keen weekend cricketer for all the "right" clubs – the Butterflies, I Zingari and Free Foresters. When he noticed that in the 1984 edition he had written nearly 10,000 words he was moved to question the notion that this should remain a labour of love. Woodcock blushed and raised his fee to £300.

With the amount of overseas travel increasing all the time, Woodcock had little time to make any major changes to the Almanack, but as it happened he never harboured such wishes. "We were always trying to cut things back, for space reasons," he said. "The Index, for example. But I never moved things. The truth is, I liked it the way it was." And all the while he was receiving enough advice from well-meaning readers to make his head spin: "I am almost 100 per cent sure that this should read J. H. B. Waite and P. L. Wilmslow," wrote one pedant. "The Parfitt-Allen stand was unbroken and therefore requires an asterisk ... Is it not time to remove the brackets round initials? ... Compton didn't make 207 at Lord's in 1947. It should be 208 ..." We must not forget, in hymning the beauties of *Wisden*, that it can sometimes be, like the game itself, exquisitely boring.

Woodcock realised that it was time to step back in 1986 when, one morning in Hampshire, he began work on the Almanack at dawn with a view to attacking his to-do pile before racing to Lord's in his capacity as *The Times* correspondent. "And I'm afraid I just thought, what on earth am I doing, trying to do both these jobs? I loved them both dearly, but suddenly it didn't make sense." The book was in a healthy position – the 1985 budget predicted a profit of £74,000 from revenues amounting to £290,000, a decent return. And when Graeme Wright agreed to his suggestion that he himself take over as editor, Woodcock did not have to feel that he was turning over the book to the unsafe hands of a stranger. Wright came at the job from a publishing, not a cricket reporting, angle, but by now *Wisden* was in his nervous system too. He was a cultural liberal who believed in the power of grand institutions – just the kind of contradiction *Wisden* liked. "There is no way *Wisden*'s shape will change while I am editor and a director of John Wisden," he told *The Times*. "I would rather give up both jobs than allow that to happen."

Advertisement from Wisden *1928*

13

The Collectible

In his first Notes, in 1987, Wright took his cue from Bradman by admitting that the pace of cricket, like everything else, was accelerating: "We live today in the age of the instant." He went on, honouring a well-established tradition, to outline his own "catalogue of concerns". These included, in a way that showed the extent to which he and Woodcock were well tuned, "the drift towards more limited-overs cricket", the weakness of Australia's domestic game, the steady erosion of crowds and the "great problem" of short-pitched bowling. The fact that he needed to beat the funeral drums for some great names of the past (Bill Edrich and Jim Laker) gave his first volume an elegiac flavour that was fleshed out by a tribute to Gubby Allen and a Swanton article on the MCC bicentenary. The quirky side of cricket was perhaps best captured in the obituary of H. D. Smith, one of the few bowlers to have taken a wicket with his debut ball in Test cricket, but the first for whom this was his *only* Test wicket.

His most radical manoeuvre was to omit, primarily for space reasons, the Laws. There was no real precedent for this. In the first *Wisden* of 1864 the Laws had occupied only four pages – Victorian cricket was a relatively simple sport – but by now there were enough revisions and amendments to make it a large and repetitive feature occupying over 40 pages. And since they barely changed from year to year it didn't seem too radical to lower them over the side. It went down badly, however. If *Wisden* was the Bible, then the Laws were its Mosaic utterance, and without them the book did not feel like the game's final arbiter. It was, wrote Matthew Engel in the *Guardian*, showing a possessive regard for *Wisden*'s traditions several years before he himself became editor, "a bit like *Hamlet* without *To be or not to be*". But Engel recognised that the blizzard of international cricket did need to be included somehow, and felt that "we should sympathise rather than condemn ... Everything is in safe hands". Plenty of more vitriolic voices were raised, however. In the 1988 Preface Wright mentioned that their absence had caused "both the spirit and the letter of the Laws" to be "threatened by malevolence and near anarchy"; chastened, he put them back in.

In this, his second edition, he introduced colour images, which made *Wisden* look more modern, and, with the help of Bill Frindall and others, gave the records section a gritty overhaul. On the whole he amended the statistics in line with current research, but he remained loyal to "the policy of previous *Wisden* editors" when it came to major revisions. "It has been said that history is a hard core of interpretation surrounded by a soft pulp of disputable facts," he wrote. "That is certainly so here."

In other matters too he sided with established tradition. He was a "most reluctant supporter" of television-based umpiring and disliked too great an emphasis on the commercial exploitation of the game ("money should not be the only determining factor"). He was quick to frown on sulky behaviour, observing the world-weary air of so many contemporary players: "I can't help thinking that they regard a Test match as just another working day," he wrote. In this he was speaking not as an old-style MCC amateur suspicious of the tradesman-cricketer, but as a boyhood fan for whom cricket pitches were fields of dreams, not a workplace.

The most sensational topic in his 1988 Notes was the incident that had inflamed England's winter tour of Pakistan: the burst of wild finger-wagging between England's captain, Mike Gatting, and the umpire, Shakoor Rana. Wright, inspired by a sense that the robes of his office were sanctified by over a hundred years of service, believed that the rights and wrongs of the case were beside the point: an England captain should never stoop to such boorish antics, no matter how grave the provocation ("I doubt if there is a cricketer anywhere who has not been upset by an umpire's decision"). He described the episode as "two grown men standing on their dignity with not a square inch of moral ground to support them", and was astonished when management actually *rewarded* the players with a "hardship" payment for their pains.

His Notes put all this in a stark, class-conscious context. Where some former editors might have drawn a discreet veil over such matters, he was happy to expose them to the light. And his conclusions were unusual. The *ancien régime* may have been turned over in favour of a new, more meritocratic elite, but on this bad-tempered evidence the new leaders were, like the pigs who stood upright in Orwell's *Animal Farm*, little better than the tyranny they supplanted. "The game's leadership, if 1987 is any indication," he wrote, "comes from the quartermaster's store rather than the quarter-deck … But when those who lead are unable to rise above their former station, indeed do not consider it essential to do so, those they lead cannot be inspired."

This was a pointed political utterance, coming as it did in the bad-tempered twilight years of Mrs Thatcher's government. If an Old Harrovian had said as much it might well have been assumed that he was merely defending an entrenched upper-class privilege. But Wright was coming at this from a different angle, and declined to hold it axiomatic that cricket's new ruling class had right on its side merely because it was no longer part of a tired old public-school clique. He was hinting, in a novel kind of heresy, that progress was not by definition virtuous, and that even in the seemingly comical days when cricket was run by old coves in blazers, the elite had been able to promote certain qualities of selfless sportsmanship – the fact that their successors regarded such scruples as windy trash might not be progress. "What gives a nation its civilisation is its ability to accept provocations without feeling a need to retaliate," he added, sounding more like a Foreign Office strategist than a cricket writer.

Wright was extremely conscious that as *Wisden*'s editor he was not simply speaking on his own behalf; he was representing the Almanack and all it stood for. And one of the things it stood for was a willingness to quote Shakespeare. "It's a bit like playing Hamlet," he would say later, echoing Engel's words. "Some people might prefer other Hamlets. But it's not a question of *to thine own self be true*, it's to *Wisden*'s self be true. I didn't want to be seen as some colonial upstart messing about with a great institution." It was a conscious decision to cite the Almanack's long-held faith in the amateur ideal at a time like this. And while he risked being seen as a bodyguard for the elite that had been running cricket for too long, Wright, in tipping his hat to the gentleman-amateur, the bookish cricket-lover for whom the conversation about the game was as important as playing it, had a more subtle point to make.

It was no coincidence that he was writing at the height of the deregulating inferno that was sweeping the world's financial markets. On the surface this seemed a radical free-for-all, crackling with white-hot egalitarian energy, which promised to crack open the stuffy cliques of yesteryear. But a rather pretty baby (to use one of Wright's favourite images) was being swept out with all that dirty bathwater. In this very different field it was also starting to seem that a cosy group of like-minded chaps, who may have been at school together, might even have been able to foster a more cohesive sense of belonging than a combative and lucrative meritocracy, however grave an outrage to an egalitarian sensibility that might be. Loyalty was a powerful force. In the old days the motto of the Stock Exchange – *My Word is my Bond* – was at least known to everyone, even if it was often ignored; in the humming new world of global money, only a handful of the people walking past the building even knew of its existence. And the top-hatted old-timers in the City might have been fuddy-duddy, but few even dreamed of the bonus-driven frenzy of modern times: the yachts, fast cars and ski chalets enjoyed by their supposedly less elitist successors.

No one wanted to turn the clock back – but this was a social detail worth noting, at least. Wright understood that not everything about the passage of time was an advance – sometimes the march of progress only took us backwards. He wasn't afraid to admit that the old school, silly and unfair as it may have been, may also have had one or two unexpected merits; and he knew that English cricket often functioned as a showcase for social or political tensions. In cricket's case, although MCC was sometimes presented as a caricature for many of cricket's most blatant flaws – its protective feelings towards apartheid South Africa, its unfriendliness to women, its gentle yet settled snobbery, its fondness for cocktails in the Long Room and quiet afternoons snoozing in the library – it was at least motivated by love rather than money. Small cliques are unjust, to be sure, and Wright was not arguing for their reinstatement. He was simply pointing out the surprising fact that sometimes they can be better at instilling and upholding good conduct than the new elite that has supplanted them. Wright was always aware of what might be lost.

It was a momentous time. There were cracks in the once-impenetrable Berlin Wall, and the world was hurtling into a new technological phase. *Wisden* was there to remind us that change could be a mixed blessing, that the past could be too freely ditched.

The *Telegraph* saw Wright's 1988 remarks as "an attack on the captaincy of Mr Mike Gatting", but *The Times* wrote a leader in praise of his stance. In fact he was banging *Wisden*'s oldest drum: "Winning is not everything". The MCC bicentenary game, he pointed out, had been a showcase for everything the game seemed anxious to forget. "Good manners prevailed, batsmen walked, bouncers were used sparingly and so were effective in surprising both the batsman and the spectator. In terms of technique, the game was a delight; from batsmen and bowlers there was variety. And throughout there was friendliness." This was old-school cricket, the way it ought to be played.

It certainly pleased venerable figures like E. W. Swanton, who wrote in the *Telegraph* that "our bible has never reflected the game more clearly than in the last decade". A former England captain, Tony Lewis, agreed: "It is the sameness of the book which comforts," he wrote. Several papers ran reviews entitled "The Wisdom of *Wisden*", and John Woodcock himself, in a review in *The Times*, agreed that in the Gatting-Rana stand-off "Test cricket had perhaps its darkest hour". He also took the opportunity of declaring a close personal interest. "When, during my six years as editor of *Wisden Cricketers' Almanack*, I woke up in a cold sweat," wrote Woodcock, "I knew my assistant, Graeme Wright, would clean up the spillage."

In his final volume, the 1992 *Wisden*, Wright gave the Almanack a further nudge forward by including the results from two girls' teams – Roedean and Denstone College – for the first time. This was not exactly leaping in front of the King's horse on Derby Day, but it was still a mild feminist rebuke to tradition. He argued that "the women's game embodies many of the qualities I admire ... They have the right attitude and enthusiasm." This too managed to sound old-fashioned while being rather radical, but a more far-reaching alteration was effected when, in October 1990, Wright brought another woman into the *Wisden* fold. Her name was Harriet Monkhouse, and Wright had met her some years earlier, after a talk he gave to the Lancashire and Cheshire Cricket Society at Old Trafford. Monkhouse approached him and, in an unconventional declaration, confessed a relish for cricket statistics. She even plucked up the nerve to wonder whether *Wisden* might, um, have an opening of any sort. Wright had nothing to offer, but when, a couple of years later, they met again at a similar junket at Lord's, he remembered her. She was the Didsbury-born daughter of a former deputy editor of the *Guardian*, had studied classics at Oxford ("not really relevant, though I suppose taking apart Latin sentences is quite a good training for subediting") and was at that time working on *Computer Weekly*, a high-tech journal of the digital age that in 1990 was still (don't tell anyone) assembled on typewriters.

Though she claimed to know nothing about cricket ("I see it in numerical terms – I get excited about things like eight maidens in a row") she had been a sharp observer of the game since school ("I was no good at playing, and one day at a parents' meeting my mother told them I would be happy to do the scoring"). She took her book to Old Trafford to watch county games and keep ball-by-ball track of the match in progress ("I concentrate better when I score, and it was a way of getting involved – people would ask me things"). When Manchester United lost the 1976 FA Cup final to Southampton, Monkhouse burst into tears and her mother, as a consolation prize, took her to the bookshop to buy – nothing else could have helped in such a crisis – a copy of *Wisden*.

It was not quite all plain sailing from there. The cricket world did not yet know that Christine Forrest was calling shots in *Wisden*'s workshop; though there had been a Women's World Cup at Lord's in 1973, it still fancied itself a man's game, suspicious of any feminine involvement that did not involve tea and cakes. But Wright met Monkhouse for a curry, wandered off the subject ("I think we talked mostly about literature in the First World War"), gave her a subediting test to check her skills, quickly saw that this was superfluous, and invited her to join the team. She moved to the Guildford office of *Wisden Cricket Monthly* and became a key – if not *the* key – cog in an odd machine. Wright and Forrest worked in neighbouring houses in north-west London; Monkhouse was in Surrey; the typesetter was in Essex. Things grew even more dispersed when Wright passed on the editorship to Matthew Engel in 1992, because Engel lived on a beautiful hillside in Herefordshire. This was long before the age of email and blink-of-an-eye data flow; *Wisden* used the Royal Mail, especially when Monkhouse began to work from home in Manchester. No one thought to append a fashion-house label ("Paris – Milan – New York") to the title, but it would have had a quaint ring: *Wisden Cricketers' Almanack*: Eastcote – Didsbury – Newton St Margarets.

Monkhouse has been a stern editorial longstop ever since – copper on the bottom of the ship. The words "Harriet to check", in Matthew Engel's handwriting, decorated miles of proofs. "It's not too much to say," he said, "that if it weren't for Harriet, *Wisden* might not come out at all." Others agreed. "If Harriet took a year off, so would *Wisden*," wrote Simon Briggs in 2000, when he left to join the *Daily Telegraph*. And Scyld Berry, when he became the fourth editor she had worked with, spoke of the "superhuman intensity" she brought to the final weeks of the process.

It is clear that *Wisden* owes volumes, in all senses of the word, to Forrest and Monkhouse (until then the most influential lady in the game was often, jokingly, held to have been W. G. Grace's mother). "I drove them mad," said Engel, "because I liked changing things. But my major concern in my years at *Wisden* was what would happen if Harriet sneezed. She was the person who finally made *Wisden* live up to its reputation for accuracy. We were dangerously dependent on her."

There is more to this than the straightforward novelty by which *Wisden* should have relied – as it still relies (Monkhouse continues to sieve through the Almanack with her fiendish fine-tooth comb) – on two relatively unsung women. The tradition laid down by Pardon, in which a high-and-mighty editor would give a lordly blessing to the players of the year while distributing lesser bouquets to the game's humbler subjects, has obscured the extent to which *Wisden* has always been a collaboration – a team game. This account too is guilty of emphasising, for storytelling reasons, the role of editors, but the truth is more various and unknowable. *Wisden* is built on the eye-straining labours of numerous, often anonymous, servants and disciples: scorers, fact-checkers, reporters, photographers, printers, designers, proofreaders, typesetters, teachers and booksellers. It may be repetitious to compare them to the masons and sculptors who carved the nooks and niches of the cathedrals that tower over England, but the similarity is strong.

As it happens another new face joined the *Wisden* team during Wright's tenure. In January 1988 a Kent University graduate called Christopher Lane started work in the London office of *Wisden Cricket Monthly* as a general administrative assistant. "London office" might have been too a grand name for the arrangement: in truth, Lane and an advertising sales manager were using some spare desk space in the Smithfield office of one of the magazine's directors, a headhunter called Patrick Allen. Lane didn't care overmuch, since he only intended to stay a few months. A fine player in his own right (he represented the Universities) his chief ambition was to play as much cricket as he could and see where that led; if anything, he saw helping out at *Wisden* as a way to get through the winter. When April came, however, he changed tack, realising that he had landed on his feet.

Lane soon noticed that the magazine was not running as well as it might, and shared his thoughts with Frith and Gray (the magazine's other directors) at the end of his first summer. Things changed fast after that. He moved out of London to the Guildford office of the magazine, and soon found himself relieving Wright of some of the Almanack's administrative chores as well. Less than a year after taking what he thought was a temporary job, Lane found himself, a young cricket-lover on the first rung of his career, with a significant role in the country's premier cricket publications. "I was promoted to general manager," he said, "and began to see that there was something in this publishing lark."

Wright liked biographical sketches and published affectionate portraits of Graeme Pollock, Derek Underwood, Geoffrey Boycott, Graeme Hick, Sunil Gavaskar, Graham Gooch and Richard Hadlee during his years in charge. His Notes continued to address structural features of the game – umpiring, business failings and the administrative matters raised by various reports and inquiries, modestly leaving the descriptive cricket writing to his contributors. In 1989 he celebrated the centenary of *Wisden*'s Cricketers of the Year feature, recognising that this had become one of the Almanack's most successful items. In one way he was unlucky: there were signs that county cricket was losing its grip on the audience, and it was also a low period for the national team, which had been pulverised by the West Indies and was again struggling against the revived Australians. Wright was rarely optimistic: "There is no reason why, in a country where it is often impossible to have building work done or a motor car serviced properly, its sporting tradesmen should perform any better."

By 1992 he felt he had done all he could, and stepped down. Not surprisingly, perhaps, in his final editorial he predicted a dark future for the game. "There are those, it seems, who think that the future belongs not to the spin bowler but to the man who paints logos on the outfield." He announced his departure at the *Wisden* dinner at the East India Club in April 1992. "The things I value, such as sporting play, are no longer valued," he said. "Cricket has become too much a business ... Cultural rot has set in." He then wrote a book on the subject – a good one, too – called *Betrayal*, though *Wisden*'s 1994 reviewer, Geoffrey Moorhouse, found it a little *too* gloomy – "I just hope I never have to read Mr Wright on the decline of Western Civilisation."

This powerful sense, shared by so many *Wisden* editors, that cricket was failing to live up to its high ideals, is too acute and persistent to be a coincidence, or trivial. Perhaps we need to think of it not as a form of commentary on actual events but as a wish, a quest, a dream. The idea that cricket ever was a shining model of fair play and gallantry may have been constructed, if anything, as a way of camouflaging the opposite urge – a raw and primal desire to win. Just as the handshake evolved as way of hiding hostile impulses (it occupied the sword hand in a peaceful gesture), so cricket chivalry grew up to blur the ferocity of the aggressive mentality in the engine room of Britain's imperial swagger. In a typical Victorian compromise, cricket was ashamed of its greedy lust for winning, so it affected instead a Kiplingesque indifference to such minor concerns. In this light the ceaseless moan that standards were slipping, one of cricket's most reliable noises, was not an observation but an expression of fear.

The search for a new editor settled on an existing contributor, Matthew Engel. Born in Northampton in 1951, he had worked for the *Guardian* since 1979. He began writing about cricket for the *Northampton Chronicle and Echo*, and was given his first *Wisden* in 1958 ("I scrawled all over it"). He loved the game ("the atmosphere, the feel, the sound, the noise it made ... the duffel bag, the banana sandwiches, the autographs"), had relevant publishing experience (having co-edited, with Ian Morrison, three editions of a reference work, *The Sportspages Almanac*) and was just finishing a history of Northamptonshire CCC when he was called up. More to the point, he was an exceptional writer. In 1984 he had composed a Cardus-like tribute to his own boyhood hero from Northampton, Colin Milburn ("nine Test matches – that's all he had time for. He changed four beyond recognition") for a Queen Anne Press collection, *Cricket Heroes*. When the old Bakelite phone rang in his rambling house overlooking a soft, golden-green Herefordshire valley, he thought that Wright might be asking him to take on the *Wisden* book reviews (John Arlott had died, leaving a legend-sized gap). "It never occurred to me that he would invite me to consider the whole thing. But it appealed to me immediately, to the side of my character that quite liked being in charge."

It was obvious when he met the chairman – over tea at a hotel – that he had a more than keen grasp of both *Wisden*'s past and its future. Engel likes to say that he "blathered on" about all the things he wanted to do, sensing that no one had "the faintest interest". He was wrong; they were much impressed. Wright and his team had polished the Almanack into a streamlined vessel; now Engel could add an extension or two, shove the furniture around and put some bravura new art on the walls.

The *Telegraph* called him an "iconoclast … a somewhat surprising" choice – which Engel took as a compliment. "I *was* an odd choice – irreverent, bolshy, argumentative. And after a few weeks I thought I might not last long. I remember thinking, God, I don't know how long I can do this." As if to contradict the idea that he had no respect for continuity, he wrote John Woodcock a dry, good-humoured letter asking for a contribution to "the above-mentioned volume, of which I believe you have heard".

Then he rolled up his sleeves. In his first year he thanked Graeme Wright for leaving him such a well-oiled machine – "My admiration for his achievement has grown by the week." He pushed the Index to the back, reintroduced a more orthodox Contents page, moved MCC games and Other Matches at Lord's from their "long-established positioning" ahead of County Cricket, welcomed J. L. Carr as the first incumbent of a rotating book review section, and announced that the Almanack had been rearranged into six parts: Comment, Records,

English Cricket, Overseas Cricket, Administration & Laws and Miscellaneous. He also initiated one of the signature items of the modern book: a rucksack of titbits from the wider shores of cricket called "Cricket Round the World"; it would soon feature over a hundred cricket-playing countries. Engel was careful to stress that it did not in itself lead him to believe in the much-touted globalisation of the first-class game. If he ever found himself witnessing a China v England Test in Guanzon, he wrote, he would "eat sweet and sour hat".

Aside from these structural reforms, which showed the extent to which he hit the ground running, his first edition also adopted a tone of voice that would become characteristic. He nailed his colours high on the mast when it came to one-day cricket, calling it "a mutant game" and "essentially shallow" – a dramatic dismissal of the format that, while obviously less rich and nuanced than a five-day Test, was the only form of cricket that most people, and most *Wisden* readers, had ever played.

In a review in the *Daily Telegraph* Tony Lewis, troubled by the severity with which Engel had previously condemned England's rebel tourists to South Africa, said that the new work resembled "the complaints book at a golf club". He must have been a member at an unusually erudite club. Engel began with a reference to his "damn bothersome" insomnia, but within a page was quoting Milton's *Paradise Lost* ("Chaos umpire sits / And by decision more embroils the fray"). Just as Wright had broken new ground by quoting the American writer Ring Lardner in his first Notes, so Engel was smuggling a 17th-century religious and political epic into the cricket picture. The intention was plain: high-minded literary allusions were free to rub shoulders with demotic asides – it was like the best conversation you could have in the Long Room, but never quite did. In due course Engel would stir in *Wisden*'s brand of scholarly abstraction, so he could quote a breezy John Betjeman quatrain set in Cheltenham –

> *I composed these lines when a summer wind*
> *Was blowing the elm leaves dry,*
> *And we were seventy-six for seven,*
> *And they had CB Fry.*

– only to point out, mimicking the most annoying pedant in the row behind you, that according to the records, C. B. Fry, though very much the *mot juste* from the poetic point of view, had not as a matter of fact ever played at Cheltenham. Sorry.

Engel had a credo: "Cricket can appeal to the athlete and the aesthete alike." His first volume included an article on cricket's close ties to the theatre, which quoted C. L. R. James's belief that "cricket is first and foremost a dramatic spectacle ... it belongs with the theatre, ballet, opera and the dance." From now on the Almanack would see it not just as an absorbing game, but as a vivid part of the cultural scenery. Not that he took the game lightly. In 1996 he wrote that cricket managed "simultaneously to be absurdly trivial and desperately important". Later he would add that, in general, "the more cricket there is, the better the world". But his ever-sensitive historical antennae reminded him that "cricket has always been in crisis of one sort or another", and that it paid to take the long view. Either way, it was *Wisden*'s good fortune that he was taking so firm a grip on the wheel at this time, because there was yet another change of ownership just over the horizon.

———

When Wright stepped down as editor he remained on the board of John Wisden & Co, and in this capacity he was again invited by William Gray to seek a buyer. Gray wanted to take his investment out – the equipment side had long been folded into Grays, and owning half of a cricket book was not quite his company's natural line. The other part-owner, Bowater Plc, was also happy to sell: there was little logic in owning just half of a small enterprise that had little bearing on the firm's other activities.

It was John Woodcock who suggested to Wright, when the subject cropped up in the Lord's press box one day, that the man they were looking for was "right over there". He pointed across to Box Number 3 in the Mound Stand, where Paul Getty, the cricket-loving son of the oil magnate J. Paul Getty, was entertaining friends. Getty had already financed the building of the modern, tented-pavilion stand in which he was holding court. Perhaps he would be interested in owning a piece of England's cricket folklore. Wright had visited the box and had met one of Getty's business advisers, Malcolm Ridley. Conscious that MCC felt somewhat proprietoral about Getty's largesse (which in truth had many beneficiaries) he went home with a polite letter taking shape in his head.

The timing was fortuitous. A few months later, Graeme Wright received a phone call indicating that Getty was indeed interested – very much so. It took a while to wrap up the details, but in 1994 it was announced that Paul Getty, scion of an American oil fortune, had bought England's leading cricket publication. "I don't know how it happened, to tell you the truth," Getty told his friend Brian Johnston in a *Test Match Special* interview. "It just sort of overwhelmed me, and there it was."

Wisden was under new ownership once again. And there was something appropriate about the change, because Getty was intrigued by *Wisden* not just as a book, but as a national treasure. Though a topical publication, it was also an heirloom, featuring in salerooms as often as bookshops. Indeed, in 1994, when Kim Philby's wife auctioned the old spy's library at Sotheby's, there, among the Victorian novels, the Marx and the Engels, was a copy of the 1972 *Wisden*. It was an emblem of his homesickness, and if Philby had kept his books in alphabetical order it could have sat beside the history of his own alma mater, Westminster School. It is nice to think of Philby, in a state-owned Moscow flat, peering across the frozen city and summoning up, by turning *Wisden*'s pages, memories of John Edrich shouldering arms, Derek Underwood sidling past the umpire, feet splayed and wrist coiled, or John Snow bounding through the early-morning sea-fret at Hove. Did he sigh when he read Arlott's obituary of Learie Constantine ("He made his mark in the only way a poor West Indian boy of his time could do, by playing cricket of ability and character")? Did he frown when he read about Snow barging into Sunil Gavaskar at Lord's, leading to his omission from the next Test as a punishment? We will never know.

But he was in some sense responding to the zeitgeist in seeing *Wisden* as a reservoir of old moods, as an artefact. Cricket-lovers had long been filling shelves with it – Grace himself had a set, Sir Pelham Warner continued to add to the one he had been given, and many others did the same – but now, as the liberalising spirit of the 1960s inspired an urge to preserve the past, markets began to develop in everything from oil paintings and wine to stamps and books. Through *Wisden*, cricket began to engage with serious money. Partly thanks to this boom, but chiefly because a set of *Wisden* was becoming ever more substantial and rare, the auction rooms began to hum. Gaston's original catalogue of

1892 (updated in 1894, 1900 and 1923) mentioned that a full set – then numbering 35 volumes – had fetched 10 guineas; in 1936 it was estimated that the first 15 editions could still be had for £20; but in 1954 a full set was sold for £145, and in 1963 it would have cost (according to *Wisden* itself) £250. Even in the centenary year it was possible to pick up old volumes for next to nothing.

Assembling and cherishing *Wisden* remained a matter of fishing about in second-hand bookshops and exploring attics. Only those in the know could have named the small group of early collectors and traced the ancestry of the extant cricket archive. Most of that first generation had died between the two wars – A. D. Taylor in 1923, A. L. Ford in 1924, A. J. Gaston, the Brighton bookseller who compiled the first bibliography of cricket literature for the 1892 *Wisden*, in 1928, F. S. Ashley-Cooper, the renowned cricket historian and *Wisden* contributor, in 1932, and the Rev. R. S. Holmes in 1933 – and Charles Pratt Green followed them in 1950. Before he died, Ashley-Cooper* had sold his collection to Sir Julien Cahn, an enthusiastic cricket philanthropist who ran his own cricket team and used his handsome inheritance (from his father's hire-purchase business) to finance, among many other things, the new stands at Trent Bridge, the ground where as a child he had sat under George Parr's famous tree. All of these lineages became both known and valuable to genuine aficionados.

Cahn himself died in 1944, leaving the second half of the 20th century to a new generation of collectors. Of these the most prominent was Joseph Goldman, a London lawyer who, after being wounded at Passchendaele in 1917, had to give up playing cricket and become a spectator instead. He began to amass books in 1926, the year of Hobbs's hundredth century, and, bit by bit, roaming England's shops and auction rooms, he assembled the most significant cricket library in the land (Sir Pelham Warner spent three days browsing in it without making much of a dent). In 1937 Goldman compiled a 200-page bibliography that was

---

* Poor health and weakening eyesight led Ashley-Cooper to retire in 1931, and he died soon afterwards. The obituary in the 1932 *Wisden* declared: "Everybody interested in the chronicle of the game is under a deep debt of gratitude to him."

the standard source for 40 years. As a sign of how small a world this was, one of his cousins was actually married to Sir Julien Cahn.

The sale of Joseph Goldman's remarkable collection in 1966 (at Hodgson's auction rooms in Chancery Lane) was something of a disappointment even by the standards of the day. It generated only £3,747, no great sum. One of the keenest buyers was a London bank employee called Geoffrey Copinger, who had been collecting since he was 11 years old, had known Goldman and now prepared to take his place as the foremost collector of his day. An out-and-out cricket nut, Copinger put together the twice-weekly averages for the PA (and therefore the national newspapers) from 1947 to 1983 and supervised the cricket records for *Wisden* for nearly two decades.

Even in the early 1970s there was no vein of gold in the literature of cricket. But new antiquarian dealers – Ted Brown in Cornwall, J. W. McKenzie in Ewell,* and Christopher Saunders, first in Wells and then in the Forest of Dean – were setting up in the trade, and a genuine market was starting to emerge. In 1973 Sir Tim Rice spent £750 of his earnings from West End musicals on a complete set from J. W. McKenzie, and, though some thought him profligate, it was a smart move. "I suspect the most voracious hedge fund manager," he wrote in the *Telegraph* in 1988, "would be quite relaxed about my investment." Although in 1977 Norman Preston guessed that a set of *Wisden* was worth only £1,000, things were beginning to fly. In 1980 Sir Pelham Warner's (signed) set fetched £7,800 – an arresting sum at which, according to David Frith in 1981, "even the auctioneer gulped".† Two days after Botham's amazing 149 not out at Headingley, the euphoria fed into the auction room when an 1867 *Wisden*, expected to command up to £150, went for £420. England's historic victory, thought *The Times*'s reporter, had "brought home to every cricket historian the importance of owning every issue". A few months later, an 1869 *Wisden* went for £800.

---

* In 1983 McKenzie became the first person to pay over £1,000 for a *Wisden*, and in 1987 he was almost certainly the first to top £10,000 for a set.

† When John Woodcock needed a working set, he heard that there was one going in the Blackwells antiquarian bookshop, and pounced. The price was £3,000 – "though when I part-exchanged the ones I already had it came out at about half that."

It was the beginning of a new cycle. In 1991 John Arlott's collection passed through Christie's for £22,160;* and in 1995 Phillips sold the first 15 for £24,000, and certain individual volumes (1864, 1869 and 1875) for just under £3,000 each. The following year the "ultimate combination" appeared in Exeter – a run of early numbers signed by W. G. Grace that was sold off by his descendants for £94,100. This time David Frith was even more lyrical; these were "the most desirable *Wisdens* ever offered". In 2007 a set at Sotheby's fetched £120,000, while the prices for the rarest volumes boomed. A rebound 1875 took £24,000 in 2006; an 1896 (the first hardback) made £21,000, and Sir Pelham Warner's first three, rebound into a single volume, fetched £42,000. His grandchildren might well have wished they had hung on to the dusty old things for a few more years.

This new world spoke a language unconnected with cricket. *Wisden* was now an antiquarian product whose contents mattered less than the quality of the binding, the condition of the photographic plates, the strength of the "hinges" that held the book together at the *fin de siècle*, the clarity of the Erratum or other inserts (such as the bat-shaped bookmark attached in some 1930s editions), the authority of any signatures, and all kinds of other aesthetic-historical considerations. Browsers would check for nicks or discoloration; they would be attuned to minute variations in the tan cloth binding or gilt embossing; they would know without looking that 1938 was the year of the first Ravilious woodcut, that 1965 was the first appearance of the yellow dust jacket for the "cloth-bound" version; or that Rex Pogson's "Index to *Wisden*" appeared in 1944. Naturally they would need no reminding that 1864 and 1875 were the rarest of them all (for reasons not entirely known), or that certain signatures – Grace, Warner, Arlott, even Goldman – carried their own store of value. Above all, they knew that even tiny details can became commodities. Of *course* 1887 was the first edition to put the date on the spine; surely no one needed to be told

---

* Bill Frindall, in his autobiography (*Bearders: My Life in Cricket*) described how Arlott, close to the end of his life, asked for his *Wisden* collection to be brought to his bed so he could sign it, volume by volume, thus increasing its value for his heirs.

that in 1904–5 the "k" fell out of the word "Almanack" (only on the paperback, thank God); and weren't we all aware that the linen editions of 1938–40 "bow to the spine"? The drama of the story has an effect too: the 1934 is prized because it tells the story of Bodyline, just as the 1957 had the good fortune to feature Laker's 19-wicket haul.

Even *Wisden* by-products were becoming sought after. In the years before the First World War the company had published a series of 14 scarlet notebooks (edited by F. S. Ashley-Cooper) that contained a diary, some records and laws, a few curiosities and a fixture list. A full run of these, a century later, was worth over £20,000.

The most evocative *Wisden* transaction of recent years, however, concerned W. G. Grace's signed set which, when it came back onto the market in 2004, inspired a new collector, Tim Bunting, to race from Hampshire to Minehead, cheque book in hand. He had seen the books back in 1996, but at that time did not have the wherewithal to buy them. By 2004 he did. He tried to do the deal over the telephone, but was told that he was the third bidder to enter the race, that the price was £150,000 (for a run that ended in 1914) and that the books would go to the first man to come through the door with the full sum in his hand. Bunting had been collecting cricket books for years by then, and had become well known as the most determined man in the market. He won the race. "Luckily I had a sports car back then," he said. "But I did drive bloody fast."

Bunting had already secured the basis of his own library (in 1998) by buying Copinger's collection, which numbered some 15,000 books and included two sets of *Wisden*. According to Copinger's obituary in the 1999 *Wisden,* Bunting paid over £200,000 for this bounty, but it was more than a private indulgence. "My mission," he told the *Economist*, "is to create a place where you can explore cricket history in literature in an orderly manner." He converted an outbuilding next to his house in Hampshire into an elegant library, with shelves of county records, club diaries and international lists. *Wisden* is its centrepiece – the hub through which almost all lines of inquiry inevitably lead. He even declines to subscribe to the notion that the Schools section (with its public-school emphasis) is an anachronism, since it stands at "the heart" of *Wisden*'s archive, capturing information found nowhere else, and plugging a gap without which the detailed heritage of many cricketers could not be traced.

By now the price of solo volumes was exploding in line with this growth of a market in cricket literature as an investment. The fact that there was one especially eager buyer (Bunting himself) did nothing to depress prices: he made no secret of his ambitions, and the antiquarians were not too unhappy to see prices rising. In a 1983 Phillips auction an 1865 and 1867 edition were each priced at £520. A decade later, a slightly tattered 1864 *Wisden* – "lacking front wrapper, torn end paper, some pages loose and taped, some foxing" – was knocked down for £2,700. This was a startling increase. Of course there were wide variations inside any *Wisden* set, but the rarest and most precious editions looked as though they would soon be fetching more than £5,000 each, depending on their condition. *Wisden*, implausibly, was gold dust.

Of the 20th-century volumes it is often said that the 1916 – with its baleful roll call of obituaries and the tributes to Grace and Trumper – tops the list. That is why the book trade jumped when the 2006 prankster offered half a dozen of them on eBay. But there were other anecdotes bubbling to the surface. In 2010 the first four books were spotted in the cut-price bin of an Oxfam shop in Hertford. When they realised what they were, Oxfam had them rebound and they sold for £8,520 at Bonham's. No wonder that in the TV series by Keith Waterhouse, *Charters and Caldicott*, *Wisden* was at the heart of a crime scene. Some bounder had run off with an Almanack – talk about not cricket!*

By the 1980s even the reprinted facsimile editions were becoming precious in their own right: the original 1961 boxed set, by Billings & Sons, was selling for up to £500 (it had been a strictly limited edition: only 150 of each volume was produced). There had been a follow-up issue in 1974 (with a similar print run), but this was a delicate matter: for the sake of existing collectors, *Wisden* was reluctant to countenance the kind of quantitative easing that would improve the supply of early copies but erode their value. In 1983, however, a cricket-mad teacher in Staffordshire called David Jenkins, motivated by his own

---

* John Wisden & Co provided its own set of Almanacks for the day's filming at the Reform Club in London, with Graeme Wright on duty as umpire and minder.

desire to own a full set of *Wisden* (an unaffordable dream) produced a thousand facsimile copies of the 1885 edition, and soon heard from John Wisden & Co. But rather than seeking to strangle the upstart, the company chose to support Jenkins, and Willows Publishing went on to produce numbered limited editions of the entire early library from 1879 onwards.

Collecting *Wisden* appeals to the boy in men, like the wish to collect stamps, coins or cards. Graeme Wright was touched to be contacted by Micky Stewart, the England team manager, who wanted to know how to go about finding all the copies of *Wisden* in which his son Alec appeared. "Whatever you think of *Wisden*," he said, "it remains the only place where cricket history is properly preserved." David Sheppard, one of the leaders of the campaign to stop England's tour of apartheid South Africa, ended a letter to Norman Preston on a warm note: "You have helped me to get back into the way of taking *Wisden*, which I have done since I was seven years old."

There is a word for the truly dedicated collector, however – a "completist". This insatiable soul wants every available dust jacket of every volume of every edition, with all the variants duly logged.* He (usually a he) is even on the lookout for mistakes, simply because they are rare. He knows that the 1963 Index stated that the image of S. H. Pardon was on page 74, when it is on page 77. Even a misprint can make a completist's pulse race (especially if it involved an eminent cricketer): the volume in which P. F. Warner became W. P. Warner is much treasured.

By the late 1980s there were more dealers in this market, notably Martin Wood in Kent, Ian Dyer in Birmingham (whose son Robin was batting for Warwickshire) and Giles Lyon in London. But their world was about to be abruptly changed by another technological miracle – the invention of online retailing. As one century folded into another, the buying and selling of *Wisden*'s began to migrate on to screens. "It changed the perception of scarcity," said Christopher Saunders, who

---

* *Wisden* acquired a dust jacket only in 1965, but since 2003, when a photograph was printed on the front, alternative dust jackets in the traditional format were also made available.

hastened to develop an online catalogue of his own. "There might be only five copies of a book in the world, and that makes it rare – but if they are all right in front of you on a website then they don't *seem* rare, and that of course affects prices."

The arrival of Paul Getty came as a surprise to the editor, Matthew Engel. Getty spoke proudly of his purchase to E. W. Swanton, so the news duly appeared in the *Telegraph*. "I wasn't party to anything," recalled Engel. "In fact I was in Dublin, and the first thing I knew about it was when it came under my hotel door on the front page of the *Telegraph*. I was scooped on my own story – by an 86-year-old."

In most other respects the emergence of Paul Getty in the story of *Wisden*, while consistent with the range of fluctuations in its long life, was serendipitous. The book did not need "saving" as such. It was a perfectly viable, though small, business. But Getty's backing was like a promise or a guarantee of its continuance, especially after the corporate twists and turns of the 1980s. For the first time in years *Wisden* would be supported by an owner motivated primarily by an affection for cricket and a desire to see its traditions upheld. It had a purposeful and ideally qualified new editor already in place: it looked, as a cricketer might say, like a good wicket to bat on.

The seed of Getty's own interest had actually been planted many years earlier. In 1971, following the death in Rome of his glamorous second wife, Talitha Pol, from a heroin overdose, Getty returned to London as a semi-recluse. Two years later one of the two sons from his first marriage, John Paul Getty III, was kidnapped by Italian criminals (his severed ear, in a famous and gruesome twist, was hacked off and sent to his stricken family). Depressed and addicted to drugs, Getty moved to Chelsea's Cheyne Walk, where his neighbour was Mick Jagger, whom he had known from his jet-set party years. It might not have been good for the Rolling Stone's counter-cultural image had it been known that Jagger liked little better than to spend afternoons slumped in front of the cricket – but that was the surprising case. Jagger, Getty told an interviewer for the *Independent* (Frances Edmonds) in 1993, would "come over to my house" and want to watch it. "And so," said Getty, "I'd have to watch it too." He soon found it hard to stop.

Through inheritance Getty was one of the world's wealthiest men (his oil-magnate father, who once topped the world's rich list, famously said: "The meek shall inherit the earth, but not the mineral rights.") He was donating immense sums to cherished British causes such as the National Gallery, Hereford Cathedral and the Conservative Party. But in 1985, when he checked into the London Clinic to address his drug addiction, he met Gubby Allen. A friendship sprang up that soon extended to other cricket personages such as E. W. Swanton, Colin Cowdrey and Brian Johnston. The last of these he first encountered when the commentator's son, Ian, installed a 30-foot radio aerial in his flat overlooking Green Park. When it became clear, through cricket talk, who his father was, Getty invited them both for tea. He was already financing new architecture at Lord's; now, in an even more quirky burst of enthusiasm, he asked Johnston to help him create a Gatsbyish cricket ground on his beautiful Chiltern estate, Wormsley. Johnston helped him scout out the terrain and put him in touch with the right people (particularly Harry Brind, the highly-respected groundsman at The Oval). Getty thanked him by putting Johnston's famous beaky profile in the weathervane on top of the pavilion; Johnston responded by donating a bronze bell, inscribed with the coded reference MFWOGP – My Friend Who Overlooks Green Park.

Colin Ingleby-Mackenzie, the Old Etonian ex-Hampshire captain, became Getty's cricket manager and between them they began to host the most picturesque games in the calendar. Both the prime minister (John Major) and the Queen Mother attended the opening day. There were clean white towels in the thatched changing rooms, beautiful mown stripes on immaculate grass and even an olde-worlde ice-cream stand for the children. Lucien Freud's daughter, Jane, sculpted souvenir tokens for guest players. Anyone who spotted a weed could have been forgiven for calling security.

Wormsley rapidly became a place of pilgrimage for the cricket world: a wonderful venue for relaxed games between upmarket players. The first fixture, in 1992, was between a J. P. Getty XI and an MCC team, and that first year saw six matches. This soon developed into a full-blown "season", with elite fixtures staged on a beautiful green hillside, with a picture-perfect pavilion, airy marquees awash with iced champagne, fine food and well-connected guests. In one sense it was a recreation of the grand old society matches of cricket's Golden Age – the fixture list included games against Oxford, Cambridge, Eton Ramblers, I Zingari, Arabs and Combined Services. It indulged well-mannered wandering sides such as Tim Rice's Heartaches and Harold Pinter's Gaieties with a taste of the cricketing high life. Keen cricketers could rub shoulders, at lunch, with the Duke of Edinburgh, Jerry Hall and John Major, and then find, waiting out in the middle, world stars like Lamb, Gower and Randall. For good measure Getty helped sponsor a team of ornithologists to fetch red kite eggs from Spain and reintroduce the once-common bird of prey back into England. Breeding pens were built in the sheltered woodland of Wormsley. Within a few years the skies over his cricket pitch had a Pyrenean, fan-tailed flavour; a few years after that the verges of the M40 were alive with the shadows of predatory birds.

Cricket at Wormsley wasn't just messing about in flannels. Getty took it seriously and, according to Ingleby-Mackenzie, liked his team to win. Touring elevens were expected to play properly – to put up a top-notch show. Lucky guests counted the stylish centuries by Martin Crowe and Brian Lara as among the finest they had ever seen: Lara's was commemorated with a burgundy-coloured plaque in the pavilion.

Getty loved it all beyond words. "Cricketers are heroes to me," he told Swanton. "I come alive in their company." His sporting salon afforded him "the happiest summer since my boyhood". Though new to the game he had all the instincts of a genuine old-timer. "I loathe the thought of coloured clothes," he said, when one-day ideas began to encroach on the white-linen world that had seduced him. "I'm horrified by things like this that cheapen cricket. Every retrograde step should be fought."

Wisden could not have found a more like-minded benefactor. Getty was a book collector in his own right; the library at Wormsley was stocked with rare first editions of Chaucer, Shakespeare and much more. "But he saw cricket as life," said his son Mark Getty. "It transformed him. It was more than just a game. He thought it represented a certain type of England, a certain type of behaviour – a sort that was endangered maybe, and maybe even doomed. But he loved it. He loved the people, especially. He just thought they were marvellous human beings. They populated his life and made it interesting."

Paul Getty was no businessman; at board meetings he would stir his tea in silence, let others get on with the discussion and sometimes, rather abruptly, get up and leave. He invited his financially alert son Mark – who was busy turning some of the world's photographic archive into Getty Images – to join the board as the family's voice in *Wisden*'s affairs, and Mark in turn (aware that he had no direct publishing experience himself) invited Richard Charkin to join the team. Charkin was at that time a cricket-loving publishing executive, and he started going to meetings in Paul Getty's new flat (overlooking Green Park) and wondered what to do with a 120-year old book.

The ingredients for major change were all in place. And that is what was on the way.

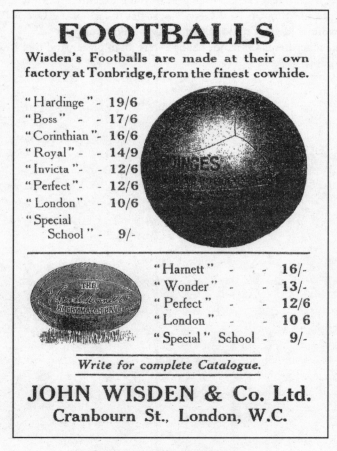
Advertisement from Wisden *1917*

14

Fin de Siècle

Of all the alterations in Matthew Engel's early years at *Wisden* nothing caused so much trouble as his decision to drop the list of Oxbridge Blues. The public schools remained an untouchable part of the syllabus, but the list of Blues had, Engel felt, become "the biggest anachronism in the book". The days when the universities were a top-grade proving ground for the best young amateurs had long gone. Though the England captain Mike Atherton, formerly of Cambridge, was proof that fine players did still pass through the ancient quadrangles, university cricket was no longer a senior element of the game – not least because the days when cricketers were waved in, irrespective of their academic ambitions, were a misty memory. Better, tougher cricket was being played elsewhere. "There was a standard of first-class cricket around the world which we were ignoring," said Engel. "And it was distorting the averages, as county batsmen helped themselves to cheap runs. Even the *Oxford Mail* and the *Cambridge News* stopped sending reporters."

This last point might have said as much about the state of regional journalism as it did about cricket. It is possible that the centenary of the Lancashire League in 1992, and the fact that its grand roster of world-famous cricketers had for so many years played such a slender role in *Wisden*'s cricket coverage, brought home the anomaly. In his final Notes Graeme Wright had suggested that the TCCB "examine the first-class status of cricket" at Oxbridge, and now his successor did precisely that. Engel, who had made the same point more than once in the *Guardian*, took a deep breath and let a little piece of *Wisden* heritage slip overboard.

Inevitably, since he was cutting one of the threads that bound the Almanack to its own past, outsiders were quick to carp. The cricket master at Eton warned that *Wisden* would "lose its value as a reference book" if it also dropped from the Oxbridge cards the name of the schools the players had attended. And a snide article in the *Sunday Telegraph* described Engel as "a political scientist from Manchester University" who harboured "bitterness" towards Oxford and Cambridge as part of a "crusade" to strip them of first-class status. "It made me out to be some redbrick dissident," said Engel. "Which didn't matter. But Paul Getty was deeply upset. It cut him to the quick. He had developed a coterie of old cricketers at Wormsley; he befriended them, became one of them. It went to the heart of his idea of the game. He asked me to think again."

Engel did think again, but came to the same conclusion. In the *Guardian*, he floated the idea of a genuinely competitive league made up of the six top universities: Oxford, Cambridge, Durham, Loughborough, London and Southampton (who in recent times had been the "Combined Universities" in the Benson & Hedges Cup) – to play high-quality three-day cricket through the summer on good pitches. This was no mere attempt to turn the clock back to the good old amateur past – nothing could be achieved, he argued, by "comic book dilettantism" of that sort; on the contrary, it was a way of creating an additional tier of high-quality cricket for young players.

In truth, this was neither the only nor even the most substantial item on the new editor's agenda. The release of Nelson Mandela in 1990 signalled an end to the sporting boycott of South Africa, and in 1992 South Africa sent a team (for the first time) to the World Cup in Australia and then the West Indies. It had rejoined cricket's top table, and Engel invited Donald Woods, the journalist whose work on the ANC martyr Steve Biko had inspired the film *Cry Freedom*, to address the subject of his country's readmission. Engel was as clear as mineral water on the moral aspect of this long-running saga: "Nothing in cricket has disgraced the game over the years so much as its relationship with South Africa," he wrote, adding that it had lured many otherwise fine people to collude with a "fundamentally evil" political idea. He found it typical, in this context, that the stylish David Gower should have been sidelined by England (the implication being that he was uncommitted to the cause) when John Emburey was picked despite having been on two rebel tours. "Short of standing on the square at Lord's and giving a V-sign to the Long Room, it is hard to imagine how anyone can have shown greater unconcern," wrote Engel. Yet while Gower was abruptly and pointedly ignored, for Emburey "forgiveness was instant".

Engel himself had reported on several rebel tours. Though a staunch opponent of apartheid, he found Pretoria's attempt to cling on to power "riveting". He did not intend to lay down a predictable editorial line, so anyone who expected *Wisden* to be pleased when the ICC ruled in 1993 that the records of these old rebel tours should be struck off had to think again. On scholarly grounds, Engel was unwilling to alter numbers that the ICC had once declared legitimate. It was paltry to make such a gesture now that it had been defused as a live issue. He refused to go along with it: "Our records thus remain unchanged."

In the years that followed, the essential ballast of his book remained what it always had been: the detailed reporting of the English season, the week-in, week-out rhythm, ups and downs, ins and outs and upsets of the county grind. "Rain delayed the start until 4 p.m. ... Hampshire were overwhelmed ... Kent's reply began badly ... the early honours belonged to Gloucestershire." A whole summer's cricket was condensed into print. And on to this background were pinned the individual moments from which the larger pattern was made: "Nicholas suddenly declared ... Fairbrother pulled a hamstring ... Watkinson switched to off-spin ... De Freitas hit Batty for five sixes ... Bailey made the most of some good fortune." Posterity would be able to recall the whole thing.

This aspect of *Wisden* rarely came into its own so strikingly as in 1995, when the Almanack's chief duty was to narrate the remarkable achievements of Brian Lara the previous year. In April 1994 he had broken Sobers's Test record with 375 against England in Antigua, and he followed it up by flying to England, joining Warwickshire as an overseas player and embarking on the most amazing run-spree in history, including the highest-ever first-class score: 501 not out against Durham.

Engel began by assembling an expert portfolio of essays on this stunning purple patch, in which a range of onlookers described Lara from different vantage points. Warwickshire's coach Bob Woolmer was thought to have been the only man in the world to have seen both Hanif Mohammad's 499 and Lara's 501 ("I said to Dermot [Reeve, the Warwickshire captain], 'Let him go the whole way'"). Anderson

Cummins was twelfth man for the West Indies in Antigua for the 375 before actually bowling at Lara for Durham during his record-breaking innings at Edgbaston ("He was on ten when I bowled him with a no-ball"). There was the word of a journalist, John Thicknesse of the *Evening Standard* ("We arrived at Edgbaston in time for the last 130"); and a statement from the Man of the Moment himself ("I knew I had a chance of making history"). Keith Piper, the wicketkeeper who partnered Lara to 501, gave the view from 22 yards, and there was a tribute from the scorer ("the general feeling was it wouldn't be much of a day").

This was cricket as theatre, cricket in the round. The reader could circle grand events and inspect them from all angles. But the more traditional way to track such events in *Wisden* was catered for too in the routine match reports that were still the Almanack's staple diet. "Lara's debut dominated the match," began the first such precis. He had been in England for only two days, and this was his first outing since that historic 375 in Antigua, but he scored 147 against Glamorgan to confirm that he was "the hottest property in the game".

He was only warming up. He made two centuries in the match against Leicestershire ("with flashing square cuts and pulls leaving the fielders helpless"), skipped the game at Oxford, notched his fifth in a row against Somerset ("the fastest century of the season"), took another off Middlesex ("looked in a different class") and made it seven out of eight on the first day against Durham, before blazing into the record books the following afternoon. He then dashed to London for a Benson & Hedges semi-final against Surrey. "Spectators flocked to The Oval," reported *Wisden* (a fact I know to be true, since I was one of them, sneaking off work early to catch a glimpse). Lara dozed in the pavilion before rattling up 70 in, oh, about three blinks of an eye. A week later he tried his luck against Curtly Ambrose in Northampton (it had been said that he was lucky that he did not have to face his lethal compatriot too often) and scored a run-a-ball 197 before perishing to "a hook that was going for six". In that seven-week blaze of form he scored eight centuries (and 1,798 runs) in 11 first-class innings, and his appearance in the Benson & Hedges final two weeks later caused "a box office stampede". His runs that season (2,066 at an average of 89.82) powered Warwickshire to the Championship and two other titles (leading to their being called "Larashire") though he came only second in the annual batting averages (John Carr's ten not outs for Middlesex just tilting things his way).

Video highlights of these amazing performances were soon available, but they were strangely numbing – a tedious run of vacuous boundaries. Only in *Wisden* could the full, steady, game-by-game procession be relived in detail. It took a "certain cast of mind", wrote Engel in his Lara-dazed Notes, even to aspire to such things.

So far as the structure of the book was concerned, Engel tinkered away like a man stripping down a classic car before reassembling it part by part. He chopped Births and Deaths into two, one of them a "Register" of current professionals, the other a list of the game's great and good. In recent years this had become an increasingly hard club to join, but Engel allowed himself a degree of "editor's discretion" in order to keep some great names in. "It seemed to me incongruous," he wrote, "that being dead for ten years should be a reason for removal." Bit by bit, as the years passed, he added new segments: on equipment, grounds and the media (in 1993), on cricket and the law (in 1994) and even a glance at cricket computer games (in 1999). This allowed the Victorian annual to observe, of *Brian Lara '98*, that it "outsold Sonic the Hedgehog", not a phrase that would have sprung readily to Sydney Pardon's lips.

Recognising that *Wisden* could be a campaigning force as well as an admonitory one, he proposed a significant initiative of his own. In 1996 his Almanack actually went ahead and created a World Championship of Test Cricket, by the simple (Engel always swore by simplicity) expedient of awarding points for wins. It was not officially recognised, though it made a stir in 1999 when, after losing to New Zealand, England hit rock bottom in the nine-nation *Wisden* list. The idea was subsequently adopted (in a slightly more abstruse form) by the ICC in 2003 and is now a routine fact of cricket life: when England reached number one in 2011 it was headline-making news.

None of this was making the Almanack any smaller, and having introduced Cricket Round the World in his first volume, in 1994 Engel expanded the book further by creating the Chronicle of the calendar year. This was an enthusiastic trove of "remarkable and eccentric cricket happenings". This player had hit 11 sixes in a row; that one had been bitten by an adder; Australia's captain Allan Border had been presented with a whortleberry pie in Taunton, Somerset; a 15-year-old boy at Ribbleton Hall High School (a powerful lad named Andrew Flintoff) had hit 234 not out in 20 overs. This dentist-batsman had thumped a six through his own car window ("I heard the crack and thought, Oops"); that 18-year-old in Mysore had set fire to herself when she heard that Sachin Tendulkar might be retiring. A Sri Lankan festival in Southall, London, was abandoned when Tamil gunmen opened fire; and the chief executive of South African cricket, Ali Bacher, failed to deliver a speech during the Lord's Test because he was "trapped in the ladies' toilet". He had "wandered in there in error" in order to go over his notes.

There was more to all this than simple knockabout fun. Engel was sliding *Wisden* into the world beyond the first-class game, the wider arena of league, school and village cricket where the Almanack's readership lived. "Some people think *Wisden* has always covered such things," he wrote. "That is unfortunately not true, but I see no reason why it should not be true in the future." Alongside articles on the nature of reverse swing and Ashes battles there were pieces on cricket societies, cricketing pubs, reflections on cheating and a tribute to 150 years of I Zingari (by John Woodcock). There was even a discussion of the fact that it was now possible to study cricket as an A-level subject.

Engel knew that cricket's centre of gravity was drifting east. In 1997, picking Sri Lanka's Sanath Jayasuriya as the first Cricketer of the Year to have played no actual part in the English summer (though his dynamic efforts in the 1996 World Cup had most certainly influenced the national game, especially in the quarter-final, when he smashed a helter-skelter 82 off Mike Atherton's luckless England team), he recognised that it was "an affront to tradition" but that "each year the cricketing world revolves a little less around St John's Wood". Those days were over; *Wisden* had spoken.

As always, the obituaries were full of famous names, some with sad stories to tell. Denis Compton, Ray Lindwall, Wilfred Wooller … *Wisden* had counted them all in, and now it counted them all out. In 1994 *Wisden* was finally able to make its peace with the Reverend Archibald Fargus, a Cambridge Blue and Gloucestershire cricketer whose death had been reported in 1915 only for it to emerge that he had, thanks to a missed train, escaped drowning. Now it emerged that when he really did die, in 1963, the Almanack missed it. Thanks to the "tireless work" of Robert Brooke, who tracked down an assortment of missing obituaries over the years, *Wisden* was also able to honour Sidney Adams, whose first wicket in first-class cricket had been – the name meant little at the time – the playwright and novelist Samuel Beckett. Adams was killed crossing the Rhine in 1945, but *Wisden*'s tribute was quiet. "Adams's career was less illustrious than his victim's, though he played nine games more for his county."

By the end of the decade Engel had led *Wisden* through a thorough transformation, but the magic ingredient was his own style. One of Woody Allen's alter egos once said that when it came to seeing the glass as half-full or half-empty, he doggedly saw it as half-full – but half-full of bitterness. Engel was equally able, when the fit of gloom came upon him, to don the darkest set of widow's weeds. There was a gleam of black comedy even in his most trenchant remarks, and along with his dry and self-aware literary manners it allowed him to develop a singular voice – "Engelish", perhaps – that gave *Wisden* a fetching new level of wit and punch. He would later call the Notes by the Editor "the most wonderful pulpit in sport" and his own sermon became a newsworthy treat – one could almost sense him climbing the circular steps, setting his text down on the eagle-shaped lectern, tugging in his sleeves and clearing his throat as he surveyed the flock below.

"The simplistic think England lose cricket matches because Boggins was picked instead of Snoggins," he wrote. "More subtle reasoners think it is because the counties are doing everything wrong. The roots of the problem are much deeper." This was one of many such pronouncements: "The script for English cricket now seems to be more like the Book of Job than anything else: the Sabeans have stolen the oxen; the Chaldeans have stolen the camels; and the fire of God has burned up the sheep." In a line that could have been his catchphrase he declared: "In the long run, I fear the worst." He wasn't too thrilled by the short run either. English cricket was a "hopeless mish-mash" played by "undermotivated cricketers on terrible pitches"; surely it could not survive for long: "The English crisis is now the greatest crisis in world cricket."

The biblical references were only partly a joshing allusion to *Wisden*'s own status as cricket's holy book. In echoing so vehemently one of the Almanack's central assumptions – that things were going to hell in a handcart – he was aligning it with one of Western culture's most powerful messages: the one which swore that humankind was living in a fallen state, that it had been banished from some long-lost Eden. Engel himself had been to a Jewish school, but was happy to see echoes of Christianity's core myth in cricket; indeed he hinted that this might be why a book so devoted to the game was also so willing to compose elegies to its endless decline.* No wonder people liked to think of it as a bible: it was a sacred text about the fall from grace – or Grace.

But in case anyone thought he was being too dogmatic, Engel would lob in the odd self-deprecating pleasantry as well. In 1995 he confessed that as editor of the game's senior record-keeper he had selected a team in a fantasy cricket competition, and that, thanks to his rare skill and famous cricket intelligence, he had come 36,952nd.

It was a tease, this voice. Readers could not tell if he was a clown with a sad side, or a misanthrope with a twinkle in his eye. There was nothing new about *Wisden* editors moaning, but Engel was the first to suggest that cricket had actually *arrived* at the dogs. There was a classical symmetry in his put-downs, which gave them a playful edge. "The Championship's prime trouble is not that it is unwatched," he wrote in 2000, it is that it is "largely unwatchable". Years later he added: "The current set-up is not merely the worst that has yet been invented, but possibly the worst that can be imagined." In a tribute to Hobbs he could not help being grateful that the Master had not lived to see modern

---

* One of the hallmarks of *Wisden* is that the game, it seems, has been going to the dogs for a very long time. In 1900 A. G. Steel wrote that it was in the "direst peril"; in 1910 Sydney Pardon, in one of many such utterances, said: "a good many people have come to the conclusion that first-class cricket is losing its hold". In 1952 Colonel Rait Kerr asked: "Can the game in this country really survive the emphasis on security first and last?" And in 1986 Bradman argued that new bats were making leg-spin obsolete (Shane Warne was 16 at the time). It has also been common for newspapers to see poor shows by the England team as a symbolic depiction of national decline. For some reason they were slower to present England wins as emblems of resurgence.

times – "an age of chancers and graspers and slackers and hustlers". And gaping in disbelief over yet another implausible proposal to "expand" the game into pastures new, he muttered: "I am not against the expansion of the game, far from it; I am against the propagation of nonsense." He promised, as he mourned the end of "walking", that if he ever saw "an out-of-form Aussie batsman" give himself out to an imperceptible nick at a decisive moment in the final Test match of the summer, then he too would walk – "home from The Oval in my underpants".

This last topic – umpiring – would become one of his longest-running causes. He was an implacable opponent of television-based umpiring, on the simple grounds that it broke the bond of trust, the consensus that operated between players and officials. Being given out unjustly was, he felt, an indelible part of the game, even – especially – if it stung. "I remain utterly convinced," he wrote in 1994, "that this is a disaster ... The heart of the game, the finality of the umpire's verdict, is being eaten away." The idea that the umpire was the representative of the players, not their supervisor, that the players' role was to *help* them reach correct decisions (rather than seeking to outwit them) – this was unfashionable. By 1998 he himself could see that it was a forlorn gesture. "I have never been an enthusiast for the third umpire," he wrote, "but I know when I'm licked." He did, however, continue to fire off poison-tipped arrows, remarking, when one-day umpires swapped their white coats for polo shirts, that they looked as if they had "wandered in from a game of crazy golf with the grandchildren".

There were other matters to attend to. When the Australian Cricket Board admitted, during the prosecution of Pakistan's Salim Malik for match-fixing, that Shane Warne and Mark Waugh had accepted money from Indian bookmakers for what the players insisted was "innocuous" information, he could see that it was "the rocky outcrop of the mountain range of corruption that almost certainly still lies shrouded in the mists elsewhere". He commissioned a series of articles on the subject, all of which echoed his sense that there were probably plenty more such skeletons in cricket's cupboard. He nodded approvingly when MCC at last (in 1998) abolished the ban on women members – "a generally stupid, mostly peevish and entirely selfish" policy. He was alert to the sense that cricket involved character and mental speed as well as technical skill – thus Derek Pringle was "far too lateral a thinker" to be thought of as "the new Botham". And he continued to expand both the comment section at the front and the miscellaneous items at the back, making an already big book even bulkier. "The survival of *Wisden* as a single volume is becoming a matter of concern," he wrote in 1995, but four years later the Almanack went past 1,500 pages for the first time, and with the volume of cricket growing all the time it was hard to see how it could easily be condensed.

While Engel pushed ahead with his vision for the Almanack, change was beginning to sweep through the rest of the John Wisden properties. In the summer of 1995 there was a ruction at *Wisden Cricket Monthly* when it published an inflammatory article by Robert Henderson suggesting that England's foreign-born (not to say dark-skinned) players were insufficiently patriotic to play for their country. It attracted some hostile publicity and presented the new management with a challenge. In the end the editor (and founder) of the magazine, David Frith, was replaced by Tim de Lisle, who was invited to bring the publication into the modern age (it was still a scissors-and-glue operation). The production contract was given to John Brown Publishing, whose own founder and chief executive would eventually join the John Wisden board.

In 1998, after nearly two decades of making herself indispensable, Christine Forrest decided the time had come for her to step down. Hers was no longer a job that could be done by a friendly neighbour with time on her hands – she had turned it into a full-on position – and her place as production editor was taken by Hugh Chevallier, a one-time student of medieval literature who had been working on the AA's travel books (the right shade of yellow, at least) before seeing an advert in the *Bookseller* for the role at *Wisden*. It was a publication he respected "enormously – it's the horse's mouth of cricket", and though he had already missed the deadline he fired off an application. He was soon rushing away from a university reunion on Exmoor to be quizzed by Matthew Engel in a motorway service station near Bristol. After passing tests both on his cricket knowledge and, more significantly, his technical know-how, Chevallier was offered the job. It was hoped that he could also bring some digital expertise to the Almanack's procedures, which, like the magazine's, were the opposite of up-to-date.

While all this was happening the "soul" of cricket – by which people chiefly meant its financial pulse – was migrating to the Indian subcontinent: that was where the cash, the fervour and the television audience lived. This had been obvious for a while. Scyld Berry's *Cricket Wallah*, an account of England's trip to the subcontinent in 1981–2, ended by saying that "the future of the game will be decided in India", and he was not alone in his thinking. When the World Cups of 1987 and 1996 were staged there, it exposed the cricket fervour in those parts for all to see. Was it troubling that cricket's new heartland seemed to be intoxicated with the shortest and noisiest form of the game? Was India too susceptible to nationalistic hero-worship? Questions such as these would drift to the surface in the years to come, but at this time it seemed merely that a vast population of cricket-lovers was beginning to make its presence felt.

Wisden knew it had to respond to such changes in the cricket landscape, but wasn't sure how. Getty had promoted Christopher Lane to managing director and made him responsible for developing the business as well as looking after the Almanack and the magazine. The most obvious step forward was to broaden the company's range of publications, and in 1998 *Wisden* went ahead and launched an Australian version of itself. The idea had been aired 17 years previously, in 1981, when Ian Botham was laying waste to Kim Hughes's team. It had taken a while, but now, as one newspaper put it, "*Wisden* is coming to Australia." In most ways it was a deferential reproduction of the classic English model (though with a bright green dust jacket). Graeme Wright wrote the Preface to the first edition, and Engel himself contributed some Notes from the Northern Hemisphere in which he sardonically narrated the way in which MCC had finally agreed to admit women members. The Australian edition, seizing a chance to go one better, actually made a woman, Belinda Clark, its Cricketer of the Year.

The first book was warmly received, and the second (edited by Gideon Haigh, with Notes by Peter Roebuck) also went well. Engel, on the lookout for things to prune, cut back the coverage of Sheffield Shield cricket in his own Almanack, leaving the finer details of Australia's domestic game to the down-under edition.

There were other *Wisden*-related publications in the pipeline, along with the limited-edition, leatherbound version of the Almanack that had been introduced in 1995. But Christopher Lane continued to feel there was more to be done. "In retrospect we were waiting for the big idea," he said. "Things were going well, and personally I felt privileged. It was like being given the keys to the kingdom. There were remarkable people on the board, so I was getting a marvellous business education, and holding the reins of two very different horses. Matthew was going great guns with the Almanack, and Tim was modernising the magazine. But I didn't want us to tread water. I knew there was something else out there, something we hadn't found – the next big thing if you like. It wasn't until the internet got going that I began to appreciate what that might be."

It was easy to say, in theory, that delivering *Wisden*'s world-famous statistics online might be the path he was looking for. But where on earth might it lead? Back in 1996, in a tentative first step, Lane, Engel and Richard Charkin visited Simon King, an English chemistry academic and MCC member who, in exile at the University of Minnesota in 1993, had come up with a new way to follow cricket. It was a dedicated space for match scores in the brave new world of the web. Supported by computer-literate cricket-lovers in universities around the world, it could transmit up-to-the-minute information to anyone with a silicon chip and a phone line. Devised as "a cure for homesickness", King believed it was revolutionary. It was called Cricinfo.

Like starched Royal Navy officers rowing ashore on an uncharted Pacific Island, the Wisden party met King in a dusty outpost of University College, London. It was a gloomy evening in February, and King's office was a poky backroom at the top of a bleak staircase. It didn't feel like the humming centre of a new world, but King said that what he had to show them would "change everything".

He leaned forward, tapped a keyboard and ... nothing. He tried again. Nothing. After two or three minutes the screen filled with illegible spots of light. King said it seemed to be running slow this evening – maybe they should try another time. The *Wisden* team looked at one another and sighed: it looked as though their game wasn't going to change that much after all. "It was," recalled Lane, "one of the worst presentations ever." They went away unconvinced and unimpressed.

Before long, however, they had to face the vexing fact that they had passed up an amazing opportunity. As Cricinfo grew into a dominant force, Wisden set up a new company – Wisden Online – in partnership with a company called Quintus. Since Cricinfo was concentrating on up-to-the-minute scores, Wisden.com would offer a more reflective set of instant match reports and comment. It launched at the end of 2001, looking for subscribers willing to pay £25 a year for access.

In the event they found only a few hundred. The reflex culture of the web was that it was an anarchic free spirit – no one wanted to *pay* for information. Simon King's seemingly dysfunctional idea, meanwhile, was being hailed by the *Financial Times* as "one of the biggest, sexiest dotcoms in the world". Cricinfo was already a multimillion-pound global operation which in 2001 was even able to ride in, like "a knight in shining, high-tech armour", to sponsor the County Championship.

"It certainly looked as though we had missed the boat," said Lane. "We believed that if we could put *Wisden* on the web we'd unlock a vast audience. We thought we'd found the vehicle to take *Wisden* to the world. But we were like Captain Scott; Cricinfo had already planted their flag, and we couldn't compete. The best you can say is that we were investing in the learning curve. We were going in the right direction, but we took a wrong fork."

In 2002, however, fortune suddenly smiled on *Wisden*. The much-vaunted dotcom boom ran out of energy, sputtered and stalled, and even Cricinfo went into a tailspin. Its value plummeted, and in February 2003 John Wisden & Co, armed with Paul Getty's deep wallet, was able to take control of it for less than £2 million, a fraction of the euphoria-driven valuation of two years earlier. In less than a decade since the arrival of Paul Getty, *Wisden* had joined the modern world.

———

As the end of the century approached, Engel was planning one of those special souvenir editions at which Wisden had always excelled. He wanted it to be a literary event in itself – "the Millennium edition". His headline idea was to name *Wisden*'s Five Cricketers of the Century. "I don't believe there has been an honour like it in this sport or any other," he wrote in the *Observer*. The annual selection was a decision taken by the editor alone, but for this one-off Engel created an electoral college of a hundred cricket people – well-known former players, journalists and historians. "It was so exciting," he said, "counting the votes as they came in. It was like Christmas." Bit by bit, nomination by nomination, the list took shape. The unanimous choice was Don Bradman ("How did anyone ever get him out?"). Then came Garry Sobers ("the last Corinthian"), Jack Hobbs ("there is only one Master"), Shane Warne ("his bowling is simultaneously a technical and a dramatic master-piece") and Vivian Richards ("never content with mere survival ... bowlers had to be subjugated"). A few others came close, but this was the Famous Five. It would prove a highly engaging talking point.

It was inevitable that an issue such as this should have its eye fixed on the past – that is what commemorations are for – but the untimely deaths of two great contemporary fast bowlers gave the Obituaries an unusually topical wrench. Malcolm Marshall and Sylvester Clarke had both died very young (at 41 and 44 respectively). Marshall, who married his girlfriend just weeks before succumbing to cancer, had five West Indies captains for pallbearers at his funeral, while Clarke, in some ways an even more fearsome opponent, was recalled by a characteristic anecdote. On England's tour of the Caribbean in 1993, four years after Clarke had left Surrey under a rum-flavoured cloud, he had sauntered into the nets in a pair of trainers without socks, and bowled a few balls at Graham Thorpe. "It was as quick as anything England saw all tour."

Elsewhere the cricket century was celebrated in style. There was a gallery of famous images; the game's literature was scanned; there were thoughts on "vintage summers" and even "a hundred matches of the century". There was also a stream of minor treats and nuggets tucked into empty corners here and there: a trio of photographs of Darren Gough's hat-trick in Sydney; a list of captains who won five tosses in a series; the first-class cricketers who lived to be a hundred; a comparison of speed-gun scores; MCC presidents and youngest triple-centurions. A table of county memberships showed a surprising increase from 120,000 in 1989 to nearly 150,000 ten years later. For some reason there was no mention of all-rounders who starred in Christmas pantomimes, but just about every other cricket-related topic was represented. Indeed there were so many of these diverting "fillers" that they needed their own two-page index. Engel was able to write that finally, thanks to the accumulated work of 137 years, *Wisden* really was the "almanack" it had always claimed to be.

And, of course, there was the usual poker-faced comedy from the wider world: "Moroccan cricket made encouraging strides ... Cricket in Bahrain has been described as the hardest – perhaps the worst – in the world … Spanish cricket continues to be dogged by lack of funds … Moon stopped play in Picardy." There were snippets on cricket charities, dealers, auctioneers, umpires, groundsmen and other "cricket people". There was smart original work on cricket and the weather, in which Philip Eden proved, through his *Wisden* Weather Index (which balanced rain, temperature and sunshine) that 1976 really had been the finest summer, and that the vile season of 1987 was nothing like so bad as the washouts of 1879 and 1888. And the fact that cricket could still produce new and unexpected trifles was manifest in the news that a single no-ball had somehow managed to produce 12 runs ("two for the initial penalty, four for the boundary hit … and six from the subsequent free hit"). *Wisden* was sad to report that two of the famous Oval pigeons had been killed during the World Cup match between Australia and India – "leading to speculation that pigeons also had problems seeing the white ball". But it was braced by news that a pair of identical twins, Hamish and James Marshall, had opened the batting for Northern Districts and shared partnerships of 80 and 60. Whether these scores were right was anyone's guess – twins in helmets were the ultimate scorer's nightmare.

Fortunately for Engel's reputation as an impish curmudgeon, there had been enough controversy in 1999 to inspire bleak sentiments as well. *Wisden* wouldn't have been the same without them. "Sometimes English cricket looks shambolic and amateurish," he wrote. "But sometimes it looks far worse than that." A pattern was emerging. By now no one could be surprised that a cricket-loving book should be so endlessly dissatisfied by the game it professed to love; it was clear that the annual breast-beating was only strengthening *Wisden*'s reputation as a taskmaster (firm but fair, as the saying went). But Engel's *Wisden* more than ever resembled the chorus in a Greek tragedy, chanting out its laments in resonant lines as it witnessed the agonies of the heroes it was supposed to be celebrating. In response to news that the Sheffield Shield was being renamed the Pura Cup, he wrote: "This is not sponsorship. It is an act of vandalism." And when it looked as though cricket was morphing into football, thanks to the use of the TV replay, he was blunt: "Oi, umpire! That's a penalty." The fact that the decision was correct was beside the point. It was perilously close to mob rule.

All of this took a tremendous lot of space. Graeme Wright's final *Wisden* in 1992 had been a hearty-enough 1,344 pages, but Engel's 2000 Almanack was 1,600 – roughly the size of the first ten *Wisden* editions put together. It was a landmark for *Wisden*, though, and Christopher Lane marked it by seeking new premises for the Almanack. In the end he found them not far from his own home in north Hampshire, at a kink in the roads west of Farnham called, appropriately enough, Golden Pot.

The 2000 edition was a hard act to follow, and Engel knew it. As it turned out he would not be making the attempt himself, because he was flying west to become the *Guardian*'s correspondent in Washington. "It seems like time to let someone else have a crack," he wrote in the same paper, noting that even his tireless predecessor Sydney Pardon "did not have to report and explain defeats against New Zealand". The Washington posting was a major professional opportunity, and his two children were the right age (young, and portable). But he did not want to sever his involvement with *Wisden* altogether, so was pleased when Graeme Wright agreed to hold the fort in his absence. "I knew that it was in knowledgeable hands," he said. "And there was an understanding that I would come back, so things wouldn't change too much." The one thing he couldn't anticipate was what a sensational story he was about to tumble into. He arrived in Washington at the end of August 2001; a fortnight later, two planes slammed into the World Trade Center in New York, and TV umpiring abruptly ceased to feel like the worst thing that could befall civilisation.

According to a famous anecdote in Quentin Bell's biography of Virginia Woolf, the modern world began in a single instant, early in the 20th century, when Lytton Strachey, lounging in the doorway of an elegant drawing room, pointed at a stain on Vanessa Bell's dress and said "Semen?" The entire company burst out laughing, and in a streak of dark lightning a breach was made in the stern wall of inherited etiquette. A new culture of irreverence and frank self-assertion marched on to the centre stage.

As it happens, the *Oxford Dictionary* cites 1922 – a great date in modernism: the year in which *Ulysses* and *The Waste Land* were published – as the moment when the f-word was first used "profanely as the coarsest equivalent of damn". In the blink of an eye, real life and language gatecrashed the secluded party that was polite literature. The celebrated vulgarisms of James Joyce and the plain speaking of D. H. Lawrence slipped through the gap and wedged the door open for good.

No one has ever accused *Wisden* of being avant-garde, so we should not be surprised that its own leap forward seemed to take place many years later, in the 2010 edition, when Tim Bresnan was quoted as using the word in a tweet – thus bringing *Wisden* (trailing some decades behind the Bloomsbury aesthetes) into the 20th century. There were some prominent complaints about this lapse of taste: the *Daily Telegraph* felt that standards were slipping and that a once-proud currency was being debased.

Few wanted to spoil a nice story by pointing out that it was not in actual fact the first time the oath had stained the Almanack's decorous pages. A 2006 obituary of Kerry Packer mentioned the moment when

Packer lay "clinically dead" for eight minutes before coming round and announcing that there was "fucking nothing" on the other side. The idea that cricketers effed and blinded was no surprise; the thought of their doing so in *Wisden* felt more than averagely jarring, and showed the extent to which the Almanack, in reporting the doings of cricketers over so many generations, had been a rather austere grandmother to the game it loved, brushing its hair, flicking grime off its cuffs and cleaning its mouth out.

Nothing ruffled the calm surface of *Wisden*'s reputation quite so sharply, however, as the larkish moment in the summer of 1999 when a little-known left-arm spinner called Matthew Brimson decided, as a prank, to improve on the usual rabbit-ear salute behind a team-mate's head by exposing his, um, middle stump in the Leicestershire team photograph. No one noticed and the revealing image ended up in the following year's volume. This was no ordinary Almanack – it was the Millennium Edition – so the gesture felt even more like a two-fingered salute than usual. Naturally it inspired a gale of public mirth at the idea that so staid a publication should feature such a bawdy up-yours. The puns flowed freely: "New Balls!" ran the headlines, "That's out!" It was, ho-ho-ho, a right cock-up. Remarks such as these assumed that *Wisden*, like a prim Victorian matron, would be outraged, but its sense of humour did not fail: Engel responded in time-honoured fashion, mocking Brimson's "credentials" and suggesting that anyone seeking to pull such a stunt needed to be "more impressively arrayed ... Even when we increased the size of the picture, we couldn't be certain that we'd seen what we thought we'd seen." Smiling aside, the incident was good publicity.

It might not have been quite the sort of celebrity the Almanack was courting but, as Oscar Wilde said, the only thing worse than being talked about was *not* being talked about. It certainly felt, as Wisden entered its third century, as though there was a radical change in the cultural conversation surrounding it. In the years to come it would also chime with the way cricket was intruding on other rude-mechanical areas of popular culture. Who would have thought that *Wisden* would be needed to supply relevant background information on various television reality shows – so-called because they pinned "guests" in the most unreal surroundings imaginable. But it was to the old yellow tome that armchair dance fans had to turn to learn about Darren Gough, Mark Ramprakash, Chris Hollins and Harry Judd, all cricketing winners of the BBC's *Strictly Come Dancing* – the first two for England, Hollins for a century in the 1994 Varsity match, and Judd for 252 runs at Uppingham. *Wisden* 2005 had noted that Judd had also "topped the UK singles chart twice" as the drummer for "the pop group McFly". The England spinner Phil Tufnell, meanwhile, took left-arm over the wicket into the Australian jungle en route to becoming the nation's favourite reality TV character.

In marked contrast to all of this, Graeme Wright's return was greeted with two rock-solid news stories. The death of Bradman was a classic *Wisden* event, but since it came when the book was at the printer there was time only for a brief note in place of the 2001 Preface. Wright still managed to find an apposite pun for the towering century-maker, gone at the age of 92: "It seemed inconceivable that he would not reach three figures." The Don would be given a more expansive fanfare the following year.

The other news was shocking in a different way. South Africa's captain, Hansie Cronje, had confessed to his involvement in match fixing, giving a fresh kick to the idea that cricket had any right to be synonymous with fair play and good conduct. Wright separated the two in a way that allowed him to be severe: "Cronje's worst crime was not against cricket ... but against morality and decency. It was the way he ensnared the two most vulnerable members of his team ..." He went on to expand on the arguments set out in his book, *Betrayal*, which brooded on the commercial and administrative threats to cricket's traditions. He stopped short of asserting that gambling and match-fixing were the inevitable by-products of a game that had been commandeered by short-term financial interests – but he hinted as much. And he commissioned Mihir Bose to write a survey of the scandal, which was full of dark suggestions that Cronje was only the beginning.

There were other tremors of novelty, not least in the way the Almanack advised readers that there was more on this story in the magazine (*Wisden Cricket Monthly*), and that up-to-date results could be found on the new website. But in other respects this was a straightforward, old-fashioned edition with a host of big names to

honour and mourn. Two great West Indians – Curtly Ambrose and
Courtney Walsh – had retired; and two giants of the English game –
Colin Cowdrey and Brian Statham – had died. Frank Keating, at his
most rhapsodic, saw their end as a darkening of the sky, an eclipse: "A
radiant era, rich in recollection, seems in a rush to pull down the blinds
and shut out the sunlight."

The volume also featured considerations of coaches and pitches – the
actual rather than figurative "grass-roots" of the game. "The coarser
rye grasses," *Wisden* told its readers, briefly sounding like a contributor
to *Gardeners' Question Time*, "were recommended ahead of the fine
fescue." As if reacting to the avalanche of famous players in the 2000
Wisden, Wright invited Jonathan Rice to peer into the crevices of the
Almanack for famous names whose lives had only briefly touched on
cricket (he found plenty). In honour of Swanton's death the previous
year, there was an account by David Rayvern Allen of the way his 1939
Wisden lifted the morale of prisoners in Thailand – "Never had the
'Cricketer's Bible' more suited that description."

Unusually, when the 2001 *Wisden* was published, it was already clear
what the chief subject the following year would be, and when the time
came Bradman was recalled with an enthusiastic volley of essays and
personal recollections. In other respects 2001 had been a routine year:
England were beaten 4–1 by Australia and county cricket was a
fragmented blur of new sponsors: hardly anyone could keep track of
the Cheltenham and Gloucester Trophy, or the Norwich Union League.
"Cricket may not be living on borrowed time," wrote Wright. "Some
counties clearly are." English cricket was "a Victorian institution" that
had become "a confederacy of mediocrity". Of course, by now it was
evident that *Wisden* readers liked this sort of head-shaking – the
Almanack was their favourite grumpy old man. But ... oh dear.

In previous times the Queen's Golden Jubilee might have been seen
as a major cricketing event, but this year the talk was all of Saddam
Hussein, UN Resolutions and the Euro. When England lost four
wickets for two runs in Johannesburg it seemed in keeping with the
downbeat mood to produce a chart of "worst starts" – readers could
relive the day in 1888 when Australia were 7 for six, or the time India
slumped to 6 for five against England in 1952. There really wasn't an
awful lot to cheer about.

In this context it wasn't altogether surprising that Wright decided, once again, to step down as editor, even though Engel was still in Washington and not yet ready to return. His parting Notes suggested that the county structure be supplanted by a competition between city-based teams, a notion that had been drifting around the cricket zeitgeist for a few years, but which still felt radical. Perhaps the romance had gone out of his vision of the English game; certainly cricket had changed greatly since his previous tour of duty. But it put *Wisden* in a delicate position. Another temporary editor was needed. After considering several possibles they invited Tim de Lisle, who had moved on from modernising the magazine, to take the reins.* Although he knew that his tenure would be brief (he called himself the "most fleeting of editors") he did not consider that he was a safe pair of hands ("If anything I was an *unsafe* pair of hands") whose role was to keep the seat warm until Engel could return. Quite the contrary: his work on the magazine had given him a taste for wholesale redecoration, and he set about giving the Almanack rather more than mere continuity.

He drew inspiration from three unusual sources. First of all he was mindful of the motto Max Hastings had deployed to embolden him when he sought to refresh the much-loved but staid *Daily Telegraph*. Disregard all complaints about changes, he would say, until they number more than 300. There will always be some who oppose change, but they should not be allowed to prevent it. In any case, more often than not the most controversial alteration would end up being the new most-loved feature.

The second light bulb flashed when de Lisle attended a soirée at the Ashmolean in Oxford. The first thing visitors to the museum encountered was a large board – a guide to the interior. It struck him that *Wisden* lacked signposts of this sort – it was a huge and baffling maze. He resolved to create a pictorial map on the way in, and to add a crisp statement of *Wisden*'s values, like the legend on a welcome mat: "The book's watchwords are love of cricket, good writing, integrity,

---

* A one-time cricket correspondent of the *Independent on Sunday,* he was also notable, as his profile on Cricinfo put it, as being "the only rock critic to have edited *Wisden*".

independence and accuracy." It was a bold motto, the first time in 140 years that *Wisden* had ever attempted to summarise its philosophy, and it gave him quite a lot to live up to.

The third clue came from the Albert Hall. In order to create room for elaborate modern events such as the Cirque du Soleil and touring opera productions, they had chopped out a cavernous underground space, transforming the concert hall without appearing to change it. This is the future de Lisle saw for the Almanack. Three great institutions had taken the plunge; it was time to take a fourth over the same edge.

The first and most obvious change was his decision to put, for the first time ever, a photograph on the cover – an image of Michael Vaughan, the England captain. The well-loved Ravilious etching, showing two gents in top hats crouching in front of a hedge, became a smaller motif on the spine. Not surprisingly, there was plenty of muttering that this was "change for change's sake", even though – anticipating this – the company prepared traditional dust jackets for collectors who wanted to preserve the time-honoured appearance. And some saw it as an overdue reform. One critic claimed he had "dragged *Wisden* kicking and screaming into the 1920s".

Actually, it was part of *Wisden*'s heritage to exploit new photographic advances – the Cricketers of the Year had been launched on the back of just such an innovation in 1889. And the new look was more than faddish, because de Lisle also hoped that it would develop into a way of congratulating "the person to whom the year belonged". This was a pleasing notion; sometimes one man really did define a year – in 1927 it could have been Hobbs, in 1948 Compton or in 1982 Botham – but this never became a firm commitment. In 2004 two men players were depicted (Ricky Ponting and Steve Waugh) and the 2005 edition showed the entire England team in a celebratory huddle.

Inside, the changes were equally obvious. There was a wider range of typography and a collection of symbols – Keys! Arrows! – to direct readers into distant corridors of the book. All that was missing was a bright pointer saying "You Are Here!" There were several new items, too. World View began with an introductory comment on each international team, Arrivals and Departures said hello and goodbye to cricketers as they came and went, and there was a section on coaches. The Schools report was given an overhaul, with a consolidated list of the best averages across the national board, a Book of the Year was selected for the first time, and the story of *Wisden*'s acquisition of Cricinfo told in full. De Lisle, who had been editing Wisden.com and appreciated the significance of the online market, had first-hand knowledge of the deal.

By *Wisden*'s standards these were major changes, and some of the editorial team (now including a future editor, Lawrence Booth) feared de Lisle had bitten off more than they could easily chew. After Christopher Lane was forced to delay publication by a month, a new problem arose: the revised deadline now made summary scores of the 2003 World Cup a possibility.* It was a reminder that producing *Wisden* was like putting up a tent in a gale; unfasten one corner, and the other side starts flapping too. And it put pressure on the dedicated team at the Colchester typesetters – Mike Smith, who keyed in the mountains of copy, and Peter Bather, the unflappable master of quality control (who first worked on *Wisden* in 1976). At the eleventh hour, Hugh Chevallier and Smith put in a 24-hour shift to get the 2003 edition to the printers on time, or thereabouts. The Laws fell out through sheer lack of room. "It's amazing there weren't more mistakes," said Chevallier afterwards. "It's always a *bit* mad, but that was hair-raising."

Wisden sometimes seems permanent, but it is always a work-in-progress. And it is not just that one must change in order to progress. In *Wisden*'s case it is more subtle; as de Lisle said, paraphrasing Lampedusa's maxim in *The Leopard*: "You can't stay the same *unless* you change." But it turned out that the 2003 *Wisden* was striking not because of these editorial tweaks – many disappeared on Matthew Engel's return the following year – but thanks to the story it had to tell. De Lisle's reflexes as a journalist responded to the fact that cricket had speeded up. Steve Waugh's Australians had been setting new standards for the rate at which they attacked the bowling, and England were forming similar plans. For years cricket had been played "at a leisurely

---

* It also allowed, indeed obliged, the Notes to dwell on the protest staged at the World Cup by Zimbabwe's captain, Andy Flower, and fast bowler, Henry Olonga. Both wore black armbands to show their unhappiness with Robert Mugabe's government. It was, wrote de Lisle, a "shining moment" in cricket history. "Two strips of black tape breathed life back into the game's battered spirit."

pace ... the standard tempo was sedate". Now, partly because of the acceleration in one-day cricket, but also thanks to a larger quickening of the zeitgeist, "the name of the game is speed".

De Lisle was more correct than he knew. In England, a few weeks after his new-look *Wisden* appeared, the first Twenty20 Cup was in the offing, while in India Virender Sehwag was starting to think that four an over looked tepid, and soon businessmen were drawing up plans to carve Indian cricket into city-based "franchises". When it came to speed, de Lisle had seen only the first outriders of a racy new world.

With typical generosity, John Woodcock wrote to congratulate him. "It makes my own efforts in the 1980s look very puny," he said. Later he expanded on this: "These days it's become so much more than just a reference book – it's a major book of prose. I certainly couldn't be editor now. When I look at what today's editors do ... In my day it was pretty clear what you had, a few articles, Five Cricketers of the Year, how to save a few pages maybe. I was brought up with a *Wisden* of continuity and I do find myself looking for things that aren't there. But it's a major undertaking now ..."

This was true. The comment section at the front of Woodcock's first volume in 1981 ran to 51 pages. Forty years later it had more than doubled, and the editorship of *Wisden* could no longer be treated as a diverting part-time position on the side.

By the time Engel returned to *Wisden* it wasn't just the Almanack that felt new. In normal circumstances it might have seemed, after Washington, like a going-back, a retirement to familiar pastures. But the entire publishing landscape looked different. "The internet had changed everything," he said. "Everyone was writing and filing by email except hard-line Luddites. And the whole concept of a reference book was being rethought. It was an entirely new challenge. First time around, my task had been to modernise the book. Now it was to adapt to a whole new way of doing things."

Wisden too was breathing different air. It was now part of a group that owned not only the world's leading sports website (Cricinfo), but also the only significant magazine on the market: in 2003, again bankrolled by Getty, it had bought out its lone competitor, Ben Brocklehurst's *The*

Cricketer, and folded the two publications together. "In the last decade the circulation of both magazines had almost halved," said Christopher Lane. "Merging them was the only thing that made sense." After a long, fraught innings since the first pamphlet was published in 1864, John Wisden & Co was now a multimedia business.

"The more I thought about it," wrote Engel in the 2004 Preface, "the more I came to feel that this [the digital world] was not a threat but an opportunity: the chance to be more creative." Far from settling himself back into a comfortable and familiar chair, he set about the book with renewed zeal.

The first and most telling of his changes (leaving aside de Lisle's typographical and design additions, which he largely abandoned) was to break open the calendar in which *Wisden* operated. Until now it told the story from the end of one English season to the end of the next – September to September. But the rush of international cricket played in the winter months meant that *Wisden*, published in the spring, was starting to look slow on its feet. Engel decided to heave the Almanack into a new schedule based on the calendar year. It meant tighter deadlines, and also forced the 2004 edition to be a "15-month book", which led to a lot of late nights in the office ("Matthew never takes the easy option," shrugged Lane) and which made it another bumper issue.

Engel decided to extend the Cricketer of the Year concept as well, naming the Leading Cricketer in the World – an award for the world's outstanding player in the previous 12 months. Unlike the Five Cricketers, this *could* be won more than once. National pride didn't come into it: the first winner was Ricky Ponting, the second Shane Warne. In 2007 Engel went further, recruiting some dinner companions in Adelaide and backdating the accolade to 1900. It turned out that, in their view, Bradman would have been the Leading Cricketer ten times, Sobers eight, and the other three *Wisden* Cricketers of the Century (Hobbs, Richards and Warne) three apiece.

Engel had not left his waggish streak on the Potomac. He raised an eyebrow at the popstar timbre of modern cricket fashion ("I am reliably informed that Copson and Pope did not wear Alice bands when they bowled Derbyshire to the Championship in 1936"). And he was delighted to announce, in 2004, that a Sri Lankan bowler called A. R. R. A. P. W. R. R. K. B. Amunugama had "established a commanding lead" over his compatriot, A. K. T. D. G. L. A. S. de Silva, in the important arena of initials – "an area where England used to imagine it could hold its own with any other cricketing country".

As it happened, he had found a new hobby horse: the purchase in 2004 of television rights to home Test matches by the satellite broadcaster, Sky. It wasn't, he told an interviewer from Cricinfo early in 2005, that he thought they would do a bad job; it was simply that removing the game from terrestrial television would pin it into a niche: "The game will cease to reach out to those who do not already follow it."

He was content, however, in his 2004 Notes merely to smile at the latest innovation in English cricket, the Twenty20 Cup. Naturally he saw it as a travesty of the real thing – "an entertainment based on cricket" – but he declined to sound off, greeting it with an indifferent shrug: "Actually, Twenty20 went on a bit too long for my tastes. I shall try to hang on for Ten10 or maybe Five5." Hugh Chevallier, in his report on the inaugural county finals day, which packed in two semi-finals and a final (almost 11 hours in all), enjoyed the pleasing irony that this new whizz-bang form of the game had, it turned out, provided "the longest day of cricket anyone could remember".

But a genuinely sad duty fell to Engel, in 2004, when he had to report the death of *Wisden*'s owner, Sir Paul Getty. He had died in April 2003 – just weeks after Wisden had completed the purchase of Cricinfo and *The Cricketer*. The obituary treated him not as a billionaire proprietor but as a friend. "He sprinkled cricket with some of the stardust that his wealth made possible ... Those who knew him valued him as a generous spirit, a quality that has nothing to do with money. And cricket repaid him a little by giving him a sense of his own self-worth as a man, not just as a benefactor."

Engel had never shied away from the personal touch; each year he thanked his family for their indulgence towards *Wisden*'s overburdened and obsessive editor. In 1993 he shared with readers the pleasant news that his son Laurie had been obliged to share his first year with *Wisden*'s 130th, and took advantage of the coincidence to remind readers that the "the most important task for everyone involved in cricket is to ensure that Laurie's generation will in time get the same pleasure out of the game that we do." A few years later he admitted that Laurie had already, at the age of just six, "discovered, like many before him, that his dad's bowling was very hittable".

In this he was living out the ancient *Wisden* vision of cricket as a family matter, for the most part a forum for fathers and sons, but now, in the 21st century, for mothers and daughters too. But in 2005 he had awful news to deliver. On the very day he had been supposed to try out for an under-12 team Laurie was diagnosed as "seriously ill", and Engel's own year was then "dominated by this crisis". His firm expressions of thanks for the friendly support of his colleagues were even more heartfelt than usual.

The fact that large swathes of Asian coastline, including some of cricket-loving Sri Lanka's, had been swamped by a deadly tsunami gave another apocalyptic shudder to the 2005 volume. Engel's Notes began by apologising for the fact that England's run of recent success (they won 11 out of 13 Tests in 2004) could not inspire the carefree euphoria it deserved.* But it was hard for Engel to join in the fun. "Our game is so time-consuming that those involved in it often forget there is a world outside," he wrote. Outside events showed "how unimportant cricket was – and how important".

He went on to decry "the worst administrators in the world" who had sold cricket to satellite television. And in so doing he delivered one of the most pained *cris de coeurs* in *Wisden*'s life: "The overwhelming majority of the British population will never come across a game of cricket in their daily lives," he wrote. "Never, never, never, never … I think we're looking at a potential catastrophe." It was an aching allusion to the death of Cordelia in *King Lear* ("She'll come no more / Never, never, never, never, never …") and it was hard not to see it as inspired by the horrendous cloud hanging over his own son. It was, and still is, a heart-rending lament for a game, a tradition and a way of life that seemed to him to be slipping away for good.

---

* The 2005 edition paid due honour to the feat: the cover photograph showed a happy team, and, for the first time in 45 years, the Cricketers of the Year were all English: Ashley Giles, Steve Harmison, Robert Key, Andrew Strauss and Marcus Trescothick.

Then what happened? That summer, for unfathomable reasons of its own, cricket did not just rise from the ashes, it burst into flames. In front of cricket's last live TV terrestrial audience, Flintoff came charging in at one end, Giles wheedled and needled from the other, Harmison, Hoggard and Jones threw themselves into their straps like shire ponies, Pietersen marched out like a cartoon wrecking-ball, and Michael Vaughan's England beat Ricky Ponting's Australians to win the Ashes in one of the most dramatic and memorable Test series anyone could remember.

Wisden's editor saw it through red, distant eyes. He spent most of that epic summer in a children's hospital in Birmingham, willing his son to pull through. It wasn't to be. Just ten days after The Oval triumph proved that England was still a country where cricket could stop the traffic and dominate the horizon, Laurie Engel died.

His father's extraordinary response was to put together one of the best – and one of the bestselling – editions of the Almanack in history. Somehow, in that coldest of winters, he wrote hymns to a gilded summer. In the Preface he apologised if he sounded "muted" and explained the reason why: his son had been taken by cancer, leaving his stunned family to "miss him every minute". But no one could have guessed, from the tone elsewhere in his Preface, that he had suffered such a blow, because he didn't just put a brave face on it – he painted a happy one. Thanks to "the wondrous Ashes", he said, the book was rather "more celebratory" than usual. In stating that it was now available in four formats – hardback, softback, large and leatherbound – he joked that "our scientists are working on a salsa and mesquite flavour" version too.* He was adamant that the series had been not "probably" or "one of" the best: it was "the Greatest" – and not only

---

* In his 2006 Preface Engel also welcomed Steven Lynch to the Almanack, after 20 years of working for the company in other capacities. He had been deputy editor of *Wisden Cricket Monthly* under David Frith and Tim de Lisle, and then editor of Cricinfo. Engel added: "I am not sure how the book came out on 142 previous occasions without his zest and knowledge." The knowledge of the whole editorial team was publicly tested in 2005 when Engel, Lynch, Monkhouse and Chevallier formed a *Wisden* team which took on the Romantic Novelists' Association in a televised episode of *University Challenge: The Professionals*. The novelists won.

from the cricket point of view. In a sad reference to the task he had set *Wisden* (and himself) at Laurie's birth, he relished the fact that the national game had been re-awakened: "Around the country, kids who had never picked up cricket bats were suddenly pretending to be Freddie or Vaughany or Harmy or KP."

This was demonstrably true. The last days at Old Trafford and The Oval were packed to the rafters. More to the point, millions of part-time cricket-watchers gathered around television screens to see Kevin Pietersen clatter England to – of all things – an exhilarating draw. It was a ripe eruption of cricket enthusiasm. A generation of eager boys skipped into their local clubs and, according to some excitable reports, advance bookings for the following Ashes tour of Australia, which normally amounted to around 500, were reported to have hit 1,200 even before the schedule was announced.

Maybe Engel was fortunate, despite his own aching heart, to have such a tale to tell. "Could stuffy old cricket really have caused all this?" wrote Chevallier, marvelling at the size of the crowd that filled London to watch the victory parade. "The answer was yes." But *Wisden* was also lucky to have an editor so conscious of the greater scheme of things. "The main purpose of *Wisden* 2006," he wrote, "is to savour what happened in the summer of 2005 and try to pickle its essence, because one day we will be hungry for it again." The best thing about it, he felt, was that it had been "a triumph for the real thing" – this was old-fashioned cricket "routing its enemies", among which he counted all the wicked trappings of the bastardised "modern game". There was, he announced, "no artificial flavouring, no added sugar". It was simply an expression of the drama that cricket could still provide if left to itself and played with intensity by two good teams. As always he couched it in laconic terms. For 22 days "one hardly dared fetch a beer, have a beer, or sometimes even think".

Given what he himself suffered that summer, these count among the most stirring set of Notes ever written, and he gave them colourful backing by hanging newspaper quotations alongside the stirring events like bunting. "There is a palpable sense of England as a country alive again … a summer odyssey that has brought fathers and sons closer together … epic grandeur … it has been like seeing the barbaric hordes repelled by the forces of decency and civilisation." This was a good old broadsheet ruse. Engel, who in 1996 published a history of tabloids called *Tickle the Public*, knew how to sneak in such sentiments without quite stooping to them himself. In the same vein he placed boxes of suggestive facts next to the match reports: tickets for The Oval had been sold on eBay for £1,115 the pair; news of England's win was announced to 6,000 applauding spectators at the Albert Hall for Verdi's *Requiem*; and when fans at Edgbaston threw an inflatable shark at John Major, he threw it right back. Against this giddy background the actual summaries could be as calm as ever ("Giles consolidated his reputation for reliability with 59, his highest Test score ...").

Engel rarely needed emboldening, but the upbeat atmosphere gave him licence to be more scornful than ever of cricket's money-minded administrators as they moved from Lord's to what he called their "Dubaivory tower". "Year after year," he wrote, "the wonderful folks at the ICC assemble the world's best players and get them to play bad cricket." Other boards had so muddied their domestic arrangements that even loyal fans no longer knew what was going on, when, or why they should care either way. "A complex game needs simple structures," he wrote, repeating what was by now a semi-mantra, and adding that "the attendance for one Sri Lanka provincial match in early 2005 was reported as zero; I'm surprised they got that many".

It was as well that the Almanack, like a refurbished art gallery, had walls that were stripped and ready. The Cricketers of the Year were all Ashes heroes (three from England, two from Australia); there was a cheery article on the merits of the post-match drink; and three colourful descriptions of a typical Twenty20 day out. One of these was by the ex-MP and radio comedian Clement Freud, who, bemused by the "marauding gangs of teenage girls", settled down to enjoy a game without repetition, deviation or hesitation. He thought of stopping by the burger stand to ask for "a lobster cocktail, easy on the Tabasco", but thought better of it. There were signs too that the strands in the new *Wisden* "empire" were beginning to link arms. The book included three pieces by Cricinfo writers – on the toss, Pakistan, and India's Ranji Trophy – that gave a new dimension (and hoped to lure new readers) to the Almanack.

The 2006 *Wisden* was, thanks to all these factors, one of the biggest selling editions of all time, rivalling the peak figure reported in the mid-1970s: it sold over 50,000 copies, making it, since the cover price was now £38, a very respectable profit centre.* But just as it is in the nature of fireworks to fall to earth after they have flared, so too the energy behind *Wisden* was stuttering. The death of Sir Paul Getty did not leave *Wisden* in limbo – his cricket possessions passed to his son Mark, who had been a director since 1993 – but there was inevitably a shift of tone. John Betjeman once said that the things we take for granted are the things we miss the most, and when Paul Getty died something went with him. He had never been a hard-driving or even an attentive managerial force, but he had given the Almanack the kind of benign and devoted leadership that could not easily be replaced.

In his absence the board became much more commercially focused. Mark Getty, more businesslike and less keen on the concept of a Victorian-age Almanack, formed his cricket properties into the "Wisden Group", and added to it *The Oldie* magazine (which his father had also bought). In 2006, the Group acquired the ball-tracking system Hawk-Eye, which was expanding very effectively out of cricket and into tennis. The board at this time was strikingly high-profile for such a small concern: Mark Getty, his business partner Patrick Maxwell, Tom Gleeson (Group chief executive), Richard Charkin, John Brown, Christopher Lane and Matthew Fleming (of the banking family, and an ex-captain of Kent). And it was quick to see that while the marriage between *Wisden* and Cricinfo was in theory made in heaven, in practice the two businesses had all too little in common. The book was unhurried and reflective, the website fast and gossipy. While the Almanack wrung its hands over Hansie Cronje, Cricinfo was a portal for online betting. *Wisden* made a fetish of accuracy; Cricinfo did not. They were, as they say in the corporate jungle, different beasts.

In February 2005 the board met at Wormsley to discuss strategy for the future. It did so in terms that hardly anyone in *Wisden*'s past would

---

* According to Grays, the owner, when *Wisden* was bought by McCorquodale in 1985, the *Financial Times* reported that the annual sale was 55–60,000. This may be an exaggeration. In *Wisden* 2007 Matthew Engel wrote that the figure was not known, but that the 2006 sale might have been the best ever. Perhaps he was right. Whether the other figure had first-class status was a question even *Wisden* could not answer.

have recognised, but according to Lane "it was one of the most important meetings in the company's history". There was a fork in the road ahead; the decisions taken on this day would determine which path the Almanack followed. The subject under discussion was how "to own and develop market-leading multi-platform brands in sport and other content/data-driven commercial niches". There were charts showing cricket in an umbrella formation along with various other sports, all looking to find new audiences through television, print media and digital "delivery". The idea was to grow "enterprise value" across a range of cricket-related information products. This was not language likely to quicken the heart of a Pardon or an Engel – it was more likely to induce an ulcer.

Translated into English, it meant that the board had a sharp choice: should the Wisden group of businesses continue to amalgamate, looking to lean on each other and become one significant sports-information supplier, or should they splinter into their component parts? "We considered rebranding Cricinfo as Wisden," said Lane, "and if we had done so, the future would probably have followed a different course. In the end we decided to retain individual brands for the website and the magazine, which ultimately made them easier to sell." Richard Charkin, by now chief executive at Macmillan, actually wrote a memo the next day, suggesting to his co-directors that the website would most likely soon find itself in competition with the game's television broadcasters, and that it would never be able to compete with them. Live coverage of cricket was set to be the key ingredient, and broadcasters could acquire the necessary rights more easily than Cricinfo. His recommendation was to sell Cricinfo.

Engel, for one, was nervous, and feared that the changes inside *Wisden* would echo the shifts he saw in the cricket world itself. Up to the 1990s, when the headquarters of the ICC was at Lord's, the world game was run in effect by the MCC secretary "on the odd afternoon where there wasn't anything else to do". That was no longer true. The move to Dubai, and the emergence of India as *the* cricket power, had brought an abrasive new edge to the game. "Cricket now had what football had," he wrote, in an echo of what Graeme Wright hinted at in his 1998 comment on Faisalabad. "Politicians, often with no stature in the game, but with strong commercial motives, political skill and ambition. Too late, we began to see the advantages of the old MCC blazers, the stuffed shirts. For all their manifold faults, they cared deeply about the game."

Closer to home, Engel also found himself missing Getty *père* sooner than he thought. "Paul had bought *Wisden* to protect it – self-evidently," he said. "But Mark wasn't so interested in the book. He was more interested in Cricinfo and those possibilities. The Almanack just wasn't his thing. And for my part, I began to be seen as an old fuddy-duddy. In the space of a decade I'd gone from rampaging bullock to dinosaur."

Mark Getty himself spoke glowingly of Engel ("just fantastic"), but conceded that cricket did not enjoy the favoured place in his own life that it occupied in his father's. "I like it – but I like other sports too." He was guided by business logic, not whims.

It was enough to make Engel feel that another break was in order. After his son's death he had launched a charitable fund in his name – the Laurie Engel Fund – to build a new teenage ward at Birmingham Children's Hospital, where Laurie had been treated. It was a notable success (it aimed to raise £100,000, and in time raised over a million), but a draining one. His deputy editor, Hugh Chevallier, and Paul Coupar, the Almanack's former assistant editor, led a 150-mile sponsored walk from the *Wisden* office in Hampshire to Engel's home near Hereford. The Ashes-winning team of 2005 signed a bat for the cause. And Engel produced an anthology of his favourite quotes – *Extracts from the Red Notebooks* – for the project. Then, on completion of the 2007 Almanack, he stepped down once more. His place was taken by the *Sunday Telegraph*'s Scyld Berry. The fact that Engel intended to return one day meant it could not yet be seen as the start of a new era, but in concert with the other shifts in the wind it did feel like the end of the old one.

─────

It was ironic that what Paul Getty loved most about *Wisden* – its direct line of descent from the antique motherland of Englishness – struck many others as a cause for complaint. It was all too easy, for instance, to see its steady coverage of public-school cricket as an elitist reflex belonging to a bygone time. In July 2005 the Labour MP for Worcester, Mike Foster, joined the chorus of those who urged that *Wisden* extend its coverage of schools cricket to embrace the state sector, on the reasonable-sounding grounds that it was out of date to concentrate only on private institutions.

Wisden, though it had a long affinity with these schools, no longer wished to be their official cheerleader (in Woodcock's time the name changed from Public Schools to Schools, and the 2005 Almanack stressed that "state schools and girls' schools" were "especially welcome"). And no one could have seen Engel, a lifetime *Guardian* man, as a poster-boy for the old school tie. But with his *Wisden* hat on he responded to Mike Foster's charge by insisting that the Almanack was open to anyone playing "an acceptable level" of cricket. What constituted an "acceptable level" was a moot point, but it was true that in continuing to give public schools generous space, *Wisden* was not so much bowing to tradition as highlighting a contemporary fact.

It was a paradoxical one. When John Wisden launched his first Almanack he had in mind, as we have seen, a journal of professional, artisan cricket; but it swiftly became clear that the market for such a book was in upper-class England, in the well-heeled world of amateur cricket at the schools and universities. Plenty had changed since then, but the resilience of the Schools section in modern times showed that the old quandary remained: cricket was not, and never had been, a mass-market pursuit. And if it turned away from the elite it risked losing its paying customers. The Schools section was still important not because it represented some old-fogey pang for the world of privilege, but for sound commercial reasons. The boys in its lists (150 runs or 10 wickets earn a mention) were both a market (proud relatives bought copies as souvenirs) and a new audience. Even in the early years of the 21st century *Wisden* had to respect not just its past but also its present constituency.

Still, there was no denying that the state of public-school cricket had been a fetish in *Wisden*'s past. "Eton were a side whose capabilities as a combination it is not easy to gauge," ran the end-of-season report in 1911. "Can it be that that insidious game golf is playing havoc with the Wykehamist style of batting?" At other times *Wisden* sounded very like a schoolmaster itself: "I should judge," it wrote, "that a certain *vis consilii expers* [force without wisdom] was rather too frequent among the Bradfield players." There was no need to translate the Latin. Its readers, having been to the establishments in question, would know their way round a well-known proverb.

By 1992, things had changed, and Graeme Wright was lamenting the fact that 78% of the schools submitting results to *Wisden* seemed to be "unable to fill in the form correctly". It was hard to say which he found more distressing – the spelling or the arithmetic – and he concluded: "I am less concerned with the state of cricket in schools than I am about the state of education."* This was entertaining, but skirted around what was rapidly becoming a major national talking point: what *was* happening to cricket outside these historic if illiterate cradles, in the public sector?

In 1994 Engel wrote of "the disaster that has overtaken sport in our state schools", adding that it had "long been recognised, but rarely addressed". In 2002, when Ian Botham railed against the trend, the England and Wales Cricket Board replied testily that 85% of state schools did "provide" cricket in some shape or form, and it was true that there were some well-intentioned initiatives to boost the game in the inner-city areas. More such moves were on the way, such as the Wisden City Cup, a lively Twenty20 competition founded in 2009 by Scyld Berry. But not everyone believed that sending a pack of cricket "resources" to a school was the same as actually forming a team, learning the game and playing grown-up matches. Tim de Lisle's 2003 *Wisden* pointed out that even in its traditional heartlands the game was panting for oxygen. The modern exam culture (earlier, more frequent and more important) meant that even the famous public schools, with their enviable pitches and professional coaches, were playing fewer games. In 1983, *Wisden* noted, a quarter of schools played 20 matches; in 2003 only 7% did so. It was becoming rare for modern schoolboys to amass the run-totals of the past: the season wasn't long enough.

---

* This was not a recent phenomenon. The public schools had long been less grateful than they might have been. One *Wisden* contributor, Terry Cooper, recalled that in the 1970s and 1980s, when schools were asked to submit end-of-year figures, the results were variable: "On the whole, the smarter the school, the worse they were at working out their averages. I remember that clearly – I had to go out and buy a calculator."

Wisden could hardly be ashamed of its long support for these schools. Over the years they had produced a dazzling list of famous names. To flick through old editions was to trip over Jardine, Duleepsinhji, May, Dexter and a thousand others who made their mark as schoolboys. Here was Tom Graveney with an unlikely 26 wickets for Bristol Grammar in 1943, there was Trevor Bailey scoring 851 runs for Dulwich in 1941. Even if one disliked this connection between cricket and privilege (and many did), it was, however inconvenient, a fact. And *Wisden* always reported facts.

On the surface it was reasonable to think that in the new millennium the influence of the traditional breeding grounds might be diminishing. As the 2012 *Wisden* explained, however, private-school cricket was getting more influential, not less. An ECB report revealed that the ratio of first-class players from such schools had risen from 25% to 36% in two decades. And when Surrey beat Somerset in the Clydesdale 40 final at Lord's in 2011, five of the players on the pitch had been to just one school: Millfield. The team striving to be number one in the world (England) was drinking from a small well. It may have been untrue that the Battle of Waterloo was won on the playing fields of Eton, but English cricket was becoming more, not less, dependent on such places.

It all meant that one of the oldest conversations in the Almanack, regarding the class nuances embedded in cricket, still had life in it. Schools cricket provided an enduring stage on which such tensions could be displayed. So while a bit of angry banter between two county sides was no longer worth mentioning – it was too common – as late as 1998 *Wisden* was featuring an entire article (by Andrew Longmore) about a spat between two public schools, Marlborough and Radley: the game was "marred" by "verbal abuse of the batsmen", while on the boundary "tempers flared". It was as if a hundred years had never passed – close your eyes and you might have slipped a cog in time. Did it really matter, in this day and age, that two sets of bad-mannered and possibly spoiled children had been horrid to each other on a cricket pitch?

Put like that, it didn't. But the piece ("The End of Chivalry") used it to address one of the Almanack's oldest causes: sportsmanlike behaviour. Woodcock had said much the same thing in 1984 when he ticked off the old boys of Malvern and Repton for the "lamentable" behaviour that marred their match. In seeing the latest outbreak as seeping from the first-class game, it was echoing all those *Wisden* writers who saw "professionalism" as the enemy of fair play. Nasser Hussain, no less, of Forest School, Durham University and England, was quoted as saying that we had to get "a bit of nastiness" into our game to compete with the rude rascals elsewhere.

Longmore shook his head. "England did not lose to Australia because they were too well-mannered," he wrote. "They lost because they were not good enough." But the truly remarkable thing was that, in 1997, a loutish incident in a public-school match could still inspire such scrutiny. The end of the amateur/professional divide back in 1963 had been supposed to usher in a new, less class-conscious cricket culture, but if anything the opposite had happened. For a while it seemed that a suburban culture might take over – in players like Gatting, Gooch, Emburey and Stewart. And there was a touch of the shires about England's 2005 Ashes winners, thanks to Trescothick, Flintoff, Harmison and Hoggard. There was a marked South African flavour, too. But there was no hiding the fact that English cricket was still, in the 21st century, a public-school game.

Wisden could only look on and sigh. The chief culprit, almost everyone agreed, was the fundraising policy, launched by Mrs Thatcher's government, of selling school playing fields. A Cabinet that might have been expected to favour *conserving* such things approved the disposal of some 10,000 pitches, a wanton sell-off of the family silver that continued under the New Labour governments that followed after 1997. This political pressure chimed with a quasi-egalitarian dislike of competitive sport in the schools themselves. The result was that a generation of children was allowed (indeed obliged) to grow up without any connection to the once-national game. Yet *Wisden* 2009 quoted the Department of Children, Schools and Families as stating that, with the Olympics coming to London in 2012, school facilities had "never been better protected". This was an unusual use of the word "better", to mean "worse".

The odd thing about unintended consequences is that they are sometimes easy to predict. It would take a lot of energetic "Chance to Shine" initiatives to repair such grave damage: state-sector cricket survived only in isolated outposts, thanks to the devoted efforts of committed enthusiasts. As a result, England still relied on privately educated players such as Strauss, Cook, Broad, Prior and Bell; and so too did the commentary box – Agnew, Atherton, Blofeld, Gower, Hussain, Nicholas and Martin-Jenkins. The schools, in turn, used scholarships to attract the best young players, and had seasoned pros like Martin Bicknell (Charterhouse), Nigel Briers (Marlborough), David Byas (Pocklington), Richard Ellison (Millfield) and Frank Hayes (Oakham) to coach them. In the half-century since the abolition of the amateur, with its tacit promise that cricket would in future reflect a wider social mix, the game was turning the clock back. *Wisden* had no option but to record what was happening.

No one could have been more perfectly bred for the *Wisden* chair than Scyld Berry (pronounced 'shild'). He owed his distinctive first name to his father, a professor of English Literature and a poet: it is the name of the first warrior mentioned in the Anglo-Saxon epic *Beowulf*. And he had been a cricket-mad *Wisden*-lover ever since, as a six-year-old growing up in Sheffield, he had scrawled "I LOVE YORKSHIRE" in red ink on the inside page of his first ever copy. He had written a cricket report for the *Observer* while still at Cambridge, and went on to enjoy a distinguished career as the cricket correspondent of first the *Observer* and then the *Sunday Telegraph*. By 2006 he had attained doyen status in the press box: he had written a number of books on the game, and was widely held to be the most perceptive reader of a match in progress anyone knew.

He was also, unusually for a *Wisden* editor, a keen club player himself, and it was this quality he resolved to bring to the fore when his chance came. If anything, he wanted to nudge the book away from its gentlemen's club roots and turn it into a more specialised work: almost an academic journal. "How many *Wisden* editors have been cricketers?" he asked. "Hardly any. It is very strange. I wanted to make the book do what it said on the tin, as it were – to be an almanack for and about cricketers, and indeed by them, with a greater emphasis on the actual playing of the game."

He was as good as his word: he commissioned essays on the neurological basis of batsmanship, the nervous tics that afflicted left-arm spinners, the impact of video referrals and many other technical matters. "I was trying to get it back to the playing of the game, not just the watching of it." He knew that cricket was a matter for judicious historical inquiry, and was proud to shepherd into print a long and original description of the first Indian tour of England in 1911. He knew too that *Wisden*'s own past was a subject in itself, and in 2008 rescued from oblivion the finest players who had never been Cricketers of the Year (in truth the Almanack had not missed all that many). But he also saw the game as a branch of science, a body of knowledge. "There is so much that is not known, that has not yet been discovered."

It was with this in mind that he named Virender Sehwag as his Leading Cricketer in the World for two years running in 2009 and 2010. Sehwag, he stated, had "broken cricket's sound barrier" by scoring his year's harvest of Test runs (in 2009) at an average of 70, which was very hot. At better than a run a ball (his strike rate was 109 runs per 100 balls) it was a pace that till now had been thought sizzling even for the one-day game. At a time when some pundits continued to see him as a limited-overs slogger on a hot streak, Berry saw that, like Sri Lanka's Jayasuriya or Australia's Gilchrist, Sehwag had spotted a bracing truth – adventurous play might not be riskier than obduracy, lofting the ball over the infield might be safer than prodding. Actually, this was antique wisdom: any Grace, Fry or Compton knew that attack was the best form of defence, that a batsman had to knock a bowler off his length and force the field back. But Sehwag was taking it to a terrific extreme.

Above all, Berry responded to the jitteriness of the modern game (and modern life) by publishing longer-than-usual essays on the grounds that *Wisden* was literature, not Twitterature. Instead of aligning himself with the hyperactive habits of the digital age, Berry inclined the opposite way, producing a scholarly compendium aimed at the game and its past. And while he did not set out to ruffle feathers, he did perform cosmetic surgery on the structure of the book, pushing the records to the back and bringing the obituaries forward. In 2008 he poured extra information into the list of Test cricketers and turned those pages sideways.

But Engel's shadow remained. Both Graeme Wright (in his second stint) and Tim de Lisle had felt conscious that they were keeping his seat warm, and so, in his first year, did Berry – Engel was in theory on sabbatical. Though his brief was to "keep changes to a minimum", it didn't stop him introducing, in 2008, the Schools Cricketer of the Year. The idea had been trialled in Wisden.com – in 2002 they awarded it to James Morrison, of Reed's in Surrey, who celebrated by becoming a professional golfer. Now, Berry's *Wisden* chose Jonathan Bairstow (son of the Yorkshire and England wicketkeeper David Bairstow) who in 2007 had scored 654 runs for St Peter's York, the school where Guy Fawkes had once learned to question royal authority.[*]

Berry was swiftly on to the front foot in his first set of Notes. "Twenty-over cricket in India is shifting the tectonic plates of the professional game as never before," he wrote. Like a dog let off the leash, he indicted the world's cricket administrators for failure to get a grip on the threat this represented. He pointed to the empty stands at the recent World Cup in the West Indies ("joyless and long-winded"), a bungled affair that alienated the local audience, and insisted, like his predecessors, that "cricketers in most countries do not have administrators they can respect and trust ... never yet have I seen one of them watching the game through binoculars". He listed the failings of the English set-up (was the 2005 Ashes victory only three summers ago?) and, like Engel, focused on the "patent economic absurdity" of a situation in which spectators were excluded from watching England by the sale of television rights to a satellite broadcaster and a rise in ticket prices to Covent Garden levels. "A family day out," he wrote, "is now for millionaires only" – and all so that county cricket could pass on pretty sums to overseas players performing in an unwatched domestic league. This did not endear him to county clubs (he even urged the ECB to keep cricket on terrestrial television by slashing the subsidy to counties), but it was rhetorically true to *Wisden*'s finest traditions as a Defender of the Faith: clear, frank and well-informed.

During his four-year editorship Berry was rarely hard up when it came to cricket stories. The rise of the Indian Premier League (IPL) continued to dominate the skyline – it was "the single biggest change ... since the invention of international or Test cricket". He deplored the

---

[*] *Wisden*'s judgement was rewarded when, in 2011, Bairstow made his England debut. His immediate successors as *Wisden* Schools Cricketer of the Year, James Taylor and Jos Buttler, also made their international debuts in the same year.

fact that "leading cricketers can now earn more by representing an Indian city" than in any other form of the game. The age of the IPL had arrived, and its implications were grave: it promised an "annulling" of the game's traditional habits; county cricket, in particular, might be "a relic". He did his duty by it, and found a way to present the IPL, in *Wisden*, through a compressed set of match summaries. But he could not hide his lack of enthusiasm. "Hector v Achilles could not have been a Homeric contest if limited to five minutes", he wrote. And he warned that soon "the cricketer of the future would be a mercenary, flying from one 20-over tournament to another without ever playing Test matches for his country".

One repercussion of all this was the embarrassing Allen Stanford affair, the lowlight of which was the tycoon's arriving at Lord's like a saviour, in a cash-laden helicopter; but this was balanced by the wonderful success of England's Test match cricket, first under Fletcher and Vaughan, then with Flower and Strauss. And in 2009 (11 years after *Wisden Australia* had taken this step) he had the pleasure of naming *Wisden*'s first ever woman Cricketer of the Year, Claire Taylor. "There is no element of political correctness or publicity seeking about this selection," he wrote in his Notes. She had earned her place by "batting England through to victory" in the Bowral Test, with 79 in the first innings and 64 not out in the final run chase. "In men's Ashes cricket," ran the profile that accompanied her selection, "only half a dozen England batsmen have dictated the course of a deciding Test with the same mental strength."

She was an amateur (she worked as a management consultant) and she graciously described her selection as "a huge honour". The BBC called it "momentous news", and the *Guardian* saw it as "a defining moment". The *Mirror* felt that *Wisden* had, at a stroke, "swept away 120 years of male exclusivity", while Taylor herself, in the *Telegraph*, permitted herself a broad smile: "W. G. Grace, Don Bradman, Shane Warne ... and now me! It shows how far the game has come." In the same paper, Berry suggested that her selection could be seen as a tribute to the work the ECB had been putting into women's cricket, but that it had not been complicated: "She is the best of her kind that there is."

In 2010 the mood changed: thanks to the fearful machine-gunning of Sri Lanka's cricket team in Pakistan, Berry had to write like a war correspondent, "hoping that a terrorist attack on a cricket team will never be attempted again, and fearing that it probably will". In keeping with the sober mood, he also commissioned an essay on cricket in the Second World War, which included an extract from Gubby Allen's diary on the fateful week in June 1940 when he took nine for 23 at Lord's, and saw *Gone with the Wind*, just as France was falling.

In 2011 Berry uniquely named only four Cricketers of the Year, claiming that one of his original five (widely assumed to be Mohammad Aamer, the brilliant young Pakistan fast bowler who had been banned for five years after bowling deliberate no-balls against England the previous summer) was now an "unsustainable" selection. The story was at that stage still *sub judice* ("never has *Wisden* been so constrained by legal dictates"), but Berry still managed to cover it in forensic detail. *Wisden* was not known for investigative journalism, but these were strange times.

Of course, there was plenty of business-as-usual to be done too. The leading cricketer of the year was Sachin Tendulkar (an Indian for the third year running). Berry introduced a Photograph of the Year award (in partnership with MCC); and he pressed an old panic button by highlighting a survey of London primary schools which found, when it asked children to rank sports in order of preference, that cricket came 21st. He also found space for the eulogy delivered by a former prime minister, John Major, at the memorial service for Alec Bedser. Berry still saw the game as "astonishing, unique" and had another cracking Ashes triumph to narrate, after the heady success of Andrew Strauss's team in Australia. But he also celebrated the role of the county reporter, the place of the tea interval and the umpire who headbutted a fielder (How's *that*?) – all part of the game's colourful tapestry.

The Almanack still needed constant attention. It was like mowing grass: shocking how much labour went into making it look smooth. And Berry didn't find any of it easy. "No cricketer has ever worked as hard at his game as the *Wisden* staff do to record it," he said. "In January and February you go to a place most people never go – it's a succession of 12-hour days, seven days a week. How they keep doing it no one will ever know. One can't praise the editorial team too highly."

Berry's 2011 editorial broke with tradition by applauding, rather than frowning at, the football-fan habits of England's Barmy Army, which had been in loud voice during the victorious winter in Australia. It was a tolerant departure from *Wisden*'s usual stance as the guardian of cricket manners, and though some readers felt that it was all very well for someone who didn't have to pay for a ticket or sit near the Barmy Army to think it harmless fun, others were relieved to see *Wisden* distancing itself from the stand-offish county members who refused to join in Mexican waves.

There were larger commotions closer to home. Since the decisive meeting of the board at Wormsley in 2005, Mark Getty had been brooding on the future of the properties he had gathered into the Wisden Group. In November 2006, at a board meeting in Bangalore (where Cricinfo now had its head office), things were looking good. The 2006 Almanack had been a commercial and editorial triumph; Cricinfo and Hawk-Eye were extremely profitable and had clear strategies for the future. Even the magazine, *The Wisden Cricketer*, was going in the right direction (circulation was rising). It was clear to everyone, though, that the magazine industry was in its twilight. When Mark Getty raised the possibility that it could be sold, there was barely a murmur of opposition. "Within half an hour it was agreed," recalled Christopher Lane. "It made sense, but it was very sudden."

It was like a first crack in a dam: that one decision triggered a larger disintegration. The *Wisden Cricketer* was sold to Sky, and before long the *Oldie*, Cricinfo and, in 2008, the Almanack itself had also been sold.* It was an abrupt flurry of changes that left some members of the *Wisden* team winded. The Almanack's new owner was Bloomsbury Publishing Plc. Though an upstart in publishing terms (founded in 1986) Bloomsbury was, thanks to the wizard earnings of Harry Potter, in acquisitive mood, and what could be more appropriate than an ancient book of spells? The papers were pleased. "Harry Potter and the Bible of Cricket" ran one headline. But the founder and Chief Executive of Bloomsbury, Nigel Newton, had to soothe the nerves of those who

---

* The Almanack and *The Wisden Cricketer* were sold for a combined total of almost £6 million. Cricinfo was sold to ESPN for £27 million, more than 10 times what it had cost four years earlier. This was by any standards a remarkable deal.

feared that *Wisden* might be turned into a rollicking children's adventure by declaring firmly that it was "an honour to be the new custodian". *

One of Bloomsbury's executive directors was an old friend of the Almanack: Richard Charkin. The thought of buying *Wisden* had actually crossed his mind as long ago as 1992, while he was working at Reed. But when he learned that Paul Getty was interested, his own aspiration faded – he knew he would not be able to compete. Since then he had been a board member for 15 years, so was well acquainted with both the strengths and the weaknesses of the enterprise ("I knew the warts"). He had left Macmillan to join Bloomsbury in 2007, and had not been there long when he was asked (in his capacity as a Wisden director) how best the disposal of *Wisden* might be approached – through a discreet private sale or via an active and visible public auction. Charkin recommended the latter, on the grounds that it would flush out the highest bidder and also create significant publicity for *Wisden*. He did point out that the highest bidder might not necessarily turn out to be the best curator of the heirloom that *Wisden* had become. But he was pleasantly surprised when, a few weeks later, he was invited to submit a bid on behalf of Bloomsbury, on the understanding that if terms could be reached then the rigmarole of a public auction could be avoided.

Bloomsbury, with no competitors, paid a price that Charkin described as "probably a little over the odds, but not by too much". And he was delighted to have obtained a 24-carat gem. "There are very few jewels in the publishing world," he said. "But *Wisden* is one of them. It has been there for 146 years. It's a glorious archive of cricket, of history, of derring-do and empire – there's so much there, and much of it is hidden. The thought of helping to make it more available in the future, both through the book and through other technologies – it was all very interesting."

---

* When Bloomsbury itself moved offices from Soho Square to Bedford Square, in 2011, it was a wheel turning full circle, since that same London square had been *Wisden*'s home for most of the years it was published by Sporting Handbooks and Whitaker's. It was, moreover, only a short walk from the original John Wisden & Co premises near Leicester Square. The more things change, the more they stay the same.

He had no patience with the idea that a fat volume of cricket details was in any way anachronistic. "I don't think you can ever say that quality is anachronistic. It fits in an umpire's pocket, just." He himself treasured the 1949 edition (the year of his birth) he had been given for his 60th birthday: "I can lose myself in its pages for hours."

Not everyone was excited by the break-up of the Wisden Group. Shorn of its sister businesses, the Almanack in particular felt vulnerable. And the first person to feel the cold wind of change was Scyld Berry. In October 2010 he visited the office of the new owner for what he thought was a routine meeting. He was on a one-year rolling contract and he had no inkling that, this year, it would not roll. He had done a splendid job, he learned, but a new editor had been sounded out, one perhaps more attuned to the digital age. Everyone was extremely grateful for all he had done.

"It was," he said, "a bit of a shock." No one suggested that he had done a bad job; it was just that *Wisden*, so long sheltered, had entered a world with sharper elbows than it was used to. "It was not an easy decision," said Charkin. "Scyld was very well respected. But we were looking at the long-term, and felt that it was right to get a new younger editor on board as soon as possible." With the 150th edition looming it was desirable for a new editor to have an ordinary year on which to cut his *Wisden* teeth.

It caused quite a flutter in the press box, of course. No one knew that *Wisden* editors could be fired – it felt a bit like sacking the Pope. And for Berry himself it had been more or less an ideal job. "I suppose I wanted to combine the cricket authority of Woodcock's *Wisden* with the readability that Matthew brought to it," he said. He was well on the way to doing that when he found himself stranded at the wrong end.

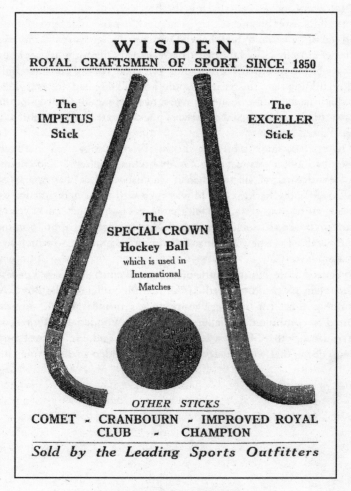

Advertisement from Wisden *1929*

Footprints

In 2007 Matthew Engel actually went to Getty and pleaded with him not to split up the entire business. With Cricinfo being sold, couldn't the Almanack at least keep the magazine as a partner?

Getty's mind was made up, however, and Engel was left feeling deflated. "I always saw it as my main job to ensure that *Wisden* was still around in fifty years' time," he said. "By the time I left I felt I might have failed." Graeme Wright echoed his words: "If I have a regret it's that I didn't do more to make sure it was set up as a trust. In my early years we used to talk about nothing but money, but under Paul Getty it became irrelevant, basically. It didn't become relevant again until after he died."

In fact, in the late 1990s, Christopher Lane made a concerted attempt to persuade Sir Paul Getty to endow Wisden as a trust, to safeguard its future as an independent voice, backed by the philanthropist's financial weight. His lawyers drew up the documentation and he did consider it. But in the end he decided that he would leave Wisden to his son. It is likely that he thought of it as a treasured gift – something mere money couldn't buy. But Mark Getty, for understandable reasons of his own, had decided that his life would not be run on such lines. He had the same traumatic family history behind him, and his response was not to take refuge in the glories of cricket but to become a full-time, hands-on businessman – in *Wisden*'s terms a professional, rather than a titled amateur. He had spent a decade turning Getty Images into a brilliant success as the leading online photographic agency in the world. He had plenty of his own fish to fry.

That didn't stop Engel criticising the deal. In December 2008 he wrote a waspish article for the *Financial Times* that left few words unminced. Mark Getty, he said, had "inherited his forefather's entrepreneurialism rather than his father's sentimentalism" – a way of saying that he had put commercial considerations above human ones.

Mark Getty was firm. "I took the decision deliberately," he said, "because it just seemed the right thing to do. The sale of the Almanack came later. *Wisden* was a great, predictable, reliable, collectable, manageable publishing enterprise ... but so small. To be honest it didn't truly warrant the board's time."

He knew that there was more to this than business logic, however. It was a bit like inheriting your father's classic car, but deciding instead to de-clutter the garage. "Would my father be happy that it was being sold?" he asked. "Perhaps not. But I hope he'd feel we took care to make sure it was in good hands – and we did."

Richard Charkin was as keen an admirer of the nostalgic aspects of *Wisden* as anyone. At the *Wisden* dinner he liked little better than to sit next to long-retired cricketers and have fun dredging up the names of Middlesex players from 40 years ago. But he wasn't about to put business considerations on the back burner either. Lawrence Booth had been involved with *Wisden* long enough to have impressed Christopher Lane ("It was clear several years ago that he had all the attributes") and it was to him that Bloomsbury turned.

Charkin was clear, in appointing Booth, about the overriding need to respect the footprints in which he now stood: "His main, his absolute number one priority is not to pollute the brand." But wanting *Wisden* to remain what it was did not mean that nothing could be touched: "The collectors are dying – at the rate of about a thousand a year. We have to try to replace them. And there are various other things we think we can do."

The first of these was an online magazine called *Wisden Extra*, the first issue of which appeared in July 2011.* "It may not seem so," wrote Lawrence Booth, echoing de Lisle, "but *Wisden* has always changed with the times." The idea was "not to replace the Almanack, but to complement it" by keeping its voice active the whole year round. There

---

* Another innovation in 2011 was to launch a new imprint, Wisden Sports Writing. The idea was to stretch *Wisden*'s reputation beyond cricket and into other sports.

were colourful Patrick Eagar photographs, and the leading article in the first issue was a history of England v India Tests by Suresh Menon, the Indian cricket columnist and biographer.

Menon would soon be involved in a more ambitious project, when he was asked to become editor of *Wisden India*. Publishers had been eyeing the vast, cricket-loving population of India for some time. It was what business-school types call a no-brainer – India was the game's powerhouse, and *Wisden* was its memory. There had to be some way to take advantage of the union. It wasn't an entirely new idea. In 1946 a *Wisden*-style almanack called *Indian Cricket* was published by Kasturi & Sons of Madras (owners of *The Hindu*). Produced by the official statistician of the Indian Board of Control, it was more or less an exact copy of *Wisden*, right down to its detailed coverage of university cricket ("The Bombay batsmen took a heavy toll of the Mysore attack"). Like *Wisden* itself it called for "brighter cricket" and named five players of the year.

When this frail paperback was first published, India was still the jewel in Britain's imperial crown, but by its fifth edition *Indian Cricket* was a decolonised voice. It retained friendly links with *Wisden*, however: Norman Preston and other Almanack regulars contributed articles, and by the 51st edition in 1997 its detailed run of reports and scores was occupying nearly a thousand pages.

Its closure in 2004 created a gap that *Wisden India* intended to fill. It was a nerve-racking adventure, not least because the previous attempt to license itself overseas, in Australia, ran for only eight editions before giving up the ghost in 2006. Some thought it followed the *Wisden* line too faithfully, failing to find a distinct Australian idiom. Others thought that as a brand-new publication it lacked collectors to keep it alive. The loss of the Ashes in the summer of 2005 might not have helped either.

Wisden India was planned on new and more audacious lines. Acting under licence from London, it would be part of a multi-media platform, a long way from *Wisden*'s own beginnings on a steam-age press in south-east London in 1864.* No one expected it to be easy – it was not

---

* While it took the original *Wisden* eight years to present its Cricketer of the Year accolade to W. G. Grace, *Wisden India* wasted no time in giving its maiden Outstanding Achievement award to Sachin Tendulkar, at a ceremony in Dubai.

obvious what would happen if India wanted to contradict England on some important point (such as the future of Test cricket), but Bloomsbury declined to lay down a strict chain of command. "They are not supposed to do things without our approval," said Charkin. "But although there was talk of a rulebook or some such, we decided that the things that come up are bound to be unpredictable. The important thing is to have a good team in India, which we have." Sourav Ganguly was appointed president of the *Wisden India* board, and the book would have a blue rather than a yellow cover, but in spirit it would be modelled on the original. "There is a certain inevitability to it," said Menon. "India is the centre of the cricketing world and *Wisden* is the 'bible of Cricket'. The two had to come together."

This was logical. But some voices in England saw India not only as an opportunity, but also as a threat. The 2011 *Wisden* dinner actually featured a prickly panel-debate on the sensitive question "Is the influence of India ruining cricket?" – an idea inspired by its fervent love affair with limited-over shootouts. The hectic growth of one-day cricket was supported by some statistics in *Wisden Extra*, which showed that by 1987 there had been over 1,000 Test matches, and only 500 one-day internationals, but that in 2010 the 3,000th one-day match took place, ahead of the 2,000th Test.

In the event the first edition of *Wisden India* was launched at the end of 2012, nearly 150 years after the Little Wonder himself, festooning his New Coventry Street store with bats and racquets, first inspected his own new book. The idea that there might one day be an Indian version would have seemed as remote as the faintest star.

———

In one sense the Indian incarnation of *Wisden* was a grand departure; in another it was nothing new. The Almanack had by then spent one and a half centuries in different pots, with new soils and a range of different watering systems – yet somehow it had managed to flower every year. One of the beauties of each edition is that it bears the footprints not just of the cricketers who stride in its pages, but also of editors who have fed, grafted, clipped, trained and otherwise tended the original plant. John Wisden himself dug the first spade into the soil, and the Pardons turned it into a vigorous perennial. Caine and Southerton maintained it,

Brookes reshaped it and Whitaker nursed it through a war. The Prestons guided it into a new world; Woodcock and Wright cleared away the weeds and enhanced the literary quality. Engel added panache, and Berry reminded it of its cricketing roots. By the 21st century it was more like a monument than a plant – a cairn, with each of them managing to create, by adding single stones, something richer than they could have managed alone. It was not yet clear what sort of rock Booth had in his hand, but he had a clear line of footsteps to guide him.

One thing was certain: he was taking over at an interesting time. Both the game itself and the media that surrounded it were vibrant with new ideas. Some would thrive; others would not. One of *Wisden*'s historic roles was to be a voice of calm authority, but this in itself was an unfashionable mode of address. Among the chief lessons of its long history, however, is that while the game it celebrates often seems to be heading for rack and ruin, it has always stopped short of getting there. The Almanack might have to bend with the wind, but it did not have to expire.

It was even possible that there might, in the hurly-burly helter-skelter of modern communications, be a refreshed role for an authoritative voice. The 1864 *Wisden* aimed to be the first place a cricket enthusiast might turn to for accurate information about the game he loved; 150 years later the goalposts, or the stumps, were no longer in the same place. In 2012, *Wisden*'s role was no longer to be the first port of call – the internet had colonised that role – but the last: the longstop, the final word. At a time when electronic media thrust fans ever more closely into the action, *Wisden* could make a virtue of detachment, of standing back.

———

Wisden has imposed itself on the cricket world in many forms – most obviously as the game's encyclopedia and oracle, but in other, more delicate ways as well. Naturally, as the primary source of factual information, it has been quoted from, and leaned on, in countless other books about the game – the words "according to *Wisden*" or "as *Wisden* put it" resonate through cricket's literature like a musical strain. We can also see reflections of the Almanack in the responses of the players it has honoured or chided. Peter May was "mildly surprised" as a young cricketer to read in *Wisden* that it was his "poor fielding" that cost him a place in the English Schools XI, while Fred Trueman was "very proud and grateful" to have been a Cricketer of the Year in 1953. "I hate the cold," wrote Denis Compton in retirement; "My refuge against the howling wind is to pull out an old *Wisden*, settle deep into my chair, and reflect ..."

This kind of thing has been a staple of cricketing autobiography ever since. Len Hutton said that being called "the best batsman" on the 1950–1 tour of Australia was "one of the compliments I treasure", and Michael Vaughan also referred to "the great compliment of becoming the first player ever to appear on the front cover". The umpire David Shepherd wrote that "on my long plane journeys around the world I am apt to thumb through my latest edition of *Wisden*", while John Arlott attributed his discovery of the "marriage" between books and cricket to the time he leafed through a "dog-eared, grimy, jettisoned 1922 edition of *Wisden*". Viv Richards and Shane Warne reacted warmly to being Cricketers of the Century (Hobbs, Bradman and Sobers were done with autobiography by then), and *Wisden* popped up in more out-of-the-way places as well. When a group of cricket writers needed a name for their golf group, they opened *Wisden* and settled on the first name they found: H. H. I. H. (Doc) Gibbons.*

It may be, however, that one of *Wisden*'s most profound legacies is that, by gathering the game's scores and crunching them, year after year, into averages and records, it has made it hard to "read" cricket in any other way. In part thanks to *Wisden*, the reverence for cricket averages seems an immutable fact of life. In truth, it is only one of several ways of enjoying cricket; it is the dominant one partly because it has been fiercely maintained for so many generations that it now seems natural. Yet averages are not quite natural; they are a nice numerical convention that has been buttressed by long time and use (and *Wisden*). The batting averages for the 1999 World Cup, for

---

* And when the architect John Pawson was invited to design a new cricket pavilion for St Edward's, Oxford in 2009, one of the key requirements, along with providing a good view of the game, was a prominent place for the school's complete set of *Wisden*.

instance, were headed by South Africa's Lance Klusener, with a commanding 140.5 runs per completed innings. He was a thrilling hitter, to be sure; but his *top score* in the tournament was only 52 – it was thanks to the convention surrounding "not outs" that his "average" was nearly triple his best effort. There is logic to this, but it is a rather specialised interpretation of the word "average".

Obviously we can't ascribe the respect for cricket averages to *Wisden* alone. They are an intrinsic part of the texture of the game. Every school and club, each village and county, every regiment and international "unit" – all measure themselves according to the same numerical reflex. But by tallying the scores for so many years, *Wisden* has helped shape the way the world thinks about and plays the game. It was not inevitable that cricket conceive of itself in this way – it could, in theory, have promoted a more carefree attitude to individual statistics, on the grounds, if nothing else, that the team came first. As it is, some might argue that cricket's regard for statistics has actually spoiled the game by turning batsmen into greedy hoarders, protecting their not outs and making their average their chief claim to fame. In this argument, the Almanack has somehow (not intentionally, of course) undermined the entire team concept by placing individual productivity on its highest pedestal.

Nothing can erase the magic of Don Bradman's final Test match average (99.94), evoking as it does the shocking drama of the day he failed to nudge it into three figures.[*] By the same token, few cricket figures are so ambiguous as the fact that Geoffrey Boycott (in 1971, his first season as captain of Yorkshire) scored a colossal 2,503 runs at the holy grail average of 100.12. We can relive the moment when this was achieved by consulting *Wisden*'s report on Yorkshire's final match, in which Boycott scored 124 not out to clinch three figures. But there is another important number in this story: 13. This was where Yorkshire

---

[*] In the Fifth Test of the 1948 Ashes series at The Oval, Bradman was bowled by England's Eric Hollies for nought, needing only four to retire with a Test average of 100. Hollies took 44 Test wickets for England, but this one has resonated more than the rest put together. With respect to Bradman's final average we might note that, if it weren't for the accepted convention by which not outs do not register as completed innings, it would have been "only" 87.45, and that fateful final innings would have been drained of its historic suspense.

finished in that year's County Championship – at that time the worst-ever position in their history. Little could better show the uneven connection between individual excellence and the team outcome. While Boycott was breaking records, his county went 17 matches without a win. Bad luck? Extraordinary coincidence? Either way, the numbers do, taken together, tell a story.

Wisden can take credit for many things, so it can endure the notion that it has also, for almost 150 years, upheld the value-system that produced this ironic contrast. It has often sounded trumpets on behalf of team spirit and fair play while simultaneously banging a statistical drum for self-promotion. In this, of course, it was only refracting the contradictory tension at the heart of the game itself, and passing it on to the greater multitude that either didn't play, or used to play and now just read about it.

Numbers aside, it remains the case that being "in" *Wisden* is a robust aspiration. And since not everyone is skilled enough to be included as a player, some enter the club by writing, coaching, scoring, tending grounds, umpiring, administering or through any other cricket-related pursuit. Sharp-eyed readers of the annual advert for Christopher Saunders's book dealership can just make out, at the foot of the page, a tiny name: Jules Akel. It identifies the designer of the artwork (who also happens to be the ticket draughtsman at Lord's). He put his name to this modest work purely so that he could say, truthfully, that he too was in *Wisden*, not quite alongside names like Grace, Hutton and Compton, but between the same covers, at least.

At the black-tie dinner to launch his first volume as editor Booth announced the 2012 Cricketers of the Year before handing over to the novelist Howard Jacobson, who spoke, on behalf of all authors, about the despair he felt when leafing through a book in which he himself was not included. He went on to insist that the dinner was a literary rather than a sporting occasion. *Wisden* was not cricket; it was what we had instead of cricket.

Booth's first Notes began by observing with studied irreverence that the year had begun with "grown men rushing around Sydney patting each other on the bottom" – a reference to the touchy-feely nature of the two Ashes teams. Noting that England's celebrations were short-lived (they were soon losing to Pakistan in Abu Dhabi), Booth nevertheless saluted an England unit that "knew its own mind inside out and probably had the pie-charts to prove it". As the number one ranked Test team in the world, England were carrying a torch for a form of the game – five-day cricket – that was, Booth feared, threatened by India's sweaty love affair with more melodramatic variants.

By standing up for cricket's traditions he was channelling *Wisden*'s ancestral voice, and the remainder of his debut Notes continued in the same vein, looking askance at the torrid antics of the IPL, groaning over the sluggishness of Test match breaks or the smoke-and-mirrors world of match-fixing and insisting on the enduring merit of the county game. A severe critic – a Pardon – might have wanted the Almanack to lay out some stirring picture of cricket's future, to mount some high-profile crusade or other. But if *Wisden* had learned anything in its sesquicentennial life it was that there is no need for hasty judgements. Thoughtfulness takes time.

His Notes were followed by 225 pages of serious cricket-writing all now placed before the averages or match reports. *Wisden* had come a long way since it opened with nothing more than a brief word to its subscribers.

As usual, the Cricketers of the Year were the first talking point. And while it has at times seemed a weakness that a player can be picked only once, on this occasion it threw up the kind of player the scheme was born to salute. Alan Richardson was no glamorous megastar, lauded by the leaping floodlit crowds of a Twenty20 gala. He was a none-too-gainly fast bowler who had, in the twilight of an unremarkable career, become the highest wicket-taker in the first division of the Championship. Of his timely move from Warwickshire (where he was the "tenth choice seamer") to Worcestershire, he said, showing himself to be quite the cricket moralist, that he had worked hard to make the move a success: "It's not a question of making the right decision; it's about making the decision right."

Moments of impish observation – England's well-built all-rounder Tim Bresnan was described as having "the air of a man with an emergency cheese sandwich in his back pocket" – were cemented in place by teasing historical studies. One (aptly enough, in the year London was hosting the Olympic Games) described the Olympic cricket final of 1900, when Great Britain beat France by 158 runs in Paris in the days when cricket was (like poetry) a gold-medal sport.

Another dwelt on the dissolution of the topic that had filled *Wisden*'s sails for most of its life, the amateur–professional divide.

In this context it was fitting that the 2012 edition should include a vision of the most shrouded figure in *Wisden*'s grand roll call, S. F. Barnes. The author, Peter Gibbs, had once escorted the ageing wizard to a Staffordshire match in Walsall in 1964 (when Barnes was 91), and now he brought to life a wintry figure demanding teaspoons, a fountain pen or a biscuit. Suddenly it was easy to imagine the austere, intimidating man of whom Archie MacLaren had once said, when told that his ship might sink, that "at least that bugger Barnes will go down with us". It was a useful reminder that the Almanack never forgets. Barnes's unorthodox career led him out of *Wisden*'s sight, but the book had been making up for it ever since. In 1968 John Arlott, in a book review, described him as a great man "about whom the general public has probably known less than about any other cricketer". The 1969 *Wisden* reported that Barnes's ashes (he died on Boxing Day 1967, aged 94) had been put in the pavilion at Edgbaston, home of the county in which he was born, but for whom he scarcely played. Even now, more than four decades after his death, *Wisden* was continuing to leave no stone unturned in its quixotic, impossible pursuit of completeness.

Countless such ghosts drifted from the records pages of the 149th *Wisden*. The great men were in their proper places, engraved in time-honoured records down which they were slowly sliding, as modern players (in bold print, to identify them as still active) clambered past them. But so were the not-so-great. The smallest amendments to the Laws were explained (though the Laws themselves were dropped) and the oddest lives commemorated. Through it all ran a thread of unusual events: the white tiger that stopped play in Hampshire (it turned out to be a stuffed toy); the four run-outs off three balls (the fourth was a wide) when Holland played Ireland; the cricket balls that pinged into the bin Laden compound in Pakistan; the marriage that took place in the Lord's pavilion, bang behind the bowler's arm.

Lawrence Booth was young, as *Wisden* editors go (35 – by chance the exact number of editions over which Sydney Pardon presided). In other respects he fitted the mould. He studied French and German at Cambridge before working on *Wisden*'s magazine and website. For three editions from 2003 he was a contributing editor to the Almanack itself, so was no stranger to its ways. And in recent years he had been a cricket writer for the *Guardian* and the *Daily Mail*. The invitation to take on the Almanack came "out of the blue – I wasn't expecting it at all". He would not be working alone: Hugh Chevallier was promoted to "co-editor". But he was excited by the prospect of giving shape to what he had long thought of as "the conscience of cricket". The topics he expected to keep him awake at night included the prime value of Test matches as the game's gold standard ("does cricket know what it is doing to itself?"), the growing evidence of gambling-inspired trickery in the sport ("can we believe in what we see on the field of play?") and the perception of cricket as elitist ("more so in England than anywhere else"). He accepted that certain sacred aspects of the *Wisden* formula – some records and the Laws – would have to migrate to the web, and believed that the Almanack's future would depend primarily on the quality of its writing. The comment section at the front would be a collection of high-class writing – "long-form journalism of a sort you won't find anywhere else".

Squeezing the records? Dropping the Laws? These were bravura moves, and it was possible to hear, in the polite remarks that greeted this first go, the sound of elderly teeth grating. But not many. When Tim de Lisle and Graeme Wright tried to save space by leaving out the Laws in *their* first editions, it was as if they had butchered mockingbirds. Fifteen years later the sighs were muted. Anyone could see that losing 50-odd pages in a 40,000 print run amounted to a cutback of two million printed pages, a clear business expense, not to mention a sizeable chunk of forest. Though they gave the book gravitas – Scyld Berry suggested that *Wisden* without the Laws was a bit like the Bible without the Ten Commandments – they varied little from year to year and were, so far as anyone could tell, only rarely consulted, not least because *Wisden* had become too huge to be easily portable. "When I started in the press box," said Booth, "you would see a dozen copies of *Wisden* lying about. Now you might only see two."

It was a similar story with the records. They had never been set in stone: in 1864 there were just three pages; in 1900 they occupied no more than 12, and were a very irregular sample. By 2011 they were stretched over 211 tightly packed pages (with their own six-page contents). But in truth even this was only what Engel had called a "skim". Cricket numerology was vast – a statistical wizard could cut it a thousand ways in search of a new facet. In the years to come, the Almanack would publish only a small selection of the game's magic numbers, and let computers massage the rest.

It all meant that, once again, *Wisden* had changed while somehow managing to look the same. "*Wisden* is like a tropical garden," Engel had said once. "Stuff just grows. It can only look beautiful with incessant pruning and chopping away." It has indeed been a long and winding route since those early editions, with their reports on the "doings" of the Elevens and the hunting-shooting-fishing dates. By the same token, we do not know which of the recent innovations will be permanent, which idea will be prophetic, which hero will go on to win renown – and which will wither and die. One of the most likeable qualities of the Almanack is that it matures over time, like a famous wine, gaining subtle new depths and flavours as the years pass.

As it reaches its 150th year *Wisden* continues to be new wine in an old bottle. In June 2012, when *Country Life* listed the qualities that marked a fellow out as a gentleman both a hundred years ago and today, *Wisden* appeared in each of the lists. Tobogganing in St Moritz, shooting at Elveden, Epsom salts, kedgeree … these all fell by the wayside. *Wisden Cricketers' Almanack* made the point that class really was permanent.*

---

* John Wisden has been memorialised in several unusual ways. He was the subject of an Alderney postage stamp in 1997; a Brighton double-decker bus was named after him; and in 2012 he was the subject of a commemorative panel in an underground tunnel at Leamington Spa railway station. There's immortality for you.

Epilogue:

150 Not Out

It is somewhat against my own interest to say so, but the true history of *Wisden* lies not in an account such as this but between the famous yellow covers of the Almanack itself. A mere summary, ignoring the tonnage of detail that makes *Wisden* what it is, fails to represent it. In the last year I have often been reminded of the short story by Jorge Luis Borges in which a perfectionist cartographer, hoping to create a definitive map of his empire, ends up making a map *exactly the same size* as the empire itself – all attempts to reduce it having come to seem a misrepresentation. I never did dream of producing a history as big as *Wisden* itself – it would have topped 130,000 pages, and few would have thanked me. But I was always aware of the weight of material I was passing over. In a most unusual way *Wisden* has, in telling the story of so many thousands of cricketers over so many summers and winters, written its own story too.

Today, a complete set may cost more than £100,000 (indeed the early volumes are now so hard to find that one way to acquire them is to buy a full run and sell off the overspill). It will also require many yards of shelf space and a spine-tingling insurance bill. Its sheer scale has earned it a place in the Barmy Army sledging manual, where Shane Warne can be deemed "thicker than a set of *Wisden*". But the result is worth more than the sum of its parts. *Wisden* is a unique encyclopedia that moves through time like a living organism, repeating itself at times (like all old people) but in a perpetual state of refreshment. "What more alive," as the poet Brian Jones wrote, "than shelves of tomb-like *Wisdens*?" The editors might not have thanked him for the sepulchral image, but they would have been pleased by his notion that an inert collection of dead facts can be quickened by a rare poetry all of its own.

The collection is Borgesian in another way: it is one of the labyrinthine libraries (full or forking paths, secret passages and cul-de-sacs) of which the Argentine fabulist was so fond. There is no fixed or recommended way to read it, but in the age of the search engine, which invites us to know in advance what we are looking for (the better to divide us into target markets), *Wisden* offers the pleasures of uncertain discovery; to rove among its pages is to ramble through a jumble store of treasures. In the *Barclays World of Cricket* (1986) one of the contributors, Bob Arrowsmith, wrote: "It is a bad book to turn to in a hurry, not because it is hard to find what one wants, but because in looking for that one's eye is sure to fall on something which suggests another fascinating line of inquiry, and soon one is off, like a dog with his nose to the ground, investigating one smell after another, forgetful of all else, forgetting even for what purpose one originally took a volume from the shelf." This is an updated version of Cardus's "magic casement", but what is true of a single edition is even more apposite when it comes to inspecting the collection as a whole. We can enter the set at any point and rapidly lose ourselves in an infinite skein of echoes and associations.

Let us dip into the 2012 edition, for instance, the 149th in the series, armed only with a straightforward question: who, in the history of Test match cricket, has scored the most runs? It doesn't take long to find the answer: Sachin Tendulkar, with 15,470, a hefty margin ahead of his team-mate Rahul Dravid (with 13,288). But before we close the book we might notice that the great Don Bradman stands at 39 in this all-time list, behind a raft of other batsmen who have, thanks to the nature of the modern game, played many more Tests. The man just behind Bradman (Sanath Jayasuriya of Sri Lanka) has played 110, more than twice as many as the Don.

Suddenly, we don't feel like closing the pages just yet. Perhaps we are intrigued by that name Jayasuriya, and want to remind ourselves of the time he batted like a threshing machine in the 1996 World Cup (making him the Player of the Tournament as well as a *Wisden* Cricketer of the Year). We might go on to explore (by flicking to and fro) the rise of Sri

Lanka as a cricketing power, or to chart the history of the World Cup itself. In the meantime our glance might be snared by a "17-year-old Londoner" named Robert Key, who scored his maiden century for Kent 2nd XI, and this might make us turn to the 2004 Lord's Test in which he scored 221 against the West Indies. And on the page describing that terrific feat (which he achieved with "chunky straight drives") our eye would fall on the fact that his partnership with Strauss (291) was well short of Compton and Edrich's 370 in 1947 – and just like that we would find ourselves reaching for the 1948 *Wisden* to read about that most famous of seasons.

Heavens – is that the time? But as we discard the 2005 edition the pages might fall open to reveal a photograph of an antiquated Englishman with a fine moustache: none other than Sydney Pardon himself, being toasted by Matthew Engel as "the greatest editor" of all. On reaching for the 1913 *Wisden* to see how Pardon celebrated the 50th birthday, we will almost certainly be waylaid by another famous image, the portrait of John Wisden himself, the 50th edition of whose publication was celebrated that year. That might tempt us to pick up the original volume, if we have it to hand, shake off the invisible dust of almost 150 years and sift through the very earliest days of Gentlemen and Players – that embarrassing day in 1827 when 11 Players beat 17 Gents, for instance – while noting the fact that in all the games up to 1863 not a single century was scored. And here, in the very first *Wisden*, we can see the Little Wonder himself taking eight wickets for United All-England Eleven against his rival cricket caravan, All-England.

The minutes have flown by, and somehow we have drifted back to the very first stirrings of the Almanack, into an utterly different time and a markedly different country. Naturally we have been waylaid, as we wandered, by other nuggets in the margins. But before we know it we can start meandering forward again, towards the present day. We might linger over one of George Parr's big scores and, wanting to know more about him, track down his obituary in *Wisden* 1892, which noted that a branch from the tree in the outfield at Trent Bridge was tenderly laid on the coffin at his funeral. Looking at the page opposite Parr's obituary we might read about the ill-fated Dick Pilling, who died in the very year that he was chosen as a Cricketer of the

Year (1891).* His obituary mentions that he twice toured Australia with England, and this might send us sniffing like hounds in search of other early encounters between England and Australia. And soon we will be ignoring the phone and reading about Bodyline, and that in turn might prompt us to look up *Wisden*'s response to the fearsome West Indies fast bowling of the 1980s, and the next thing we know we will be shaking our heads over Michael Holding's thrilling performance at The Oval in 1976. From there a thousand alternative paths lead us forward to the later heroics of Botham, Warne and the luminaries of the modern game. We can look up days at which we were present and days we missed, days we will always remember and days we have tried in vain to forget. If we are that way inclined we might even look up ourselves, or people we know, or the children of people we once met.

Throughout this wander along memory lane we know that we are barely scratching the surface of a rich and tangled landscape, and that there are innumerable other paths down which we might have ventured, nose to the scent of some stray memory or thought. We might have wanted to read about Bradman's fateful last innings in Test match cricket, when he failed by a whisker to secure the magical career average of 100. We could have rummaged around for glimpses of Strauss and Cook as schoolboys (discovering that Cook scored a mighty 1,287 runs for Bedford School in 2003, at an average of 160.87),† or lost ourselves in descriptions of the summers Tendulkar and Dravid spent in England for Yorkshire and Kent. Who knows what we might have fetched up as we pushed through rarely visited parts of the undergrowth? We could all too easily have become, as Arrowsmith predicted, dazed and forgetful.

---

* Pilling was almost (but not quite) the first player to be honoured posthumously by *Wisden* – he died three months after being named. But in 1936 South Africa's Jock Cameron *was* made a Cricketer of the Year, even though he had succumbed to enteric fever the previous November. Aged only 30, he had just returned home after helping his team become the first non-Australian touring side to defeat England. Alas, he never knew that a modest yellow book, in a faraway country, had given him this little gleam of immortality. We can only guess whether Pilling knew of his honour.
† Cook's music teacher at Bedford School proudly recalled, in an interview with *Test Match Special* in 2012, giving the future England captain "his first *Wisden*".

It is like rummaging through an old garden, and here and there in the long grass we will have turned up stray, discarded emblems not just of English cricket, but of the imprint the game has left on other parts of the national scene. The George Bernard Shaw who took wickets for Glamorgan in the 1950s was not the author of *Pygmalion*, and the William Shakespeare who played for Worcestershire in the 1920s never conceived of *Macbeth*. But most of the other great names are the genuine article. Here is Captain Oates, who "played cricket for his house while a lower boy" at Eton before dying near the South Pole; there is Douglas Bader, the wounded pilot-hero of the Second World War, scoring 65 for the RAF in 1931. Here is the devout cricket-lover Harold Pinter, who once said that cricket was "the greatest thing that God ever created on earth" and who, *Wisden* recorded in his obituary, took the trouble to write to David Gower after he was dropped by the England selectors: "You remain the best batsman in England, and the selectors a bunch of ignorant apes." Here is Cardinal Manning (a leader of the Oxford Movement) playing for Harrow against Winchester at Lord's. Here is Admiral Jellicoe, hero of Jutland and a "very good fieldsman at cover". King Edward VII is here ("It cannot be said that he ever showed much aptitude for the game") while Victor Eberle reminds us that failure is immortal too – he dropped a Cliftonian schoolboy on 20, a ghastly lapse that allowed A. E. J. Collins to go on and score a world record 628 not out.

Within the confines of its historic class boundaries the Almanack can't help being a meritocracy: the greatest prominence is given to the most successful performers. But it delights in tracking down well-known personalities whose claim to fame lies in the fields beyond cricket. No one knew, in 1926, that "Mr S. V. Beckett", the lanky opening batsman for Dublin University at Northamptonshire (he scored 4 and 1, and also opened the bowling without taking a wicket) would grow into the Nobel prize-winning writer Samuel Beckett.* Nor could the boys of

---

* "It is reasonable to theorise," wrote Matthew Engel in the *Guardian* in 1989, "that Beckett's work – obscure but deeply poetic, full of dramatic longueurs, inaccessible at first glance but with hidden meanings that slowly reveal themselves – could only have been written by a cricketer." Appropriately enough, the first International Beckett Festival at Enniskillen in 2012 featured, among theatrical events, a game of cricket.

Bedford School, long before Alastair Cook's time, have guessed that in John Fowles, who took 34 wickets in 1943 with "a ball that swung away late", they had a first-class novelist in their midst.

The villagers of Shipton-under-Wychwood were certainly aware of the luminary in their middle order when Sam Mendes strode to the crease in the 1997 Village Cricket final at Lord's. Not yet an Oscar winner, he was still a noted theatre director with a production of *Othello* poised to tour the world. *Wisden* noted his details (bowled for 8), but saw no need to add that at the time he was also directing Nicole Kidman at London's Donmar Warehouse. Flick back a few years, to the early 1980s, and there he is again, scoring 1,454 runs in three seasons for Magdalen College School, with 120 wickets for good measure.

Many other legends of this sort had been unearthed by Jonathan Rice in the 2001 *Wisden*. In 1962, he found that the footballer Geoff Hurst had played for Essex, scoring nought not out and nought on his only appearance before achieving a slightly more famous hat-trick against West Germany in the 1966 World Cup final. Michael Bonallack, the amateur golf champion, was in the book as a schoolboy cricketer, and H. W. Austin was a "sound and correct" batsman at Repton before adopting the name "Bunny" and reaching two Wimbledon finals.

The captain of Harrow in the 1919 match at Lord's had the evocative initials W. A. R., but it was his surname, Collins, which went on to achieve renown in publishing. In *Wisden* 1969 Prince Charles, a schoolboy at Gordonstoun, was pictured playing "the Compton sweep", and the school captain 11 years later, scoring 212 runs and taking 11 wickets, was his younger brother "HRH Prince Andrew", later the Duke of York. An even more ripping royal effort came in 1953, when the obituary of King George VI revealed the fact that he had, as Prince Albert, achieved a hat-trick on the "private grounds below Windsor Castle". This was a notable haul: he dismissed three kings (Edward VII and the future George V and Edward VIII) to complete an extremely royal flush. Rice was obliged to point out that this notable haul had been achieved by "a young boy against three people who never showed any aptitude for the game". Either way, the ball was mounted in the mess-room of the Royal Naval College, Dartmouth.

In 1929 the opening pair for Harrow against Eton were the future banker N. M. V. Rothschild and the playwright-in-waiting Terence

Rattigan. And look: a lad at St Paul's who later became Field Marshal Montgomery of El-Alamein managed to put on "over 100 for the last wicket when a severe defeat seemed impending" in 1905. Poor Erwin Rommel: he had no idea what kind of sporting grit he was up against.

Naturally we cannot know how many of the young cricketers named in the most recent editions of *Wisden* will one day glitter in this way, but the enticing glimpses of future stars remain one of the Almanack's reliable pleasures. Graze back through the set and you can pick out stray first sightings. Sometimes they are only hints. In 1996 a panel of cricket VIPs was asked whether cricket was "getting worse" and one, Chris Broad, the former England opener, mentioned that his nine-year-son liked to watch the television highlights – and suddenly we were granted a vision of a young boy, later to be the blond arrowhead that is Stuart Broad, curled up on the sofa with his dad.

It is at moments such as this that we seem to have peeked through a crack in time to inspect the wider shores of cricket. When we were looking for the account of the 1996 World Cup, for instance (in the 1997 *Wisden*), we might have paused to enjoy both the kind-hearted verdict of our own newspapers ("End of the World for Pathetic England" – the *Sunday Mirror*) or the way that even American journalists noticed that Sri Lanka's victory was startling: as the *New York Times* put it: "Cricket is 'not cricket' any more".

We would also have tripped over plenty of minor news from the around the world. "The ravages of war have brought cricket to Afghanistan ... cricket thrives in Bahrain ... cricket is not endemic in the High Andes ... France made a bright start to 1996 ... Israeli cricket took a step closer to finding a home ... Enthusiasm for cricket is high in Japan..." If the news that France had played two one-day internationals against Germany in 1996 made us want to flick forward to see what happened the following season, we would have come upon one of cricket's strangest matches. It was the final of Europe's Nations Cup, and Germany (who in a previous round had scored 467 for one) lost by a single run. It sounds, in *Wisden*'s sober summary, unusual. In the first innings France's last man, David Bordes, "was hit on the forehead and staggered through for a single before collapsing with a fractured skull". Fifty overs later, with two balls to go and eight needed, Germany hit a six when third man spilled a high catch, but fell at the final hurdle when a skier was held at deep mid-on. "The Bordes head-bye proved a matchwinner," wrote *Wisden*. "He had to spend the next two weeks in hospital, and was ill for some time but, happily, was able to resume playing indoor cricket before Christmas." He usually wore a helmet, but "did not bother this time".

Have we got time for a quick look at the chronicle of bizarre incidents? If so, here is the Shropshire groundsman whose false teeth shot out of his mouth when he sneezed, only to be crushed by the heavy roller. Here is Garry Sobers winning £200,000 in a Barbados lottery only to find that his name meant nothing to the schoolboys to whom he was giving a coaching clinic at his old haunt in Nottinghamshire ("Garry Who?" said one ungrateful wretch). And here is the friendly game in Lincolnshire that was interrupted when a hang-glider crashed into a fielder, inspiring, once the bruises faded, the perfect local newspaper headline: "Bad Flight Stopped Play".

We *must* stop. But what is this? Graham Gooch's final game for Essex? He had recently become the heaviest run-scorer in the history of the English professional game, heavier even than Hobbs – surely he went out with a bang? Alas, his last innings merely caught the damp, pork-pie flavour of English cricket. "The MP for Colchester, Bob Russell, tabled a Commons motion listing Gooch's achievements, and the Chelmsford town crier rang a bell, but Gooch's leg stump was uprooted by the 26th ball he received." This, in *Wisden*, is how the mighty fall.

Echoes such as these lie dormant just beneath the staid surface of these little yellow bricks, but we only have to turn a page to awaken them. We can roam the corridors in as many different directions as we please; we can grow dizzy and lost to the world. So perhaps it adds to the charm of the Almanack that its own story is also in many ways hidden. When the cricket historian Murray Hedgcock was researching the "Mortlake era", seeking first-hand accounts of the *Wisden* factory on the Upper Richmond Road, he found few traces of its existence – it was "surprisingly unrecorded". Richmond and Wimbledon libraries had "no reference at all"; the one in Barnes was "equally uninformative"; and local researchers knew "virtually nothing". The Public Record Office, only a mile and a half away in Kew, was "mute", and the archive of the Co-operative Wholesale Society in Rochdale (which had bought the company just before the factory was bombed in 1944) had "no *Wisden* information". Even John Wisden & Co's own company minutes had the address down wrong, listing it at 28 Fitzgerald Road instead of in the yard between 14 and 16, which is where it actually was.

This silence, this drift of snow on *Wisden*'s past, may be an apt symbol of the Almanack's charm. To the outside world it seems monumental, down to its four-square annual appearance. It is solid, a bristling rampart of facts. Yet anyone who thinks that it dwells in marble halls is way off the mark. For 150 years it has been published by a fraternity of cricket-loving reporters and printers, most of whom have had other jobs at the time. Its editorial headquarters has moved from pillar to post, from parlour to back office, from rural cottage to suburban lounge. It has had 16 editors and a strangely convoluted succession of owners – sometimes it has been the prestigious bauble of a failing sports company, and at other times it has been a tiny stowaway in some much larger corporate vessel. Its circulation has bobbed like the scoring rate in a one-day international; it has been bombed twice and survived bankruptcy, corporate crossfire and countless advances in technology.

Somehow, it has managed to cling on to its singular form and nature. Like an actor reeling behind the painted scenery of the theatre, it has contrived, even when punch-drunk by events outside its control, to present a confident front to the outside world. In the process it has attracted fervent admirers. The biographer Michael Holroyd, writing about his own youthful bowling, once said that "years of close study of *Wisden* went into each delivery", while the philosopher Freddie Ayer, a devoted Middlesex man, said that he "regularly bought and studied" the Almanack. It makes sense that Kim Philby had a copy in Moscow, since 13 castaways on the BBC's *Desert Island Discs* also named it as the book they would most like to take into exile. Nor were they all cricketers. It was no surprise that Geoff Boycott, Colin Cowdrey, Alec Bedser, Dickie Bird and Tony Greig might enjoy the Almanack, since it featured the highlights of their own lives. But the rest – Nigel Kennedy, Stuart Rose, Gary Lineker, John Biffen, David Puttnam – were motivated only by love for the game.

The past is indeed a foreign country, but its shades are always flickering to and fro, dancing in the shadows of the present. When Dravid or Tendulkar glide the ball off their pads they can't help evoking, across the bounds of time and place, and only for an instant, the spirits of Ranji or Pataudi; when Botham or Pietersen batter the ball into the grandstand, the big-hitters of the past judder on the boards where their feats are written. Not every drive recalls Hammond, nor every pull Bradman, but cricket's history shimmers in the background, and *Wisden* is the chest where its memory lies.

It is a creative work as well, in that it has advanced and sustained a mythical view of English country life. This was the spirit in which a small cricket tableau was included in the vast 2012 Olympic opening ceremony. But in truth cricket does not really evoke the countryside, except in pastiche: it presents it not as working farmland or wild heath but as an orderly playground of neat pavilions on well-trimmed lawns.

Not everything about *Wisden* is misty-eyed, however. It has also – in an inverted honour – been the butt of jokes. Just as it was once a privilege to be a *Spitting Image* puppet, or the subject of a four-eyed portrait by Picasso, so the Almanack can be proud to have been mocked, in recent years, by a certain D. Podmore, Esquire, an imaginary all-rounder whose column (ghostwritten by Christopher Douglas) often referred to *Wisden*. On one occasion he recalled a trip to the "Doritos-on-a-paper-plate shambles calling itself the *Wisden* dinner" where, wounded by the fact that he had not been honoured as a Cricketer of the Year (the concept of which, he felt, did him "no favours whatsoever"), he mused: "I know from conversations with the lads in the dressing room that they'd be a lot more inclined to read *Wisden* if it contained a Players' Wives section, a horoscope and a review of cricket computer games."

Even in his own column the Almanack had its revenge, patiently correcting his Test average of four – "an edge through the slips against Sri Lanka, and they cannot take that away from me, except in *Wisden*, which says it was leg-byes". But it may not be a coincidence that Pod, the "evergreen trundler who put it there or thereabouts" has his own roots in the book: Austin Podmore presided over Public Schools in the 1930s, and helped select the Public Schools XI for the match at Lord's (another silver-spoon showpiece event in which Pod, true to form, would never figure).

―――

The death of the printed word has been announced many times, and it is common to hear the book trade referred to as a twilight industry mortally threatened by screen-based reading. This notion has a particular piquancy with respect to *Wisden*, because the winking growth of digital info-seeking would seem to undermine nothing so thoroughly as a reference work. Yet even now *Wisden* retains some advantages over a website. It better sponsors the serendipitous browsing so central to the *Wisden* aesthetic. As we have seen, to flick through the records section of *Wisden* is to find answers to questions we never thought to ask in the first place. Some facts you cannot search for; they must be stumbled on, and for that we need an Aladdin's cave, not a silicon chip.

Sometimes there are different answers to the same question. If we are looking for the best batsman in Test history, for instance, we need to define our terms a little. Tendulkar has the most runs, but by no means the best average (Bradman) and so it goes. Highest score? Lara (400 not out for West Indies v England, 2004). Best series? Bradman again (974 v England in 1930). Most runs in a year? Mohammad Yousuf (1,788 in 2006). Fastest century? Viv Richards (in 56 balls, West Indies v England, 1986). Fastest double-century? Nathan Astle (in 153 balls, New Zealand v England, 2002).

We might pause to wonder why such records seem so frequently to be set against English bowling, but there is no consensus over which is the senior measurement, the yardstick by which a batsman should be judged. It depends on the context. The fastest batsman may not be the one we would want to hang on for a draw, just as the one with the best average may not be ideal if we need six off the last ball. *Wisden* takes care to cover these and many other bases. It knows who has scored the fastest fifty, the most runs off an over, the most in a day, the most sixes in a career. Since cricket is a game of many eventualities, it knows who are the *slowest* scorers as well. Taken together, all these landmarks describe the boundary of a game that has stirred its disciples for centuries. The semiconductor may well be an uncanny miracle, but the richest path through cricket's undergrowth is still, in many instances, the oldest technology of all: the single finger, the opposable thumb, and a fat yellow book.

This is one reason why it has managed to survive so long; another is that, at the end of the 20th century, at the very time it might well have vanished, *Wisden* became a valuable object – an investment opportunity.

It allowed the Almanack to attract a devoted and compulsive readership that few books have been able to reach. And it wasn't only cricket fans buying into its charm: *Wisden* carried flashes of England's domestic history as it moved down the generations, from father to son to grandson, and from library to saleroom and back again, circulating in the English bloodstream.

Sometimes, like an old desk with initials scratched inside the lid, it has nursed its scars and hopes in secret for years. But it is never too late: *Wisden* has an expanded sense of time. The 2012 edition featured the touching story, by Andrew Renshaw, of a schoolboy called "Niel" who gave a copy of the 1912 *Wisden* to his father bearing the inscription: "Wishing Daddy a very happy birthday, and many happy returns of the day from Niel." In another hand was a line from Wilfred Owen – *Dulce et decorum est pro patria mori* ("How sweet and fitting it is to die for one's country"), plus some unexplained numbers. Renshaw, the volume's new owner, set to work to unravel the mystery and, after painstaking investigation, discovered that this kind spirit was a boy called Niel Fagan, whose elder brother Brian had topped the bowling averages at Rugby School in 1911 – the numbers were the pages on which Brian's exploits were to be found. In 1916, Niel, aged 20, was killed at the Somme, and a grieving parent added the line from Owen. Renshaw even tracked down Brian's son, who knew nothing of the gift. It took a hundred years for the tale to play out but, in the Wisden scheme of things, that is not so very long.

Wisden looks after its own, and does not forget. In keeping with its power to confer immortality, it is happy to plunge into the underworld to revive some long-forgotten soul – even when it involves a very distant relation. Hence its sometimes sorrowful tone. It is a book about the past, dealing with death as much as life. It appears in spring, like a primrose or daffodil, and has a green sense of renewal, chiming with the sap rising in the blossoming cherry and the smell of new-mown grass. But it trembles with pathos too, reminding readers that they are, once again, a year older.

If the Almanack conducts a conversation with the passing of time, so does cricket: it is a notoriously time-consuming game. Captains gauge run-rates, over-rates and the right time to declare; umpires signal the beginning and end of each session. What time will the rain arrive? How long till it gets dark? For how many hours did that fellow bat? These are all part of cricket's workaday nature. And how else to describe a pretty shot other than to say it was perfectly timed. Old Father Time has swayed over Lord's for many generations now. Just as the pencil marks on bathroom walls display the increasing heights of children, so each *Wisden* adds a new stone to the monument of its own past.

———

When we speak of the English sensibility we imply also the echoes of this in the regions it once colonised. The rise and fall – perhaps better to say the advance and retreat – of Britain's Empire is one of the most amazing stories of the last few centuries, and like all the best stories it involves both base and high-minded behaviour, both cruelty and courage. The way in which one small rain-washed island exploited so vast a tract of the world … it would be hard to believe it possible if it had not happened. But in imposing its dominion across the world Britain exported many aspects of itself – steam engines, railways, religion, legal ideas, language, literature, a supercilious attitude to social hierarchy and, of course, the peculiarly English game of cricket. The bat-and-ball game was stowed in the knapsacks of soldiers and settlers, merchants and teachers in Australia, New Zealand and South Africa; it wormed its way into the imaginations of the Caribbean and India, and became one of the stages on which tensions of class and race in imperial days were played out. When the dissolving Empire drifted back to the so-called Mother Country, when migrants from the West Indies, India, Pakistan, Sri Lanka, Australia and South Africa brought their own ardent vision of the game back to Britain, they threaded new strands into the fabric. Winston Churchill once remarked that "we shape our houses, and then they shape us". He had in mind the parliamentary buildings at Westminster, but it applies to *Wisden* too. It began life as a child of the fair-play ideology behind Victorian sport, but went on to become one of the institutions through which that dream, that system of values and hopes, was (with all its faults) preserved, polished and expressed.

The history of cricket is a delicate saga, and nowhere better told – with such a scrupulous respect for individual deeds and unsung detail – than in *Wisden*. In this context, 150 years is neither such a long time nor, as it happens, a complete landmark. The first prose in the Almanack was a history, by W. H. Knight, of the double-century – even then, 200 was the true measure of distinction, and *Wisden* needs only another half-century to reach it. Who knows – by 2063 international cricket may be a hectic ten-over thrashabout, with scores routinely topping 300. Fans may be recalling, with wistful smiles, the golden age of Twenty20 that we enjoy now, those long, lazy evenings when the "hitters" used those funny wooden bats, bowlers had to keep their arms straight (amazing but true!) and those comical old fellows in the white coats – umpires, was that what they were called? – actually walked out to the middle instead of watching the game on replay screens in air-conditioned television studios by the Arabian Sea. Perhaps, by then, cricket will have changed its name to *Crack-it!* and be staged in bright indoor leisure-domes, and be an Olympic sport – with China, Brazil and the United States wrangling with one another for gold. It will inspire a few letters to *The Times*, we can be sure. But if *Wisden* is still around to remind us that it has all evolved from the game of Grace, Bradman, Lara and Tendulkar, then it will still, however changed, be cricket. It will be in the book, and that's what counts.

Advertisement from Wisden *1917*

WISDEN TIMELINE

1826 – John Wisden ("JW") is born in Brighton.

1845 – JW's first match for Sussex.

1850 – JW takes ten wickets in an innings for North v South at Lord's (all are bowled – still a unique feat in first-class cricket). He also sets up in business selling cricket gear in Leamington in partnership with George Parr.

1852 – JW and Jemmy Dean form the United All-England Eleven.

1855 – JW opens his "cricket and cigar" shop at 2 New Coventry Street, London, in partnership with Fred Lillywhite.

1858 – JW becomes the sole proprietor of the business after his partnership with Fred Lillywhite is dissolved.

1859 – JW plays in the USA and Canada as a member of the first overseas tour by an English team.

1863 – JW retires from the game.

1864 – JW publishes his first *Cricketer's Almanack*. The editor (or "compiler") for the first 16 editions is W. H. Knight.

1868 – JW publishes the Almanack in partnership with Frederick Maynard, but the partnership is dissolved after the 1869 edition is published.

1870 – The book's title is changed to *John Wisden's Cricketers' Almanack* (*Cricketer's Almanack* had been changed to *Cricketers' Almanack* (plural) in 1869).

1872 – Wisden's shop moves to 21 Cranbourn Street, London. JW & Co is now a sports goods manufacturer and retailer as well as a publisher.

1880 – The Cricket Reporting Agency ("the CRA") is founded by Charles Pardon.

1880 – The first of seven editions of *Wisden* edited by George West.

1884 – JW dies in his flat above the Cranbourn Street shop. The business is bought from his estate by Henry Luff.

1887 – The first of four editions of *Wisden* edited by Charles Pardon and the first to have its content compiled by the CRA.

1889 – *Wisden* selects its first Cricketers of the Year ("Six Great Bowlers of the Year") and includes a page of "portrait" photographs for the first time.

1891 – The first of 35 editions of *Wisden* edited by Sydney Pardon.

1896 – The first edition to be published in hardback ("cloth-bound", in addition to the "limp" version). Also, the Almanack exceeds 500 pages for the first time.

1896 – JW & Co open a second London shop – in Great Newport Street.

1901 – Sydney Pardon starts "Notes by the Editor".

1910 – Henry Luff dies. His son, Ernest, takes over the business.

1911 – JW & Co receive a Royal Warrant to certify their "appointment as Athletic Outfitters to the King" (George V).

1913 – The 50th edition of *Wisden*.

1914 – JW & Co are incorporated as a limited company with their shares divided among several investors.

1916 – Ernest Luff is sacked.

1916 – The Almanack suspends its Cricketers of the Year feature due to
war (it resumes in 1918 with Five School Bowlers of the Year).

1920 – JW & Co merge with Duke & Son, a "sports goods
manufacturer" specialising in cricket balls.

1923 – JW & Co publish their first Rugby Football Almanack (it is
discontinued after only three annual editions).

1924 – The Almanack exceeds 1,000 pages for the first time.

1924 – JW & Co acquire the Taylor-Rolph Company, a bowls
manufacturer.

1926 – The first of eight editions of *Wisden* edited by Stewart Caine.

1928 – The shop in Cranbourn Street is closed.

1934 – The first of two editions of *Wisden* edited by Sydney
Southerton.

1936 – The first of four editions of *Wisden* edited by Wilfrid Brookes.

1938 – J. Whitaker & Sons Ltd ("Whitaker's") become *Wisden's*
publisher under licence from JW & Co and immediately
conduct a thorough overhaul of the Almanack. Their changes
include a rearrangement of the content, interspersed images on
early pages, dropping "John" from the title (to be simply
Wisden Cricketers' Almanack), the introduction of yellow
linen covers (for the "limp" version) and adding Eric
Ravilious's woodcut of top-hatted cricketers to the front cover.

1939 – JW & Co go into receivership.

1940 – Whitaker's offices in Warwick Lane, London are destroyed in
the Blitz.

1940 – The first of four editions of *Wisden* edited by Haddon
Whitaker (the Notes in all his editions are written by
Raymond Robertson-Glasgow).

1941 – The Almanack suspends its Cricketers of the Year feature due to war (it resumes in 1947).

1943 – JW & Co are bought out of receivership by the Co-operative Wholesale Society.

1944 – Wisden's factory in Mortlake is destroyed by a bomb.

1944 – Although still published by Whitaker's, *Wisden* moves to the Sporting Handbooks imprint, in which JW & Co have a half-share.

1944 – The first of eight editions of *Wisden* edited by Hubert Preston.

1952 – The first of 29 editions of *Wisden* edited by Norman Preston.

1957 – Whitaker's buy JW & Co's half-share in Sporting Handbooks, who continue to publish *Wisden* under licence.

1960 – Facsimile editions of *Wisden* are produced for the first time, when Billing & Sons are licensed to produce the 1864–78 editions in a limited edition of 150 sets. Over the next 52 years other facsimile editions are produced, including Willows reprints of every edition up to 1946.

1960 – The shop in Great Newport Street is closed.

1961 – JW & Co amalgamate its Duke and Wisden cricket-ball manufacturing business with those of Gray-Nicolls, Surridge and Ives in a joint venture company, Tonbridge Sports Industries.

1963 – The 100th edition of *Wisden* is marked by the introduction of the Wisden Trophy, to be contested in all future Test series between England and West Indies.

1965 – The CRA merge with the Press Association (the PA).

1965 – The hardback ("cloth boards") version of Wisden has a dust jacket for the first time.

1968 – Norman Preston retires from the PA (thus ending the PA/CRA editorial arrangement with the Almanack which had been responsible for 82 editions) but Preston continues to edit *Wisden* on a freelance contract.

1970 – Grays of Cambridge Ltd purchase JW & Co (including their stake in Tonbridge Sports Industries) from the Co-operative Wholesale Society.

1979 – Queen Anne Press (a division of Macdonald and Jane's Publishers which, in 1982, came under Robert Maxwell's control) succeed Sporting Handbooks as *Wisden*'s licensed publisher.

1979 – The magazine *Wisden Cricket Monthly* is launched, published under licence from JW & Co.

1981 – The first of six editions of *Wisden* edited by John Woodcock.

1984 – The centenary of John Wisden's death is commemorated with the unveiling of a new headstone for his grave in London's Brompton Cemetery.

1985 – McCorquodale Plc purchase JW & Co from Grays and re-establish JW & Co as *Wisden*'s own publisher.

1986 – Grays of Cambridge buy back 50% of JW & Co to become joint owners with McCorquodale (who are later acquired by Bowater Plc).

1987 – The first of eight editions of *Wisden* edited by Graeme Wright.

1988 – *Wisden* includes colour photographs for the first time.

1993 – Paul Getty purchases JW & Co from Grays and Bowater.

1993 – The first of 12 editions of *Wisden* edited by Matthew Engel. The combined total of pages in all editions of *Wisden* now exceeds 100,000.

1995 – A limited-edition leatherbound version of *Wisden* is introduced.

1998 – An Australian *Wisden Almanack* is launched (it is discontinued after only eight annual editions).

1999 – The Almanack exceeds 1,500 pages for the first time.

2000 – *Wisden* names Five Cricketers of the Century (Don Bradman, Jack Hobbs, Garry Sobers, Viv Richards and Shane Warne).

2001 – Wisden Online is launched.

2001 – Graeme Wright returns as editor of *Wisden*, while Matthew
      Engel takes a three-year sabbatical.

2003 – JW & Co buys *The Cricketer* magazine (which it merges with
      Wisden Cricket Monthly to form *The Wisden Cricketer*) and
      the website Cricinfo (into which it integrates Wisden Online).

2003 – Paul Getty dies. His son, Mark, takes control of JW & Co.

2003 – The only edition of *Wisden* edited by Tim de Lisle, the
      Almanack features a photograph on the cover for the first time.

2004 – Matthew Engel returns as editor of *Wisden*.

2004 – *Wisden* introduces a new annual accolade: The Leading
      Cricketer in the World.

2006 – A large-format version of *Wisden* is introduced.

2007 – Cricinfo is sold to ESPN and *The Wisden Cricketer* is sold to
      BSkyB.

2008 – The first of four editions of *Wisden* edited by Scyld Berry.

2008 – Bloomsbury Publishing Plc purchase JW & Co from Mark
      Getty.

2008 – *Wisden* introduces a new annual accolade: The Schools
      Cricketer of the Year.

2009 – Claire Taylor is the first woman to be named as a Cricketer of
      the Year.

2011 – *The Shorter Wisden* ebook is introduced.

2012 – The first edition of *Wisden* to be edited by Lawrence Booth.

2012 – *Wisden India* is launched.

2013 – The 150th edition of *Wisden*.

Compiled by Christopher Lane

Acknowledgements

When I began this book one of the things I knew most firmly about *Wisden* concerned its enviable reputation for accuracy: it was by far the safest pair of hands in the cricket world. So the slurred and unreliable nature of my own first draft was both alarming and a noticeable slight on the name of the publication to which it owed its existence. It was caused in part by a few technical mishaps, and was influenced too by a *Wisden* characteristic (its clock runs a year late, so that in *Wisden* time Bradman's Invincibles appear in 1949, and the end of the Second World War is celebrated in 1946). In general, though, it was down to little more than authorial dizziness (this was a book about books – a maze in which it is all too easy to lose one's sense of direction). If the finished product feels purged of such confusions it is thanks to the knowledgeable, energetic and devoted efforts of four expert readers: Charlotte Atyeo, Christopher Saunders, Graeme Wright and, to an extent that proved the writing of books to be a team sport, the tireless Christopher Lane. No writer ever had a more skilled cordon of slip catchers. It is a tribute to the great affection the Almanack commands that they were willing to rake through my own fallible manuscript so keenly and with such grace. Any mistakes and misjudgements that remain are, it goes without saying, my fault entirely.

Many grateful thanks are due also to Stephen Baldwin, Scyld Berry, Catherine Best, Lawrence Booth, John Brown, Tim Bunting, Richard Charkin, Hugh Chevallier, Terry Cooper, Simon and Maggie Davies, Matthew Engel, Julian Flanders, Christine Forrest, Michael and Pat Gee, Mark Getty, John Gray, Richard Gray, Murray Hedgcock, Nicholas Heroys, Nick Humphrey, David Kynaston, Tim de Lisle,

John McKenzie, Ken Medlock, Harriet Monkhouse, David Preston, Andrew Renshaw, Simon Wilde and John Woodcock; Adam Chadwick and Neil Robinson at Lord's; Patrick Healey and Helen McIntyre at Bank of England Sports Club; and the staff of many libraries. Christopher Lane steered the project with spectacular friendliness and zeal.

As has often been said, no sport has been annotated with such a devoted attention to detail as cricket, so the bibliography that follows is highly selective. The key source, of course, was *Wisden* itself. Final thanks are due to the many reporters down the years who have filled its pages so faithfully, so well, for so long.

Select Bibliography

Allen, R. D., *Arlott: The Authorised Biography*, HarperCollins, 1994

Allen, R. D., Ed., *A Word from Arlott*, Pelham, 1983

Arlott, John, *Basingstoke Boy*, Willow, 1990

Arlott, John, *How to Watch Cricket*, Sporting Handbooks, 1947

Barty-King, Hugh, *Quilt Winders and Pod Shavers*, Macdonald's, 1979

Benaud, Richie, *On Reflection*, Willow, 1984

Birley, Derek, *A Social History of English Cricket*, Aurum, 1999

Birley, Sir Robert, *Sport and the Making of Britain*, Manchester University Press, 1993

Blunden, Edmund, *Cricket Country*, Pavilion, 1985

Bose, Mihir, *All in a Day*, Robin Clark, 1983

Bowen, Rowland, *Cricket: A History of its Growth and Development throughout the World*, Eyre & Spottiswoode, 1970

Bright-Holmes, John, Ed., *The Joy of Cricket*, Secker & Warburg, 1984

Buruma, Ian, *Playing the Game*, Cape, 1991

Cardus, Neville, *Autobiography*, Collins, 1947

Cardus, Neville *Cardus in the Covers*, Souvenir, 1978

Daft, Richard, *Kings of Cricket*, J. W. Arrowsmith, 1893

Duckworth, Leslie, *S. F. Barnes: Master Bowler*, Hutchinson, 1967

Fingleton, J. H., *Cricket Crisis*, Cassell, 1946

Fraser-Sampson, Guy, *Cricket at the Crossroads: Class Colour and Controversy from 1967–1977*, Elliott & Thompson, 2011

Frindall, Bill, *Bearders: My Life in Cricket*, Orion, 2006

Frith, David, *The Golden Age of Cricket*, Lutterworth, 1978

Graveney, Tom, *The Heart of Cricket*, Arthur Barker, 1968

Green, Benny, Ed., *The Lord's Companion*, Pavilion, 1987

Green, Benny, Ed., *The Wisden Papers of Neville Cardus*, Hutchinson, 1989

Hadfield, John, *A Wisden Century 1850–1950*, Sporting Handbooks, 1950

Haigh, Gideon, *Endless Summer: 140 Years of Australian Cricket in Wisden*, Hardie Grant, 2002

Haigh, Gideon, *Silent Revolutions: Writings on Cricket History*, Aurum, 2007

Hamilton, Duncan, *Harold Larwood: The Authorised Biography*, Quercus, 2009

Hammond, W. R., *Cricket My Destiny*, Stanley Paul, 1946

Hornung, E. W., *Raffles: The Amateur Cracksman*, Penguin Classics, 2003

Hutton, Len, *Fifty Years in Cricket*, Stanley Paul, 1984

James, C. L. R., *Beyond a Boundary*, Serpent's Tail, 1963

Johnston, Barry, *Johnners: The Life of Brian*, Hodder & Stoughton, 2003

Kynaston, David, *Bobby Abel: Professional Batsman*, Secker & Warburg, 1982

Kynaston, David, *WG's Birthday Party*, Chatto & Windus, 1990

Lane, Christopher, Ed., *A Century of Wisden*, John Wisden & Co, 2000

Lee, Christopher, Ed., *Through the Covers: An Anthology of Cricket Writing*, Oxford, 1996

Lillywhite, Frederick, *The English Cricketers' Trip to Canada and the United States*, World's Work, 1980

McKistry, Leo, *Boycs: The True Story*, Partridge, 2000

Major, John, *More than a Game: The Story of Cricket's Early Years*, HarperCollins, 2008

Martin-Jenkins, Christopher, *Ball by Ball: The Story of Cricket Broadcasting*, Grafton, 1990

Martin-Jenkins, Christopher, *CMJ: A Cricketing Life*, Simon & Schuster, 2012

May, Peter, *A Game Enjoyed*, Stanley Paul, 1985

Meyer, Michael, Ed., *Summer Days: Cricket Writing*, Methuen, 1981

Midwinter, Eric, *Quill on Willow: Cricket in Literature*, Aeneas, 2001

Midwinter, Eric, *The Lost Seasons: Cricket in Wartime*, Methuen, 1987

Oborne, David, *Basil D'Oliveira*, Little, Brown, 2004

D'Oliveira, Basil, *D'Oliveira: An Autobiography*, Collins, 1968

Rae, Simon, *W. G. Grace: A Life*, Faber, 1998

Ranjitsinhji, K. S., *The Jubilee Book of Cricket*, Blackwood, 1897

Rice, Jonathan and Renshaw, Andrew, *The Wisden Collector's Guide*, John Wisden & Co, 2011

Robertson-Glasgow, R. C., *Crusoe on Cricket*, Pavilion, 1985

Ross, Alan, Ed., *The Penguin Cricketer's Companion*, Eyre & Spottiswoode, 1960

Shepherd, David, *Shep: An Autobiography*, Orion, 2001

Sheppard, David, *Steps Along Hope Street: My Life in Cricket, the Church and the Inner City*, Hodder and Stoughton, 2001

Swanton, E. W., *Sort of a Cricket Person*, Collins, 1972

Trueman, Fred, *As it Was: The Memoirs*, Macmillan, 2004

Warner, Sir Pelham, *Cricket Between Two Wars*, Chatto and Windus, 1942

Warner, Sir Pelham, *Long Innings: The Autobiography*, Harrap, 1951

Warner, Sir Pelham, *Gentlemen v Players 1806–1949*, Harrap, 1950

Webber, Roy, *The County Cricket Championship*, Phoenix House, 1957

Webber, Roy, *The Phoenix History of Cricket*, Dent, 1960

Wilde, Simon, *Ranji: A Genius Rich and Strange*, Kingswood, 1990

Williams, Marcus, Ed., *Double Century: 200 years of Cricket in the Times*, Guild, 1985

Wilton, Iain, *C. B. Fry: An English Hero*, Metro, 1999

Wisden Cricketers' Almanack 1864–2012

Wright, Graeme, *Betrayal: The Struggle for Cricket's Soul*, Witherby/Cassell, 1993

Wright, Graeme, Ed., *Wisden at Lord's*, John Wisden & Co/MCC, 2005

Wright, Graeme, Ed., *Bradman in Wisden*, John Wisden & Co, 2008

Advertisement from Wisden *1936*

Index

Advertisement from Wisden *1879*